THE CHARITY OF WAR

THE CHARITY OF WAR

Famine, Humanitarian Aid, and World War I
in the Middle East

MELANIE S. TANIELIAN

Stanford University Press
Stanford, California

Stanford University Press
Stanford, California

© 2018 by the Board of Trustees of the Leland Stanford Junior University.
All rights reserved.

No part of this book may be reproduced or transmitted in any form or by any means, electronic or mechanical, including photocopying and recording, or in any information storage or retrieval system without the prior written permission of Stanford University Press.

Printed in the United States of America on acid-free, archival-quality paper

Library of Congress Cataloging-in-Publication Data

Names: Tanielian, Melanie S., author.
Title: The charity of war : famine, humanitarian aid, and World War I in the Middle East / Melanie S. Tanielian.
Description: Stanford, California : Stanford University Press, 2017. | Includes bibliographical references and index. |
Identifiers: LCCN 2017028678 (print) | LCCN 2017030864 (ebook) | ISBN 9781503603776 (electronic) | ISBN 9781503602403 (cloth :alk. paper) | ISBN 9781503603523 (pbk. :alk. paper)
Subjects: LCSH: World War, 1914-1918--Civilian relief--Lebanon. | World War, 1914-1918--Food supply--Lebanon. | World War, 1914-1918--Health aspects--Lebanon. | Famines--Lebanon--History--20th century. | Humanitarian assistance--Lebanon--History--20th century.
Classification: LCC D638.L43 (ebook) | LCC D638.L43 T36 2017 (print) | DDC 940.3/5692--dc23
LC record available at https://lccn.loc.gov/2017028678

Typeset by Bruce Lundquist in 10.25/15 Adobe Caslon Pro

To Hrair and Nikita
with love and gratitude

CONTENTS

Acknowledgments — ix

Note on Transliteration — xv

Introduction
Total War: Politics, Power, and Benevolence — 1

1. A City and Its Mountain, a Mountain and Its City — 23
2. Wartime Famine: Strategies, Logistics, and Catastrophe — 51
3. The Politics of Food: Wartime Provisioning for Civilians — 79
4. Prayers and Patrons: The Politics of Neutrality — 109
5. Rats, Lice, and Microbes:
   The Struggle against Infectious Diseases — 141
6. Local Relief Initiatives: Civil Society, Women, and the State — 173
7. Beneficial Benevolence: International Wartime Relief Efforts — 201

Conclusion
Beirut 1919: The Chaos of Memory and Politics — 235

Notes — 259

Bibliography — 309

Index — 327

ACKNOWLEDGMENTS

A Moslem family arrived in Egypt from Tripoli, Syria, about a couple of weeks ago. The account of their escape reads more like fiction than reality. During many a long night, patiently and secretly, the work of building a small skiff was carried on inside the house; and, as soon as it was completed, the frail boat was launched on a rather rough sea. Even the old mother was dumped down in the boat under the cover of darkness, and the journey to a place of safety—the name of which is withheld for obvious reasons—was a long drawn agony; the occupants of the boat were almost all the time waist deep in water, and it was only through tireless and desperate bailing that the constant danger of sinking was averted. To have thus braved such a voyage the situation left behind must have been as bad indeed as death.[1]

This book is about famine, death, the inhumanity of war, and, most important, the humanitarian desires and efforts of those watching a catastrophe unfold more than a hundred years ago in what is today's Lebanon. As I complete this book in 2016, I can't help reflecting on the changing meaning of this work. Accounts of a secretly carpentered skiff, treacherous waters, tireless bailing, and astonishing endurance are today's reality, the violent experience of the twenty-first century for far too many. Crossing the Mediterranean Sea in unsafe vessels is one of the few options left for those fleeing the horrors of the Syrian war of our times. We witness the sea, an unforgiving mediator, taking its toll, as thousands have drowned and their bodies washed ashore. Those who survive the journey find themselves caught as refugees in the maelstrom of a humanitarian disaster. Witnessing the despair and suffering in the present has generated in me a different sensitivity toward my historical subject. As I revisited the fragmented sources of a time long past in preparing the book, I read differently. I could not ignore the pictures and words of the daily news cycle. A news story of a mother selling her child for a pound of flour published in the Cairo press in 1916 reminded me of the headline I read on a morning in January 2016 in the *New York Times*: "In Syrian Town under Siege, Dinner Is Soup Made of Grass."[2] I felt as if the voices of those who suffered then were so much louder, and I heard their agony just a bit clearer. And writing became more urgent.

The research for and writing of this book have been supported by a number of grants, fellowships, and awards, including the Faculty Fellowship of the Eisenberg Institute at the University of Michigan, Ann Arbor; the Sultan Fellowship for Arab Studies from the Center of Middle Eastern Studies at the University of California, Berkeley (UCB); the Allan Sharlin Memorial Award, UCB's Graduate School of Arts and Science's Dean Dissertation Fellowship; the Foreign Language and Area Studies Fellowship, UCB's Mentored Research Award; as well as travel grants from the German Academic Exchange Service, the Andrew Mellon Foundation, UCB's History Department, and UCB's Center of Middle Eastern Studies.

This book would not have been possible without the support of my many mentors, peers, students, friends, and loving and patient family. At UCB, I had the great privilege to work with an exceptional group of mentors. I owe much to Beshara Doumani, who taught and guided me as I embarked on this project. His generous advice, support, and critical feedback have made me a better historian. Margaret Lavinia Anderson's commitment to mentorship, methodological precision, and analytical acumen has been a model for me. Saba Mahmoud's academic rigor and intellectual creativity set examples I can only aspire to. I benefited greatly from the guidance of my mentor Keith David Watenpaugh, whose work on humanitarianism in the Middle East and beyond has been a guiding paradigm. The late Susanna Barrows's humor and commitment to collective intellectual growth never failed to make me feel at ease. Her kindness combined with her judicious intellect will always be a model that I seek to emulate. Words cannot express the loss our community experienced from her premature death. I was fortunate to learn from and work with Salim Tamari, Stephan Astourian, Eugene Irshick, Samera Esmeir, Thomas Brady, Leslie Peirce, Emily Gottreich, Osamah Khalil, Murat Dağlı, Amy Aisen Kallandar, Malissa Taylor, Heather Ferguson, Alan Mikhail, Nora Barakat, Hilary Falb, Ryan Calder, and Nick Kardahji.

My colleagues at the University of Michigan deserve a special thank-you: Kathleen Canning, not only for her intellectual support but also for countless winter car rides; my dear friend and swimming partner Nancy Rose Hunt, whose rebellious writing and bold inquiries have been my inspiration; Kathryn Babayan, whose home and heart have been a warm open place for me and my family; Helmut Puff, who has inspired forthcoming madness; Farina Mir, whose strength and kindness have set an example for me; Will Glover, whose understated brilliance and humbleness should be the model for every academic; my dear mentors Mrinalini Sinha and Joshua Cole, who have been most generous with their time, reading drafts and providing feedback; Geoff Eley, who has listened and guided me with his intimate knowledge of the academy; Hussein Fancy, Erdem Cipa, Ellen Muehlberg, Brandi Hughes, Michelle McClellan, and Perrin Selcer, all of whom have been supportive friends and colleagues.

The book has greatly benefited from the feedback I received from many colleagues and friends. In addition, the Department of History at the University of Michigan generously sponsored a book manuscript workshop. I thank Elizabeth Thompson, Roger Chickering, Juan Cole, Pamela Ballinger, Ronald Suny, Kathryn French, Douglas Northrop, Jonathan Marwill, and Devi Mays for commenting on the manuscript and taking the time to discuss it in a formal setting. In addition, I would like to thank Jens Hanssen and Talha Çiçek for their feedback along the way. I thank Mustafa Aksakal, Judith Tucker, and Osama Abi-Mershed for hosting me at Georgetown and providing insightful recommendations. My gratitude also goes to Isabelle de Rezende and my beautiful sister Wendy Taylor-Tanielian for their editorial comments.

It has been a great pleasure to work with the Stanford University Press editorial and publication team. I would like to express a special thank you to Kate Wahl, Micah Siegel, Cynthia Lindlof, and Gigi Mark, whose tireless work and helpful commentary made this a better book.

In Beirut, I was blessed with overwhelming hospitality, friendship, and support for my research. I thank the archival staff at the American University of Beirut, in particular Samar Mikati-Kaissi and Imam Abdallah, and the staff at the Bibliothèque Orientale at Université Saint-Joseph, the Near East School of Theology, Beirut University, Lebanese University, and the Université Saint-Esprit de Kaslik. I also thank Loulou Saybaa and Suad Slim, who were kind enough to facilitate my work in the archives of the Greek Orthodox Archdiocese; the staff at the Lebanese National Archives, the archives of the Maronite Patriarchate at Bkirki, the Greek Catholic Bishopric in Beirut, and the Missionary Society of Saint Paul in Harissa. I also express thanks to Bishop Joseph Kallas for his knowledge and suggestions; Elie Azzi, who shared his ongoing research with me, and Elias Agia of the Missionary Society of Saint Paul; Mr. Maalouf at the Greek Catholic Charity Association; Fawaz Traboulsi, Tarif Khalidi, Maysun Shukari, George Sabra, Hasan Hallaq, and Khalil Matta for their time and help. I thank in particular Stefan Leder at the German Orient Institute in Beirut for taking an interest in my project and welcoming me as an affiliate. Julia Hauser and Christine Lindner have been inspiring colleagues.

Most of all, however, I am indebted to Marie Chahwan, who assisted me in my research, introduced me to archivists, took me under her wing as a researcher, and opened her house to me and my daughter as a great friend. The friendship of Jill and Naji Butrous and their wonderful children turned Beirut from a place we visited into a home filled with memories of laughter even in the most difficult times. Their care, concern, and hospitality were more than anyone could ever expect from friends. It was the Butrous family who made Lebanon a home away from home, who opened their house and hearts to us and became lifelong friends.

But none of this could have happened without the support of my family. My mother, Ingrid, inspired me as the strongest and most uncompromising woman I know. She never questioned my decisions but supported me in every new adventure with her love and curiosity. My dear mother-in-law, Yvonne Tanielian, with her great wisdom, stories of Palestine Jerusalem, and amazing cooking has fed my spirit and stomach all through graduate school. And she spent endless hours babysitting; I could have not done it without her. My daughter, Nikita, has grown up to be a wonderful human being and never complained too much over my absences and having to move to Beirut, leaving her friends and family behind. And my husband, Hrair, has not only been my best friend through the ups and downs of this project but also has been my biggest cheerleader. His confidence in me and loving support gave me the necessary stamina, and his sense of humor and unparalleled joie de vivre made me laugh and push on when the task seemed impossible. To him, my partner in life, I owe my most sincere and unequivocal gratitude.

NOTE ON TRANSLITERATION

Arabic words are transliterated according to the simplified system employed by the *International Journal of Middle East Studies*. Although diacritics have been omitted, ayins and hamzas have been retained. In addition, modern Turkish diacritics have been retained in proper names.

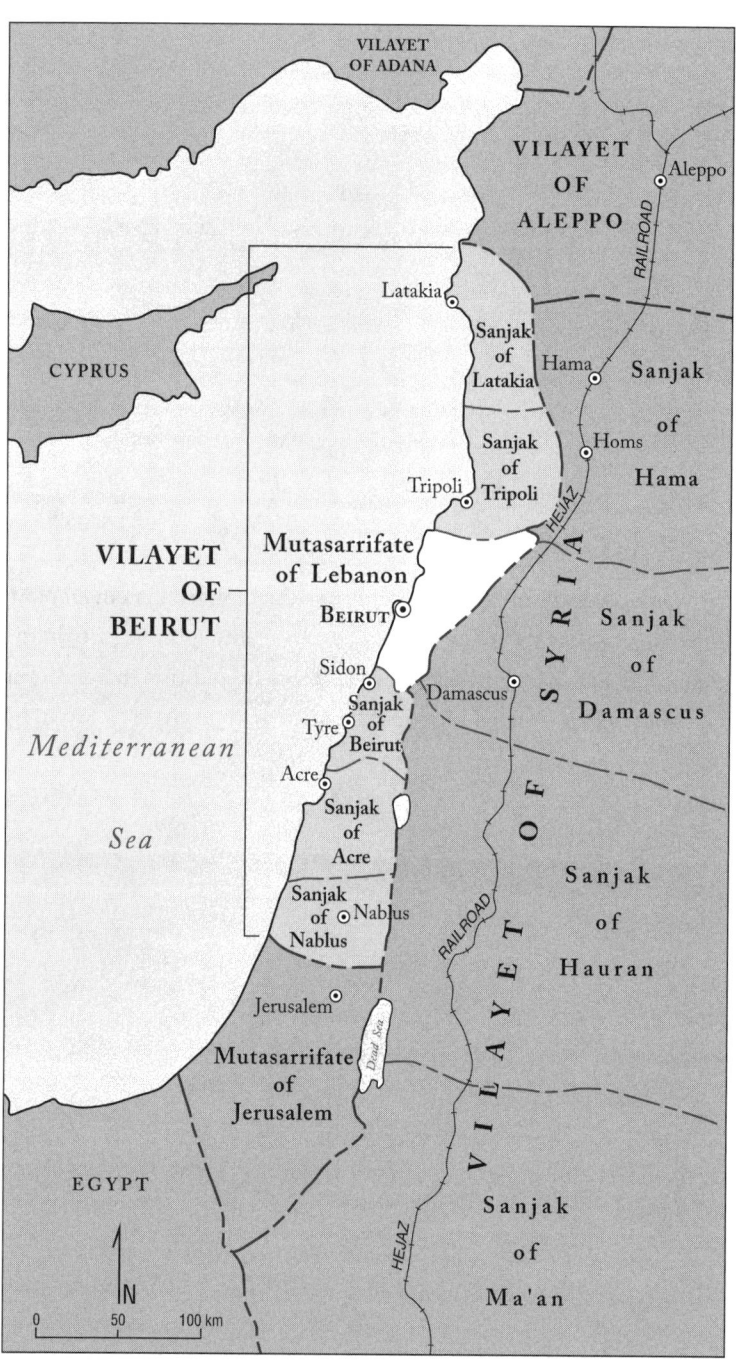

Map 1. The Ottoman Levant: Administrative divisions before 1914.

THE CHARITY OF WAR

Figure 1. Deux pleureuses (Two mourners) by Yusuf Huwayyik (1883–1962). Source: The Fouad Debbas Collection / Sursock Museum, Beirut, Lebanon. Reference No. TFDC/CPA/ScavoJanto/5959.

(INTRODUCTION)

TOTAL WAR

Politics, Power, and Benevolence

In 1952, the Lebanese government held an international design competition for a national monument to commemorate the nation's experience of World War I (1914–1918). A watershed in the country's history, the war had marked the end of the four hundred–year-old Ottoman Empire. And for many Lebanese looking back at the Great War from the vantage point of the 1950s, the war signified the beginning of national resistance, a moment of communal martyrdom for independence from Ottoman rule, even if this independence was to be delayed by decades of French colonial rule.[1] The winner's statue would be erected in the heart of the country's capital of Beirut, at the center of what was then and is still called Martyr's Square (Sahat al-Shuhada').[2] The new design would replace an existing sculpture, controversial and by then also vandalized, the work of prominent Lebanese sculptor and painter Yusuf Huwayyik.[3] Sculpted from locally sourced limestone, Huwayyik's monument was a somber and understated centograph framed by two modestly dressed upright women. The only difference between the two female figures lay in their head coverings, which clearly identified one as Muslim and the other as Christian. With outstretched arms, the women faced each other, their hands and gazes fixed on a funerary urn, which symbolically held the ashes of those who perished in the war. Titled *Deux pleureuses* (Two mourners), the stoic women were alternatively interpreted as mourning the loss of their sons, their children and families, or the many who had fallen victim to a devastating man-made wartime famine.

The upheavals of World War I were felt early on in Beirut and in the adjacent Mount Lebanon, the former a provincial capital and the latter a semiautonomous district of the Ottoman Empire. It was at the end of June 1914—when affluent Beirutis escaped the heat of the city, and with the tourist season in the cool resort towns of the neighboring mountains in full swing—that news of the Austrian imperial heir's assassination set off a "firestorm" in Mount Lebanon.[4] Upon hearing the reports, vacationing families from Cairo, Damascus, Europe, and the United States instantly gathered up their belongings and hurried down to Beirut to catch the next boat, train, or carriage back home.[5] This swift flight stirred locals' worst fears. Was war imminent? Their concerns were to be substantiated in short order. The Ottoman call to arms came on August 3, 1914, several months before the empire's central government in Istanbul publicly announced its ill-fated decision to enter the war on the side of the Central Powers—Germany and Austria-Hungary.[6] According to official figures released in 1921, in the course of four seemingly endless years of war, the Ottomans mobilized an extraordinary 2.85 million men between the ages of fifteen and fifty-five to fight, what historical hindsight now makes plain, a losing battle.[7] By the end of the war, the empire had lost a fourth of its army and suffered many more casualties among its civilian population.[8] Ottoman military engagement, as is well known, was limited to the peripheries of the empire. Except for a few targeted aerial bombardments of its harbor, the cosmopolitan Mediterranean port city of Beirut and the coastal and rugged mountain terrain of Mount Lebanon did not see direct combat.[9] Although they were far removed from the Ottoman battlefronts, high estimates of noncombatant mortalities for both city and rural mountain areas, however, are clear indicators that the war happened here too.

When considering the empire as a whole, it is evident that the war hit civilians living in Beirut and Mount Lebanon especially hard. In the course of four years, approximately half a million people perished in Greater Syria.[10] While there are no reliable statistics, historians have estimated that Mount Lebanon lost somewhere between 150,000 and 300,000 people.[11] Beirut, the capital of the Ottoman province of Beirut, alone is said to have lost approximately half its residents.[12] While many fled, the extraordinary human loss was a direct result of war calamities; the biggest killers were hunger and disease. As early as October 1914, Ottoman civilians complained of food shortages, diminishing supplies of seed grain, and a disproportionate rise in the cost of living. In Beirut and Mount Lebanon, both places of limited agricultural production, the food crisis soon escalated into "a famine of epic severity."[13] As Ottoman authorities closed the Beirut harbor to imports from abroad, the Entente Powers (Britain, France, and Russia) blocked nearly all Mediterranean trade; transportation of food from the grain-producing regions of Greater Syria to the coast became increasingly difficult, and the coastal areas' most important supply lines were effectively cut. Bad harvests due to heat waves, lack of rain and workers, followed by an infamously destructive locust invasion, exacerbated the situation. Basic necessities, if they did not completely disappear from the market, rose in price beyond the reach of the average person. Famine struck!

The Horrors of Famine on the Provincial Home Front

It was the bloodless incursion of starvation and the silent assault of fatal microbes that defined the experiences of war on what I refer to as the provincial Ottoman home front. First propagated during World War I, the term "home front" is useful here. It was initially intended to differentiate a masculine *battle* front from a female *home* front, but here the term "home" is used to describe the military term "front." This suggests a blurred line between soldiers and civilians and introduces violence into the civilian realm.[14] Lacking the high drama of bombs and bullets, it was a different, silent violence that defined life on the home front in general, and in this provincial home front in particular. As an employee of the American Syrian Protestant College (SPC) in Beirut, Edward Nickoley observed in early 1917 that "there is more evidence of distress and suffering at those places [soup kitchens, meaning the home front] than there is on any battlefield."[15] With an already dire situation worsening in Beirut and Mount Lebanon, starving bodies, now easy targets for deadly infectious diseases, turned into everyday sights. Visiting Beirut in 1916, Turkish feminist Halide Edip described the scene in her memoir: "In the rich streets of Beirut, men in rags with famished faces, solitary waifs and strays of both sexes wandered; lonely children, with wavering stick-like legs, faces wrinkled like centenarians, eyes sunken with bitter and unconscious irony, hair thinned or entirely gone moved along."[16] Individuals turned into survival machines, defying all human dignity; women and children scavenged for food in Beirut's garbage bins; like animals, they grazed on the fields and mountain meadows, devoured dead animals, and, in final acts of desperation, even picked grains from horse dung.

The situation in Mount Lebanon, as in Beirut, was dire and no doubt was growing worse each year. Hunger's wreckage was confirmed by the accounts of American canvassers, who traveled into Mount Lebanon, compiling lists of people in need. Upon their return to Beirut, the men testified to the appalling state of affairs caused by starvation. One surveyor, after making a list of poor people in the villages assigned to him, returned to the same villages to ensure their accuracy. In the meantime, so many people had died that his lists were useless, and he had to compile new ones. In one village, forty-seven people had died during the twelve-day interval between his first and second visits. In another, nineteen were dead after only three days, most of them from "out and out starvation."[17] The account of an unnamed American eyewitness published in a Cairo newspaper further confirmed the disproportionate fatalities. In the village where he had spent the summer months, more than thirty people had died of hunger.[18] In other cases, entire villages had been abandoned. For example, one small village near the Damur River was "empty except for one old man, who was burying his dead friend."[19] Here, the war was, without a doubt, a battle endured, fought, and eventually lost on the home front. Civilians were the victims.[20]

The inhumanity of war and famine became a catalyst for indescribable behaviors. The most horrifying example, framed as a moral disease that accompanied "body disease," was the moment when "mothers ate their children." According to an eyewitness, starvation reached such heights that people employed "just about any means to get food to survive, means which ordinarily their upbringing and pride would have ruled out."[21] Eating human flesh may have been such a means. Yusuf Rufa'il, a resident of a small town in northern Mount Lebanon, claimed to have known of two such incidents: one in the northern Kisrawan and another in the central Shuf district of Mount Lebanon.[22] Ibrahim Kan'an included a section in his history of wartime Beirut titled "The Eater of the Children's Flesh." In it, he recounted the story of a man who had reportedly slaughtered and eaten one of his sons. When interrogated by police, the man admitted his crime and blamed hunger.[23] Antun Yamin's eyewitness account published in 1919 offers, as the historian Najwa al-Qattan put so well, "not stories or even anecdotes, but a register of horrific still lifes in bite-size bursts of arresting detail."[24] He quickly rattled off a list of the violations, never pausing, as if to avoid lingering on the moral implications. He enumerated: "In Damur, Kattar Shahdan al-Salafani ate three human corpses; in Matn, Helena daughter of Salibi Abd ate the corpse of her nephew, Najib Salibi 'Abd. And 'she was not the only one who ate a corpse.' In Tripoli, four women cannibalized four children."[25] It is impossible to parse fact from fiction. But there is no doubt that this "epic" famine turned food into most people's *primary* concern.[26] The chroniclers of the famine used the "unthinkable" to describe what they saw as nothing less than a demographic catastrophe, an attack on human existence, an existential crisis. The accounts of first-generation eyewitnesses and historians alerted their readers and listeners that this famine, like so many others, had exposed sentiments, instincts, and behaviors that not only revealed, unflatteringly, a universal abandonment of ethics but perhaps represented the darkest moment of their people's history.[27] It was, as the Syrian poet Nasib 'Arida signaled, a "tale of weakness and disgrace" best erased from history.[28]

Reminding the public as it did of the horrors of famine, Huwayyik's *Deux pleureuses* became the focus of heated debates and disapproval in the Lebanese press immediately after its inauguration on May 6, 1930.[29] The monument depicted the beginning of the Lebanese Republic's national "birth" as the unacceptable passivity of female suffering and male absence or, perhaps more aptly, impotence. As one critic noted, it "did not represent the manhood [*rujula*] of heroes." Another lamented that the sculpture "symbolized tears and resignation rather than courage and heroism."[30] And while the most horrific effects of the famine were recorded during and immediately after the war, this sinister episode was perceived as a stain on the memory of a newly emerging nation. It seemed best forgotten, which had the remarkable effect of turning this catastrophic devastation into an insignificant detail in the larger history of World War I in the Middle East. This book insists that the famine was anything but irrelevant. Instead, it argues that this man-made wartime famine opened a space for local, national, and international actors to reshape the wartime and postwar political landscape as they responded to starvation and disease. Indeed, the position of state and nonstate actors in the chain of civilian provisioning, their willingness or refusal, their capability or failure, and their altruism or greed in feeding the poor and destitute affected their social and political standing during and after World War I. The great potential for sociopolitical benefits and, in turn, losses rendered civilian provisioning a highly contested field.

Uncovering a Forgotten Story: The Famine in Lebanese Memory and History

When I was conducting research for this book, state-sponsored memory of the war years chose to highlight the martyrdom of a select group of Arab notables, intellectuals, and nationalists who were framed as having resisted the tyranny of Ottoman rule. This memory was *also* rooted in wartime events. Under the umbrella of martial law, the regional and local representatives of the Committee of Union and Progress (CUP), the ruling party of the Ottoman state, regulated the smallest and seemingly most insignificant civilian matters in Beirut and Mount Lebanon. Jamal Pasha, a high-ranking member of the party, arrived in Syria as the commander of the Fourth Army Corps soon after the Ottomans entered the war on October 31, 1914. The military commander more often than not was described as an unsavory character. The American ambassador to Istanbul, Henry Morgenthau, found "there was little about Djemal [Jamal] that was pleasing." On the contrary, he saw him as cunning, remorseless, and selfish to "an extreme degree. Even his laugh, which disclosed all his white teeth, was unpleasant and animal-like."[31] As the CUP had entrusted Jamal Pasha with full reign over Greater Syria and the Arabian Peninsula, he ruled unchecked and with an iron fist.[32] According to the ambassador, he governed Syria "as independently as a robber baron," becoming "a kind of sub-sultan, holding his own court."[33] Jamal Pasha dealt ruthlessly with any opposition that advocated ideas threatening to Ottoman sovereignty, such as Arab nationalism and demands for the continued autonomy of Mount Lebanon. Jamal Pasha ordered suspected traitors to be exiled, imprisoned, and in the worst cases executed. The public hanging of thirty-three prominent Arab men accused of anti-Ottoman scheming in Beirut and Damascus in 1915 and 1916 earned Jamal Pasha the titles of "blood-shedder" (*al-saffah*) and "butcher" (*al-jazzar*).[34] It was this public spectacle of violence that became the focus of the state's commemoration of World War I in 1938, when May 6, the date of the men's "sacrifice," was proclaimed an official day of national mourning. There was no plaque, no statue, and no mention of the famine in the state's official memory of World War I. But the famine's memory lingered right below the surface.[35]

During my many casual conversations with Lebanese citizens, I never missed an opportunity to ask what they knew about the experience of World War I. Most if not all men and women framed their answers by stating that there had been *no war* in their country, no *real* war at any rate. There had been, however, starvation, hunger, no food, or as some would say, the people fought a "war of famine" (*harb al-maja'a*).[36] The experience of the Great War in the second- and third-generation memories of ordinary Lebanese seemed to be primarily identified with either famine or its semantic associates, hunger and food shortages, and with people's reactions to the famine, even though Lebanese textbooks generally dismissed this historical episode within a paragraph or two. Whether emphasizing family histories of feeding, provisioning, and compassion or focusing on the suffering of the many, the famine loomed large in what we might call popular memory.[37] Intrigued by the discrepancy between official and contemporary popular memory—the latter partially influenced by the famine's domineering presence in the accounts of eyewitnesses and first-generation historians—this book retrieves the story of this Ottoman provincial home front through its encounter with the famine.

A number of historians have recently begun to write the social and economic history of World War I in the Middle East. Unsurprisingly, their focus has been on the war's dehumanization and perpetual disruption of normalcy.[38] This book, however, is not only about the injurious inhumanity of famine or the war's destructive force. Indeed, the horrors of the famine will eventually fade into the background. It is clear, as Janam Mukherjee points out, that "famine preys on the poorest of the poor, the weakest of the weak, those whose very lives and life-stories are erased by marginality and neglect."[39] It is of little use to present sensational perhaps even pornographic pictures and accounts of suffering. However shocking, sad, and startling, such images and texts contribute little toward explaining the long- and short-term processes that bring about famine. Instead, I am interested in the reactions of those men and women who saw, heard, or read the accounts of starvation and were motivated to help, whether for pity, piety, politics, prospects, power, or profit.

The Creative Power of War and Famine: The Politics of Provisioning

I argue here that the exigencies of World War I in general and the famine in particular also constituted a productive force. War, conflict, violence, and famine are spaces of generative powers wherein realities are forged, and "what comes after rarely resembles what came before. . . . It is a rift that illuminates elsewhere and creates new states of being."[40] Theorists of war have long expounded on the understanding of war as formative and as a particular opportunity for state intervention. In recent years, a number of works on the war in the Ottoman Empire have started to highlight the war's creative role in consolidating national identities, urban development, and state power.[41] Viewing the war from a local perspective and through the lens of famine, this book follows this trend and engages war relief and welfare activities, understood here as constantly changing enactments and performances of society, gender, family, and local communal relationships, as arenas in which we can see war as a generative force. In this sense, the book's purpose is to portray the war of famine as simultaneously, and perhaps paradoxically, destructive and formative.

War and famine relief in the form of provisioning and humanitarian aid to Ottoman civilians in the Arab provinces has received little attention.[42] Historians have focused their attention on foreign efforts in the Anatolian provinces, in particular the tremendous work of international missionaries and relief organizations in response to the Armenian genocide. For Beirut and Mount Lebanon, the war years often have been dismissed as a period of communal, international, and state failures in regard to taking care of civilians. This is not surprising, since relief work in the region was not only overshadowed by the cruelty of the famine but also in the end proved unsuccessful in preventing mass starvation. Moreover, when considering state officials' roles in providing wartime relief, the callous legacy of Jamal Pasha's military dictatorship left little room to even contemplate Ottoman aid work. Yet a closer study of the war years shows that in response to tragedy and the initial absence of state-sponsored civilian provisioning policies, international and local actors worked to provide relief and stepped in where the central state, at least early on, was unable or perhaps even unwilling to intercede.[43] As Bayard Dodge, an employee at Beirut's SPC, insisted, everyday violence in the form of starvation triggered a response by "the finest people in Beirut" and beyond.⁴⁴ The responses to violence and suffering, however, were not without contention. On the contrary, I argue that the provisioning of food and the struggle against infectious diseases were contested domains wherein political power was negotiated and asserted, won and lost.

My main objective is to demonstrate how war relief and humanitarian aid to victims of starvation and disease involved fierce political battles among state, local, and international actors. Humanitarian relief workers, in the words of historian Rebecca Gill, "operated in a crowded field with numerous impromptu committees and sympathetic individuals offering their services," all of whom at times competed for space.⁴⁵ It is this crowded field, as the "site of a more or less overt struggle over the definition of the legitimate principles of division of the field," that sets the stage for this work.⁴⁶ To draw out what I call the "politics of provisioning," the book focuses on the efforts of local communities (in particular, philanthropic, women's, and religious organizations), the state, and municipalities, as well as international efforts, to ameliorate the situation on the Ottoman provincial home front.⁴⁷ While highlighting the field as a local, national, and international space, the politics of provisioning primarily uncovers the workings of these organizations as key to shaping the everyday experiences of ordinary citizens, thereby enhancing our understanding of social realities on the Ottoman home front. Exposing the strategies of these various agents of benevolence, and considering the challenges they encountered, this locally situated micro-study shows the centrality of the war in an area peripheral to the European and Ottoman battlefields; it complicates normative accounts of Ottoman decline and tyranny; and, most important, it argues that wartime competition, integral to the politics of provisioning and resulting in the deep reorganization of society, contributed to the shaping of the postwar political landscape.

The Centrality of the Periphery: Ottoman Civilians at War

The Great War in the Middle East immediately evokes three particular diplomatic stunts. Historians have filled rows of library shelves with accounts of the Arab Revolt (1916–1918), with stories about T. E. Lawrence (1888–1935), and with the secret negotiations between the British high commissioner Sir Henry McMahon (1862–1949) and the sharif of Mecca, Husayn Ibn ʿAli al-Hashimi (1853–1931).[48] The Sykes-Picot negotiations of 1916, in which the Russian, French, and British parceled out the Ottoman Empire based on European political, cultural, and economic interests, has dominated much of the discussion.[49] The third maneuver—whose bequests proved equally durable and damaging—was the Balfour Declaration of 1917, which promised the Zionist movement a Jewish homeland in Palestine.[50] Given their significance in shaping the geopolitics of the region, such prominence comes as no surprise. The troubling result, however, is that the Ottoman Empire has been inscribed in the history of the war as victors' spoils and thus devoid of historical agency.[51] The war in the empire was seen as a peripheral happening, acquiring meaning only in the context of European colonial competitions and desires. Among military histories, the accounts of Ottoman battlefields pale in comparison with those of the Western trenches. While in recent years, scholars of World War I have acknowledged that the experiences of non-European societies are essential to understanding the global scope of the war, the latter's incorporation into the war's history has been slow. Even the most recent historiography, which advocates for a global or transnational account of the war, largely continues to present the Ottoman Empire as a sideshow. But the war was not peripheral to those who lived in the Ottoman Empire. Here one soon realized, as an American observer did, "what a terrible thing war was." Moreover, he claimed, "It not only means unspeakable suffering on the battlefield but also starvation, sorrow and fear amongst the populace, which can hardly be described."[52] The periphery, the home front, was a main stage.

Viewing the war through the lens of the famine necessitates a decentering of the history of the war. It is impossible to understand the famine without situating it in two operational fields—the international and the local. The famine and responses to it resulted from and were shaped by the Ottoman state's actions in the world arena, where it interacted with other leaders and transnational actors such as foreign diplomats, missionaries, humanitarians, and educators. The macrolevel international politics, as they pertain to the politics of provisioning, are important to consider given that Beirut and Mount Lebanon, as discussed in Chapter 1, were integrated into the world economy in ways that would present particular challenges to Ottoman wartime provisioning. Their incorporation into a larger global market made both Beirut and Mount Lebanon more vulnerable to famine and undermined the state's ability to control its population, as external actors meddled in business and politics. In the most general terms, the Ottomans' position in the international system meant that certain international actors could place constraints on it. The war was an opportunity to shift this power balance. The Ottoman government's move to enhance the empire's position in the international system and to establish itself as an ally to the Central Powers affected local food supplies and the government's ability to distribute food, as shown in Chapter 2.

The war on the provincial home front was not an exogenous political, diplomatic, and military event but rather an endogenous socioeconomic and political process. It is requisite for us to shift our gaze away from the cigar smoke–filled bureaus of the European continent and the military horrors of the Ottoman battlefields to the streets, municipal and church offices, headquarters of volunteer organizations, and the pages of newspapers and to catch glimpses of the dinner tables of ordinary people wherever possible. World War I was a *total war*, so the home front was crucial to the war effort and essential to a comprehensive study and analysis of the war.[53] Scholars have long acknowledged the importance of the war's home fronts to the war effort and as areas of historical inquiry. While historians have raised questions about proper chronology and debated the validity and utility of the concept of "total war" extensively, two defining features make the concept useful here as a comparative analytical tool.[54] First, it embraces the "total mobilization" of society, "utilizing all the resources of the state and the economy."[55] During World War I this meant that all belligerent countries demanded increasing sacrifices not only from their men fighting cruel battles on the front but also from their civilians. In the Ottoman Empire in general, and in Beirut and Mount Lebanon in particular, this involved an unmitigated mobilization of civilian resources. The Ottoman state callously collected humans (conscription) and the animals and materials (requisitioning and increased taxes) required to serve and feed its armies. Indeed, civilians on the Ottoman home front were mobilized to a greater degree than ever before, so much so that mobilization, as in Europe, became "cynosure of the home front."[56] Second, the home fronts of the Great War became critical to the material and moral support of combat troops, progressively obliterating the distinctions between spaces of war (fronts) and not war (homes).[57] The lines between civilians and soldiers were blurred, as the former came to experience the war firsthand.[58] In this process toward totality, civilians became legitimate targets of military violence, enduring direct attacks and, more often, strategic blockades of people, money, and materials.[59] Besides becoming enemy targets, civilians came under the scrutiny and surveillance of their state. Restrictions of movement, censorship of the press, urban restructuring, and increased military presence in cities, towns, and villages were everyday occurrences and were framed as collective ways of aiding the war effort. Total war here describes a development in warfare that demanded increasing civilian sacrifices, turning civilians into targets of aggressions systematically meted out by the enemy and by the state; most important, it engendered everyday forms of violence. Or, as Bayard Dodge lamented, "starvation, sorrow and fear" were at the heart of the war's totalizing nature. In this circumstance, the famine was both an outcome of total war and a defining *central* characteristic of the experience of war.

The Ottoman Provincial Home Front: State in Society

The Ottoman home front was central. Still, the wartime experiences of Ottoman civilians on the home front have received little scholarly attention, especially when compared to the large volume of literature chronicling everyday life on the various European home fronts.[60] Turkish historiography deems World War I as a dark period. Other than the victory at Gallipoli (January 6, 1916) and the defeat at Sarikamish (January 15, 1915),[61] the war, until recently, was simply a nonevent.[62] Eclipsed by the "heroic" victory of Mustafa Kemal's forces during the War of Independence (1919–1920), the losses from the war and, more important, the stain of the genocide perpetrated against the empire's own Christian population were of limited use in the nationalist discourse of the "birth" of the Turkish Republic (1923).[63] Working against this trend, historians conducting research in the central Ottoman archives have begun to write diplomatic and military histories of the war, including the experiences of soldiers, and are increasingly paying attention to state-citizen relations in wartime.

It must be noted that the empire's geographic, linguistic, and ethnic diversity does not allow us to speak of a uniform home-front experience. This book tells the story of *one* Ottoman provincial home front's encounter with total war by highlighting the evolving relationship between the state and provincial actors during the war, as well as the state's function *in* society. Following Joel Midgal's *state in society* approach, the politics of provisioning showcases both state and society as fluid constellations with indistinct boundaries. My goal is to complicate state-centered accounts by dismantling the state's often-presumed coherent, monolithic, and autonomous character. By placing the state within society, the story presented here challenges one-sided accounts of Ottoman tyranny and of the war as a time of top-down state building. By focusing on the negotiations, competitions, and cooperation involved in provisioning, we can draw attention to the state's *becoming* as a process involving, in its provinces, both conflicts and alliances with society. I argue that local provincial elites and circumstances have a stake in triggering, molding, and negotiating wartime politics and policies—that is, talking back to the state. Local actors' engagements, reactions, and negotiations, as they crossed paths with representatives of the state, will not only provide a more holistic view but also force us to rethink once again the position and processes of power as it functions in society.[64]

War, no doubt, stimulates juridical power, here understood as the power of the state or its official representatives to assert or expand its sphere of operation. For example, Charles Tilly has argued that war, as a moment of organized violence, engages state agents in four activities: war making, state making, protection, and extraction.[65] Each of these activities—eliminating external and internal enemies and threats to the state's representative clients, and extracting the means needed to carry out these activities—assumes the use of violence. It is here, in the context of violence, that the productive power of war appears most obvious. The formation, establishment, and restructuring of armies, their supporting institutions, means of surveillance, efforts of extraction, and fiscal accounting mechanisms, however successful, all underlie organized violence.[66] Such articulations are characteristic of what Nancy Rose Hunt, in the context of colonial Congo, has called the "nervous state," a state that polices and secures, dreading both external enemies and internal rebellions.[67] In the case of Beirut and Mount Lebanon, it will become immediately clear that the motivation of those who represented the top-down powers of administration and law—Jamal Pasha and his underlings—was to maintain, broaden, and inhabit institutions linked to the state.[68] There is no doubt that the actions of Jamal Pasha and his subordinates, such as carrying out executions, forcing people into exile, and declaring martial law, were central in framing experiences on the home front. Talha Çiçek convincingly makes this point in his notable history of wartime Ottoman Syria. Çiçek presents an intricate account, proceeding outward from the empire's capital, and highlights the war as a moment of accelerated state formation. It is the history of Jamal Pasha working to consolidate a state that could "conduct the conduct" of its provincial citizens. For the military commander, Çiçek writes, this was a struggle to control, lead, and shape a particular loyal Ottoman citizen.[69]

The state's power, however, works not only through violent deduction, extraction, and restrictions (censorship, conscription) but also in the delivery of services (urban development, education). Food and health provisions in times of famine, I argue, were equally as important. Power that seeks to "generate, incite, reinforce, monitor, optimize, and organize the forces under it" does not work through deduction alone.[70] Wartime provision and relief was another sphere where this becomes clear. In Beirut and Mount Lebanon, representatives of the state saw the war as an opportunity to assert state power through wartime provisioning and the extension of public health measures. Charles Tilly's idea of "protection" as part of what a state does during war is helpful here. He asserts that protection includes, on the part of state representatives, the "elimination or neutralizing of their clients' enemies."[71] (I would add "perceived" or "real" enemies.) The act of protection can take on violent form, or, as in the case of shielding clients' bodies against hunger and disease, it can be humanitarian. Suffering turned into "the principal 'call for alms'" on the home front.[72] This clearly suggests that at times power over life, the biopolitical, is benevolent and not "unambiguously nefarious."[73] Hunt outlines the dual function of the state: The nervous state "policed and securitized as it sought to contain menacing forms of therapeutic rebellion," whereas "the biopolitical [state] worked to promote life and health."[74] The former functioned driven by fear, and the latter by guilt. *Charity of War* brings this important point to the fore. However, it would be rash, Hunt argues, to think that these dual functions forge a dichotomy or even parallel processes; instead, the biopolitical/humanitarian and the nervous/securitizing interact with mobility, so the two functions exist as relational processes. In the case of Beirut and Mount Lebanon they were at times so entangled that any distinction between them becomes difficult. Moreover, distinguishing between the nervous and the biopolitical does not imply that the latter did not use violence to accomplish its goals. Still, it seems shortsighted to understand the state as somehow separate from society.[75] Neither the Ottoman state nor its representatives ever worked in isolation. Instead, men such as the newly appointed Jamal Pasha entered into a society, both urban and rural, made up of a complex network of power relations that could not easily be oppressed, ignored, or appeased.

A close look at the politics of provisioning not only allows us to see different types of power but also forces us to account for the natures of state and society and their relationships with each other. The state cannot be reduced to an unchanging, solid, harmonious object, whose autonomy relies on its clear separation from society and its control over it. Instead, as Midgal argues, both state and society are "not static formations but are constantly becoming as a result of struggle over social control."[76] Their boundaries are always shifting. Hence, I argue that the state cannot "stand apart from society";[77] the state functions within society through a mélange of formal and informal social organizations.[78] The governmentalized state of the nineteenth century (the Ottoman Empire can be seen as such an entity) took shape through, or at the very least was influenced by, the "prior formation of ever-growing apparatuses of knowledge collection and problematization that formed alongside the state apparatuses, often in conflict with it, in the emergent terrain of the 'social.'"[79] Michael Watts and Hans Bohle posit that "prescriptive and normative responses to vulnerability" reduce exposure, enhance coping capacity, strengthen recovery potential, and bolster damage control (i.e., minimize destructive consequences) through both private and public means.[80] This means that not all modes of protection originate with the state. But some existing social organizations have at their disposal some of the "same currency of compliance, participation, and legitimacy to protect and strengthen their enclaves" as the state.[81]

In the Ottoman provinces, we see that exigencies were dealt with through both private and public means. For example, philanthropic organizations, foreign missionaries, local notables, and religious institutions that exercised demands and constraints on the metropole in the prewar period, asserting a certain amount of power over life, strove to counteract the destructiveness of the war, or at the very least ameliorate its effects. With this goal in mind, local, state, and international wartime relief efforts mobilized existing networks and forged new ones to help those in need. This process was marked by fierce competition over the loyalties of local civilians, which in turn would guarantee the maintenance or even expansion of their social positions. For example, urban notables' struggles to maintain their social standing as benevolent agents and the state's attempts to assert its role as benefactor to the citizenry, were driven by local and international competition over people's stomachs, that is, over loyalties, as discussed in Chapters 3 and 5. Consequently, this book asserts that while the interventionist wartime policies of state representatives shaped everyday life on the home front, we must also bear in mind that the relationships between the empire's diverse social groups and the state affected ruling strategies as well as resistance to them. *Charity of War*, therefore, expands on work that has long seen provincial notables as instrumental to processes of reforming the empire's social and political structures.[82] Paying particular attention to provincial actors and social organizations, this book insists on their agency as they competed for political power and status in Beirut and Mount Lebanon, and sought to assert themselves in the face of an increasingly centralizing state.[83]

The Politics of Provisioning: Fashioning Legitimacy beyond the War

War simultaneously controls and silences, as well as empowers and lends voice. Historians of Europe have long discussed this aspect of the war, but among Ottoman and Middle East historians, this "total war paradox" has not been fully explored.[84] The historian Geoff Eley argues that war means increased state interference in the form of restrictions (censorship, emergency legislations, etc.). But Eley pushes further, insisting that juridical power at the same time legitimized the voices of certain groups, opening areas for popular participation and generating demand for entitlements from the state.[85] This aspect of state-society struggles during wartime opens another set of questions. Examining social organizations in Chapters 4 and 6 that neither originated in wartime nor in the state but functioned as regulatory mechanisms at the substate level, as well as their changing relationship with the state during the war, allows us to answer a number of important questions. Who was silenced? Who silenced themselves? Who was empowered? And who empowered themselves by participating in the politics of provisioning?[86]

The answers to these questions will not only tell us much about the dynamics of wartime social and political hierarchies but can also provide important information about how the politics of provisioning contributed to the staging of a postwar political landscape.[87] First, we can assume the power of giving. The historian Amy Singer, for instance, has provided much evidence for the political character of charitable giving, demonstrating how giving is intrinsic to performing, defining, and strengthening power relationships.[88] Provisioning, like charitable giving, is a relational process that defines the bond between provider and recipient and cannot be dismissed as merely the strategy of wealthy individuals for maintaining unequal relationships with those on the receiving end.[89] Famine victims, then, were not simply "docile bodies" that could either be abandoned or nursed back to health and, through the process of feeding, molded and educated. Instead, provisioning buttressed power by creating allegiances. We might say that the recipients of provisions possessed social capital in the sense that their political allegiances guaranteed the maintenance or the reconfiguration of power relations.[90]

Starting from the assumption that neither state nor society is a stand-alone entity, an account of their changing nature and a focus on their interactions, as well as the processes that constitute social control and power, will reveal who could use provisions as power currency. In the eyes of ordinary citizens, feeding people and ensuring their health during the war signified power and legitimacy for leadership. Its lasting legacy, as shown in the concluding chapter, influenced political positionality in the aftermath of the war of famine. Midgal, further, proposes that social control may be measured by *compliance*, *participation*, and *legitimacy*. Compliance not only refers to the degree to which a population obeys state demands but is also the outcome of the capacity of distributing resources and services, which in turn "determines the degree to which the state can demand compliance."[91] Furthermore, the state gains strength through participation, by legislating contributions to the war effort, and by empowering either nonthreatening or unavoidable allies on the ground and enfolding them in state-sponsored provisioning schemes. For example, women, seen as a political asset, were enlisted to contribute to the well-being of society during the war, as were CUP-friendly provincial notables.

Both compliance and participation were driven by a state of emergency, wherein many people simply had no choice, and by a rewards system. A good number of people benefited from an alliance with the state, many of whom would be listed as war profiteers in the aftermath of the war and lose legitimacy in the eyes of the population. Legitimacy, as a measure of the state's strength, was far more complicated, as it implies that the population would readily accept a particular social order. One can imagine that people comply and participate without automatically accepting a given state of affairs. Provisioning was one measure state officials thought would guarantee the goodwill of the population. As some leaders of social organizations rejected the state's interference—the Maronite Church, for instance—their ability to continue provisioning would determine their legitimacy in the aftermath of the war. Other groups like the American Red Cross, which organized sizable relief work, helped strengthen the role of the United States in framing the "politics of welfare" in the region and internationally. Others who lost credibility based on their inability to provide would struggle to maintain their social position, especially when the victors rolled out well-organized and well-funded humanitarian campaigns after the war.[92]

Archival Encounters: Fragments, Enchantments, and Vagaries

The historian Roger Chickering has argued that any historical narrative of total war must consider that this kind of war by definition touched "everyone who lived through the conflict." Hence, sites of total war deserve nothing less than a "total history," a history that includes all of the war's political, economic, social, and cultural aspects.[93] Writing a total history for Beirut and Mount Lebanon would be an ambitious goal under normal circumstances. The absence of a functioning central archive and the fact that many official and family records were destroyed during the most recent Lebanese Civil War (1975–1990) presented significant challenges for archival research. Consequently, this account relies on a unique set of sources collected from archives in Lebanon, Germany, France, and the United States. Attempting to get as close to "the ground" as possible, it combines published and unpublished sources, memoirs, diaries, private correspondence, diplomatic records, and the files of charitable societies, international relief organizations, and religious institutions in and outside Beirut. Reading them against published Ottoman sources, I am fully aware of the limitations of this diverse, and in the end incomplete, source base. Without a doubt, there remains much room for further research.

The archival record I have used, or rather its fragments, is untidy and opaque and presents a number of problems. For example, the famine, while always present, oscillated between ubiquity and nonexistence. The term "famine" was generally avoided in wartime correspondence and local publications. There were also few mentions of the word "famine" in the sizable collection of private letters of SPC president Howard Bliss and his American colleagues throughout the entire duration of the war.[94] A handwritten draft of the college's *51st Annual Report* (1916–1917) shows the careful consideration the words "famine" and "hunger" received; these were crossed out on the draft and replaced with "insufficient food supplies" and "supperless," respectively. The entry reads:

> The problems [of supplies to the college] were solved and we are profoundly grateful that no member of our large family of 700 have gone ~~hungry~~ supperless to bed during these long dark years of ~~famine~~ insufficient food supplies.[95]

However, references to scarcity, deprivation, and price hikes appeared on nearly every page. Discussions about the production and procurement of food supplies, as well as the dire direct or indirect consequences of their absence, lurked within every crevice of an otherwise disparate archive. Yet in other instances, "famine" was announced loud and clear. Eager to inform their communities about the suffering back home, in particular after 1915, the Arabic diaspora press in Egypt and the Americas ran such headlines as "The Famine in Syria and Lebanon" and "Between Hunger and Disease."[96] "Famine," moreover, was amplified in postwar reports and eyewitness accounts locally and internationally. The archives spoke, and the suffering of the many emerged front and center.

The archives were of various types, and their discovery, more often than not, was tortuous. I encountered the usual enclosed spaces, where documents, institutionally affiliated and sometimes catalogued, were kept, a sense of pride about their preservation in the air. Archivists lurked to make certain no unauthorized photographs were taken or too many words typed, while hours of operations and identification cards policed access and credentials. In today's Beirut, however, this normative limited archive is the exception. The more common archive is infinite and requires persistence, patience, and curiosity. Remembering the boxes upon boxes of photographs and letters stored in my grandmother's attic, the hours I spent interrogating her about unfamiliar faces, some of whom she did not know herself, I anticipated that family archives offered yet another possibility for uncovering the past. I decided I would begin knocking on the doors of institutions, organizations, and families with whose names I had become familiar in the previous year. It was a great idea in theory, but its execution proved challenging to say the least. For many people, to open their door, their homes, and in particular their private family history to a stranger would be uncomfortable. Imagine someone knocking on your door. So naturally, I had my work cut out for me. Any potential visit was preceded by meeting a family member, perhaps through a friend or an acquaintance, or simply by chance, and was followed by time spent building relationships. Days, weeks, and sometimes months passed, and whatever was packed in wooden drawers, neatly collected in family albums, piled into boxes, or simply stuffed into old suitcases would be a surprise. A picture or a diary; newspaper clippings; birth, death, and marriage certificates; letters; all the things a historian desires, I soon realized, were rare. Emptiness, nothingness, a vague story remembered by a family elder was instead the norm. The Lebanese civil war had robbed many families' storage areas, drawers, and shelves of their past. The past, after all, was an unnecessary luxury in the contest for survival. Memories had traversed at least a generation and survived the test of time to become part of family history, memory, or myth. Historian-turned-ethnographer, I listened to the unconventional archive.

Soon my own entanglements "with real-life experiences of the past, memory, myth, fantasy and desire" reminded me of Raphael Samuel's warning about the promiscuity of "sources" and that "history has always been a hybrid form of knowledge, syncretized past and present, memory and myth, the written record and the spoken word."[97] The work before me was one of weaving. It involved intricate processes that would string together patches and fragments of vastly different textures and colors. It is in those places, where oral and textual archives agreed, contradicted, negotiated, and compromised, that the plotlines of the civilian drama could be drawn. Although a finite tapestry or narrative is presented here, it is important to remember that history is "an organic form of knowledge."[98] The "Lebanese" archive will continue to change as new relationships open new doors and individuals and institutions begin to digitize their own records and various family documents and photographs donated to them. Access and availability are expanding, and the distant past is opening to the researcher, albeit incrementally and contingent on circumstance. The story will change accordingly.

For the present, this book proposes an alternative narrative to one-sided interpretations of wartime Ottoman tyranny, the complete collapse of society, and top-down state formation, not that these were not realities. At the same time, its focus on the Arab provinces highlights the importance of on-the-ground localized policies and practices put into play by provincial governors and local elites in setting the stage for centralization. From there, the discussion moves between levels of analysis that include international, state, regional, and "micropolitical contexts of social relations, locality, and the everyday" as these became affected by changes in governance.[99] The book complicates the process of wartime state intervention as a top-down unidirectional measure by lending agency to local actors in shaping the process and by paying attention to local networks, actors, and individuals, all of whom negotiated, formulated, and implemented wartime policies. In the end, international, state, and local efforts to alleviate suffering proved futile, as thousands of civilians lost their lives, and the war marked the final collapse of the Ottoman regime. Eventually, all that that was left were cities filled with starving refugees and villages emptied of their young men (if not of all their residents) and a society drained of political opposition and exhausted from hunger.[100] In light of the large number of starvation deaths and overall civilian suffering, *Charity of War*, as a study of these largely futile responses to the Lebanese famine, may seem a counterintuitive project. If war relief was unable to save large numbers of people from starvation, why write about it? The answer, I argue, lies in the processes, practices, and failures of various aid, relief, and provisioning campaigns. However inconsequential in preventing a demographic catastrophe, the history of a dynamic politics of provisioning not only shaped wartime power constellations but also contributed to shaping the political landscape of the postwar period. It will become clear that the four years of crisis cannot simply be understood as a series of state or local failures, neatly fitting into the paradigm of a declining empire. And instead, in its consideration of the war and the end of empire, the book traces an uneven trajectory.[101] In short, the Great War was not simply another nail in the coffin of an already sick man of Europe. There is no teleology.

Figure 2. View of Beirut and Mount Sannine from the American University of Beirut, 1924–1925. Source: American University of Beirut / Library Archives.

{ CHAPTER 1 }

A CITY AND ITS MOUNTAIN, A MOUNTAIN AND ITS CITY

Sitting on the second-floor balcony of the new Near East personnel house, Nellie Miller-Mann breathed in her new surroundings. "Everything is lovely and the goose hangs high," she wrote to her sister. Nellie's new home was a typical upper-class house situated on the hillside overlooking the bay of Beirut. The Beirut harbor, nestled into a cove protected from the usual southwest winds, was visible in the distance. Spanning the entire building, the balcony immediately became Nellie's favorite spot, as it was a "lovely cool place to sit out at night and watch the sunset behind the palms and the moon rise over the Lebanon mountains and peek through the fir trees."[1] With great enthusiasm, Nellie described the scene: "The Lebanon Mountains, which extend far out into the sea in front and the distant peak of Sannin Mountains, the highest peak of the Lebanon, was like a huge shining coral. It was the most wonderful sight."[2] The Mennonite missionary was not the only one impressed; many before her had marveled at the scene. Six decades earlier in 1858, Lady Strangford, a British writer and nurse, saw an "amphitheater of mountains," at center stage a city that rose from the water's edge, crawling up the slopes of the foothills. It fascinated "the eye in the first moment," forging an "everlasting memory of loveliness."[3] The women's view must have been similar to that captured by the photographer from the Bonfils studio at the beginning of the twentieth century: majestic snow-covered mountains as the backdrop for a city at the edge of the Mediterranean Sea. The city as foreground to the distant limestone peaks and the ubiquity of the mountains have been described by travelers and replicated in countless images of the nineteenth and early twentieth centuries. One arrived in Beirut via train from Damascus, by sailboat or steamer from the Mediterranean Sea, or by carriage from the northern and southern coastal towns, such as Tripoli and Sidon. Whether crossing the mountains from the west, traveling alongside the peaks from the south and the north, or approaching them head-on from the east, one's encounter with Beirut meant traversing, brushing up against, or simply observing the snow-covered peaks. City and mountain, as in the women's accounts, were visually indivisible.

There, however, was more than met the eye, as the connection between the urban center and its rural hinterland was existential as well. During most of Ottoman rule over the Levant, Beirut and Mount Lebanon constituted two distinct and independent administrative units, but the city and the mountain district maintained close political and socioeconomic ties. These ties mandate a combined history, as war, famine, and the politics of provisioning took place within the context of an entangled history of Beirut and Mount Lebanon that affected the relationship between them. A key argument of this book is that the wartime politicking around providing food and in the struggle against infectious diseases challenged, renegotiated, and reshaped preexisting power constellations that opened a space for the political union of an already visually and existentially united city and mountain in the postwar period. To fully understand the special relationship of Beirut to its hinterland during war and in the postwar period, it is necessary to first outline their changing social and economic linkages, administrative setup, and demographic makeup leading up to 1914.

In the 1980s, famine theorists moved away from explaining mass starvation as an act of God or nature to its being the outcome of human action and inaction.[4] It was a late revelation. Fourteenth-century Arab scholars, though couching the point in religious rhetoric, had long insisted that humans caused famine. Arab philosopher and historian Ibn Khaldun (1332–1406) was among the first to consider famine (*maja'a*) the outcome of bad government,[5] when he drew a clear link between poor governing and high grain prices.[6] Ibn Khaldun blamed famine on the government's "coercion of the subject" and its failure to intervene successfully to remedy the decrease in agricultural production and the food shortages that resulted.[7] Fifteenth-century Mamluk chroniclers such as Ibn Taghribirdi (1410–1470) and the Arab historian Taqi ad-Din al-Maqrizi (1364–1442) took up Ibn Khaldun's interpretational frame.[8] For al-Maqrizi, famine, which he referred to as "*ghalā'* [increase in prices] that causes *jū'* [hunger] and *mawt* or *mawtān* [death]," was the outcome of high prices, oppressive taxes, and the debasement of currency, all of which, as we will see, played a role in the war of famine in 1914–1918.[9] He also indicts governmental mismanagement for further causing people's distress during famine.

In modern famine studies, the fact that famines are the result of human action or inaction gained currency after economist Amartya Sen published his study of the 1942–1943 Bengali famine in 1981.[10] The study demonstrated that famine was not the outcome of lack of food due to harvest shortfalls. Instead, Sen saw famine as the outcome of "a crisis of exchange entitlements, legal, economically operative rights of access to resources that give control of food devoid of yields." It was not the food itself that was important but "the relationship of persons to the commodity." He famously asserted, "Starvation is the characteristic of some people not having enough to eat. It is not the characteristic of there being not enough to eat. While the latter can be the cause of the former, it is but one of the many possible causes."[11] Since the publication of Sen's *Poverty and Famine*, many social scientists have used his entitlement-based theory to highlight the changing socioeconomic and institutional relations between food and people during famine.[12]

In recent decades, entitlement-based approaches have been criticized on at least two counts. First, there is a general focus on the event itself, often neglecting long-term historical processes, conjunctures, and contingencies that produce starvation.[13] Second, entitlement theories are not interested in what follows in the wake of disaster. These are serious oversights. Famine, after all, happens in society, which, as Rebecca Solnit reminds us, rests on the "idea of networks of affinity and affection."[14] Suffering, she argues, evokes altruism and caring. A more skeptical approach of course may argue that the distress of some is an opportunity for others. Michael Watts and Hans Bohle suggest a threefold "vulnerability" theory that invites both a historically grounded approach and one that takes into account famine responses, recovery, and relief.[15] The three basic defining coordinates are the risk of exposure to crises, the risk of inadequate capacities in coping with them, and the risk of severe consequences and hence slow or even limited recovery from crises.[16] Together they make up a particular space of vulnerability. More important, each element making up this space is dependent on historically specific social, political, and economic structures. The famine and responses to it then can only be fully understood in the context of long-term socioeconomic developments and locally and historically specific configurations that both rendered Beirut and Mount Lebanon vulnerable to famine and determined the social position of various local, state, and international actors that would dictate their capabilities to participate within the political field of provisioning.

This chapter situates the war of famine not as a rupture but as the historical context in which local politics happened. Nineteenth-century economic changes not only rendered Beirut and Mount Lebanon particularly vulnerable to wartime famine but also, combined with increased access to education and the emergence of mass politics following the 1908 Young Turk Revolution, broadened access to politics. This resulted in a particular set of local actors in both state and civil institutions who had various degrees of access to power and, from the outset of the war, had the potential to mitigate or exaggerate the horrors of the famine. The following then is both an administrative road map and a socioeconomic survey that paints the mise-en-scène and introduces the relevant actors of the wartime provisioning drama.[17] The goal is to historicize the wartime agents of provisioning in their operational spaces so that change over time is clearly visible as we move into the war years.

Economic Changes: Forging a Space of Vulnerability

The visits of Lady Strangford and Nellie Miller-Mann to Beirut straddled six decades. Their descriptions of the physical landscape suggest few if any changes. In reality, the years between the women's visits were arguably the most tumultuous decades in Lebanese history. The intermittent years accounted for significant administrative, political, economic, social, cultural, and demographic changes and witnessed violent intercommunal conflict, war, famine, and eventually colonial occupation. The long nineteenth century no doubt was a time of profound change for the Ottoman Empire and its multiethnic population. The empire not only had to contend with the globalization of a capitalist world market, accompanied by increasing Western encroachment on its territory, but also faced local strongmen and newly emerging nationalist independence movements that challenged Ottoman sovereignty.[18] The years leading up to 1914 were filled with conflict, war, revolution, and significant territorial losses. The Ottoman state, while it was the only sovereign Muslim empire to survive in an era of aggressive nineteenth-century imperialism and nationalism, was caught in a seemingly irreversible downward spiral. Selim Deringil describes the situation well: "The Ottoman state, together with its contemporaries, Habsburg Austria and Romanov Russia, was engaged in a struggle for survival in a world where it no longer made the rules."[19] In the Syrian provinces, the changes were notable in an ever-growing missionary movement, an increased presence of European investors and diplomats, and a lengthy Egyptian-Ottoman struggle culminating in the invasion of Egyptian troops, followed by Ottoman centralization efforts of and international intervention in the politics, economy, and administration of the region.[20]

Since the sixteenth century, the Ottomans had ruled the Levant through a decentralized system based on middlemen who pledged loyalty to the sultan and paid yearly tributes.[21] Mount Lebanon, a semiautonomous region, was administered by local strongmen from the Ma'an and Shihab families. Notable Maronite and Druze families served as intermediaries between tax-paying common folk (*ahali*) and the ruling emir and enjoyed significant autonomy, as long as they preserved order in their domains. These tax-farming families (*muqata'jis*) commanded the political landscape in support of or opposition to the emirs and would prove to be a politically resilient group.[22] It was for the most part a system of nonsectarian patronage, which began to crumble with the Egyptian occupation in 1831.

The imperial ambitions of Mehmet 'Ali, an ethnic Albanian strongman and Ottoman governor of Egypt since 1805, drove him to expand his domain into Greater Syria in 1830. For commoners in Beirut and Mount Lebanon the new regime meant high taxes, a monopoly economy, violent repression, military conscription, corvée labor, and forced disarmament.[23] The oppressive and exploitative policies meant that the population was even more disappointed when its reigning emir Bashir II al-Shihabi (1788–1840) threw in his lot with the invaders.

By the late 1830s, disillusion had turned into local unrest and uprisings, as locals demanded an end to the exploitation followed by administrative reforms, including the formation of a representative council.[24] Faced with growing regional instability and Mehmet 'Ali's expansionism, the Ottoman sultan sought help from the European powers. None was too eager to help. Only when Russia made overtures to intervene on behalf of the Ottomans did Britain bother to address the tension between the governor of Egypt and the Ottomans. But their help would not come for free. In exchange, the British demanded trade advantages. The Ottomans agreed. The resulting Treaty of Balta Liman (1838) effectively gave Britain full and unrestricted access to the Ottoman markets.[25]

Unsurprisingly, Mehmet 'Ali refused to recognize the treaty, and his military successfully resisted the Ottomans' attempt at expelling him from Greater Syria. It was only after Britain and Austria dispatched a military vessel to the eastern Mediterranean in support of the Ottomans that Mehmet 'Ali withdrew his troops.[26] The British took advantage of this moment, compelling the Egyptian governor to accept all present and future treaties signed between the Ottoman sultan and "friendly powers."[27] This included the Balta Liman Convention of 1838, which not only benefited foreign powers but also accelerated already-occurring economic changes in the region: namely the integration of Ottoman territories into the global market. The resulting economic shift is of utmost importance for us here as it ultimately increased the distance between people and food, rendering Beirut and Mount Lebanon particularly vulnerable to wartime disruptions.[28]

Beirut, some say paradoxically, benefited from both nineteenth-century Ottoman reforms and European encroachment. In the early years of Ottoman rule, the city was a small port town of a few thousand souls, insignificant when compared to the large inland metropolises of Damascus and Aleppo. Toward the end of the nineteenth century, it had become exemplary of Ottoman modernism and a center for European cultural, political, and economic expansion.[29] Beirut proved to have great potential within a rapidly changing global scene. And when the city's harbor was expanded to become one of the most important ports in the eastern Mediterranean, it seemed there was no limit to its growth. If approaching from the sea, fin de siècle Beirut's prosperity was visible in newly built opulent homes of foreign and indigenous entrepreneurs that adorned the low slopes of the mountains. Each house was surrounded with beautiful gardens and verandahs.[30] The old castles lay in picturesque ruins at their feet. Beirut had become the place to be, and by 1914 its population had grown twentyfold.[31] Beirut was a Mediterranean boomtown.

Recurring violence in the adjacent districts, the city's reputation for religious tolerance, increasing economic opportunity, and continuous improvements in sanitation and governance made the city an attractive destination, and neither merchants nor migrants could resist the city's pull. The majority of new arrivals in the city were middle-class Christians from Mount Lebanon, implicitly strengthening the link between the city and the mountain. These new arrivals made considerable economic and cultural contributions and tipped the demographic balance toward Christians.[32] According to Leila Fawaz, the number of Christians increased threefold between 1849 and 1865. By the 1870s, travelers remarked, "The Muslim element is gradually being displaced by the Christians."[33] Eventually, Christians would make up just under two-thirds of the population. Greek Orthodox constituted the largest number, followed by Maronites, a sect of the Eastern Catholic Syriac Church, and a much smaller community of Greek Catholics.[34] Beiruti Muslims were mostly Sunni. Small numbers of Shiites, Jews, Druze (a sect that has its roots in Isma'ili Shiite Islam), and foreigners made up the remaining population.

Beirut's explosive demographic and economic growth in the decades before the war and the resulting prosperity were partly the outcome of a general growth in sea trade, driven by European imperialist desires and in accordance with a mercantile system that dictated the rules of the European-dominated global market.[35] Import-export in Beirut was *the* booming business. Foreign trade in the empire as a whole increased by a factor of ten between 1820 and 1914.[36] For example, the tonnage of goods entering the Beirut port grew from 50,000 in 1830 to 600,000 in 1886, and to 1.6 million in 1911. Although import trade took a hit during the Balkan Wars, the economy in 1913 showed a return to normal.[37] In terms of weight, coal was the most important import to Beirut. Imported from Britain, it fueled the railways and was used by Beirut's electric-power, gas, and tram companies.[38] While there were some attempts to mine coal in Lebanon, they had failed to produce adequate amounts.[39]

Other imports came, in order of importance, from France, Germany, Austria, and Italy. By 1911, a daily average of nine large vessels, powered mainly by steam, called on Beirut's buzzing port.[40] At that time it was the only port on the eastern Mediterranean where smaller ships could unload directly at the quay and the only one operating a steam crane. Larger ships anchored offshore, unloading and loading their wares one dinghy at a time. The port's customhouse, the first stop for all merchants and traders, stretched along the shore visible from a distance. At its quay, countless small rowing boats, in an array of colors, delivered their wares and passengers.

Export articles from Beirut were wool, cotton lace, olives, olive oil, apricot paste, oranges, lemons, wheat barley, wine, and most important for people living in Mount Lebanon, raw spun silk.[41] The raw silk, in the form of silk threads and, later, silkworm cocoons, for the most part came from Mount Lebanon and the coastal plains around Beirut, Tripoli, Sidon, and the Bekaa Valley. Responding to increasing demands from a growing European silk manufacturing industry, farmers in these areas planted mulberry trees to feed the temperamental and gluttonous crop of silkworms. The new industry not only changed agricultural production but also killed native textile manufacturing businesses and significantly altered the physical landscape. By the outbreak of the war, the number of mulberry trees had risen to twenty-eight million from three million in 1840.[42] Lebanese silk production peaked between the 1860s and 1890s.[43] It was such a lucrative venture that by 1873, silk made up 82.5 percent of the exports and accounted for an industry that earned 275 million piasters that year (equivalent to approximately US$12 million at the time).[44] Most important, the demand for this commodity meant that peasant farmers grew a cash crop and had to purchase most of their food on the open market.

As a cash crop, silk naturally was vulnerable to a fluctuating global market and global competition. By the end of the nineteenth century, local silk producers felt this vulnerability. Artificial silk from Asia flooded the European markets after the opening of the Suez Canal in 1869. The subsequent decline in demand for Lebanese silk resulted in income loss for many Lebanese families and the closure of smaller silk reeling factories.[45] Revenues from silk export, however, continued to be important, accounting for about 50 percent and growing to 62 percent of Mount Lebanon's total revenue by 1911.[46] In

1913, 193 silk factories were among the main employers in the mountain district, producing 770,000 pounds of silk. Nearly three-fourths of the silk was exported to Lyon, where a pound of silk could fetch anywhere between $3.87 and $4.93, depending on quality.[47]

Many people benefited from the burgeoning silk trade. Foreigners owned most factories, but eventually wealthy local families also invested in them. Struggling lower-class families in Mount Lebanon began sending their daughters to work in factories, so by the end of the 1860s, young women made up the majority of silk workers.[48] The silk business was closely linked to banking and financing operations that waxed and waned alongside the precious thread's production and sale. The silk business not only connected the mountain to the financial sector in the city but also engendered a new merchant class. Serving as brokers, local merchants filled their pockets by borrowing funds at low rates from European import-export houses and lending the money out to peasants at much higher rates. This new group of intermediaries between the European market and the peasants altered pre-existing social, political, and economic hierarchies in Mount Lebanon. Fawaz understands the rise of this new merchant class as initiating a social revolution in both the city and the mountains, which undermined the position of traditional feudal families.[49]

A second nineteenth-century development changed the socioeconomic structures of Beirut and Mount Lebanon. Other than the silk industry in the mountains, manufacturing businesses were "very small and insignificant." Indeed, Beirut's growth in trade was not accompanied by a growth in industry.[50] Following an economic downturn, in particular the slump in the silk industry in the latter half of the nineteenth century and without local alternatives for work, significant numbers of men and women left Mount Lebanon to better their lives.[51] The first large-scale out-migration took place in the 1840s and 1850s. Between 1860 and 1900, approximately 120,000 persons emigrated.[52] By 1914, about 15,000–20,000 people emigrated each year.[53] Many of them sent money home to support their families. Returning immigrants invested their hard-earned money by purchasing or building homes in the mountains.[54] A report commissioned by the Ottoman governor of Mount Lebanon listed remittances as the primary source of income in Mount Lebanon, followed by income from silk, tourism, agriculture, and industry.[55] For example, remittances from the United States processed through Beirut banks amounted to between $3 million and $4 million each year, with possibly a lot more money coming from South America.[56] Remittances grew in time, and at the beginning of the war, some families relied on remittances as their sole income.[57]

Besides silk and remittances, a tourist industry, although still in its infancy, had become an additional source of income for families in the mountains. The moderate climate made Mount Lebanon a welcome escape from hot summer days. Towns like Beit Marie, 'Aley, Brumana, and Bhamdun attracted visitors from Egypt and Iraq as well as affluent Beirutis. Most foreigners residing in Beirut, such as consular staff, merchants, and missionaries, had summer residences in the mountains. The growth in tourism provided potential income in the service sector, and many Lebanese began to rent their homes or rooms to summer guests. Prior to 1914, four tourist agencies in Beirut were organizing tours to historical places on the coast and in Mount Lebanon, such as the ruins at Byblos. And the income from tourism in Mount Lebanon had risen to about 20 million piasters ($878,000).[58] Income from remittances and the service industries were important augmentations to rural families, who having moved away from subsistence farming to cash crops, increasingly depended on their income to purchase food.

Connectivity: Rails, Roads, and Roller Skates

Beirut grew to become the principal trading port in the eastern Mediterranean and the main entry and exit to the Syrian interior, as the travel routes of foreign businessmen confirm. In 1910, a "normal year" for travel according to the American consular report, nine hundred businessmen and commercial travelers, not including tourists, landed in Beirut. Among these were representatives of British biscuit manufacturers, a British businessman who sold nothing but chocolate, an Italian businessman who traded flour, another who specialized in macaroni and spaghetti, and yet another whose only merchandise was neckties. These traveling merchants would "as a general rule" visit all the important interior cities such as Aleppo, Homs, Hama, and Damascus, and apparently they did "more or less good business."[59] For most, their first stop was the Antun Bey Inn in Beirut, before boarding the slow-moving narrow-gauge train to Damascus. The inn had its own private dock as well as a warehouse and housed businesses such as merchant banks, shipping agencies, trading companies, and post offices. It was a convenient one-stop destination for foreign merchants.[60] While American merchants were seldom seen, some American products began to appear in the Beirut markets.[61] Petroleum, somewhat ironically, was the main American import to Greater Syria. It was traded through the Standard Oil Company, which had set up branches in all corners of the empire, including the Levant. But American imports, in general, were quite random. Among the wares were American roller skates. In 1910, roller skating apparently was a craze in all of Turkey, and skates could be purchased in Beirut. Other American products listed in the customhouse ledger were camping beds, office furniture, steam plows, Tennessee lumber, and mineral oil for tanning leather. Surely, none of these goods' trade compared with the Syrian-French silk exchange.

Booming business meant that means of transportation needed to be improved. Most important was to link Beirut to the interior. In the 1850s, construction of the first continuously paved road between Beirut and Damascus began, financed by a French company. The road opened in 1863, and its nearly seventy miles, passing through the Lebanon range, could be traveled with a daily stagecoach service that took thirteen hours. Stagecoach traffic, in turn, opened business opportunities. The road's economic importance is evidenced by the fact that after the 1860s most of the silk factories were built along it. However, to reach the road from outlying villages and towns, people had to traverse steep mountain ranges by small wagons, camels, packhorses, donkeys, and mules. To ease the travel, smaller roads were continuously improved. Along the coast, engineers were busy preparing to widen the thirty-one-mile-long road between Beirut and the southern coastal town of Sidon in 1911. The road was to be freshly macadamized, using broken limestone. The work was part of a large road-building and improvement contract sold to a French company. Some 380 miles were to be constructed in the Beirut province alone.[62] By 1917, there were close to 700 miles of paved road in Mount Lebanon,[63] the most important of which was the Beirut–Damascus road.

Europeans also invested in railway construction to link the coast to the hinterland, ultimately contributing to the commercialization of agriculture and the increasing integration of the empire into the world market as an exporter of raw materials. The European investment in infrastructure between

1860 and 1914 was approximately 205 million francs (nearly $40 million).[64] While there are few statistics concerning rail transport in the Arab provinces, the overall assessment has been that both passenger and freight traffic, despite growth, remained relatively small. By 1910, there were six sections of railway. The 135-mile Beirut–Damascus line had opened in 1894.[65] It ran, as one of its passengers described, through "some very fine scenery," journeying through a "constant panorama of mountain, forest, or plain."[66] From Rayak, a station between Beirut and Damascus, another line of normal-width gauge ran north through Homs, Hama, and Aleppo. Following the opening of this line, goods could be shipped between the coast and the grain-producing interior via rail. French investors also purchased the concession from the Ottoman government for a coastal line starting from Beirut to its northern neighbor Tripoli. However, by 1910 the narrow-gauge line was only about 9 miles long because a lack of "suitable labor" had slowed the progress. Apparently, Italian laborers, who had gained a good reputation, were in short supply.[67] There was further improvement when a line connecting Tripoli to Homs (63 miles) opened in 1909; its primary purpose was to ship materials for the construction of the Berlin–Baghdad Railway. The longest rail in Syria was the Hejaz line (809 miles), owned and operated by the Ottomans, which connected Damascus to Medina, servicing pilgrimage traffic. Off the Hejaz line some 77 miles south of Damascus at the station of Dara'a, another line veered off down to Haifa. Still, by 1914, the Ottoman Empire as a whole operated only one hundred small trains on barely more than 3,500 miles of tracks for an area of approximately 680,000 square miles.[68] Beirut and Mount Lebanon's economy became gradually characterized by limited food production, as the economy shifted to satisfy the global market. The region, hence, grew increasingly reliant on a functioning international and regional trade network for income and food, with the result that any disruptions in these volatile connections would be detrimental to the region's economic well-being.

Shifting Tides: Administrative Reforms and the Creation of the Prewar Political Scene

Economic changes were accompanied by important political rearrangements in both Beirut and Mount Lebanon. The previously mentioned Ottoman-Egyptian rivalry and European meddling, as well as Ottoman centralization efforts provide the larger context for a significant political restructuring. Politics and governance in the Ottoman Empire, as is well known, did not happen in isolation from local knowledge or without local agency. Thus, the nature of the state's relationship to local actors, institutions, and organizations is perhaps the most important factor to consider when untangling the complex web of wartime politics of provisioning. Historians, beginning with Albert Hourani, have emphasized the role of provincial urban notables in cultivating self-serving relationships with Ottoman officials.[69] It was a mutually beneficial relationship: local notables were allowed to expand "ties of personal dependence" among the lower classes in the provinces with state backing, and the state benefited from the men's local knowledge and connections. Local notables insinuated themselves as intermediaries into the Ottoman system of rule.[70] Ottoman Arab society, according to Hourani, was divided between Turkish Ottoman administration, Arab notables, and ordinary people.[71] This tripartite division has long been criticized and a close look at the pre–World War I period will necessitate further adjustments to Hourani's traditional understanding of the "politics of the notables." The years leading up to the war accounted for a "highly modified form of the classical 'politics of the notables'" and highlight, as Rashid Khalidi has pointed out, significant regional differences about who made up the Syrian elite.[72] In Beirut and Mount Lebanon this "modified form" was a new group of merchants who had benefited from growing coastal trade and increased access to modern education and would dominate important positions in newly formed state institutions. Moreover, the provincial restructuring of governance, expansion of a local press, and rise of party politics after 1908 significantly broadened the realm of political influence beyond the traditional landed notable referred to in Hourani's work.

Changing Politics in Mount Lebanon: A Church, a Council, and a New Man in Charge

Nineteenth-century political change in Mount Lebanon was a tumultuous affair that ended the Lebanese emirate and ushered in significant administrative reforms.[73] Following the end of the Egyptian occupation and in light of continuous intercommunal hostilities between Druze and Maronites, the European powers pressured the Ottoman government to reform Mount Lebanon's administration.[74] Considering that Maronite Christians, the largest community (58 percent), lived mainly in the mountain's northern district, and Druze, totaling 11 percent of the population, made up the majority in the southern Shuf district and lived in significant numbers in the central Matn and southern Jezzin districts, European advisers thought that partition of the mountain districts along religious lines would calm the situation.[75] However, the distribution of political power and administrative divisions based on sectarian identity was problematic.[76] The borders of the districts did not take into account that Druze and Maronites lived side by side in many of the mountain's towns and villages.[77] Elevating one group's power over significant numbers of the other community's members eventually resulted in "endless complications" in an ongoing contest for supremacy.[78] Two tumultuous decades followed, in particular in mixed Druze and Maronite districts.

It is interesting to note the paradox of this local development in the context of the larger nineteenth-century changes radiating from the Ottoman center. In response to financial and territorial challenges and in a plea for acceptance as one of the Great Powers, the Ottoman governing elites, far from being passive onlookers in a time of crisis, moved to initiate internal reforms to modernize and strengthen the Ottoman state.[79] The reforms of the Tanzimat (Restructuring) period (1839–1876) and their effects on the governance of the Arab provinces have been a central concern of Ottoman historiography.[80] Beginning in the 1990s, a group of social historians focused their attention on the unintended consequences of the reforms in particular.[81] In Mount Lebanon, the reforms, coupled with European meddling, replaced secular allegiances and loyalties based on social hierarchies with religious distinctions and differences as the district's political organizing frame. This occurred despite the Ottoman government's reform decision to abolish all preexisting religious distinctions between imperial subjects, introducing a secular equality and an official Ottoman nationalism.[82] The transfer to sectarian loyalties in Mount Lebanon benefited religious leadership and propelled one important actor of our wartime drama onto the stage, the Maronite Church.

European powers, historians have shown, made sure that the population of Mount Lebanon understood the Tanzimat decrees as promises for the protection of oppressed Christians. With support of its long-standing French patron, the leadership of the Maronite Church argued that its community's security and equality necessitated a revival of a Christian-led emirate.[83]

Maronite dominance in the political order, it was argued, was the only way to guarantee the protection and prosperity promised by the reforms of the Tanzimat. This local interpretation of the Tanzimat, supported by a foreign power, emphasized religion as the line between communities and shifted power from local notables to religious leaders.[84] The church had long been working to assert itself economically and politically. Beginning in the late eighteenth century and driven by ambitious clerics critical of its dependency on local notable families, the church implemented reforms of its organizational structures. The goal was to take full control of its administration, lands, and institutions. In this process, the church effectively sidelined its secular overlords, who lost much of their income-generating properties and some of whom were propelled into financial ruin in the process.[85] The church, in turn, rose to become the wealthiest institution, as it was able to redirect the income from its large network of monasteries, convents, and religious endowments directly into its coffers.[86] The clerics found a formidable ally in the ambitious emir Bashir II, who in an attempt to undermine powerful families, cultivated a relationship with the Maronite patriarch and strategically placed his Christian relatives in important positions of power. By the nineteenth century, the church had become the largest landowner, holding approximately a third of the district's land. The relocation of the patriarchate's seat from the remote northern region of Bsherri to the more accessible Bkirki, located on the mountainside overlooking the port of Junieh only a few miles north of Beirut, was the physical manifestation of an increasingly powerful and politically involved church. And its patriarch effectively emerged as the primary political leader of the community. Observing the church's growing size and wealth, outsiders described it as "the only social force among the Maronites" by the end of the nineteenth century.[87]

The changes of the Tanzimat also opened room for demands for popular participation in politics from below. The revolt led by the Maronite peasant Tanyus Shahin is illustrative. Beginning in the Kisrawan in 1858, the rebellion began as a protest against excessive taxation but soon turned into yet another broad challenge to the feudal order. Shahin and his followers demanded equality between the *ahali* and their overlords, specifically the Khazin family. After burning the homes of the Maronite gentry and stripping them of their property, Shahin proclaimed a peasant commonwealth.[88] The church largely supported the revolt. In the adjacent Druze district, the Maronite minority inspired by Shahin's movement demanded representation in governing the district and an end to random violence against its community. Druze overlords and neighbors resisted the requests for representation, and the resulting tension escalated into an outright civil war in 1860.

The violence, including intercommunal massacres, once again inspired external intervention. French military forces landed in Lebanon in August of the same year. Having quelled the violence, a coalition of European powers drafted a set of special regulations, the Règlement Organique. This protocol designated Mount Lebanon as a *mutasarrifiyya*, a semiautonomous province that would be accountable only to Istanbul and enjoy special taxation privileges. Its inhabitants were exempted from military conscription.[89] The *mutasarrifiyya* included seven administrative districts, each headed by a *kaymakam* (a lower-ranking governor or subgovernor). The *kaymakam* usually came from the prevalent religious group in the district. On the village level, locals elected village headsmen, or sheikhs, as intermediaries between ordinary people and the representatives of the state. At the head of the new governing system was the Ottoman governor (*mutasarrif*), who was directly appointed by the Sublime Porte (the central government of the empire) in conference with the Europeans. The *mutasarrif*'s position was complicated. He was responsible to the Sublime Porte in Istanbul, but since Mount Lebanon was now under international guarantees, his actions were also under scrutiny of the embassies signatory to the Règlement.[90] It was also mandated that a Catholic Christian occupy this post. A special corps of the gendarmerie, besides serving as judicial police, assisted the *mutasarrif* in maintaining order.

The position of a centrally appointed Ottoman official is important, since as representative of the state, the Ottoman governor would be an important person in negotiating the provisioning of civilians during the war. The political reshuffling in the 1860s also included the creation of an Administrative Council (AC), which would have a stake in the political landscape of Mount Lebanon. This elected body of twelve representative sectarian members was to aid the *mutasarrif* in ruling the district. While having limited consultative powers, the AC could veto tax increases and the intervention of Ottoman forces into Mount Lebanon.[91] The introduction of the AC marked an important shift toward modern representational governance.[92]

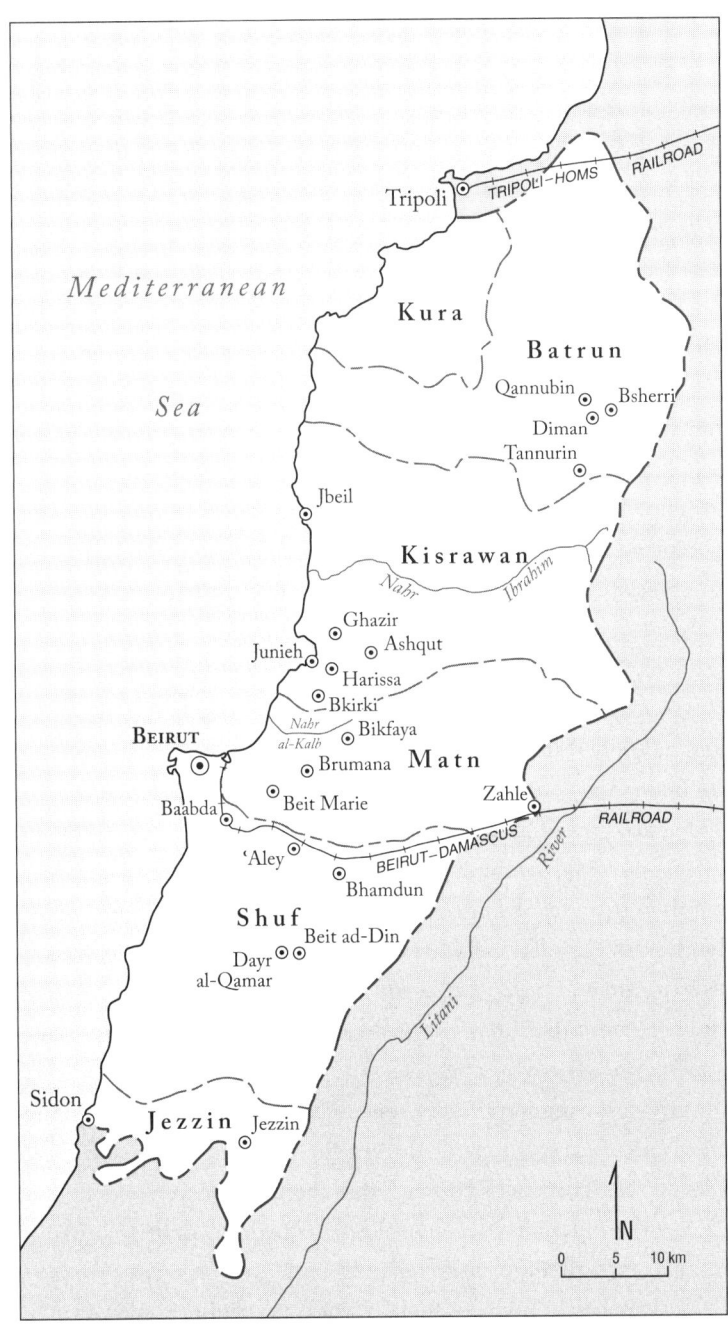

Map 2. The *Mutasarrifiyya* of Mount Lebanon, 1861–1920. Source: Based on map published in Haqqi, *Lubnan*.

The Maronite Church was disappointed with the new order because the AC had the potential to challenging the church's position.[93] In time however, religious leaders recognized the political order of the *mutasarrifiyya* as safeguarding the relative independence of their community in the Ottoman Empire.[94] In the following years, the church displayed an increasingly conservative attitude as it renewed its alliance with old notables and was mainly interested in maintaining its status quo. As the church lost some of its dynamic characteristics, the elected AC began to challenge the idea that the church represented the desire of all the mountain's inhabitants. Indeed, it became increasingly more difficult for the church and its allies to assure the election and appointments of their candidates to government offices. Instead, the popular support and electoral victories of anticlerical candidates undermined its power and prestige. In sum, the Maronite Church's conservative leadership and its lack of vision instead antagonized an increasingly educated secular elite, which eventually found its voice in the newly established AC.[95]

Changing Politics in Beirut: Reforms, Representation, and Rule by Council

Istanbul not only reshuffled the administrative system and Mount Lebanon's district boundaries but also reconfigured Greater Syria's provincial borders. The Provincial Law of 1864 redrew the administrative boundaries by forming the Vilayet of Syria, combining the provinces of Sidon and Damascus. This larger unit was subdivided into five smaller administrative units (*sanjak*) centered in Beirut, Acre, Tripoli, Latakia, and Nablus, each of which was further divided into smaller units (*kaza*) and even smaller communes (*nahiye*). The shift from Sidon to Beirut as one of the centers of provincial governance was no surprise.

The city's growing importance was officially acknowledged in 1888, when the Beirut province was separated from the Vilayet of Syria and Beirut became its capital. Historians contend that the upgrade in the city's "political scope" was the outcome of a "tenacious" struggle of Beirut's urban elite.[96] A centrally appointed governor-general (*vali*) was in charge of the provinces' departments of finances, public works, agriculture, education, police, and commerce.[97] Like Mount Lebanon's *mutasarrif*, the governor-general had to cooperate with an administrative council by the mid-nineteenth century. Membership on the provincial council was also based on sectarian representation. Supervised by the governor-general, the council was to maintain security, regulate the market, approve concessions, assess taxes, collect revenues, ratify land sales and property deeds, authorize infrastructural projects and public works, and implement quarantines in case of infectious disease epidemics.[98] Giving provincial rule a formal structure and guaranteeing formal communication between the center and the periphery, councils permitted a degree of administrative decentralization while at the same time concentrating and enlarging decision-making power in Istanbul.[99] Representative (even if not entirely democratic) governance was extended to all levels of the local administrative hierarchy in the 1860s and 1870s. On the city level, this translated into municipal councils that were established both in response to local needs and as part of administrative restructuring dictated from the center.

Representative councils, in general, became important arenas for provincial politics and would become important instruments of provisioning during the Great War. Beirut's municipal council is of particular interest. Beirut's population growth not only changed the physical appearance of the city as it grew beyond the old city wall but also necessitated changes in its governance. Prior to the nineteenth century, Beirut, like all other Ottoman towns, was governed by a complex system of privileges. It was generally dominated by traditional notables, leaders of confessional communities, guilds, and the military, which came together in civic assemblies to instigate, regulate, and supervise public order, the markets, building projects, taxation, and so on. A formal municipal counsel was established in 1863 partially as a communal response to a stream of refugees fleeing the violence in the adjacent district.[100] It took another four years for an empire-wide law to dictate that all cities and villages have a municipality.[101]

Coinciding with the inauguration of the first Ottoman parliament and the proclamation of the empire's first constitution in 1876, the central Ottoman government announced a newly amended Municipal Law, which detailed the structure and function of municipal governance. The short-lived Ottoman parliament fine-tuned the legislation, resulting in the Municipality Law of Istanbul and the Provinces in 1877.[102] The law regulated the electoral process and expanded the franchise to all men above the age of twenty-five who paid a minimum of 50 piasters (about $2.18) of (unspecified) taxes and had no criminal record.[103] Comparing the amount to the income of unskilled laborers, which was somewhere between 3 and 8 piasters a day, clearly shows that elections were not affordable to all. The law excluded foreign citizens from holding office by restricting its membership to Ottoman subjects. While imperial laws were important, Malek Sharif highlights the importance of local notables in framing the work of the municipality.[104] Its responsibilities expanded into urban planning, market control, health, public morality, and public welfare.[105] Thus, the elected council would play a significant role in economic and political decision making, asserting a degree of provincial autonomy. For example, negotiating with the provincial governor and the provincial council, members of the municipality established directives to facilitate the security and sale of properties outside the city center. The council bargained with European capitalists over the construction of the Beirut port in the 1870s and negotiated with Ottoman authorities to make Beirut a provincial capital in the 1880s.

Both Beirut's municipal council and Mount Lebanon's AC, at their inception and throughout World War I, had a distinct sociodemographic profile. The twelve men staffing Beirut's municipal council, for example, had alternative sources of income. Most members were involved in local, regional, or international trade and business and were generally part of a new political elite, who owned substantial property in the city. The predominance of the landowning merchant class in local politics may be explained by the unique nature of Beirut's merchant community. Unlike other North African or Ottoman Mediterranean cities where foreigners dominated trade and commerce, Beirut had a homegrown cadre of local, religiously mixed merchants who controlled international and regional trade and constituted a powerful fiscal class that invested in real estate in the city and its surroundings. Since the Municipality Law of 1877 linked candidacy for the municipal council to the payment of a significant amount of property taxes, only notables who possessed properties worth at least 50,000 piasters (about $2,180) could run for office.[106] This not only limited the number of qualified candidates but also privileged this new wealthy, propertied merchant class.[107] As a result, most council members occupied a peculiar position as participants in both the market economy and the legal and administrative apparatus that regulated the market.

The Rise of an Opposition:
Provincial Party Politics, Power, and Protests

The officially organized participation of the local upper- and upper-middle-class population in public affairs expanded after the 1908 Young Turk Revolution, which reinstated the Ottoman constitution of 1876 and parliamentary rule that had been suspended by Sultan Abdul Hamid in 1878. Representative party politics that defined at least the early years of the Second Constitutional Period (1908–1918) resonated with those who had practiced electoral municipal governance for the last three decades. Activists in and outside the empire were eager to participate in the progressive spirit that seemed to be coming from the new regime in Istanbul.[108] Intellectuals and "men of capital," to borrow Sherene Seikaly's term, joined parties, wrote opinion pieces, sponsored papers, and sought power in the elected bodies on the municipal, provincial, and imperial levels.

Historians have summarized emerging and often competing political currents by assigning "isms": Ottomanism, Islamic revivalism, Arabism, Syrianism, and Lebanism. While these categories are not entirely helpful, we may say that the common goal of such movements was the reform of the Ottoman system. Syro-Lebanese associations, while eager to maintain and even strengthen local autonomy for the Syrian provinces, did not present national independence as a clear priority.[109] One of the most significant political organizations of the Levant was the Beirut Reform Society (Jam'iyyat Bayrut al-Islahiyya). Founded in 1912, it brought together Muslim and Christian intellectuals and community leaders advocating for a decentralized government that would leave local affairs of the provinces in the hands of their residents. A number of other political parties, such as the Decentralization Party (Hizb al-Lamarkaziyya) and the Young Arab Society (Jam'iyyat al-'Arabiyya al-Fatat), were also insisting on reform and decentralization.[110] Burgeoning party politics, formation of ideological groups, and electoral activities increasingly governed Beirut's public sphere and gave rise to a new group of urban notables, the *zu'am'* (singular, *za'im*), and a sizable and increasingly vocal local press that contributed to political debates in the provinces.

The relationship between Istanbul and provincial power brokers grew tense after the CUP staged a coup in January 1913. Asserting its power, the CUP dismissed all demands for local autonomy as a threat to the integrity of the Ottoman Empire. Instead, CUP policies were state centered and openly Turkish nationalist. Urban politics in Greater Syria after 1913, as a result, were divided between pro-CUP notables and Arabists, who worked against the centralization and Turkifying policies of the new regime. A meeting of Arabists took place in Paris in June 1913, where they debated the position of the Arab provinces in the empire. One key request everyone could agree on was to insist that Arabic would continue to be the primary language in schools and official correspondence. Presenting their demands at the Ottoman embassy, the Arabists, threatening to turn to European powers for support, were able to pressure their state for reforms. In response, the Sublime Porte ordered the Ottoman Ministry of Education to introduce teaching Arabic in the state schools of the Arab provinces and replace Ottoman officials who did not speak Arabic with men who did.[111] After some initial concessions, the CUP, Talha Çiçek notes, plotted to get rid of what had by now become an outspoken and in its eyes threatening opposition. The war would be an important opportunity to do so.

The AC in Mount Lebanon, similar to the Beirut city council, became the mouthpiece of a new sociopolitical class. The last decades of the nineteenth century here too opened educational and economic opportunities, benefiting a new, growing middle class whose existence would challenge old hierarchies. A new middle class made up of midlevel landed elites, administrators, professionals, merchants, sericulture entrepreneurs, and returning émigrés entered into politics.[112] Fawwaz Traboulsi makes an excellent point that this group of people was occupying a position not only between the notables and the commoners but also between the two political poles, the church (Bkirki) and the Ottoman-appointed *mutasarrif* (Beit ad-Din). The ideology of this group, although there was no coherence, has been broadly described as liberal, nationalist, and reformist.[113] It worked independently and often in opposition to the Maronite Church and spoke out against taxation, demanded more local autonomy, and fought against old notable families' monopoly in the administration.

Still, the actual power of the AC vis-à-vis the church was dependent on the political leanings of the Ottoman governor and, more here than in Beirut, foreign interference. For example, the secular leadership of the AC used an economic downturn at the end of the nineteenth century to assert its leadership in Mount Lebanon. Taking the lead in demanding financial help from the center, an expansion of its electoral base, and the addition of an independently elected president with "executive powers" to the AC, the leaders were eager to shift the power away from clerics.[114] Reformist Ottoman officials generally welcomed their ambitions. For example, the *mutasarrif* Muzaffar Pasha (1902–1907) not only promised genuine reforms but also publicly endorsed individuals who opposed the clergy. He also encouraged the establishment of Masonic lodges and charitable organizations as counterforces to the clerical institution.[115] Charitable societies became political gathering centers, advocating and supporting the election of anticlerical candidates to the council. It was no longer a given that the church's candidates would be elected or appointed to government offices. In the first decade of the twentieth century, the church lost ground to the secular elite, which formed committees and increasingly voiced its positions in a growing press and in widely circulated pamphlets.[116] The patriarch's threats to excommunicate supporters of the opposition had little effect on reversing, or even stalling, the trend toward secular-independent leadership.

The clerics, although facing a challenge to their power, had a formidable ally in the French government. Trying to secure access to Ottoman lands, in particular Greater Syria, France was eager to ensure that the church, a loyal asset, never completely lost its political power. Leading up to the war, French officials, who had significant influence on decision making in Istanbul, were deaf to the plight of the AC for reforms and showed little interest in any proposals that lacked the signature of the patriarch. The Ottoman administration, however, made concessions to the reformist bid in Mount Lebanon to counter French and British influence. For the church the war and its aftermath was an opportunity to reassert its position. It did so by positioning itself as one of the key agents of benevolence for hungry and desperate Lebanese.

Both in Beirut and Mount Lebanon, the political landscape relevant to the wartime story of provisioning was drawn by the interactions, relationships, and competition between Ottoman officials and local players. Through the establishment and subsequent adjustments of the provincial councils and its lower-level twins, provincial leaders had gained significant power within a centralizing regime, and their position within the governing hierarchy determined their actions, loyalties, and commitments.[117] The capabilities of the Beirut municipality and the Lebanese AC as local state-sanctioned institutions are important to consider in the discussion of wartime provisioning politics. Besides Ottoman officials, the elected members in these representative councils were important political actors for whom the war, mass starvation, and infectious diseases were both an opportunity and a calamity. Their ability to cope with the famine and ensure the well-being of the city's inhabitants was central to preserving their political power and determined whether Ottoman officials saw them as threats to the legitimacy and sovereignty of the state. Moreover, their unique social position placed council members in a tempting position that could easily lead to the abuse of power. In short, official state-sponsored institutions, made up of local propertied elites, no doubt were one arena in which the politics of provisioning would take place either in coordination or in competition with the state.

The Benevolent Landscape of a City and the Mountain

The importance and obvious utility of Albert Hourani's "politics of the notable" is reflected in the numerous works that have built on and sought to revise his argument. What has become clear in the four decades since its publication is that his "far too neat" tripartite division silences important actors such as women, foreigners, and a newly emerging educated middle class,[118] all of whom were vital members of society and agents of provisioning in the city and the mountains before and during the war. State and society, wartime provisioning illustrates, were not two fixed entities. And it is important to recognize that both were constantly changing their structure, constituencies, rules, and ability to assert social control. And as shown throughout the following chapters, the interactions of state and society forged wartime and postwar changing social hierarchies and powers. This does not mean we should simply set the state against society. But it is important to recognize that the state is an organization in society that exists not in isolation but in the context of other formal and informal social organizations, such as families, churches, and philanthropic organizations.[119] Both state and society, striving to dominate social control, recognized the ability of individuals, organizations, and institutions to offer social services; in this case most important was access to food, and community-based patronage was important in creating a loyal clientele.[120]

Charitable giving was and is an integral part of religious piety in both Muslim and Christian communities in Beirut and Mount Lebanon.[121] Beyond a culture of individual pious giving, religious endowments funded institutions to provide food and short-term shelter for the poor. Some larger imperially funded mosques, generally situated in large and important cities to assert an Ottoman presence outside the capital, had hospitals or schools attached to them.[122] Charitable giving underwent significant changes in the mid- to late nineteenth century as part of a larger, albeit often unrecognized, global shift. Whereas charity and benevolence had been part of everyday life, it increasingly became institutionalized, organized, and professionalized beginning in the late eighteenth century. Citizens' groups formed associations that took up humanitarian work nationally and internationally. The prime examples of this trend are the international antislavery campaign and, later, the formation of the Red Cross. The key characteristic of this modern politics of compassion was that its concerns reached beyond simple distributive charity, such as providing food, shelter, or money. Instead, an organized "alleviation of human suffering" addressed the real and perceived underlying causes of that suffering. This, of course, is neither to say that it displaced distributive charity as a practice nor that earlier practices were not concerned with causes of suffering.[123]

How does this modern culture of compassion unfold in Beirut and Mount Lebanon? And how did it alter existing forms of charity? In the Middle East, charitable giving took on "a new type of organization, the *jam'iyya*" (society or association) in the mid-nineteenth century.[124] The *jam'iyya* is representative of a move from local religious institutions that collected and distributed funds to organized groups, associations, and committees that not only sought to provide immediate relief but also instigated public fundraising and awareness campaigns to help the destitute. Before the *jam'iyya*, individual donations and family endowments were the primary sources of charity. Egyptian nineteenth-century intellectual al-Tahtawi, for example, noted that "associations for joint philanthropy are few in our country."[125] He lamented that such associations were needed since neither state nor individually sponsored organization were able to uphold the public good. Beginning in the late nineteenth century, however, organized philanthropic associations requiring large endowments from wealthy patrons and urban elites of all sects stepped in where state-run institutions were lagging behind or simply did not exist.¹²⁶ The first associations of this kind were generally arranged around scientific education and sharing, acquiring, and circulating knowledge. Based on these models, urban elites later shifted the focus of their philanthropic associations to directly address community interests and needs and provided medical care, education, burials, and subsistence to the urban poor.¹²⁷

In Beirut, the first of these associations were also literary and scientific associations.¹²⁸ Later associations dedicated to charity were linked to religious institutions: Among the most prominent were the Sunni Muslim Association for Benevolent Intention (al-Jam'iyyat al-Maqasid al-Khayriyya al-Islamiyya, hereafter referred to as al-Maqasid) founded in 1878; the Greek Orthodox Benevolent Society (al-Jam'iyyat al-Khayriyya al-Urthuduxiyya) founded in 1868; the Greek Orthodox Society for Aiding the Sick of the Hospital St. George (al-Jam'iyyat musa'da al-Marda fi Mustashfa al-Qadis Jirjis, hereafter referred to as Society of St. George) founded in 1878; and the Greek Catholic Charity Association (al-Jam'iyyat al-Khayriyya lil-ta'ifa al-Rum al-Kathulik) founded in 1883.¹²⁹ These associations were run by upper-class Beirut men, many of whom were simultaneously involved in city politics through councils and committees. But women as well increasingly asserted themselves in the public through work for the poor.

Whereas municipal politics was a strictly male domain, philanthropic organizations were an avenue before the war for women to participate in the public sphere. In the mountains and the city, female education and women's entrance into the workforce were an important aspect of nineteenth-century changes. Female education in general was linked to modernization discourses that saw girls as the mothers and educators of a future generation. Foreign missionaries were the main catalysts for the expansion of female education. It was a competitive affair. In Beirut and Mount Lebanon, American and British Protestants and French Catholics, who entered the mission field to uplift "downtrodden womanhood," vied for wealthy clients.¹³⁰ The Ottoman authorities, troubled by missionary education, began opening state-run schools and in the late nineteenth century declared elementary education for girls mandatory.¹³¹

Partly in response to missionary schools, local religious communities set up their own schools with the specific purpose of educating their community's new generation of proper mothers. The men of the al-Maqasid founded a school for Muslim girls in 1878 and employed female teachers and administrators to run the school.[132] The Greek Orthodox community followed suit and established schools for girls of the middle and upper classes of Beirut. In the endeavor for female education, the women of important families were often instrumental. For example, Greek Orthodox Emili Sursock, who, along with other women, founded the philanthropic society the Blossom of Charity (Jam'iyyat Zahrat al-Ihsan) to educate the girls of her community. The society was composed of upper-class laywomen and, with the support of the Sursock family, opened both a school and an orphanage. The local schools taught elementary subjects, some domestic skills, and foreign languages.[133] It is in these schools and in philanthropic societies that elite women were active in the public sphere prior to the war. Their role significantly expanded during the war through mechanisms associated with the politics of provisioning.

Conclusion

Famine scholars Hans Bohle and Michael Watts have proposed that a space of vulnerability has to be understood locally and historically, and famine must be contextualized with respect to "social, political, economic and structural-historical coordinates."[134] This chapter has drawn a map of these coordinates, with the intent of highlighting the structural properties that determined the social, economic, and political context of the wartime entitlement crisis.[135] The broad changes of the nineteenth century shifted the local economy toward trade and cash crops, rendering both Beirut and Mount Lebanon vulnerable to disruptions in local, regional, and international trade networks. In turn, nineteenth-century social, economic, and political changes produced a particular set of political actors. Prewar hierarchies of these potential agents of benevolence are important to keep in mind when thinking about how affected people dealt with vulnerabilities and risk and in contextualizing their responses aimed at mitigating hunger. They also determined the setting, or what Pierre Bourdieu has called "fields," wherein agents, their social position, and actions are situated.[136] The centralizing state for which war would be an opportunity to assert its power had to contend, compete, and coordinate with the complex preexisting network of local political and social agencies and actors. The total war of 1914–1918 upset the system.

Figure 3. The Terrible Plague of Locusts in Palestine, March–June 1915. Locusts Stealing in like Thieves through Window. Source: The American Colony (Jerusalem), G. Eric and Edith Matson Photograph Collection, Library of Congress Prints and Photographs Division, Washington, D.C.

(CHAPTER 2)

WARTIME FAMINE

Strategies, Logistics, and Catastrophe

"One warm, breathless night they were found crawling thick into our windows, which were left open after sundown," wrote John D. Whiting in an article published in the *National Geographic* in December 1915.[1] A year into the war, his subject was a devastating desert locust (*Schistocerca gregaria*) plague that had invaded Jerusalem that spring. The family had left the windows open at night, thinking that the cool spring air would paralyze the insects. But now locusts were "stealing in like thieves through window."[2] Anything but immobile, the locusts resembled speeding, rushing, whooshing invaders for whom no obstacle was large or high enough. Whiting's biblical allusions captured their great energy: "They shall run to and fro in the city; they shall run upon the wall; they shall climb upon the house; they shall enter in at windows like a thief."[3] Humans had little choice but to surrender and endure what was sent from God. For foreign missionaries and educators unfamiliar with this spectacle, the locusts' appearance not only spoke to their Christian sensibilities but also was the subject of a good news story. The *New York Times*, the *San Francisco Chronicle*, and *National Geographic* all published stories about this seemingly foreboding phenomenon.[4] Swedish immigrant to Palestine Lewis Larsson was careful not to open his windows, but from a safe distance he photographed the stubborn pests feveriously knocking on the glass, trying to find a way into his home.[5] The locusts became Larsson's obsession. He documented their movement, destructiveness, pervasiveness, and the struggle against them.[6] The locusts resemble a crawling, intricate lace in his photograph, lace that would be more than a window dressing, eventually covering "all of Palestine and Syria—that is from the borders of Egypt to the Taurus Mountains" and beyond.[7]

In April 1915, the insects congregated into a "snowstorm of mammoth flakes of yellow and black."[8] Crossing the mountainous areas of the Shuf and Matn districts of Mount Lebanon, the swarm darkened the sky. After lingering a few days on the outskirts of Beirut, the locusts continued their flight in cloud formation into the city. Moving in from the south, the insects easily crossed the border between Mount Lebanon and the Vilayet of Beirut. Bayard Dodge, an employee at Beirut's SPC, recounted his first sighting:

> We saw them coming as a great cloud flying across the sky and then swarmed by millions all about Ras Beirut. They look like giant flakes of snow being driven along by the wind over your head with their bright yellow wings flashing in the sun. On the ground, you see their shadow, rapidly moving, giving a very peculiar effect.[9]

The air became unbearably heavy, and birds fluttered frightened to the ground. The insects settled on fields and trees and began to devour "every leaf and flower and fruit.... The ground where they had rested was bare of every living plant," as they had gobbled up every green twig, permanently damaging fruit and olive trees.[10] The locust invasion convinced some that they had attracted the wrath of God;[11] men, women, and children prayed, to no avail, that the winds would sweep the pest west into the Mediterranean Sea. "Man had done his worst for his country, and now nature had turned cruel."[12]

War Famine and Famine as a Weapon of War

The people in Beirut and Mount Lebanon had been living under the dark clouds of war for some months when the locusts physically darkened the sky in April 1915. The familiar visitor only made things worse. Dramatic in their onslaught, the locusts have often been cited, if not the primary cause, as the tipping point that turned food shortages into a famine.[13] The insect was and still is a convenient culprit in that it neither differentiated among religious confessions, nor, as the Jerusalemite Ihsan Turjman proclaimed with a certain satisfaction, did it "discriminate between rich and poor."[14] It simply ate whatever came in its way. Locust plagues, like other natural disasters such as droughts and earthquakes, were common occurrences along the eastern Mediterranean coast of the Ottoman Empire. As one historian writes, they were "an integral part of people's lifetime experience."[15] Nature, generally, was tough on those living in the region, and it did not take pity in the years that followed the declaration of war.[16] Instead, the winter of 1915 was harsh: Rains had stopped in February, and hot winds, lasting twenty days, followed.[17] By June 1915, "the country [was] becoming as dry as a desert."[18] The locusts reduced the summer crops, fruits and vegetables mostly, of the coastal areas to about one-fourth the average harvest. Unfavorable climate and crawling insects continued to be an issue, as the scenario repeated itself the following year. A heat wave with temperatures of 108 degrees Fahrenheit hit Beirut and Mount Lebanon in June 1916.[19] But what we refer to as natural disasters, scholars agree, are hardly ever entirely caused by nature. Instead, human action or inaction, if not significant in determining the outcome of a natural disaster, played some role.[20] In the Lebanese case, natural disaster and unfavorable climate arrived at a time when humans were already forging their own disaster, a total war.

This chapter analyzes the totalizing process of World War I and the effect it had on food supplies and civilian provisioning on the home front. It outlines the historically specific social, economic, and political relational processes linked directly to this moment in time.[21] The focus is access to food supplies. Food no doubt has a claim to being among the most important everyday substances, which matters "most to most people for most of the time."[22] While food is indispensable both on the battlefronts and home fronts, political negotiations and military campaigns have dominated the historiography of World War I in the Middle East. But it is almost too obvious to say that to wage war and engage in political practices, people must be fed.[23] And even in wartime, when many social, economic, and political activities come to a standstill, negotiations surrounding eating—albeit in altered form—continue.[24] In Greater Syria, the famine generated an unprecedented urgency visible in talk and action around feeding Ottoman subjects.

The famine was a unique event contingent on the caprices of human action in times of war. It was neither a direct result of an absolute absence of food nor an unadulterated natural disaster. International and national wartime strategies, situations, and struggles determined much of individuals' relationships to daily necessities. And in this there are uncanny resemblances between the Lebanese case and the "paradigmatic" war famine in Bengal (1943–1944), where wartime conditions and strategies of belligerent nations converted minor food shortages into a disastrous reduction of available supplies.[25] The cutting and requisitioning of supplies and transportation for military purposes and the prioritization of supplying the empire's capital are only a couple of examples wherein the wartime famine in the Ottoman Levant resembles that of British-occupied Bengal nearly two decades later. Famine in Beirut and Mount Lebanon was also the outcome of wartime maneuvering that disregarded the need for the proper distribution of available food.[26]

The answer to the question of whether the famine in Beirut and Mount Lebanon would have happened without the war is clearly no. The disruption of international and regional trade and the total mobilization of the Ottoman military and society were the primary reasons for regional shortages, loss of income, and price hikes, effectively rendering food unattainable to large portions of the population. In general, there is no direct or universal causal relation between war and famine; after all, plenty of wars did not include famines, and plenty of famines occurred without war. Why famine accompanied war in this case may be explained in the larger context of historical changes, long-term economic developments, and the resulting vulnerabilities discussed in the previous chapter. The war happened within a preexisting space of vulnerability, and wartime uncertainties, strategies, and expediencies were the key inflationary factors that left some segments of the population without access to food, resulting in starvation and mass mortality. It is with this reminder that we turn to the war here.

Famine as a War Strategy:
The Maritime Blockades of Goods and People

Immediately following its entrance into the war, the Ottoman government tightened control of its territory and economy. Given the empire's linkages to an international system of trade and cross-border exchanges, everyone knew this wartime strategy would disrupt the movement of goods and people. How much it would affect local economies and the availability of food supplies might not have been so obvious. The CUP saw the war as an opportunity to solidify its rule, expand state power over the empire's subjects, and remedy a weak bureaucracy and its fiscal problems. Not unlike the case of 1940s Bengal, where war exigencies allowed for an authoritarian resolve to "accelerate the entrenched predatory dynamics of colonial rule—even as the empire was crumbling," in Lebanon imperial power also saw such prospects.[27] And for the next four years, war making and state making, as interrelated processes, determined the practices and priorities of the state in society.

CUP officials, justified by war, first used "emergency powers" to expand financial and military control into the provinces and used "defensive strategies" that significantly impacted food supplies. Even before the war, the Ottoman empire had stopped paying its sizable foreign debts and unilaterally abrogated capitulatory agreements with foreign powers.[28] As uneven trade agreements, the capitulations had facilitated the export of raw materials and set low tariffs on imports, encouraging their purchase and consumption.[29] In Mount Lebanon, the announcement of the capitulations' planned abrogation on October 1, 1914, caused concerns about a possible end to the district's special privileges and a foreign invasion of the coast. The French consul general in Beirut, François Georges-Picot, marveled at the power of rumors, while he witnessed a general panic. According to the consul, Muslims who could afford it purchased train tickets to Damascus, Beirut's Christians were moving into the mountain district, and foreigners left, abandoning their schools and missions. He estimated 30,000 people had left Beirut in the last two weeks of September 1914. With the date of the official end of the abrogation of the capitulations approaching, Georges-Picot intervened with Beirut's Ottoman governor-general, Bekir Sami Bey. He warned the governor that any public demonstration would cause further panic. The governor-general assured him that everything would be done to avoid "an incident." The government prohibited any popular demonstration from taking place on September 30 and October 1. Thus, stores remained closed and only a few people could be spotted in the streets of the city hurrying from one place to another. The emptiness of the streets on these days, according to the consul, felt like a genuine public mourning of the end of their many international trade relations. In his eyes it also demonstrated government's power in controlling its public.[30]

The Ottomans, at the same time, dispatched troops to control the coastline, including the eastern Mediterranean territories belonging to the *mutasarrifiyya* of Mount Lebanon. The presence of Entente warships surveying the coast in 1914 stirred up bitter memories of the previous century. European powers' intervention on behalf of non-Muslim communities during the crisis of 1860 and France's continued meddling on behalf of Mount Lebanon's Christians, in particular, had long been a thorn in the side of the government.[31] While sympathies toward France were not limited to Mount Lebanon's Maronite Christians, as is often believed, the Ottomans most prominently directed their suspicions at Christian "colluders."[32] The empire's defeat in the Balkan Wars had increased tension between Muslims and Christians, and this war seemed to strengthen the general sentiment about Christians as European sympathizers and disloyal subjects of the empire.[33]

Jamal Pasha, while maintaining some of the mountain's privileges (such as military exemption), imposed martial law, established a military court, and forbade shipments of grain between provinces.[34] The latter, of course, is the most important to this discussion. The Ottoman war ministry apparently had received intelligence reports of a scheme by the French to smuggle foodstuffs out of the empire via Beirut.[35] The German consul stationed in Beirut, Gerhard von Mutius, expressed his concerns. While Beirut was of no military importance, it was vulnerable to an enemy attack. Hence, "one would not want to leave provisions in such a place." Fearing a possible depletion of military supplies, as grain would surely be exported for a superior price "to supply enemy fleets active in the eastern Mediterranean," Jamal Pasha closed the ports, limited the grain supply shipped to the coast, and ordered close surveillance of Entente ships so that sending in any contraband was impossible.[36] An Ottoman blockade of its coast was in effect.

Ottoman paranoia eventually prevented the landing of enemy merchant vessels not only in its Mediterranean ports but also in those of neutral nations like the United States. The American ship *Indiana*, carrying a precious load of 150 tons of flour, is a case in point. In January 1915, the *Indiana* was scheduled to arrive in the Lebanese port of Junieh to unload its cargo. Just before landing, the captain was informed, "The *vilayet* prohibited categorically the unloading of said flour in the port."[37] The shipping company contacted the American consulate in Beirut, which took up this matter with Mount Lebanon's *mutasarrif* and Beirut's governor-general. While the former agreed to the landing of the ship, the latter responded "that it is prohibited for any vessel to stop over on the coast of Lebanon."[38] The American embassy had assured its commercial vessels that "all ports on the Ottoman coast after Smyrna to the Egyptian frontier" were open to them.[39] The American consul in Beirut was not surprised by the change in terms: "The *vali* of Beirut never obeys orders from Constantinople when they are in conflict with orders issued by Jamal Pasha, who has practically constituted himself as the dictator of all of Syria."[40] After the American ambassador in Istanbul presented the confusion to Minister of War Enver Pasha, the latter set the record straight, announcing that "no vessel would be allowed for the present to touch at ports in the Lebanon."[41] In due course, "no business" was conducted between the Ottoman Empire and neutral countries like the United States.[42]

Intervention in trade was not simply a measure of protecting borders and supplies, but it could, so CUP leaders thought, resolve the empire's dire financial situation. Ending the capitulations allowed the Sublime Porte to finally "levy customs and excise."[43] In June 1915, the government in Istanbul began by raising the customs duties to 30 percent. The secretary of the American Mission Press (AMP), Margaret McGilvary claims, perhaps in exaggeration, that the military authorities in Beirut increased the "duty on imports a hundred percent" and closed the city's customhouse, which was filled with goods worth more than $1 million. When the owners of these goods were unable to clear customs, the military authorities commandeered the inventory without issuing receipts or payments. McGilvary described the whole proceeding as "a mob-plunder carried out by soldiers and by government representatives."[44]

The ability to control customs, however, did little to remedy the fiscal situation of the empire. The government did not alter the pre-1914 provisional tariff structure. The biggest mistake, according to Hew Strachan, was that the government continued to rely on tariffs based on weight, not value. Since the former decreased and the latter increased, it was a missed opportunity in the end.[45] Still, the CUP officials saw the tightening borders as a necessary step to protect the empire's supplies, prevent an enemy landing, and undermine possible collusion of Ottoman subjects with the foe. They gave little consideration to the fact that both Beirut and Mount Lebanon were reliant on food imports and that the region's wealth, as well as many people's income, relied on international trade. In time, the empire's external trade was almost entirely limited to its wartime allies, Germany and Austria-Hungary. But even here seaborne commerce was constantly interrupted if not "impossible with British, French and Russian men-of-war continually patrolling the coast."[46]

Entente war vessels controlling the eastern Mediterranean were part of a broader European maritime blockade aimed at halting all international trade with the enemy. For the Ottomans, as Linda Schilcher writes, the Entente blockade was "unmercifully constant." She speculates that it must have been the primary cause of the famine. However, due to what she calls a dearth of sources discussing this deadly maneuver in European archives, she has little to say about the blockade as an international strategy of war.[47] It warrants a closer look. European powers, with the assumption that war was not a question of if but when, drafted intricate war plans in the decades leading up to August 1914. These plans included movement of troops, invasion routes, and logistics and targeted the enemy's entire economy, resources, and populations.[48] Disruption of international and especially maritime trade was part of their schemes.

Britain, in particular, fearing Germany's increasing power in international waters, reviewed its wartime naval policy in light of the Second Hague Conference in 1907. Should there be war with Germany, the review committee suggested, the British navy should block all German ports.[49] The plan's details were worked out in the following years. When on August 4 Britain declared war on Germany, the Entente secured control of the sea and gradually shut down Germany's international maritime trade. In military terms, it was a successful strategy. The blockade of Germany (1914–1919) led to severe food shortages on the entire continent. Continuing for more than six months after the cease-fire (to coerce Germany into signing the Treaty of Versailles), it eventually contributed to the starvation of hundreds of thousands of Germans.[50]

In World War I studies of economic warfare, the Entente blockade of Germany looms large. But the blockade was not simply a British ploy to counteract Germany's naval power. The policy simultaneously targeted Germany, Austria-Hungary, Bulgaria, and, most important here, the Ottoman

Empire.⁵¹ At the end of 1914, the Entente powers dispatched a "blockade fleet" made up of French, British, and Russian ships and two aerial squadrons to patrol the Mediterranean coast, initiating an unofficial embargo. Official proclamations of a maritime blockade followed months later, by the British on June 2, 1915, and the French on August 27. The blockade fleets conducted military operations, including attacking suspicious vessels, dispatching reconnaissance planes and agents on spy maneuvers, engaging in submarine warfare, and bombarding suspected supply and petroleum depots in the coastal cities. In addition to the Mediterranean coastline, the Entente shut down the coast along the Red Sea, cutting the Arabian Peninsula off from its trading partners in Egypt, India, and Australia.⁵² Blockaded items included not only weapons and ammunition but also what international law of the time referred to as conditional contraband, items for military and civilian use, including food. In short, the blockade prevented everything that could sustain the armed forces and its supporting economy from entering the empire.⁵³ It was a deliberate policy. While the European powers did not always agree on the usefulness and application of this strategy concerning the Ottoman Empire, both France and Britain employed famine as a weapon of war.

The combined Ottoman and Entente war maneuvers paralyzed trade and resembled a full-fledged siege.⁵⁴ By January 1915, the American consular agent in Tripoli reported business as "absolutely nil." Most businesspeople were "idle." By May, the landing places in the port of Beirut were deserted, the customhouse was empty, and the "stevedores and boatmen have all departed."⁵⁵ In September, American consul in Beirut Stanley Hollis writes, "No merchant steamers have entered our ports for months."⁵⁶ His yearly economic report, although made up of "meager general statistics," sheds light on the decline of international trade. Exports decreased in value from $9,400,000 in 1910 to $2,005,126 in 1914 and a meager $114,497 in 1915.⁵⁷ While exports were a much smaller proportion of trade, the disruption was still devastating.

Silk trade was hit especially hard, leaving many without a stable income. That silk was vulnerable to fluctuations in the international market by now was not news to anyone. The war, however, was an entirely new challenge for its merchants and producers. The industry's collapse began with "great difficulties in marketing the 1914 crop owing to the disturbance in banking and transportation facilities," especially the closure of the Beirut port, the center for silk trade.[58] The blockade also had cut off the import of silkworm eggs from France and Italy.[59] Consequently, producers in Lebanon relied on eggs from Bursa, which did not do well in the Lebanese climate. The 1915 harvest was about half that of a normal year. A heat wave the following summer further reduced the yield.[60] Unpredictable wartime circumstances left merchants hesitant to extend the usual credit to local spinning factories for the purchase of cocoons from the peasants. Hollis noted the great risk merchants would have to take even at low prices, since it was impossible "to ship any goods out of Syria."[61] Peasant producers could demand only a quarter of the price for their cocoons that they had demanded the previous year. Other agricultural export goods, such as lentils, vegetables, figs, and olive oil, also could no longer be shipped.[62] Considering the near halt of international trade, the initial raising of customs duties seemed "facetiousness. Commerce was dead and no merchandise was entering the country."[63] It in the end did little to fill the Ottomans' coffers.[64]

The disruption of international trade contributed to shortages, if not complete absence, of imported goods. The value of imports landing at Beirut drastically decreased from $18,753,137 in 1913 to $8,810,675 in 1914 and $489,060 in 1915.[65] The effect of the war on imports is most apparent when we compare the average monthly imports of 1913 ($1,562,761) to those of January 1915 ($4,830). As a result, local warehouses were empty, and "the stock of imported foodstuffs [was] about exhausted."[66] Rice imports declined from 5,088 tons to a meager 4 tons.[67] Imported luxury items like sugar, coffee, and tea were hard to find anywhere in Beirut and Mount Lebanon.[68] Wheat imports that had amounted to 14,385 tons in 1913 fell to only 360 tons in 1915.

The increases in foreign exchange rates and price hikes of imported goods are another good indicator of the destabilizing effects of the blockades on international trade. The value of both the British pound and the French franc, which were used in trade along with Ottoman currencies, rose. At the outbreak of the war a French franc could be exchanged for 86.5 piasters, but in 1915 for 109 and in 1918 for 135. The exchange rate of the British pound increased from 110 piasters in 1914, to 137 in 1915, to 200 in 1918.[69] For Lebanese merchants this was a clear disadvantage in addition to their already devastated business. The prices of imported goods, not surprisingly, also rose almost immediately. In December 1914, it was common for the prices of these goods to double from one day to the next, and at times, they even fluctuated over the course of a day. For example, a *rotl* (2.5 kilograms) of sugar could be bought for 12 piasters on December 2 and sold the next day for 20. An *uqqa* (1.3 kilograms) of coffee rose from 35 to 50 piasters, and a standard-sized can of kerosene rose from 60 to 70 piasters. As sugar prices rose, sweets became more expensive; the price of kanafeh and baklava reached about 60 piasters per *rotl* in 1916, an amount that "exceeded the earnings of even the rich in those days." By 1916, "only the rich" could drink coffee and only without sugar. Those who frequented the few remaining coffeehouses were served an unpleasant brew made from roasted chickpeas and lupine seeds. Most of Beirut's coffeehouses closed during the war.[70] Foreign liquors were sold at high prices, and chocolate had completely disappeared from the market. Imported canned goods such as tuna, sardines, and biscuits were hard to find and often too old for consumption. It is important to note that any available price indices are incomplete, come from a variety of sources, and can reflect only a very general trend or a very specific moment in time in one locale. Still they provide a glimpse of the general disorder of the region's market.

The dual maritime blockade also disrupted the flow of people and money. Remittances, one of the main income sources for families living in Mount Lebanon, were difficult to get into the empire, as the government shut down foreign postal and bank services.[71] While remittances never entirely stopped, they often did not make it to the person in need or lost much of their value in the exchange to local currencies, leaving many families high and dry.[72] As international tourists and returning immigrants could no longer enter the empire, the service industry in the mountain collapsed. Even the movement of domestic vacationers decreased because of increased financial strain, restrictions on internal travel, and stricter military supervision of the borders between Beirut and Mount Lebanon.

Imported goods like coffee, sugar, and rice could not easily be replaced, since there was no local production of these items. However, other goods like wheat and flour, also imported in significant amounts prior to the war, were produced in the Ottoman Empire. The interior Syrian provinces generally produced an oversupply of wheat and exported it through the ports of Haifa, Tripoli, and Latakia.⁷³ Since Beirut and Mount Lebanon received grain supplies from abroad as well as from the interior grain-producing areas, if one supply line was cut, could the other make up the deficit? Local observers thought it possible. Fritz Grobba's economic survey reported Greater Syria to have been in a good position concerning food and grain supply in 1913. Wheat, the most important necessity, he wrote, was readily available throughout the provinces. Its harvest had been above average; grain prices were low, and export (due to low prices) was minimal, so a sizable surplus of cereals was carried into 1914.⁷⁴ As a diplomat and officer with the German forces, Grobba informed his superiors that the warehouses of Beirut and Jaffa's merchants were stocked with a good amount of wheat.⁷⁵

In early 1915, the American consular representative in Tripoli informed officials in Beirut that food produced in the country was still "plentiful, and about normal in price."⁷⁶ While in some regions the locusts had affected the 1915 harvest, in the Vilayet of Aleppo, it was unusually plentiful. The province's governor marveled in a report to Istanbul "that it was unlike anything seen in twenty or thirty years." He noted that even after he had dispatched grain to Istanbul, supplied the military, and sent some to Beirut and Mount Lebanon, "the province still had 10 million kilograms of wheat and approximately 5 million kilograms of barley in its tithe granaries, while the public [*ahali*] had another eight to ten times that in own possession."⁷⁷ A Syrian refugee confirmed that stocks of wheat, barley, and lentils were plentiful in Aleppo in November 1915. Wheat, he recounted, was stacked pile upon pile; there were thousands of bags of grain heaped on the platform of the Aleppo train station, in the caravanserais, and on the rooftops, although many of them were rotten.⁷⁸ Another "reliable source" described the situation as a "veritable siege that prohibited us to leave our mountain and communicate with neighboring regions, where the harvest was abundant this year."⁷⁹ As late as April 1918, grain was still available. The president of the American SPC, Howard Bliss, wrote, "The crops in all this region are very abundant and His Excellency [Jamal] Pasha has kindly promised to furnish us with provisions next year at government rates."⁸⁰ Shortages and starvation in Greater Syria, according to Fritz Grobba and others, were *not* inevitable. And while each year the food production decreased, the crop could have fed, if not everyone, a large portion of the population, even when imports from abroad were interrupted in 1914. It seems to be a classic Amartya Sen scenario, as there was never an apparent complete lack of food. So why did Beirut and Mount Lebanon experience shortages as early as November 1914?

Moving and Supplying an Insatiable Machine: The Ottoman Military

Mobilization for war was disruptive in all belligerent countries because it affected both legal and moral frameworks that organized and defined distributive networks.[81] The ability of governments or local agencies to carry out mobilization and deal with the resulting social and economic consequences on the home front determined the degree of change in everyday life. According to the historian Jay Winter, the balance of dividing goods and services between the military and civilians was preserved through citizens' entitlements in both Paris and London. Both cities displayed an evenhanded and largely effective system of supplying both soldiers and civilians. However, the priorities, he argues, differed in Berlin. Here the military came first, and Germany's economy "created to service it [the military] completely distorted the delicate economic system at home," to the detriment of civilians.[82] One can easily expand Winter's argument to the Ottoman Empire, where the provisioning of the military was also the priority. Measures employed to supply the army with men, animals, and provisions determined the capabilities and functions of civilians to not only maintain a particular standard of living but also, in the case of Beirut and Mount Lebanon, to survive the war.

This prioritization of the military may be understood in the historical context of an empire in trouble. A century of war, territorial losses, fiscal crisis, and the recent devastating defeat in the Balkan Wars, which was in part due to poor logistical support to the troops, all had turned this war into an existential threat. Another loss was simply not acceptable. And a victory, it was thought, would reverse adverse perceptions of the empire nationally and internationally. Everyone and everything, however, would have to be mobilized to effect it. Ensuring the supply and logistical support of the army, although poorly executed in the end, was a top priority. The military command thought, according to Grobba, that since food was plentiful in Syria, the province could feed itself and hence paid little attention to civilian provisioning.[83] The government left civilian provisioning to local officials, and only when widespread starvation could no longer be ignored did the state legislate civilian provisioning in 1916. I will return to these measures, but for now we have to ask how did provisioning the military affect civilian food supplies?

Mobilization interfered first with interregional food supply transfer. By the end of 1914, the Ottoman command in preparation for the first Suez Campaign appropriated all railway services for military purposes. That "there was one single railway (that was not complete at the time) over which the entire military transport and the entire provisioning of the country had to pass" put extreme pressure on the existing transportation system.[84] To make things worse, the sea blockade had cut off important coal imports.[85] By January 1915, the coal supply was almost depleted; "practically none" was on hand, and no coal was imported at all that year.[86] This meant that "the railway was obliged to curtail and restrict its train service to solely accommodate the movement of troops and their supplies."[87] This resulted, as the governor of Aleppo Mehmet Djelal Bey noted, in "dwindling means of transport" to the coast in 1915. While trains connecting Beirut and Damascus had run twice daily before the war, they now made the journey only once a week. Eyewitnesses lamented the unavailability of trains for transport of wheat.[88] In general, it was almost impossible to obtain railway freight cars. And when they were accessible, military commandos and the railroad commission demanded large bribes to get anything moving.[89] The transport of wheat from the interior to the coast, in any case, had become a costly nightmare, and grain shipments to feed civilians were sporadic and unreliable.[90]

If train and fuel shortages were not enough, locally stationed military and provincial and municipal authorities often interfered with shipments. The Ottoman governor of Damascus was notorious. By the end of 1914, he had banned exports from the interior to prevent local price hikes in his district. The governor of Aleppo did the same.[91] Those higher up in the chain of command, fearing the export of wheat to Beirut and Mount Lebanon would cause bread prices to skyrocket in the interior cities, supported the move. And while the military command had temporarily allowed shipments in January 1915, Damascene officials decided to prohibit the export of their grain to the coast. Even when intense negotiations between the central authorities, local Turkish officials, and municipal officers from Beirut and Damascus put the trains back in motion, shipments often were obstructed by red tape. Shipping anything without special permission became nearly impossible: the papers had to be notarized numerous times and "stamped with a great many official seals."[92] Even when the necessary stamps were procured, they still did not guarantee supply shipments or their arrival at the destination. Military authorities often confiscated grain shipments at random. Even when Jamal Pasha "was forced" to lift the ban on interdistrict trade and ordered shipments to Mount Lebanon in 1916, German military officials were concerned whether adequate transportation could be procured.[93]

The military use of trains might not have been the most important disruption.[94] In prewar years most grain and basic foodstuffs grown in the interior arrived on the Syrian coast not in freight trains but on the backs of camels, mules, and donkeys, and to a lesser extent via carriage. But now horses, mules, camels, and oxen all were called to defend the empire. The government's need for pack animals to transport troops and supplies was so great that it "consistently seized them."[95] The First Suez Campaign alone conscripted an estimated 25,000 camels to carry ammunition, food, and water to the front.[96] All regions of the empire were to contribute their share of four-legged compatriots, and failure to oblige resulted in confiscation and punishment. The outcome was an empty landscape. An American missionary reported that when he rode across the country, he "did not see a single camel or mule or horse, and only a few weak donkeys and very few men. All were hiding from the army draft."[97] Not even the Lebanese, despite their status of exemption, escaped the order to surrender their beasts of burden.[98] The governor Ohannes Kouyoumdjian Pasha temporarily delayed the requisitioning of animals. He argued it was illegal and surely not worth alienating the Lebanese in return for a small number of mules and camels. But after Kouyoumdjian left his post in 1915, Enver reinstated the order.

Orders to render valuable—and even not so useful—animals to the military were repeated constantly, and only a few exceptions were made.[99] Edward Nickoley described them as the government's attempt to go "over the country with a fine comb for both men and animals."[100] But it was a chaotic process. Bayard Dodge wrote that "men, horses, and supplies have been taken for the army cruelly and, what is more striking, very stupidly with no system."[101] The number of draft animals in the empire as a whole fell by more than half, and the number of sheep and goats was reduced by 40 percent.[102] In Beirut, one "could count them [draft animals] on the fingers of one hand," making any taxi or transportation services an expensive luxury. The fare was now at least three or four times the regular price.[103] The remaining animals generally were the weakest ones. Few people could afford the high cost of feed. Many owners had to let their livestock starve to death.[104] The lack of means of transportation was a serious problem, but not the only one directly resulting from military needs.

You're in the Army Now: Anything but a Comedy

When the names of men ages twenty-two to forty-five were read out in public on July 31, 1914, the residents of the southern town of Nabatia understood this to be the beginning of universal conscription in the preparation for war.[105] Ottoman authorities distributed large envelopes containing posters adorned with two green crescent moons, one crossed by swords and the other by a gun, indicating the military nature of the proclamation. Below the symbolically armed crescents, large letters spelled "SAFIR BARLIK."[106] Local officials were instructed to post the proclamations on the doors of government buildings and houses of worship. It was official: the men of the Beirut province had been called to fight in the war.

Enver Pasha ordered the full mobilization of Ottoman forces, animating thirty-four active divisions and the Hamidiye Cavalry reserve, on the evening of August 3, 1914.[107] Under what would be referred to as "armed neutrality," preparations such as registration and the physical examination of men were initiated. The call to arms was to be based on universal conscription, which had been the aim of nearly a century of military reforms.[108] A recent Law of Military Obligation, propagated after the losses in the Balkans, delineated recruitment districts, legislated regional army inspectorates in charge of mobilization and training to ensure maximum efficiency, and required all male Ottoman citizens, regardless of religion, to serve in the military.[109] The mobilization in the Vilayet of Beirut took place in a feverish manner. The *Weekly Irish Times* reported, "The mobilization of troops is being pressed forward here with great activity," as all men who could carry arms were "driven" to the barracks.[110] Georges-Picot described utter chaos: "Orders and counter orders are following each other hour after hour, and no one knows which order to obey and orders are constantly sent only to be rescinded a few moments later."[111] Only one order never changed: a train would be ready to transport troops to the regional army inspectorate in Damascus. At some point, the military authorities had immobilized a hundred cars for this purpose. Otherwise, no two offices responded in the same manner to the same question, and the consul saw soldiers being brought to Beirut just to be sent off again the next day.[112] The result was that mobilization proceeded at a snail's pace. The goal was to have everyone in place within twenty-one days. Only the Third Army Corps, part of which was stationed in Gallipoli, was completely mobilized as planned. The Ottomans had a difficult time filling their ranks. As late as January 1915, only 4 percent of the male population was under arms, compared to the situation France, where 10 percent had already been mobilized. As the war progressed, the recruitment of men became increasingly desperate and difficult. As a countermeasure, the government continuously increased the exemption taxes, widened the age range of eligible men, hunted down and harshly punished deserters to deter others, and reconsidered who may be exempted from service in 1916.[113] The impact of massive mobilization and its linkage to the experiences on the home front, and by extension the famine, is exemplified in the term *safar barlik*, which in its Arabic usage is understood to mean "journey over land" but more generally refers to mobilization. The term has become a metonym of the war and, in particular, the memory of Ottoman tyranny, hunger, famine, violence, and fear.[114]

The responses to mobilization were mixed in the Arab provinces. A small minority eagerly joined, but most men feared conscription. The atmosphere was agitated and confused, and if there was any national enthusiasm, it was not obvious.

> It would hardly be incorrect to say that there was not an Ottoman subject in all of Syria who was animated by one spark of patriotism. The available men of the country were scurrying to Lebanon like rabbits making for cover, and those who were obliged to remain within the vilayet were daily disappearing from view. No one knew whither they had gone, or how they lived, but many who had been familiar sights in the genial haunts of the city vanished overnight, and were not seen again for months—in some cases even for the whole

period of the war. Where they hid themselves we are only now beginning to learn, but with the desperation of the outlaw, they fled from the conscription officers of the Government.[115]

Fritz Grobba confirmed that "the population of Syria, if it was not outright hostile, objected to the measures of the Turkish government."[116] Since Mount Lebanon was exempted from conscription, many young men from Beirut and the neighboring districts fled there. They hid in the villages, in the nooks and crannies of homes, in the corners of fields, in secret caves, and among Bedouin families.[117] Indeed, the Ottoman recruitment officers had taken all "eligible Muslims, except those who escaped to Lebanon," as well as "all Christians, who could not pay the heavy indemnity."[118] Lebanon, a European paper reported, was "crowded with refugees from all parts of Syria and Palestine."[119] The British consul reported that the Lebanese authorities at this early moment protected men fleeing the conscription officers and "opened their borders to horses and mules that had been frightened away by their owners to avoid their animals being commandeered."[120] Military authorities stopped everyone of military age and requested proof of their exemption status; if the papers could not be produced in due time, the man would be taken and enrolled in the army. By August 1915, even papers proving residency in Mount Lebanon were no longer enough, as the "imperial council requires military service of all Lebanese in Beirut."[121] Men who were not trusted with guns were recruited into labor battalions.[122] Some wealthy families sent their young men abroad. In time, the escape route via the sea, however, was thwarted by the Entente blockade. Observers recounted Beirut's streets as emptied of its young men or "practically deserted" and its business suspended.[123]

The conscription of both men and beasts had an immediate effect on food production. A report of Gerhard von Mutius estimated that 28,000 men were conscripted from the province of Aleppo during the first year of the war. Damascus province supplied another 26,000 men. Apparently, the men came mainly from the grain-producing areas of Homs, Hama, and the Hauran. The numbers only increased during the war, as the government continuously expanded conscription, either by extending the age range or adjusting exemption rules. The authorities both revised the list of exceptions and raised the exemption tax.¹²⁴ To improve soldiers' provisioning, the tax was eventually to be collected in kind. This meant increasingly fewer people could afford it because of growing shortages and price hikes.¹²⁵

All That Fallow Land

The military mobilization of an estimated 13 percent of the population, and in particular of active reserve and territorial reserve men, was detrimental to the empire's economy.¹²⁶ Since most military recruits were peasants and sharecroppers, agricultural production decreased. In contrast, "rich Syrians, because of their hostility against the Turkish state and military service," continued to purchase their freedom.¹²⁷ In December 1914, Bayard Dodge wrote his family in the United States that the greatest fear in Beirut was reckless conscription. The Ottomans' policy, he lamented, might make the upcoming harvests impossible because there would be no farmers left to do the work.¹²⁸ The worst was that the initial call to arms coincided with the harvest. "Thousands of dollars' worth of foodstuffs rotted in the fields."¹²⁹ How bad was it?

The limited statistics available show a decline in agricultural production. According to the Ottoman Ministry of Forestry, Mining, and Agriculture, the estimated cultivated area of Greater Syria was 12,074,722 *dunums* (about 1,086,725 hectares) in 1908–1909.¹³⁰ The cultivated area increased from at least 921,919 to 12,996,641 *dunums* in 1913–1914, yielding about 1,238,551 tons of grain. In 1914–1915, cultivated land decreased in total by about 10 percent, and the overall yield declined to 942,319 tons of grain. There was a further decline in cultivated land in 1915–1916, but it varied by region. In Palestine, due to more direct exposure to the military, the decline was 40 percent. In the Adana province, affected by the massacres and massive deportation of Armenians, the decrease was around 30 percent, as it was in Beirut. Aleppo and Damascus each fell about 10 percent. In the Hauran, the cultivated area increased somewhat. While this seems to be a contradiction since this area was one of the key military recruiting grounds, large numbers of economic refugees had moved to the Hauran, working in now-vacant jobs for food. But the total land cultivated in 1915–1916 was significantly less, about 80 percent (9.25 million *dunums*) of that of the previous year. The crop yield was correspondingly lower, at approximately 789,765 tons of grain. Grobba blamed the decrease on the removal of able men from agricultural positions. Moreover, he wrote that peasants feared that the Ottoman military command would requisition their harvest, and many, in particular in the Hauran, simply let their land lie fallow.[131] Even if it is possible to point to a 20 percent decrease, would this mean starvation? Most certainly not in any normal year, as shortfalls would be made up by imports and interregional redistributions, both of which had become impossible in wartime. The biggest foe was the insatiable hunger of the armed forces.

Requisition Mania: Chickpeas, Clover, and Silk Stockings

Ottoman orders of civilian sacrifice and reckless and disorderly confiscation of goods added to the everyday struggle on the home front.[132] The government's inability to properly feed and clothe its soldiers had had devastating consequences in the past during the Russo-Turkish War and the Balkan Wars.[133] To deal with this obvious deadly problem, the government drafted the Law on the Method of War Taxes, which mandated the formation of commissions made up of Ottoman provincial officers, representatives of the military, local administrative councils, and municipalities to collect war taxes at the first sign of a new international conflict. After estimating civilians' needs, the commission was to confiscate only surplus supplies and, most important, to issue receipts to the owners based on price lists drawn up by representatives of local administrative councils, municipalities, and chambers of commerce.[134] The Law of Military Obligation ordered civilian authorities not to hold back any assistance to the military, in particular of supplies, food, and money. Once war was under way, however, the orderly frame outlined in the laws was swiftly abandoned. Disorder and chaos took over.

The empire-wide requisitioning of provisions and supplies was to be based on prices dictated by the military authorities. The war ministry charged its general supply department with buying food for the army from the production centers of the empire. Orders were transmitted to the military authorities stationed in Damascus and from there forwarded to provincial governors. The local officials then passed the orders down a chain of command to men in charge of urban quarters and to village sheikhs, who did the dirty work of collecting funds and materials. To deal with the administration and logistics of purchasing and distributing supplies to the troops, the army inspectorates set up general supply stations. Here, the military organized a number of committees at each station: a food storehouse committee, transportation committee, and a committee in charge of the medicine and equipment depots.[135]

No other Syrian city, according to the German consul, delivered as many supplies to the military via requisitioning as Beirut.[136] In time, and with growing involvement of Ottoman troops in battle, the formal requisitioning orders turned into commandeering and plunder. Transporting food eventually was no longer safe, as any soldier felt entitled to simply confiscate whatever he could get his hands on.[137] Requisitioning was not limited to goods that had an obvious use for military purposes. We read of soldiers and officers appropriating "women's silk stockings, children's shoes, lightning rods, and printing presses," foreign-made shoes for women, furniture, and even eau de cologne.[138] According to Mutius, articles like perfume and silk stockings would find their way onto the black market.[139] What had been framed as civilian mobilization for the war effort turned into a "requisition mania."[140] Civilians complained about the authorities not issuing proper receipts when taking supplies, fearing, of course, the promised reimbursement would be denied in light of missing paperwork. It was a systematic looting scheme.[141] Stanley Hollis's observations are illustrative. "The government here is commandeering all merchandise that it can lay its hands on, and there's little likelihood of the goods thus commandeered being paid for." Even Beirut's largest export firms, Hollis warned, would be driven out of business or into bankruptcy by the end of 1915 if the process was not regulated.[142] William Nelson, an American consular official in Tripoli, reported, "The cruelty of the officials trying to enforce the orders means beating and abuse of the men and destruction of household effects in the villages."[143] Another account described it as "the most wicked and unbridled system of plunder," chaotic and at times violent.[144] In response to criticism, Jamal Pasha in his postwar *Memories of a Turkish Statesman* insisted he had avoided requisitioning anything from Syrians. Instead, he vowed he had paid for what was needed "cash down." He reminded his readers that the first order he issued upon arrival in the province was "that nothing should be taken."[145] He did everything, he argued, not to alienate the Arabs.

War taxes, imposed to raise additional revenues, including an exit tax on foreigners leaving the empire, a new income tax of 3 percent, a road tax, a tax on private and public vehicles, a toll for entering Beirut, and others that were arbitrarily enforced.[146] And no doubt in some cases the taxes were extremely high. For example, merchants and producers were to pay their taxes in kind depending on the quantity of their merchandise and products. War taxes could be as high as 25 percent of "livestock and foodstuffs in the hands of merchants—including items such as potatoes, beans, chickpeas, onions and butter."[147] Mutius was puzzled by the situation in Beirut: "One would assume that the city would have a right that its own economic needs, as long as they did not contradict military interest, would be considered by the military and civil administrations." This, of course, was not the case. Military needs trumped the needs of civilians. As the war continued, the military proved to be a greedy machine, guzzling up men, beasts, and goods. Although it was necessary to place the region under the supervision of the military, Mutius warned that none of the Ottomans' actions were conducive to garnering the trust of a population that already had "separatist tendencies." Instead, he accused the authorities of arbitrariness and insisted chaos could be avoided even in wartime.[148]

The Predicaments of Loss and Greed: Prices, Purchasing Power, and Profiteers

There were additional avaricious competitors for whom the war proved to be an opportunity: wartime profiteers. In Beirut, the halt in the import-export business and higher exchange rates put an end to those businesses because they did not have the necessary capital to weather the storm. The disruptions eventually were felt by the poorest in the society. Those men and women who raised silkworms in their sheds for extra income; men who unloaded the merchant ships, worked in stocking the customhouse, or carried wares from the stores to the homes; hoteliers; shopkeepers; and anyone who generated income from ships docking in Beirut saw their earnings disappear.[149] At the same time, the reduction in agricultural production, the removal of products from the market through a halt in import-export, requisitioning, war taxes, monetary instabilities, and speculative hoarding caused prices of imported goods and locally produced basic foodstuffs to skyrocket.

The price index of grains, such as wheat and barley, sold on the local market in Mount Lebanon, while not a perfect indicator, sheds some light on civilians' difficulties in surviving the war. Grain prices were particularly important since bread was the main food for lower-class families, or, as one missionary put it, "Bread is knife, fork and spoon, as well as the main part of the Syrians' diet."[150] According to Grobba's estimates, each person needed 600–650 grams of wheat (or 500–510 grams of flour) per day.[151] A study of local, albeit fragmented, records by ʿAbdallah Saʿid for a few villages in the Shuf district is particularly telling.[152] Saʿid carefully analyzes prices of currency and basic commodities with changes in wages of agricultural laborers to determine locals' purchasing power. Saʿid's sources are incomplete and cannot account for regional differences, but they highlight how difficult it was for some to feed their families and survive the war. The price of wheat in the southern Shuf district, according to the study, although it fluctuated throughout the year, was an average of 4.13 piasters per *rotl* in 1914, 6.88 in 1915, 13.00 in 1916, 18.66 in 1917, and a staggering 24.00 piasters in 1918. A *rotl* of barley, often used in exchange for the more expensive wheat, could be purchased at a low 2.23 piasters in 1914. By the end of the war, following a general upward trend, a *rotl* of barley cost an average 15.00 piasters. But rising prices by themselves mean little. They have to be studied in relation to income and currency values to determine the purchasing power of individuals.[153]

A cash income was a necessity for most people so they could purchase basic foodstuffs that were no longer locally produced or produced on a very small scale. Some estimate an income decline of 80 percent in the Vilayet of Beirut,[154] which is based on the assumption that nearly everyone involved in the silk industry, which incurred an estimated 90 percent income loss, and trade saw their earnings decrease if not entirely disappear.[155] These are broad and not well-supported claims. A more concrete picture emerges only when we focus on the local. In contrast to these general assumptions, ʿAbdallah Saʿid's research shows agricultural wages as either stagnating or increasing somewhat. When they are considered in combination with price increases, however, he still notes a significant decrease in purchasing power. For example, a female wage laborer in the olive harvest and oil production business earned an average of 4.00 piasters in 1914, which meant at the current price *one* day of work would pay for a *rotl* of wheat. The wages declined in 1915 to 2.00 piasters and then slowly increased to 2.78 piasters in 1916, to 3.83 in 1917, and 4.75 in 1918. While there was an upward trend in wages after the initial plunge, the purchasing power declined as grain prices increased. Consequently, a female worker had to work 4.68 days in 1916, 4.87 days in 1917, and 5.00 days in

1918 for a *rotl* of wheat.¹⁵⁶ An unskilled male agricultural worker in the Shuf district who performed menial tasks like cutting grass, stacking firewood, or assisting in construction made approximately 6.0 piasters per day in 1914. This allowed him to purchase 1.45 *rotl* of wheat per day. He had to work 55 days to earn enough money to buy the amount of wheat necessary to feed one person for the year (assuming a low need of 557 grams of grain per day). While wages steadily climbed to an average of 9.5 piasters in 1918, the purchase power declined to 0.39 *rotl* per day's worth of labor, meaning that it now would take 303 days to earn the necessary funds for the yearly supply of grain per person.¹⁵⁷

The result was devastating. In July 1915, the *Assembly Herald* published a report from the American Red Cross chapter working in Beirut. One missionary wrote,

> I found a girl of fifteen the head of the house. She was an orphan and had not only the care of her four younger brothers and sister, but also her grandmother. She lives in a little wooden hut, perfectly bare except for some ragged bedding. The kitchen utensils have been sold for food. She and her brother next younger had earned their living by odd jobs, which are so difficult now to obtain. We were able to give the boy a little work and help them with ten pounds of flour a month. An older sister was married but her husband had been drafted into the army, leaving her, a child of seventeen, alone with two babies, one of them newborn. She is typical of a large class, lonely, heart-broken women left to care for themselves, and their children.¹⁵⁸

The story summarizes much of what the high prices, loss of income, and conscription meant for average families. Whether any of these young people survived the war is unclear. It may even be unlikely since the scarcity of jobs and the low earnings of unskilled workers would never be enough to buy adequate supplies for everyone in the family. Hunger and starvation eventually were an everyday reality for many. But not everyone.

Every war has its profiteers, and so do famines. Famine scholar Jenny Edkins has criticized both natural (Malthus) and economic (Sen) disaster explanatory frames for ignoring how famines provide potential benefits for some and how callous actions of profiteers deepened the famine.¹⁵⁹ Who benefited from the famine in Beirut and Mount Lebanon? Berthold Brecht is quoted as saying that "famines do not occur, they are organized by the grain trade."[160] In this case, merchants hoarding and profiteering have long been acknowledged as contributing to the suffering. Many first-generation Lebanese historians and politicians did not hesitate to blame "greedy speculators, former associates of Turkish officers," who even after the war still had "huge depots filled with wheat."[161] "Merchants, who were left to their whims and encouraged by an already questionable government, took advantage of everything to get rich."[162] At times the blame was directed against a particular group of merchants. In his postwar memoir, Yusuf al-Hakim devoted an entire chapter to the misdeeds of greedy merchants.[163] He listed local profiteers, both Christian and Muslim, such as the Sursock, Trad, Asfar, Bayhum, Ghandour, and Mkhaysh families, who catered to the Ottoman officials, as "did all the wealthy from one end to the other in Beirut and the Mountain."[164] That the rich of the city threw elaborate parties for government officials is documented in diplomatic sources and memoirs.

Being wealthy and on good terms with the Ottoman government meant not only survival but also potential significant economic benefits. Beirut merchant Michel Sursock, for example, has been accused of profiteering from his wartime concession over wheat. He is said to have tried to increase his profit by closing granaries and, "along with another family, the Asfars," engaged in price speculation.[165] Bayard Dodge, the chief of the American relief efforts, complained in a discussion with Mutius about Sursock's refusal "to sell grain bought at 40 piasters . . . for less than 250 piasters, even to save some of the children fed by the American relief organization."[166] Near the end of the war, a group of Beiruti merchants is reported to have sent a telegram to Istanbul, "demanding that the wealthy businessman Salim 'Ali Salam be brought to justice for siphoning 40,000 kilograms of sugar from the General Food Directorate for distribution among his constituency."[167] Moreover, considering press reports and eyewitness accounts, it seems much of the grain arriving in Beirut and Mount Lebanon after 1915 was smuggled and sold on the black market at exorbitant prices. Edward Nickoley, an employee at the SPC in Beirut, confirmed:

> It is true that businessmen have exploited to the full the situation created by the war. Many struggling merchants have become fabulously wealthy, having accumulated their wealth as a result of the dire necessity of the poor and suf-

fering. Many have abandoned their previous business pursuits to speculate in provisions and go in for money changing. Prices were raised, as stock on hand diminished each increase in the former, placing the commodities farther beyond the reach of the people who need them.[168]

This occurred even though the local government by that time had attempted to deal with profiteering and speculation. Indeed, it might have been an internal problem, as it was rumored that government officials were enriching themselves in scandalous ways "by selling [government-organized grain] to middlemen and then sharing the profit that would result from price gouging."[169] There still is little hard evidence concerning hoarding and profiteering. Many of the accusations still come from anecdotes and hearsay. By reading between the lines, we see that government actions and public debates not only indicate merchants' power to control the market but also their shady dealings. Perhaps future research in family archives will shed further light on this.

Conclusion

Famines have much in common, such as high food prices affecting mostly the poor; migrations in search of food, work, and charity; increase in crime, suicide, and antisocial behavior; and increase in mortality from disease and starvation. At the same time, famines occur in particular socioeconomic settings and are subject to specific human action or inaction in face of the immediate threat of crisis. The Lebanese famine, not unlike the Bengal famine, was the outcome of war-generated market failures.[170] The European powers deployed hunger as a weapon of war and the state prioritized supplying its military. The hunger of the Ottoman military cannot be underestimated; its politics and those of the war more generally "suffocated and diverted the supply of food" that might otherwise have fed the most vulnerable.[171] While environmental factors certainly aggravated the situation, there is no doubt that causal factors were primarily war related.

Considering the significance of the famine, it is not enough to expose its causes. It is equally, if not more, important to highlight how the disaster unfolded and how people dealt with it, since it is in this context that we can determine the famine and the war's impact on identifiable power structures. The famine happened within a particular socioeconomic constellation that would not only determine society's and individuals' capabilities of dealing with the crisis but also would be transformed as a result.[172] The focus now shifts to the actions of those dealing with the disaster to assess "human conduct under life-threatening conditions and the role of collective institutions [state, religious, and philanthropic] in shaping people's responses to them."[173] The responses to it, I argue, reveal this society's deeper difficulties.[174] The various attempts at and competition over civilian provisioning expose important sociopolitical changes that impacted both wartime and postwar power relations. In the following chapters, wartime politics of provisioning serves as the primary hermeneutic. It is a key space of competition, wherein some would be empowered and others repudiated, and the political capital and ambitions in the postwar period would be determined.

Figure 4. *The Beirut Vegetable Market before the* War. Source: The American Colony (Jerusalem), G. Eric and Edith Matson Photograph Collection, Library of Congress Prints and Photographs Division, Washington, D.C.

(CHAPTER 3)

THE POLITICS OF FOOD

Wartime Provisioning for Civilians

The Ottoman Empire had been at war only thirteen days when, in the afternoon hours of November 13, 1914, a group of destitute men knocked on the doors of the Beirut municipality building. The men, described in the Beirut daily newspaper *al-Ittihad al-'Uthmani* (Ottoman union) as "heads of households from among the poor of the city," desperate and with hungry women and children waiting at home, protested that neither flour nor wheat was to be found in the city.[1] Warning municipal council members, who were taken aback by this sudden assembly on their doorstep, the men complained that not one ounce of affordable flour or wheat was left in the markets and the usual four loads of grain from Aleppo had failed to arrive in Beirut that day. At the same time, some urban poor were ransacking neighborhood bakeries, seizing whatever hidden reserves they could get their hands on. Beirut seemed to be falling apart under the weight of hunger. Urban order was in danger, and the lack of food had generated precarious conditions that needed to be addressed to preserve peace in the city. The municipality rushed to solve what would be become known as the "flour issue."[2] Municipal council members sent a messenger to Beirut's governor-general, Bekir Sami Bey, who immediately cabled his counterpart in Aleppo to solicit provisions and urge Ottoman military authorities to give top priority to shipping grain to the coastal capital. There was plenty of grain in Aleppo, but transporting it to the coast would prove the greatest obstacle to its actual delivery.[3]

Given these difficulties, the president of the Beirut municipality, Ahmad Mukhtar Bayhum, decided to handle the situation in person. His primary concern was to take care of the bottleneck in the transportation system, which had reduced grain supplies in the city and driven prices through the roof. Fully aware that wheat and flour could be purchased in the interior regions of Greater Syria, Bayhum set out for Aleppo in the early-morning hours of November 14 via Damascus to arrange a shipment of wheat and flour to feed his city. After intense negotiations, he finally secured the necessary freight cars from the military command of the Ottoman Fourth Army.[4] With the cars lined up, Bayhum sent an urgent telegram to Hassan Effendi, a Beirut merchant, asking for the immediate transfer of 500 Ottoman liras from the account of the Beirut municipality to purchase a "great amount" of wheat. Hassan Effendi hurried to the Beirut branch of the Ottoman Bank to transmit the desired amount to Aleppo.[5] Five days later, on November 19, trainloads of grain slowly made their way down the slopes of Mount Lebanon into Beirut, and according to the report in *al-Ittihad al-'Uthmani* the poor inhabitants of the city breathed a sigh of relief.[6] Hopes, it seems, were high. The municipal president's efforts had solved the first wartime food supply crisis.[7] Little did anyone know or expect that the crowds in the city's vegetable market would soon turn from jolly children, who curiously shielded their eyes from the sun to glance at the photographer, to children in rags digging in the garbage in search of leftovers.

War, Food, and the City

In all of the belligerent states, struggles and negotiations over the procurement of food supplies for soldiers and civilians were an everyday, often contentious, affair. Jay Winter noted that wartime provisioning of civilians, and by extension securing their health, preoccupied municipal, county, and central governments and justified unprecedented state intervention into everyday life.[8] Government officials knew their state's legitimacy in the eyes of civilians depended on the successful provision of the basic necessities of food and health. Civilians would support institutions and individuals able to deliver physical and mental security. In light of ever-diminishing food supplies, an increase in diseases, and mental stress, caring for civilians became a competitive and politically charged affair.

While Ottoman authorities at times responded to civilian food shortages, the central government implemented an empire-wide civilian provisioning scheme only in the spring of 1916. In the absence of a central order to provide for hungry civilians, local actors were pivotal in organizing, or at the very least attempting to organize, provisions. Representatives of the state such as the Ottoman governor and Beirut's elites and politicians, many of whom came from a merchant background, were particularly well positioned to take up the responsibilities of provisioning because of their thorough understanding of the subtleties of the local food system. How local urban power players entered the field of wartime provisioning is the story of this chapter. A close look at local efforts to feed civilians and the opportunities and challenges presented in the arenas of provincial and municipal politics sheds light on the relationship between the Ottoman state and its citizens on the periphery. It showcases local urban wartime politics by exposing communal dynamics in times of crisis and the intricacies of existing communal and social orders that shaped the experience on the home front.[9]

As the opening scene of this chapter illustrates, members of the Beirut municipality asserted their role in the city as providers and problem solvers. Locals perceived the Beirut council as the ideal mediating body in regard to food provision in the city. It is not surprising since the municipal council had become one of the most important institutions of urban governance, and its members had significant power over the daily affairs of the city.[10] The municipality's state-sanctioned legitimacy and its expanding links to an urban clientele permitted it to intervene in the daily lives of urban inhabitants. Most important, Beirut's political elite understood the successful performance of the municipal council's officially legislated role as not only proving its general utility but as solidifying its members' legitimacy as leaders in the community. For reform-minded individuals, such as Ahmad Mukhtar Bayhum, the war was an opportunity to finally demonstrate to their local constituency and the Ottoman state that issues related to internal security and well-being of the Beirut province in general and the city more specifically could be dealt with locally. Decentralization and local autonomy could potentially be sold as functioning systems to the public and the state. The council, however, would face insurmountable obstacles in regard to food procurement, such as the continued defiance by local merchants to restrictions in the market and a growing distrust of the central authorities. Ottoman state representatives eventually saw the council's desire to display provisioning power as a direct challenge to their authority and as standing in the way of CUP policies designed to rein in the provinces and centralize state power. The political competition between the state and Arab reformers was visible in the politics of provisioning, as the center increasingly encroached on local affairs.

The Politics of Food: Prices, Profiteers, and the Urban Poor

Wartime Beirut may best be described as a city under siege. Food shortages, especially of flour and wheat, continued to be the city's most pressing issue, despite the municipality's initial efforts in November 1914 to guarantee the transfer of grain from Aleppo to Beirut. Indeed, on November 21, only a few days after the press had announced the end of the first food crisis, large crowds, once again driven by empty stomachs and bare dinner tables, gathered in front of bakeries and stores. Reporting on upheavals in the city, an article in *al-Ittihad al-'Uthmani* attributed the shortage to the "sad fact" that merchants were taking advantage of their position in the supply chain. Some Beiruti merchants had apparently diverted a few carloads of flour—those that were not directly supervised by the municipality—into Mount Lebanon, where they were able to sell them at a higher price.[11] The results were a depleted market and inflated prices in the city.[12] According to the reports, the municipality, heeding the people's anxieties and fearing widespread riots, again intervened to guarantee unhindered interdistrict trade.

The provincial administrative council, the Beirut municipality, and some members of the Beirut Chamber of Commerce reportedly met under the supervision of Bekir Sami Bey to discuss problems of transportation and speculative hoarding and how to put an end to it.[13] The men agreed the solution was to assure an abundant supply of grain to both Beirut and the surrounding districts. This, however, required the involvement of the central authorities. First, Beirut's leaders needed funds; the Beirut municipality had declared bankruptcy in 1913, and money had been short ever since.[14] Second, to ensure grain shipments from other districts, an order had to be issued in Istanbul, especially as the local authorities in Damascus and Aleppo had banned grain exports.[15] The response from the capital was positive. The director of the Ottoman Bank in Istanbul agreed to deposit 10,000 Ottoman liras into its Beirut branch, and the interior ministry promised a daily shipment of at least eight trainloads of grain.[16] Announcing there would no reason "to fear any deficiencies in terms of this basic necessity in the future," *al-Ittihad al-'Uthmani*'s editor euphorically attributed the end of yet another food crisis to the great accomplishments and negotiation skills of the provincial governor and, more important, to the president of the municipality.[17] Once again, it seemed, the political competence of the local leadership had ensured the provision of food, and a larger catastrophe was avoided. The problem, however, was far from being solved. In a report from April 20, 1915, wheat shipments were described as unreliable and never filled the minimum demand of 240 trainloads a month (or 8 train cars a day). "The Wheat Issue" was no joking matter. Considering that in January 1915 only forty-eight railcars arrived, followed by twenty-five in February, twenty-five in March, and twenty in the first two weeks of April, it is possible to imagine the shortages.[18] In May 1915, according to the German consul Mutius, the important question of Beirut's flour and grain supply still was not solved. Whose fault it was, he wrote, was unclear. But the provincial administration blamed the military, and vice versa. The fact was that the "grain supply was not secured, and at times none arrived at all." Some families, at times, went without bread for days. As a result, riots took place in front of shops and bakeries. A scandal in his eyes, since "the whole world knew that there was sufficient grain in the interior, Homs, Hama, Aleppo, and some of it was rotting." He found it incomprehensible that the needed grain, five to six railcars daily might be enough, could not be shipped to Beirut,[19] especially since Ottoman officials had uncovered irregularities and an elaborate system of bribery in the processing of grain to Beirut. A number of railway officials, including one Turkish officer, were caught and punished. Whether this was going to improve the situation, Mutius posed, was yet to be determined.

Destabilizing speculation by Beirut's merchants and consumers' panic purchases even at inflated prices also became a problem early on since producers and merchants, at least initially, were permitted to trade grain at market prices.[20] In an article on December 3, *al-Ittihad al-'Uthmani* suggested the city government would set reasonable prices for whatever limited supplies remained on the market. As demands for increased government control may have been difficult to accept, the article cautiously addressed the issue. Prices, it argued, needed to be "fair" to both consumers and merchants. It was not advisable to simply restrict merchants; rather, it was desirable for everyone to find a compromise between the interests of businessmen and consumers. "If we request a fair limit for all prices, it is only in the interests of both sellers and buyers."[21] Price hikes were not blamed on greedy merchants but on overall confusion. Merchants, the article argued, did not know at what prices to sell, and the buyers did not know when and how much to buy. Instead, there was panic in Beirut whenever an enemy warship was sighted off the coast or when grain trains were delayed. The author urged the municipality to end this confusion and encouraged the council, expressing great confidence in its ability, to determine proper sales prices. By interpreting the municipality's actions as not hostile toward the city's merchants, the article precluded any negative responses from the business community. Framing the municipality as acting in everyone's interest, the author positioned it as an incorruptible institution and opened the possibility for the municipal council to act despite its close connections to the city's merchants. That the council would heed these recommendations was almost taken for granted, as the article expresses gratitude in advance for its efforts.[22]

The municipal council first dealt with imported goods that were most affected by the Entente naval blockade, such as coffee and sugar.[23] Price fluctuations in these goods were commented on in the press, and only a day after concerns were voiced about price gouging, the municipal council ordered the most prominent sugar, coffee, and kerosene merchants into its offices to discuss trade practices for their commodities. The city authorities then set up a commission comprising members of the municipality and the Beirut Chamber of Commerce with the task of suggesting fair prices for both imported goods and necessities such as flour and wheat. Intervention in the economy was not unprecedented in Ottoman history. The state had historically played an active role in controlling the market. Suraiya Faroqhi has shown how regulations of prices played a part in creating an intricate Ottoman provisioning network in the sixteenth and seventeenth centuries. Centrally appointed Ottoman judges, in close consultation with merchants and craftsmen, set prices. The detailed price lists were publicized and enforced by specially appointed government agents.[24] Well into the eighteenth century, the state continued to play a protective role, at the expense of merchants, especially in relation to necessities such as bread. But state control over the economy decreased as the empire was integrated into the global economy.[25] The role of the mid-nineteenth-century municipal council was limited to inspecting weights and measures and quality control of goods.[26] It was to prevent fraud, but it did not intervene in setting prices. Indeed, by the outbreak of World War I, the Ottoman economy was governed by a free market, which continued to hold sway until the authorities legislated an empire-wide provisioning scheme in July 1916. The price controls implemented immediately after the outbreak of the war thus emanated from local urban settings, and the main agents directing negotiations were locally elected urban institutions rather than centrally appointed Ottoman judges. This was, no doubt, the result of nineteenth-century reforms, which empowered local elites within elected bodies. The focus was on provisioning the urban population, and local governments fixed prices in cooperation with merchants.

The fact that council members were elected, came from upper-class, often merchant, backgrounds, and were frequently involved in reformist politics meant that municipal intervention into the market in general, and in setting price limits in particular, involved a delicate balancing act. For example, the fact that the municipal council initially paid attention to luxury goods, unaffordable to average workers, perhaps partially speaks to their position. After all, council members were dependent on the franchise of upper- and middle-class men, who for the most part voted along the lines dictated by their community leaders. Nominations for council candidacy depended on the goodwill of powerful and rich community leaders and the endorsement of imams, priests, and *mukhtars*.[27] Considering these groups' lobbying powers, it is not surprising that the council prioritized luxury goods. Still, the suggested price list published in *al-Ittihad al-'Uthmani* on December 6, 1914, not only delineated fair prices for coffee and sugar but also included wheat, flour, bulgur (cracked wheat), butter, milk, and soap.[28] This move illustrates the municipality's broader responsibility to ensure everyone's well-being. The commission decided to reduce prices to levels prior to the steep increase that had occurred on December 2.

The price list, however, was not accompanied by any legal order or enforcement mechanism, which ultimately rendered it ineffective. Price fluctuations would continue to be a problem throughout the war.[29] When wheat prices rose, families began using alternative grains to grind into flour. The immediate substitute was barley, as it sold for about half the price of wheat as late as November 1916.[30] Barley was more readily available and offered similar qualities and nutritional value;[31] families of average means and wealthier ones began eating bread made from barley.[32] As barley climbed up the social ladder into the homes of affluent Lebanese families and was no longer frowned on as an inferior grain, its price increased just as its availability diminished. The outcome was that many of the poorer families resorted to stretching the flour used for baking bread with ground-up cheap legumes, such as chickpeas, lentils, and even lupine seeds, previously used only to feed livestock.[33] The price of a *rotl* of lentils was between 4 and 5 piasters; a *rotl* of flour made from wheat cost between 16 and 17 piasters in April 1916. Considering that an unskilled laborer in Beirut earned about 8 to 10 piasters per day, legumes were more affordable.[34]

In the absence of strict government controls, commodities disappeared from retail stores and were sold on the black market at the highest possible prices.[35] This problem sparked a debate in *al-Ittihad al-'Uthmani*. Prominent intellectuals, positioning themselves as voices of the public, insisted that the municipality exercise the kind of surveillance and control over prices similar to that of heads of households over their families and possessions.[36] On December 7, 1914, in an open letter to Bekir Sami Bey, the intellectual Yusuf 'Abdallah Susa expressed his concern and frustration. The practical implementation of price controls on "daily necessities" had failed, despite, as he put it, the great efforts of the municipality. Susa reminded his readers that Beirut's commerce was in the hands of a small number of individuals—one in a thousand—who took advantage of the population's most dire needs, affecting its moral and physical strength. He blamed wholesale merchants for hoarding. Sometimes, he wrote, these merchants stored goods for two to three weeks, until the market was completely devoid of the product, so that consumers would pay whatever the merchants' greed demanded. Wartime profits on grain sales was as high as 300 percent, he wrote, to the obvious detriment of the urban poor. At the same time, Susa praised the municipality for attempting to curtail rising costs of living. He reminded the public that the municipality had demonstrated that all its projects were geared toward the well-being of the city.³⁷ Nevertheless, he pointed out, the last time the municipality legislated prices, merchants continued to sell their goods at exorbitant rates. According to Susa, for some men greed trumped any moral obligation to the community.

In his attack on the profiteers, Susa employed a complex moral language contrasting the wholesale merchants' greedy personal interest with the good and "humanitarian" intentions of the municipality, which was working for the collective destiny of the city. He presented civilian sacrifice as a communal moral necessity, appealing to Beirut's upper classes to share the sacrifices of the urban poor, who could not find any affordable flour.³⁸ It was clear that the source of scarcity and shortages, at least to a certain extent, was the greed of men.³⁹

Susa, however, blamed not only the merchants but also implicitly the Ottoman governor, as he addressed his letter to Bekir Sami Bey. This public display of dismay may have contributed to the governor's loss of "public confidence." Rumors even began to circulate that Bekir Sami Bey was collaborating with speculators, surely undermining his credibility.⁴⁰ Mutius seemed to be convinced that the governor was corrupt: "It seemed to be a fact that the locally stationed highest official, the governor Bekir Sami Bey, had lost the trust of the population, which in secret, albeit in unison, accused him of receiving a share of the profit made by speculators of luxury items and petroleum."⁴¹ It is impossible to know, as Elizabeth Williams points out, whether there was any truth to the rumors. What we can say is that Susa's piece highlights a particular political strategy that plays out on the pages of *al-Ittihad al-'Uthmani* in more general terms—a distinct attempt to elevate the municipality as a well-functioning provisioning body able to guarantee the well-being of Beirutis. The municipality is imagined here as what might be described as a Foucauldian *dispositif*, a mechanism driven by an emergency, able to successfully manipulate a heterogeneous set of forces and develop them in a way that would improve the situation.⁴²

Political Strategies:
Municipal Politics between the Real and the Imagined

The strategy at play aimed at establishing political legitimacy of the municipality, and more broadly, of provincial Arab elites. At the beginning of the war, the editor and owner of *al-Ittihad al-'Uthmani*, Ahmad Hassan Tabbara, and the paper's various contributors highlighted Beirut's municipal authority as a central urban institution that could alleviate suffering in the city. The paper's local news section, despite strict Ottoman censorship of the press, showcases how local politics were practiced and, under the guise of "daily city talk," a locally governed public sphere imagined.[43] Thus, the editor's view of the immediate world around him and his local political ambitions became known. Moreover, however insignificant local news reports may seem in the broader context of the war, they also tell us what kind of news people consumed. For at least the first eighteen months of the war, the local news amplified a message of both local vulnerabilities and capabilities.[44]

Al-Ittihad al-'Uthmani's editor generally praised the municipality's efforts in guaranteeing the provisioning of civilians, in particular the urban poor. From November 1914 until the paper closed in January 1916, food shortages—despite censorship—were a regular news item. Approximately one-third of the 324 preserved editions include articles related to urgent questions surrounding food, mostly published under the subheading "Local News." Food-related news hardly ever made it onto the front page, which was reserved for international and regional war-related events. However, relegating food to page 2 or 3 of the paper did not diminish its importance. Instead, it was framed as a local issue. The captions ranged from "The Price of Sugar," to "No Fear of High Meat Prices," to "The Flour Problem," to simply "Flour, Flour."[45] Slightly more than 80 percent of food-shortage articles—those including keywords such as "food," "flour," "wheat," "sugar," "coffee," or "rationing"—focused on the "good" campaigns of the Beirut municipality and at times the locally stationed Ottoman governors in spite of their many failures.

The question must be raised: If the efforts of Beirut's leaders were in vain, why do we find such a positive representation of the municipal council in the newspaper? In the prewar period, it was not unusual for local newspapers to question the council's effectiveness in areas such as urban planning and market control. This changed during the war, as critiques were never directed at the municipality as an institution but rather at various actors who did not heed its suggestions or commands. It could simply relate to Ottoman censorship and the editor's desire not to offend the authorities, since a discussion of extreme shortages in the city would negatively reflect on both the municipality and Ottoman officials and, by extension, the state. The CUP was serious about preserving a positive image of the Ottoman state. In November 1914, military authorities had announced that news about the war could be published only if it came directly from the war ministry. Any publication of information thought to endanger the Ottoman war effort or to present the state as failing in its responsibilities to its citizens would incur the large fine of 100 to 500 Ottoman liras. Editors permitting such publication would face a prison sentence of up to three months.[46]

Government press censorship was not new to Beiruti intellectuals. Tabbara, a member of the Beirut Reform Society and the Decentralization Party, had experienced firsthand the government's intolerance of oppositional voices before the war.[47] In April 1913, Tabbara and his paper came under fierce attack from the Ottoman government. Earlier that year, the Beirut Reform Society had outlined a program detailing the various functions of local government and proposing to limit Ottoman authority in the Arab provinces to foreign, economic, and military affairs.[48] This public articulation of a reform proposal was possible under the governorship of Adham Bey, who, in line with the liberal ruling party that had appointed him, was inclined toward political compromise.[49] After its coup on January 23, 1913, the CUP, alarmed by developments in Beirut, reinstated its loyal member Abu Bakr Hazim as governor.[50] Eager to undermine the opposition, Hazim ordered the Reform Society's clubs closed on his arrival in the city on April 8, 1913. The provincial reformers, in response, called for a general strike. Both Ahmad Tabbara and 'Adb al-Ghani al-'Urasi, the editor and owner of yet another reformist newspaper (*al-Mufid*), drew the governor's anger by publishing the defiant call for the strike in their papers.[51] Hazim responded with a raid on the papers' offices and threatened the men with arrest. This encounter would appear to be a good reason to avoid future confrontation. Fear of government crackdowns, however, only partially explains Tabbara's later actions, especially since he, it seems, was not easily intimidated; during the crisis of 1913, he had continued to secretly publish his paper despite the official ban and the constant threat of arrest.[52] The editor's decision to portray Beirut's wartime municipal council as a functioning, reasonable, concerned, and moral governing body was a calculated move. Tabbara's project to use the war an opportunity for local self-governance, so promising in its early months, was extinguished when he and thirteen other reform-minded men were led to the gallows in the early-morning hours of May 6, 1916.[53]

With the war escalating, famine devastating Greater Syria, and soldiers dying by the thousands from disease, the Ottoman state grew ever more nervous, a condition that was personified in the paranoid Ottoman governor 'Azmi Bey, who had replaced Bekir Sami Bey, and his superior Jamal Pasha. During the summer of 1915, Jamal Pasha became increasingly suspicious of an impending anti-Ottoman Arab rebellion in Greater Syria. Ottoman authorities discovered documents left behind by the French consul, which named individual Beirutis, including Hassan Tabbara, as having conspired with the French against Ottoman rule.[54] According to the commander of the Fourth Army's intelligence services, 'Aziz Bey, Tabbara had been friends with the French consul in Beirut before the war and continued to be in contact with Georges-Picot even after the French were expelled in 1914. Supposed communication with an enemy nation, as well as membership in the Decentralization Party, was reason enough for Jamal Pasha to have Tabbara court-martialed.[55] In January 1916, the Ottoman authorities arrested him, suspended his paper, and closed the press. Arrests by now were a daily occurrence. Hardly a day passed without local papers publishing lists of accused or sentencing announcements issued by the military court. Tabbara's arrest was a high-profile case. According to Mutius, the Ottoman authorities had long suspected him of anti-Ottoman sentiment, but nothing had stuck. This time they must have had some proof, although it was never revealed. Beirutis deplored the disappearance of Tabbara's paper, as the editor had pleased both his own Muslim community and, "out of business concerns," the Christian community.[56] Tabbara was executed a few months later.

Between Profit and the Common Good: The Social Position of Municipal Council Members

It is important to note that whenever mention was made of merchants in *al-Ittihad al-'Uthmani*, their identities were generally left ambiguous. For example, when discussing those who diverted trains into Mount Lebanon, the November 21, 1914, report referred to them simply as "some merchants."[57] However, accounts written after the war often openly blamed merchants' greed, and most did not hesitate to name families and individuals who had profited. Yet, in regard to wartime coverage of profiteering in *al-Ittihad al-'Uthmani*, writers talked about merchants in general terms. Susa, as we have seen, simply criticized the behavior of "wholesale merchants," without mentioning any merchant by name. Instead of making a direct accusation, he relied on his audience to make the appropriate judgment, but why?

Ahmad Hassan Tabbara must have been sensitive to the council members' multiple social positions and interests. His political allegiances also colored the narrative. The majority of municipal council members were both propertied businessmen and vocal reform politicians.[58] For example, prominent merchant and alleged wartime profiteer Michel Sursock was a member of the Beirut Reform Society and thus linked both to the president of the municipality, Ahmad Mukhtar Bayhum, a reformer who also made the list of war profiteers, and to the paper's editor, Hassan Tabbara. Sursock's political connections perhaps placed him outside the scope of legitimate criticism from his associates during the war. Another prominent example is Ahmad Mukhtar Bayhum, who came from an important Beirut merchant family and had played an important role in the city's Muslim community.[59] The Bayhums were involved in the trade of agricultural products and were among a Muslim minority of export merchants. Before the war, the family had conducted vigorous trade with Europe, a business that was generally dominated by non-Muslims.[60] For example, Hasan Bayhum traded grain in the Hauran, and the family initially owned the Société anonyme ottomane de la voie ferré de Beyrouth à Damas (Ottoman Beirut-Damascus Railway Company), a railway company for which the Ottoman government granted an imperial concession in 1891.[61] The Bayhums had a long history of political involvement in the city. Mukhtar Bayhum's father's cousin Muhyi al-Din Bayhum was an original member of the municipal council. Hardly a year passed without at least one Bayhum occupying a seat on the council.[62] One of the most important changes in Beirut's municipal politics may even be attributed to the appointment of a Bayhum; after the presidency of Muhammed Bayhum, which began in 1893, the municipal council was no longer dominated by men with an Egyptian military background but by local merchant notables.[63] So historically the family was involved in commerce and politics, a duality that was epitomized in al-Hajj 'Abdallah Bayhum, president of Beirut's Chamber of Commerce and the city's mayor in the early 1860s.

Ahmad Mukhtar Bayhum, moreover, as the wartime mayor of Beirut until late summer of 1915, was exemplary of an urban elite that engaged not only in politics and commerce but also in literary and philanthropic associations. Bayhum it seems was invested in improving his immediate surroundings both through social welfare organizations and educational institutions.[64] Bayhum was a notable author, educational activist, and Arab nationalist.[65] First, he was an important member of the Beirut Reform Society and, along with Salim 'Ali Salam and others, had pressed the Ottoman government for provincial reforms. In 1913, he traveled to Paris as a member of the Reform Society's delegation with Salim 'Ali Salam, Michel Sursock, Khalil Zaynieh, Ayub Tabet, and the editor of *al-Ittihad al-'Uthmani*, Ahmad Hassan Tabbara.[66] As the scion of a merchant family, a member of the municipality, and a political reformer, Bayhum determined his interests by his complex social position. On the one hand, his family ran a trade business, which put him in the position of potentially profiting from war shortages; on the other hand, as a member of the municipal council, Bayhum had a moral obligation to ensure the well-being of the city. His close relationship with Tabbara made it unlikely that the latter would publish articles overly critical of the municipality or portray all merchants as profiteers.

Considering the position of municipal council members as both reform politicians and members of important merchant families, Susa also avoided making blunt accusations that could potentially destabilize the municipality's position. After all, it was likely that council members themselves, or some of their close associates, were taking advantage of the wartime situation. Instead, Susa employed the language of a moral code centered on communal sacrifice on behalf of the city's poor; his idea of well-being was living well, not simply in a material sense but also in a moral sense. He called for human decency. For Susa, the municipality had to regulate the marketing of all basic commodities and morality in the city. At stake was keeping the famished poor alive.[67] To achieve this goal, Susa suggested the municipality take a complete inventory of essential commodities and then set fair prices according to their availability. He recommended the municipality take control of all wholesale distribution of flour and wheat, restricting private merchants to retail transactions. This, he proposed, would bring prices back to a reasonable level and prevent wholesale merchants from monopolizing the market.

Susa rendered his critique of the municipality's inaction in the most flattering tone, reminding council members that Beirutis had not forgotten the municipality's efforts in the earlier transport crisis. Susa did not condemn trade in general; he left room for men like Bayhum to position themselves as "moral" merchants not interested in taking advantage of the situation. Susa's suggestion that the men of the municipality take over wholesale business highlights his trust that not all merchants were wartime profiteers; rather, he trusted that the merchants linked to the municipal council would work for the greater good of the city.[68] This sentiment was further elaborated the next day, this time on the front page. The author—now anonymous—insisted that merchants would respect the by-then widely publicized price list because the municipality took the cost of living of the poor into consideration when drafting it. Despite the open encouragement of the paper, the municipality did not take an inventory of wheat or flour, nor did it immediately take over the wholesale grain business to eliminate hoarding; instead, until the early spring of 1915, it resorted to jawboning, urging merchants to adhere to the prices suggested by the municipal commission.

Disciplining the Market:
Regulations, Surveillance, and Punishment

In the spring of 1915, the municipality stepped up its game. The council imposed punitive measures, including monetary fines and imprisonment, to dissuade Beirut's merchants from selling commodities, in particular grain and its derivatives, above the assigned prices. Council members had hesitated to enforce price limits, perhaps out of fear of alienating their electoral base, the city's community leaders, and their own family members or perhaps not to undermine their own profits. Likewise, the editor of the newspaper was hesitant to issue demands more stringent than his appeals to merchants' social consciousness. But in 1915, with an ever-decreasing grain supply, the paper insisted more strongly on the municipality's managerial and control mechanisms. Whether or not it matched reality, a picture emerged in the paper of a council ready to take over the wholesale distribution of grain. The municipality, at that moment of impending emergency, appeared to be a powerful institution. Reports were published that the municipal council had bought wheat and flour and set up a functioning security apparatus. When trainloads of grain and flour arrived in Beirut, the municipality stationed policemen throughout the city to receive the precious cargo. The wheat and flour were then distributed to vendors at wholesale prices set by the municipality, and store owners were ordered to sell the provisions at a fixed rate. To be eligible to retail wheat or flour, vendors had to procure permission from the police. The crowds of the "poor and desperate in front of the stores was tangible proof of the great need."[69] The municipality apparently met this need; the paper praised its efforts and cheered at the prospect of the poor being able to obtain wheat at a decent price, especially when the municipality assured the public that the retail price would not exceed the limit it had set in December 1914: 5 piasters per *rotl*. Those closest to the municipal council would, of course, still have a chance to take advantage of the situation.

Moreover, the editor stressed the council's commitment to ensure vendors obeyed the price limit and did not commit food fraud, since any arrival of wheat still presented opportunities for profiteering at the retail level. Opportunities to take advantage of those in need had indeed trickled down the socioeconomic ladder to bakers and policemen.[70] In November 1914, its finances had been so dire that the municipality was forced to let go fifteen sergeants in charge of implementing its orders.[71] As a result, the council was understaffed and had to rely on local police to supervise distributions and sales. However, policemen often looked the other way as bakers sold bread at black-market prices right under the nose of the city council. The newspaper denounced a number of Beirut bakers and store owners who could not resist the temptation to make extra cash by charging more than what the municipal council permitted or by stretching their wares; for example, some retailers mixed ground coffee with finely ground barley and chickpeas. The purchase of flour became ever more hazardous, as it was stretched at times with sand, sawdust, and more dangerous additives.[72] Food fraud was a daily occurrence, growing worse as the war dragged on. During June and July 1915, a large number of people in Beirut suffered from nausea and dizziness. One substance mixed with wheat was the darnel grass plant, which grows plentifully in Greater Syria and is often called false wheat due to their resemblance.[73] Eating darnel causes a feeling of drunkenness, and consuming large amounts can result in death; in wartime Beirut, it affected enough people to warrant mention in the press. Another common additive was bitter vetch (*julubban*), grown as animal feed.[74] There were even reports that some of the bread produced by the city bakeries contained no wheat at all but was "dirty and black; the view of it simply spoiled one's appetite."[75] People specifically complained about the bread sold by order of the municipality as being "an unwholesome mixture of barley, corn, millet, and even earth and tares." It would turn moldy within a day; white bread was black on the second day and gray or purple by the following evening.[76]

To halt the shady dealings of bakers and store owners, the municipality threatened to arrest anyone who sold above the set prices.[77] The paper reassured the public that these punitive measures were legitimate; under the headline "In Punishment There Is Life," the editor made his approval of the previous week's actions clear and issued a warning to anyone who even thought of circumventing the law. Referring to the Qur'an, he imbued the municipal council with the highest authority by linking its legal actions to divinely sanctioned and life-giving punishment.[78] In a follow-up article, the paper urged the municipality to continue publicizing the prices at least twice a week so that sellers and buyers would not forget them and expressed the hope that the council "would come down on the merchants after the arrival of shipments and set just limits to flour prices."[79] Action followed. For example, the municipality fined some bakers for selling a single loaf of bread for a *matlik* (about 8 piasters), whereas prior to the war a whole *rotl* of bread could be bought for 10 piasters or less.[80] In another instance, the Beirut police arrested two men, Ibrahim Ibn Husayn and Tawfiq Ibn al-Hajj, for selling a *rotl* of wheat for 5 piasters and 25 *para* (40 *para* making up one piaster). Exceeding the municipal set price of 5 piasters by only a fraction of a piaster, the men were imprisoned.[81] The arrests and their subsequent coverage in the newspaper were to serve as deterrents and a show of the municipality's strong executive power. However, it seems that the council cracked down only on small-time vendors, as the names of those arrested for fraud did not include the large merchant families, such as the Sursocks, Bayhums, and Salams.

Reining in the Local: Rationing

After June 1915, articles mentioning the municipality's role in feeding or attempting to feed the city decreased. The Beirut province's new and ambitious governor, 'Azmi Bey, knew filling people's stomachs would ensure their loyalties. Arriving in Beirut in the early summer of 1915, he took matters in hand almost immediately. His goal was to undermine reformist agendas in the city by asserting control over food, outlawing foreign relief work, and setting up his own (ultimately insufficient) provisioning scheme for the city. With this he wanted to eliminate political competition and assert power in the Beirut province. He had been appointed by Jamal Pasha, who "changed almost all the governors of the principal administrative units" in Greater Syria within the first year of his reign. Beirut's governor, Bekir Sami Bey, was among the first to be dismissed. Jamal, in a report to Istanbul, accused the governor of extortion and gambling with local bankers.[82] The real reason, however, might have been that Bekir Sami Bey worked closely with Arabists, such as Salim 'Ali Salam.[83]

'Azmi Bey began by sidelining the municipal council as the city's chief provisioner. According to a letter sent from the Beirut police chief to Howard Bliss, the Ottoman authority's plan to take a more active role in provisioning was in place by April 1915. The letter alerted Bliss that "the imperial government has taken certain decisions concerning the distribution of flour among all the residents of Beirut," including putting the director of the police—a loyal pawn of the new governor—in charge of registering all inhabitants of the city.[84] On June 4, 1915, an announcement was published in *al-Ittihad al-'Uthmani* under the heading "How Is Flour to Be Sold in the City?" The newly appointed director of police explained the project. First, he would conduct a census to record the sizes of families and the ages of their individual members. Then he would divide the city into seventy-two districts, and in each district, a special shop would be selected to sell flour. Each shopkeeper would be provided with a book including all the names of the families assigned to his store. To avoid fraud, each individual family was to receive a paper showing the names and ages of its members. Each day the head of the family could appear at the store and purchase the amount of flour allotted to his family. The rations assigned by the director of the police were as follows: every person over the age of fifteen would receive 480.13 grams of bread per day; those between three and fifteen would receive 320.09 grams; and children under the age of three were not assigned any ration.

Four days after the police chief's explanation, the editor of *al-Ittihad al-'Uthmani* raised concerns and criticized the governor's decision to put the police chief in charge, a decision that ultimately reduced the power of the local municipal council. The paper also questioned the chief of police's methods. Among the concerns was that the distribution shops, selected by him, were inadequate for the size of the population. How was it possible to make flour available to nearly "150,000 inhabitants" living in "close to 20,000 houses" through only seventy-two stores? Moreover, the paper pointed out, some families were assigned to shops far from their residences, even when they lived near a different distribution center. Parts of the city were outside the perimeters of distribution centers altogether, and some families were not given the proper papers. The flour sold was second rate or worse and cost 5 piasters and 30 *para* per *rotl*, which the report deemed unfair to the poor, the plan's supposed beneficiaries.[85] Other reports described the chaos that accompanied the distribution. Armed with tickets from the government, people showed up at the distribution centers, where "the utmost confusion and disorder" reigned, and after waiting "for hours, persons sometimes get one fourth of the quantity indicated on the ticket."[86]

There are very few reports of public demonstrations in response to inadequate supply, but these accounts shed light on the everyday in the city. For example, the American consul at Beirut recalled, "Yesterday, while some wagons loaded with a few bags of flour were being hauled through the streets they were attacked by a number of frantic and famished women who ripped the bags open with knives and wolfishly scooped up the flour as it flowed out into the road."[87] Edward Nickoley described bands of women and children who, "frantic with hunger overwhelmed the keepers of bread shops and vegetables and meat stands."[88] The police stood by, according to Nickoley, as women and children carried away what they could and returned the next day for more. Women and children, who easily became a menace, challenged social norms and morality. The "bands" imply lawlessness, while the description of the women as "frantic" or animal-like suggests an uncontrollable nature of the female famine victim. The international and diaspora press also reported on instances of what might be called bread riots in Beirut. For example, "some pitiful scenes are reported to have taken place at Beyrout when flour mills and depots were besieged by famished people of the poorer class."[89] Ibrahim Kan'an recounted a similar story in his postwar account. It was dangerous to join large crowds waiting to get a share of flour in front of the mill near the municipal building; the desperate souls, he wrote, in anticipation of a morsel of bread or a cup of flour, shoved and pushed to get to the front. When a woman dropped her child, it was immediately trampled to death.[90] Hearsay or truth we will never know. Another example, according to a report published in the Argentine paper *Al-Salam* on May 9, 1916, was that women and girls had gathered in front of the store of a flour merchant in Beirut. Faced with the threat of his supplies being plundered, he relented and gave everyone present an *uqqa* (1.282 kilograms) of flour.[91] Whether the rationing scheme eliminated disorder in the city is unclear. Some people like Ra'if Abi al-Lam, a medical student at SPC during the war, remembered that food distributions became less chaotic after its implementation.

Rationing certainly did not prevent starvation. The assigned portions included about eighteen hundred calories for an individual above fifteen years of age and twelve hundred for a person between three and fifteen. This, according to German army officer Fritz Grobba, amounted to about 49 percent of average prewar consumption.[92] Although not at starvation level, the rations were insufficient to prevent long-term malnutrition.

The rationing scheme illustrates the Ottoman governor's efforts to assume responsibility for feeding the city. But other measures were also taken. In August 1915, 'Azmi Bey ordered the suspension of all foreign relief work in the city and informed the American Red Cross in Beirut that "any one desiring to distribute charity could do so openly through the municipality.... Otherwise no distribution could be made."[93] What followed were arrests of relief workers, intimidation campaigns, and in some cases expulsion to Anatolia. Meanwhile, the municipality, through which the distribution was to be carried out, no longer posed a political challenge to the governor. 'Azmi Bey had dismissed the elected council under Ahmad Mukhtar Bayhum and replaced it with an appointed committee under 'Umar Da'uq, who generally was a pliant man and remained far removed from political activities.[94] Hijacking provisioning, Beirut's Ottoman governor sought to sideline any competition to his, and by extension state, power.

On December 23, 1915, the governor chaired the first of two meetings of a General Assembly of the Vilayet of Beirut. He began the meeting by stating that he would work with "altruism for the happiness and prosperity of the people of our province."[95] He immediately addressed the issue of agriculture, claiming the province was suitable for both agriculture and trade and urged that the assembly discuss a plan and time frame for a new economic policy. To inform such discussion, 'Azmi Bey ordered Rafiq Bey Tamimi, an employee of the Ministry of Education, and Bahjat Bey, a lawyer, journalist, and educator, to survey the Beirut province. The result was a detailed report of among other things education, agriculture, and trade. The two were to survey Beirut as well, but that work was never completed. The report highlighted that the rural areas of the province begged for improvements, highlighted the complaints of peasant farmers, and in general argued for "better guidance by the state."[96] The governor acknowledged the war had taken its toll and that the people of Beirut were "cursing" what was happening in the province. So what was at stake was the honor of the men assembled and the state. In the governor's words educational and economic reforms were essential to "protecting our honor." 'Azmi Bey made a distinct effort to link the sacrifices of the soldiers/martyrs on the battlefront and the honor gained from protecting the homeland to his desire to safeguard civilians in Beirut. He was eager to accomplish "economic and social victories." The army's achievements against what he called a more scientifically advanced enemy should be an example for the necessary self-sacrifice.[97]

Part of these new policies was an expansion of the governor's command over food by creating the Beirut grain syndicate in August 1915.[98] 'Azmi Bey forbade all grain trade and set up an import and sales company of Beiruti merchants under the leadership of Mustafa 'Izzadin, a grain exporter. The task of the syndicate was to purchase wheat in Aleppo, transport it to Beirut, and sell it there to the bakers of the city with the order that the syndicate should make no more than 10 percent profit. The Beirut municipality was to closely supervise the syndicate, although the latter was a private organization.

The syndicate failed because underground market forces, despite efforts to the contrary, remained largely unchecked. The possibility of making extremely large profits on the black market was too tempting for most merchants. For example, in the summer of 1915, the price of wheat in Aleppo was about 300 piasters per *qintar* (about 256.4 kilograms). 'Azmi Bey had allowed the syndicate to sell grain at no higher than 475 piasters per *qintar* in Beirut. The large margin between purchase and sales price (an added 58 percent) was mainly due to the high costs of transport. But even when transportation costs of 60 to 100 piasters and the additional 10 percent of profit were added, the legal price of wheat was still well below its black-market price, which was reported as 700 to 800 piasters per *qintar*. Due to the overall devaluation of paper money, prices rose in Aleppo by August 1915, and it became impossible for the Beirut merchants to maintain the government-stipulated price of 475 piasters per *qintar* without a loss. Aleppo merchants saw these price hikes as an excellent opportunity and formed their own syndicate. To eliminate competition, the merchants purchased all the available wheat in their district and pushed prices up to 500 and eventually 800 piasters per *qintar*. Eager to gain a monopoly in Mount Lebanon, the Aleppo syndicate negotiated with the newly appointed governor to Mount Lebanon, 'Ali Munif Bey.[99] And while the outcome of these negotiations is unclear, the Aleppo syndicate successfully took control of the grain market in its own town. Marginalized Beirut merchants, increasingly unable to make any profit and eager to circumvent government restrictions, eventually left the useless and unprofitable confines of the syndicate. Faced with the abandonment of his project, 'Azmi Bey promised 'Izzadin coverage of any losses. However, a one-man business was inadequate to import the amount of wheat necessary to feed Beirut. The ever-decreasing supply of food in Mount Lebanon meant hikes in price, which reached 1,000 piasters per *qintar* by November 1915, and eventually sidelined the Beirut syndicate in a fierce competition for grain. Corruption of railroad operators aggravated the situation. It was not unusual for the men in charge to "assign freight cars to shippers, merchants and growers only upon the payment of bribes from one to two hundred pounds" and sometimes even to change their minds if someone else offered a larger sum.[100]

However, 'Azmi Bey and Mustafa 'Izzadin believed that private merchants should remain in charge of the grain trade instead of giving it entirely over to the government, even if profit was minimal. Mustafa 'Izzadin suggested setting up a new syndicate by including merchants from all three markets: Beirut, Mount Lebanon, and Aleppo. The two traveled to Aleppo to introduce the plan. The joint-stock company was to be made up of eighty shares each to be sold at 1,000 Ottoman liras, evenly split between Beirut and Aleppo merchants. The governor negotiated with the railroad commissioner in Aleppo to set aside ten freight cars per day for shipments to Beirut and Mount Lebanon; then the men bought a total of 900 tons of wheat. This amount could have fed the city and the mountain community for some time, but none of it was ever shipped; the railroad commissioner had received a better price for his railcars. The Aleppo-Beirut joint-stock company disintegrated before it even started, and Beirut remained without a stable and regular supply of wheat.[101]

Even the military commander, Jamal Pasha, got involved in attempts to feed civilians *before* statewide regulatory orders came from Istanbul. Jamal Pasha set price limits for cereals and regularly promised shipments of fixed amounts of grain to the cities in his district. While Jamal Pasha had initially ordered a ban on trade of grain between provinces, he reversed his decision, realizing that the prohibition had increased speculation and led to extreme increases in prices.[102] For example, in March 1916, he ordered Beirut's director of police to purchase grain in Urfa and Birecik. The grain was transported to Beirut and Mount Lebanon via military transport and sold at a 5 percent profit. 'Azmi Bey eventually organized government-sponsored relief projects, including soup kitchens around the city. While the efforts of local municipal and state officials failed in feeding the city, they demonstrate the centrality of food in establishing political legitimacy in an urban setting.

Feeding Civilians: From Free-Market Policies to State Intervention

The economic historian Şevket Pamuk has highlighted several stages of Ottoman food policies. From November 1914 to July 1916, the state, he argues, maintained a mostly free market. Although one may argue that market was not entirely free, as local municipalities and the Ottoman governor sought to impose price controls and regulations, the central government did not systematically deal with feeding civilians across the empire during the first twenty months of the war. As a champion of free-market trade, Adam Smith would have lauded this Ottoman approach, as he thought periods of dearth could be remedied by noninterventionist government economic policies. Smith suggested that famines occurred due to the "violence of governments attempting, by improper means, to remedy the inconveniences of dearth."[103] In this case, there were no attempts at remedying the situation at all from the center, but the state's decision to leave food unregulated did not have the positive outcome Smith would have predicted. The increasing food shortages during 1914–1916 proved the opposite: under war conditions, the free market does not even out shortages. Yet for nearly two years, the Ottoman state relied on market forces and left local authorities to handle food supplies. However, when local attempts failed and there were widespread reports of starvation among civilians, the central government intervened in July 1916.

In coordination with German advisers, the Istanbul authorities founded the Imperial Ottoman Office for Provisioning and tasked it with recording, transporting, and controlling the empire's entire grain supply in excess of the tenth that was already to be paid to the state as in-kind taxes.[104] Realizing that a total takeover of the grain economy was impossible because of a lack of regulatory infrastructure and manpower, the state continued to rely on locally established networks and practices. As part of this early restructuring, local governments were given permission to confiscate flour and ovens, set fixed prices for foodstuffs, and regulate sales.[105] Instead of taking complete control of the market, the men in Istanbul focused on organizing the large-scale purchase and distribution of grain to the military and the most needy civilians, at least on paper.[106] For this purpose, the government passed the Provisional Grain Act on July 23, 1916, and implemented it in September.[107] According to the new regulation, Ottoman authorities were to purchase all grain from producers at a fixed low price. Peasant farmers were to sell all their grain and were allowed to keep only enough for seeds and to feed their families for the year.[108] Amendments to the Provisional Grain Act in September 1916 outlined punitive measures aimed at hoarding and smuggling. The first paragraph of the amendment ordered anyone who disobeyed state orders to be arrested and brought before the military courts, where the person could receive a prison sentence of one week to one year.[109] The government would confiscate any grain hoarded, hidden from the commission, or sold illegally at higher prices, without any financial compensation to the owner. The law was expanded to include all foodstuffs; local government commissions had the authority to confiscate any hidden foodstuffs without any monetary payment. The result was devastating. An American eyewitness reported that by October, military authorities had taken control of the entire wheat supply and even figs, grapes, and olives. The confiscated items were then "redistributed" to all districts, but the amount each received was only a third of what was necessary for survival.[110] This failed government intervention or expansion of bad government immediately reminds us of Amartya Sen's assertion that famines were not the outcome of food shortages or the unavailability of food due to poor harvest but rather an unwilling or incompetent government.[111]

Jamal Pasha Feeds Syria?

To facilitate the practical implementation of this law, an executive order divided the empire into three provisioning zones: Asia Minor, Greater Syria (including Adana), and Mesopotamia (including Aintab and Marash). The grain export from any of these zones had to be approved by the Central Commission for Provisioning specifically set up for this purpose.[112] The commission depended on local subcommittees that were organized in the provincial capitals and provinces.[113] The subcommittees were to carry out a census, counting inhabitants and domestic animals to determine the amount of grain needed for cultivation and subsistence. The Central Commission for Provisioning was then to compare the grain on hand for cultivation, the number of inhabitants, the amount of livestock, and the supply of foodstuffs in all provinces and determine the need and surplus. It was hoped that empire-wide foodstuffs could be distributed according to the estimated needs of the population.[114]

While purchases in Asia Minor were to be organized by the Central Commission for Provisioning and Mesopotamia remained free of any restrictions, Jamal Pasha was in complete control of Greater Syria.[115] The law gave him carte blanche and consolidated his position of power. But his provisioning policies were riddled with miscalculations. For example, he ordered the annual tithe to be paid in kind. Due to the lack of personnel and transport facilities, however, many people, even if willing to comply, were forced to pay in cash. To prevent smuggling and illegal sales, he banned threshing of grain until taxes were paid and permission was granted. This was a bad decision to say the least, because the Ottoman command was understaffed and disorganized, permissions were frequently delayed, and grain cultivators all too often lost their entire crop "as vermin and autumn rains destroyed it."[116] Making matters worse, Jamal Pasha ordered producers to render a second tenth of their harvest to the government to feed the troops. And on top of that, the military commander mandated small landowners to sell an additional 10 percent and large landowners 25 percent of their harvest at fixed (low) prices to the government.[117] Jamal Pasha's high demands meant that grain producers were more often than not forced to sell not only their livelihood but also the reserve grain that should have been used for the next cycle of cultivation.

In late summer of 1916, Jamal Pasha ordered delegates from the various Syrian provinces to Damascus and informed them of his plan for the upcoming harvest. Inspired by European governments that purchased grain and distributed it according to need, Jamal Pasha designated three grain purchasing zones—Palestine, the Hauran, and the province of Hama—and assigned three prominent merchants to carry out purchases in these zones. The Beirut merchant Michel Bey Sursock was responsible for the Hauran region (the region that would feed Beirut and Mount Lebanon) and was ordered to buy and deliver to the headquarters 80,000 tons of grain, an unrealistic demand.[118] The harvest in the Hauran, controlled by the Ottoman authorities, was just a bit above that, at 85,740 tons. If we take into account the needs of 204,583 civilians and 17,856 animals, as estimated by German officials, plus the necessary retention of 10 percent of grain as seeds and the payment of in-kind taxes, a surplus of only 21,226 tons was left, an amount far below Jamal Pasha's demands.[119] While these numbers are rough estimates by the German consulates in Greater Syria, they give us an idea of the discrepancies between availability, demands, and needs. There is no doubt that Jamal failed to consider the needs of civilians living in the grain-producing areas. Perhaps, as Grobba mentioned, it would have been possible to purchase the desired amount in all of the Hauran and the adjacent Jabal al-Druze. But trade was complicated by the fact that a large portion of farmers, mostly Druze, were outside the government's control and demanded gold, instead of the newly introduced and quickly depreciating paper money, for their products.[120] Purchases were eventually carried out under threat of violence, but still Sursock delivered only a fraction of the desired amount (somewhere between 15,000 and 20,000 tons).

The Ottomans' continued military campaigns further increased the pressure on food supplies. Besides having to feed troops for the continuous Suez Campaign and now in the Hejas against Arab rebels, the government was especially hard pressed to feed its primary means of transport: the camel. While by 1916, grain could be shipped via train to Beersheba, it took an additional six days by camel to reach the front lines. Camel transport meant that a third of all the cargo was fodder for the animals. Overall, Grobba estimated the necessary provision for the army stationed in Syria, Palestine, and the Hejas in 1916 (about 100,000 men and 50,000 animals) to have been 70,000 tons of grain and feed added to the strain on civilian provisioning.

The Ottomans' policy for provisioning civilians after 1916 was a failure. When the state intervened, it was unable to deal with increased pressure on the supply and with the decrease in cultivated areas and harvests. The state did little to alleviate the situation in Beirut and Mount Lebanon and instead aggravated shortages through compulsory sales of all grain beyond the actual need of the peasant farmer's family at low, government-regulated prices. Cereal producers' response was resistance.[121] Resistance to the state's wartime measures resembled what James Scott has termed "weapons of the weak."[122] Families hid their grain from government agents, attempted to sell it at higher prices on the black market, and at times tried to bribe local officials to underestimate the harvests or to let them deliver grains of lower quality. High taxes, along with increasingly hard requisitioning policies and grain seizures, undercut any positive incentives to increase production.[123] Instead, peasants manipulated production by foot dragging, concealment, and evasion. At times peasant families stopped cultivating altogether, because they could no longer make a profit.

Initially the Ottoman government and Jamal Pasha had focused on regulating procurement and distribution of grain, but eventually consistent peasant resistance and the decrease in cultivated lands inspired deeper state intervention. In August 1916, the government directly tackled agricultural production with the Compulsory Cultivation Law. It was provisionally implemented in September 1916 and confirmed by parliament on April 3, 1917.[124] The law mandated that women and all peasant men above the age of fourteen not serving in the army—in essence everyone capable of agricultural labor—cultivate a set amount of land and work at least eight hours a day.[125] The law gave the government the right to force individuals and various organizations to work in the fields.[126] If necessary, the agricultural ministry could demand that, once they had finished working their own lands, farmers communally cultivate the fields of soldiers' families or land that would otherwise remain fallow. The law designated the size of the land a farmer was required to cultivate, based on the type and gender of his draft animals. It also regulated the producers' work hours and possible profit.[127] On paper, the government now regulated the use of all remaining animals and prohibited any further requisitioning of animals needed on the land as well as their sale for slaughter.[128] The regulation also dictated what farmers were to grow and when, emphasizing the cultivation of winter crops, such as wheat and barley. Men needed to build and repair agricultural equipment, and any civil officers needed to implement the law were exempted from military service. Agriculture became *the* priority, and 20,000 men were put at the disposal of the agricultural ministry. The punishment for disobeying state-legislated orders were cash fines from 25 to 100 piasters; repeat offenders could receive a jail sentence of a day to a week.

The Compulsory Cultivation Law represented the Ottoman state's interventionist policy at its extreme; it was designed to regulate both space and time of grain producers. The government hoped to mobilize its entire population for the war effort, including women and children. The plan was meticulously drafted, and the Ordinance on the Implementation of the Compulsory Cultivation Law specified its administration from the level of the central government to the provincial authorities to the level of the village. The law, however, had little immediate impact, and the 1916–1917 harvest was only 75 percent of the previous year's. Considering the continued decrease in cultivated areas and peasant resistance, it can be argued that the state's coercive measures only exacerbated an increasingly devastating situation. Government policies, we may say, meant that people were unable, in Sen's words, "to command" food. High and unstable prices driven up by shortages due to limited means of transportation, the disruptions in interdistrict transfer, panic purchases, and speculation were not efficiently dealt with; on the contrary, they were aggravated by administrative chaos.

Conclusion

The central Ottoman government entered the game of civilian provisioning late. The early war years were marked by one-sided demands for civilian sacrifice without much in return.[129] Beirut, however, immediately became the political space wherein civilians' access to food was negotiated; at the heart of this process, at least initially, was the municipal council. Its prominence meant that for Beirutis wartime governance was not an abstract state that intervened in their daily lives but rather familiar city officials who acted with a measure of autonomy. For Arab reformists, like Hassan Tabbara, the war was an opportunity to convince local urbanites and state officials that a municipal council was the ideal political body to deal with the crisis and a local agency that could function autonomously.[130] The imagined and real potential of this local institution, seated with men critical of Ottoman centralization policies, in the eyes of the Ottoman governor and his superior Jamal Pasha presented a real threat to the state's power to control the social order. The governor worked tirelessly to diminish the power of the municipal council and undermine the social position of council members who advocated reform. As the municipality was one of the key institutions that could order provisioning in the city, membership had political capital. The governor's attempt to sideline competition in the city seems to have been successful, as he smothered local reformist ambitions. His increasing control over urban government is visible in the thematic shift in Hassan Tabbara's newspaper before its closure in 1916. We can speak of two important outcomes that would influence postwar political standings. First, being removed from the municipality meant loss of political power and legitimacy during and after the war. Second, the failure of the state and the municipality to provide for civilians after the summer of 1915 rendered the Ottoman authorities and, more important for us here, local power players who worked with the government as unworthy of political loyalties. In the end, Ottoman state and local municipal agents could claim little success in fighting shortages and certainly did not win anyone's approval.

Figure 5. View of the Diman and Kanobin Convents, ca. 1885–1895. Source: The Fouad Debbas Collection / Sursock Museum, Beirut, Lebanon. "Bonfils studio, Vue des couvents de Diman et de Kanobin, ca. 1885-95," Ref. No. TFDC 406/021/1076.

{ CHAPTER 4 }

PRAYERS AND PATRONS

The Politics of Neutrality

Sometime on May 31, 1917, Maronite fathers Louis and Butrus stepped out from the gates of their patriarch's summer residence in Diman. Turning their backs on the majestic view of the Qadisha Valley, the men headed south and then west. It was the beginning of a five-month physically and emotionally exhausting journey through the northern districts of Mount Lebanon. The purpose of their expedition was to assess the state of Maronite institutions and staff and the conditions of their church's devotees. They first arrived at the Maronite monastery of St. Anthony the Great in the village of Hub. Perched on a hillside, near the town of Tannurin in the district of Batrun, the monastery would serve as a base for their inspections of the surrounding villages. As it was expected by 1917, the priests were met with dire conditions and extreme poverty everywhere they went.[1] The pair was troubled. The villagers were starving, and their flock's spiritual deprivation was appalling. With great sorrow, the men observed the widespread "spiritual desertion" effected by the famine. Their brethren were either neglecting their religious duties or in some cases had simply absconded, leaving their parishes orphaned.[2] When Father Louis and Father Butrus arrived in Mahmersh, the temporary resident priest apologized to the surveyors. It was impossible for him to stay very much longer. He promised to wait until the expiration of his term, but then he would pack up and leave. The reason: There was no food in the village. No one could possibly survive this scarcity. To calm his fears, the fathers handed him 45 piasters in gold and an additional 40 in paper currency. The money was nothing given the high prices of necessities; it would surely run out before long. But for now it was enough for the priest to stay put.

Fathers Louis and Butrus were under way by order of the Maronite patriarch Ilias Butrus al-Huwayyik. The patriarch had repeatedly demanded reports on the state of his community in 1917 and 1918. The goal was to evaluate the work of local churches, distribute some relief, and inspire a renewal in physical and spiritual care for the needy. Louis and Butrus's report was the third such survey of the northern districts of Jbeil and Batrun. The surveyors had clear directives to first inspect the "spiritual state" of Maronites and afford them with spiritual guidance. Traveling from May 31 to November 17, 1917, the men led prayer services, heard confessions, pronounced absolution, and performed other religious services and rites. The men also had limited funds to dole out to priests on-site for the sole purpose of feeding the poor of their villages. The inspectors issued financial aid, based on their assessment, in Ottoman paper lira and in solid coins.[3] In short, both the souls and the bodies of the community were to be cared for.

The report of Fathers Louis and Butrus, who diligently recorded grievances brought to their attention and noted down the state of affairs in remote rural regions as they saw them, provides a unique picture of one of the most isolated regions of the Ottoman home front. In general, the records of the Maronite order are a largely untapped resource concerning World War I in the Arab provinces. I am most interested in those sources that account for the acquisition and distribution of material relief, which was clearly linked to caring for the spiritual needs of the community. The available documents in the archive of the patriarchate and those of individual monasteries that account for aid distribution to the poor vary from long lists of aid recipients' names, to detailed records of money spent and materials distributed, to survey reports, such as the one submitted by Fathers Louis and Butrus. These sources highlight the processes and scope of relief work, the difficulties encountered, and the particular local, national, and international position of the Maronite Church, which determined its role in the constellation of the mountain's politics of provisioning during the war and its political position in its aftermath.

Like Beirut, the mountain was a space of a complex politics of provisioning. Filling people's stomachs, as we have already seen, was a powerful force in maintaining, solidifying, and forging alliances and loyalties. Here we focus on the Maronite Church, although it was not the only agent of relief. Historians of Lebanon have argued that one of the outcomes of World War I was a shift in political power in Mount Lebanon. The Maronite Church, it is said, won a decisive victory over Mount Lebanon's secular government, which was seated with a newly configured, reform-minded secular middle class and had increasingly challenged the church's dominant political status. For the church the war presented an opportunity to reverse this trend.

This chapter argues that the church's active role in wartime provisioning, even if largely a failed attempt, contributed to the reshaping of the political landscape of Mount Lebanon. The fact that the church's existing institutions and personnel could be utilized to distribute food even in the most remote corners of the mountain inherently guaranteed its position. The church benefited from Jamal Pasha's distinct efforts to sideline its main political competitor, the AC, which, like the municipality in the city, had the potential to distribute food but was undercut politically and then dismissed before it could establish itself as a successful agent of benevolence. Yet provisioning was not an easy task; the chapter draws attention to the complications in the church's attempts at relief work because of its past relationship with the Ottoman state and the international community, as well as its relationship with other smaller Christian communities in the mountain district. The chapter not only outlines the church's practices of provisioning but also situates them in the larger context of diaspora politics; foreign influence; and the relationship between Maronites, France, and the Ottoman state, all of which shaped much of the wartime provisioning politics in the mountain district. The processes showcased here allowed the Maronite Church, despite all the difficulties it encountered, to solidify its position as temporal leader of the Christians of Mount Lebanon, which guaranteed its seat at the political bargaining table in the postwar period. The formative powers of the war of famine were undeniably at work.

Feeding Stomachs and Souls in Times of War

The war years were famine years in Mount Lebanon as they were in neighboring Beirut. One of the district's *kaymakam* lamented, "Death by hunger took close to 500 people (mainly men) every day."[4] The institutional diary of the Missionary Society of St. Paul, an order of the Melkite Greek Catholic Church, recorded the cruel details of starvation. The order's monasteries adorned the hillside of Harissa, a community of "only a few houses" a few steep miles up from the Maronite archdiocese in Bkirki.[5] In November 1915, the priests noted that "those who died of hunger were not few."[6] Death's entries continue. In January 1916, "not one day passed without us seeing many people succumbing to the pangs of hunger."[7] On March 6, the record stated, "13 people died of hunger in Junieh, 5 in Sarba, and 5 in most villages of the Kisrawan. Up until today, 196 people died in Aashqut of hunger."[8] Aashqut, a small hamlet east of Harissa, was hit hard. Its name appeared repeatedly in the records. The news was never good. By the end of 1916, two-thirds of its inhabitants were dead.[9] Parochial records of the Greek Catholic community, housed in the archbishopric in Beirut, paint a similar picture. The parish of Mar Sema'an, roughly twenty-five miles inland from Bkirki, counted 902 members prior to 1914 and only 646 in 1919. Nearly one-third of the community, or 256 people, were recorded as "dead during the war."[10] The records suggest villages "lying on the northern coast and the lower hills in the middle of the Kisrawan" suffered most, mainly because the northern areas received their "main supplies of foodstuff from Junieh, the chief Lebanese port, whose coastal trade was completely paralyzed by the blockade." In the central mountain districts, where the Druze were in the majority, famine was "less rampant than in other parts." But here too, "thousands of people" perished of hunger.[11] Survivors struggled with poverty. The Mar Sema'an survey indicates that of the 459 persons who endured the war, 75 percent were poor and in need of support from the church. This included 58 orphans (36 boys and 22 girls). In Rumia, 122 Greek Catholics had left the village to live abroad. Of the remaining 69 individuals, 57 were listed as poor.[12] As in Beirut and other regions of the mountains, many left the site of suffering attempting to find income and/or food somewhere else. The people of Mount Lebanon's central districts tended to migrate to the Bekaa and the Hauran. Men from the northern districts left their villages to find work and food in the northern Akkar region. Few of them ever returned. In most cases, they abandoned their families and villages for good. The situation in some villages was so desperate that the two priests thought it best to prepare those poor souls left behind for the afterlife by hearing confessions and granting absolution.¹³ The horrific story of a young boy digging up his younger brother's corpse to eat its already-decomposing flesh, recorded by the priests of St. Paul, highlights the despair. The boy died only a day later—poisoned.¹⁴ Who was to help? As one of the key political powers in Mount Lebanon, the Maronite Church had an obvious responsibility, even for those of other denominations.

Administering Aid:
Rules, Registers, and the Ottoman Regime

High mortality, while most often blamed on CUP intentions to starve out Christians, at times have been attributed to the Maronite Church's unwillingness, carelessness, or inability in aiding the poor. But we cannot say that the religious leaders did not express their concerns. The central church leadership circulated appeals urging its communities to aid the poor as early as September 1914. Some noted the patriarch's sluggishness in organizing aid: he did not insist on a regulated relief system until 1916. While this criticism has to be taken seriously, an exclusive focus on the patriarch and the central institution overshadows the work of the church's many monasteries and convents that distributed bread, grain, and flour at the beginning of the war. The centrally organized efforts may better be seen as an adoption and extension of practices already established on the microlevel and as a moment of the church's centralization and consolidation.

With Ottoman mobilization and requisitioning under way in the fall of 1914, some clerics foresaw the stress that the Ottomans' entrance in the war would place on the poor. Father General Ignatius Al-Tannuri, a Maronite, wrote letters to the sect's institutions, urging their leaders to help their poor in light of emerging food shortages. Tannuri noted the already-growing number of poor at his monastery's doors begging for bread. Poverty, he wrote, was increasing in all districts, and he called on his brethren's Christian obligation to mobilize all their supplies and reduce waste in anticipation of a great emergency. "It is not fitting for us and our Christian brothers," he proclaimed, "to live off money for the poor and to be withholding even food in a time of need."¹⁵ The Maronite archbishop in Beirut followed suit and issued a statement reminding the public that a war would necessitate collective sacrifice. The needy, hungry, and poor should under no circumstances be forgotten.¹⁶ The appeals in some cases translated into action. The monastery of St. Anthony at Hub, for example, began distributing money, wheat, potatoes, and corn in 1915. A summary report, *Dar Hub in the Time of Famine and War from 1914 to 1919*, submitted to the archdiocese, reveals at least 150 people daily asking for bread. The monastery spent 22,000 piasters on aid in 1915.¹⁷ The report highlights the efforts as an example of Christian spirit. Despite the great expenses and constant flow of guests that occupied the time of the monks, the brothers never failed to distribute bread to the poor. The shortages in the northern districts also affected wealthier families. Because it was difficult to obtain grain, many of them approached their local monasteries for help. The records show that some convents and monasteries decided to sell wheat to the "owners of large houses," charging them half an Ottoman lira (50 piasters) per *rotl*.¹⁸

As the queues of ragged and starving bodies knocking on the doors of the churches, convents, and bishoprics grew longer, critical voices questioning the church's commitment to the poor grew louder. Perhaps partially in response to this reproach, the patriarch felt compelled to employ strict rules concerning distribution of charity (*ihsan*) and relief work (*a'mal al-ighatha*) in 1916. A communiqué from the patriarchate outlined the principles regulating aid. Superiors of smaller parishes should record the names of the poor in their community. Village authorities would then check, verify, and certify the lists before submitting them to the bishop of the local bishopric. The bishops were to discuss the organization of weekly wheat distributions with superiors of monasteries and the managers of the schools and endowments. Communally they would decide on a reasonable number of poor that could be helped by individual monasteries and approximate the needed supplies and their costs. After that the bishops were to send statements outlining their plan and a budget to Bkirki and then forward a copy to the Ottoman governor requesting the necessary wheat. The governor had final say about prices and the actual amounts of food supplies to be delivered.

The patriarch demanded the cooperation of all Christian monasteries. Huwayyik announced that he would supervise the work personally and promised to send any wheat received at the patriarchate immediately to monasteries, schools, and endowments for distribution.¹⁹ At that time, the lists of needy community members should be adjusted, since the numbers of poor constantly fluctuated. After reception of the wheat, the superiors had to record the actual weight of the grain so that exact payment could be made to the government. The clerics knew from experience that the weight noted on the delivery documents was often more than the actual amount received, so it was crucial to sift and weigh the wheat on-site. Often large amounts were missing. The secretary at St. Paul recorded such an incident in January 1916: "The last time we took two bags of wheat said to be 75 *rotl* [192 kilograms], and after sifting it, we noted that 13 *rotl* [33 kilograms] were missing."[20] After the wheat was weighed, the bishops oversaw the distribution process, making sure to adjust the lists and report any negligence and fraud from superiors in the monasteries or the managers of schools and endowments. Offenders were disciplined on-site or referred to the patriarchate. Distributions were to be recorded in detail and on a daily basis so that the work could be presented to the military authorities if necessary at a moment's notice.[21] The registers had to be submitted to the bishop by the end of each week for inspection, guaranteeing overall accountability and preventing any fraud or insubordination regarding the patriarch's orders. The order instructed clerics to then borrow the necessary money or sell or mortgage properties to the government to ensure that food supplies could be paid for in cash. To guarantee that foodstuff and relief expenditures were properly carried out and were reaching those in need, Huwayyik sent out survey teams. The goal was to amass detailed descriptions of each community's material and spiritual state and dole out some financial help to village churches and bishoprics, especially in the most remote regions.

With the patriarch's plan in place by 1916, the amount of aid spent by the monasteries increased somewhat. St. Anthony at Hub now provided monetary and material relief worth 71,000 piasters. While this was a large increase from the previous year's 22,000 piasters, dramatic price escalations and currency inflation in the region have to be taken into account. The cost of a single *rotl* of wheat—and this may be the greatest increase recorded in any of the sources—is said to have gone up from 20 piasters in 1915 to 125 in 1917. As a result, the monastery spent 123,000 piasters on 1,465 *rotl* (3,759 kilograms) of foodstuffs in 1917. In 1915, the combined expenditure for 1,300 *rotl* (3,336 kilograms) was only 17,300 piasters. More money spent did not mean that more people were fed. A similar conclusion can be drawn for the monastery's cash distributions. As prices sharply increased, individual charity recipients received higher amounts to make sure they could purchase the necessary food for survival.[22]

Convents, Committees, and Collaboration?

The compiling of lists, registering, and surveying the poor, besides serving to draw up more or less concise budgets and providing immediate emergency funds, was a necessity to secure adequate access to government wheat. Jamal Pasha had instructed the Ottoman governor that absolutely no wheat would be forthcoming without such lists. The military government used its men in the mountains to organize wheat allotments, but the involvement was strictly limited to the procurement of wheat and its sale to local church leaders. When the missionairies of St. Paul wanted to purchase wheat from the government to feed the 330 poor who showed up at their doors on distribution days, they followed a process similar to that prescribed by the Maronite order.

> The government asked [us] to give a list of poor to whom we give the bread and the quantity that is given to everyone. The list then had to be certified by the *mudir* [director or chief] of the subdistrict. After that, the list should be presented to the governor and certified. A petition for wheat should follow, and the governor would examine the facts very carefully. If he finds it to be agreeable, he writes again to the *mudir* to give the wheat. The *mudir* then requests from the person who is in charge of the government wheat to give the *mukhtar* of the village the quantity of one load to be distributed to the poor. Until now, it was not allowed to distribute more than two bags of wheat. And every time we are obliged to follow this process.[23]

Local government officials were involved at the higher level of the distribution chain, and local religious institutions were focusing on the actual process of distribution on the ground, an arrangement that reinforced the community's vision of the church as its key benefactor.

The Ottoman governor and initially the AC—knowing their administrative limitation—relied heavily on the well-established religious networks of convents, schools, and monasteries to deal with the increasingly desperate situation. On March 12, 1916, the Ottoman governor asked that a committee be formed to provide food to the poor in the district of Ghosta.[24] The committee was made up of the superiors from seven bishoprics of various Catholic orders that surrounded the village.[25] The governor approached religious leaders, not the *mukhtars* or mayors of villages, sidelining them in the relief efforts. The committee met and decided to distribute bread, not wheat or money. Apparently, this was modeled on a committee set up by Muslim officers to provide for the starving people in the port town of Junieh. Assigning each convent one distribution day, the committee shared the responsibilities. This new arrangement meant that many of the poor who had relied on the charity of a particular monastery found their distribution days cut. In return for the committee's efforts, the government promised to send a weekly *qintar* (256.4 kilograms) of wheat at government prices set at 550 piasters.[26]

Community leaders agreed that the plan was sound, and the monasteries' superiors were ready to implement it fully. However, none of them received the full amount agreed on. The monastery at Harissa received only 71 *uqqa* (92 kilograms) instead of the promised *qintar* in the first and second weeks; no wheat arrived at all during the third week. The government delivered only 50 *uqqa* (65 kilograms) during the fourth week and after that nothing until April 24, 1916.[27] Beginning in October 1916, the priests witnessed a short period during which deliveries of grains became more regular. This may be attributed to the Lebanese grain syndicate, organized to purchase and ship wheat from the interior. At the end of 1916, the syndicate, although not perfect, had secured the regular delivery of 20 *qintar* (5,128 kilograms) per month to Mount Lebanon. As grain was forthcoming, the committee conducted a new survey, counting 545 needy families in and around Ghosta.[28] The committee then assigned each monastery, based on its size and capacity, a number of needy individuals, and the convents were free to expand the work. The Paulists, for example, took on an additional ten people who by then had been propelled into abject poverty. A few months later, the wheat supply again became unpredictable. It was so irregular that some of the monasteries were forced to end their distributions in February 1917. Smaller non-Maronite orders were worse off. The Paulists regularly noted the unreliability of the wheat shipments to their institution; deliveries to the Maronites were far more regular. The order suspected foul play from the side of the Maronite patriarch, an accusation that may not have been without merit. After all, Huwayyik was in direct communication with Jamal Pasha, and it seemed he was able to secure his community's access to government grain, at least some of the time. The government's seeming focus on supplying the Maronites may also simply have been the result of its demographic size, the church's larger and more useful network of institutions, and the fact that smaller communities lacked high-profile representatives and were looking to the Maronite patriarch as leader.

Mount Lebanon's Politics of Provisioning: Money, Food, and Strained Liaisons

Even with a plan in place, procuring foodstuffs to carry out relief was not an easy task. The Maronite community produced some food, and its leaders began taking stock and regulating locally grown crops to ease the pressure. The monasteries compiled lists of the kinds and amounts of crops they harvested, such as grain, silk cocoons, and products from vineyards and orchards, such as wine, *dibs* (grape molasses), and olive oil. Before sending them to Bkirki, the monastery's superior with their signatures and official seals authorized the list. Huwayyik warned everyone not to sell crops unless the necessary reserves were secured. He even limited the total amount that could be sold. If a monastery wanted to sell more, its superior had to submit a written request. According to the patriarchate, this policy assured a secure flow of subsistence to the poor of the community. The mandate was serious, and the church was ready to excommunicate anyone who disobeyed these guidelines.

Locally produced materials, however, were not enough. Additional grain needed to be procured from the interior grain-producing areas, which became increasingly impossible without the explicit consent of the Ottoman state and its locally stationed officials. Negotiations with state officials, as we saw in the case of Beirut, were a delicate and often fruitless task. The national and international political position of Mount Lebanon further complicated access to power and hence food. During the first months of war, a rift between the governor of Beirut and the Armenian Catholic *mutasarrif* Ohannes Kouyoumdjian Pasha made cooperation between the two districts difficult. The Ottoman governor of Beirut, Bekir Sami Bey, was irritated because Kouyoumdjian did little to prevent Beirut's military-age men from hiding in his district to avoid conscription. The French consul in Beirut, François Georges-Picot, saw Kouyoumdjian's behavior as reckless and warned that his actions might jeopardize Mount Lebanon's privileged status within the empire.[29] An angry Bekir Sami Bey eventually threatened the *mutasarrif* with an invasion of his district if he did not expel residents of Beirut city and province. After having procrastinated for some time, Kouyoumdjian finally issued an order for all Beirut residents with military obligations to leave his district within three days.[30] It was Mount Lebanon's international entanglement, however, that made negotiations with the Ottoman authorities over food ever more difficult. Fear of treachery, conspiracy, and dissent dominated the conversations.

A New Sheriff in Mount Lebanon: Suspicions, Suppression, and Policies of Silencing

Mount Lebanon's position as a semiautonomous region with powerful European patrons and the Maronite Church's long-standing connection with France raised serious concerns for the Ottomans. Margaret McGilvary claimed that "the terms Catholic and Maronite and French-sympathizer are practically synonymous in Syria, for most of the Syrians who acknowledge the authority of the Pope also look to France as their strongest hope in the attainment of their political aspirations."[31] Many thought it obvious that the "non-Turkish elements were conscious or unconscious tools of foreign designs for the dismemberment of Turkey."[32] Locally stationed government men loathed the status quo and had witnessed firsthand the French consuls' power in appointing and dismissing bureaucrats without official approval. Bekir Sami Bey warned Istanbul of possible intrigues and advised strengthening Ottoman control by dismissing pro-French officials.[33]

An active and vocal Syro-Lebanese diaspora played an important role in shaping Ottoman perceptions of Maronite loyalties. While the Syro-Lebanese diaspora was diverse in regard to age, class, religion, and its aspirations for its homeland's political future, the CUP perceived it as a homogeneous anti-Ottoman group. It was the agitation of a relatively small number of politically active émigrés that shaped Ottoman opinion.[34] In Cairo, the members of the Syrian Decentralization Party joined forces with the Cairene Alliance libanais (Lebanese Alliance); although the groups did not share an ideology, they had come together even before the war with the intent of preparing an anti-Ottoman revolt as soon as the Ottoman Empire entered the war. Moreover, the offers of Syrians and Lebanese living abroad to join the war efforts against the Ottomans on the side of the European powers was hardly a secret in diplomatic circles.[35]

Fearing possible dissent, the Ottoman government moved 3,000 of its troops from Damascus to Mount Lebanon a month into the war at the end of November 1914. Onlookers were puzzled, especially since decisions made by the troop's commander, 'Ali Riza al-Baylani, were questionable. In an attempt to take military control of the mountain district, he insisted on sending his men north in the middle of winter. At some of the highest altitudes, his soldiers were caught in a severe snowstorm, and some died of hunger and exposure. The *mutasarrif* fiercely objected to the arrival of Ottoman troops as a direct challenge to his power. Kouyoumdjian vowed to protect the coast with his own troops and assured Jamal Pasha of Lebanese loyalty to the Ottoman sultan. The Ottomans' responding claim that small guns and cannons positioned on the western mountain slopes were to deter enemy warships threatening Beirut's harbor made little sense. The cannons were located thirty kilometers from Beirut and did not have the necessary range to reach the harbor. Instead, the more probable job of troops and weapons was to deter a local uprising.[36]

The Lebanese public interpreted the stationing of Ottoman troops and cannons to be an encroachment on the special status of their district. Trying to calm concerns, Jamal Pasha issued a statement promising to maintain the status quo by not imposing any special taxes and/or military service on them. Of course, his pledge was contingent on Lebanese loyalty.[37] During his visit to Beirut in December 1914, he urged everyone to remain calm. The troops were stationed in Mount Lebanon for protection. "The Ottoman Empire is your mother," he announced, "who shows mercy upon you and saves you from the foreigners who come to you under the pretext of protecting you and defending your rights and independence. In reality they are like the leech that sucks your blood and crush the dignity of your spirit."[38] A long article published in *al-Ittihad al-'Uthmani*, no doubt dictated by the commander and his men, painted the government's actions as "nothing more than a very clear indication of the government's concern for Lebanon." The mountain's limited finances made it impossible "to administer its affairs and troops," and the troops' arrival should be welcomed as in the "general national interest."[39]

Ottoman policies left little doubt that the presence of troops would be accompanied by changes in the administration of the district. In a move to remedy the perceptions held by both natives and foreigners alike of the "relative impotence of the Turkish authorities" in Lebanon, the interior ministry and the military authorities began to directly supervise its governance.[40] The first order of business was to deal with possible internal opposition. After his visit to Beirut, Jamal Pasha invited Kouyoumdjian Pasha to his headquarters in Damascus. He expressed his concern about sympathies of AC members and other politically active Lebanese toward Britain and France He cautioned the *mutasarrif* that the Lebanese would be punished, perhaps even exiled, in case of dissent. He warned even the slightest suspicion of someone colluding with the enemy would land him in front of the court-martial tribunal.[41] Habib Pasha al-Sa'ad, president of the AC, his three brothers, and AC members Khalil 'Aqil and Na'um Bakhus were particularly distrustful in the military commander's eyes. He ordered them to report to Damascus. The Sa'ads, despite warnings not to go, went to Damascus. Only Habib returned to the mountain. His brothers were exiled to Anatolia.

An invitation from Jamal Pasha was almost never good news for men from Mount Lebanon. The historian Nicholas Ajay described Jamal Pasha's invitation of AC members as the beginning of a long series of dismissals and so-called resignations. The *kaymakams* of Batrun, Jbeil, Suq al-Gharb, and Dayr al-Qamar; Jezzin, the head of the Lebanese gendarmerie; a number of court officials; an agricultural commissioner; the president and members of the law department; chief clerks and secretaries of government offices; and even the private physician to Lebanese government officials and the translator of the AC were all called to Damascus to be dismissed from their posts.[42] From December to March 1915, *al-Ittihad al-'Uthmani* frequently published the names of Lebanese government officials who traveled to Jerusalem, via Damascus, to report their resignations.[43] The government's strategy was clear: render the local government impotent. As Jamal Pasha removed members of the AC one by one, meetings had to be canceled and work delayed. Eventually, rumors of the council's imminent suspension began circulating.[44]

Speculations became a reality on March 14. The dirty job of announcing the AC's end fell on Kouyoumdjian Pasha, who informed Habib Pasha al-Sa'ad of its dismissal. Jamal Pasha cited the pressing need to elect men to the council who were genuinely interested in the welfare of Mount Lebanon.[45]

At the end of May 1915, new elections for the AC, under strict supervision of Ottoman officials, were held quietly and without the usual "election propaganda."[46] The government ensured that all newly elected members were loyal advocates of CUP policies with no connections to the British and/or French consulates.[47] While maintaining the AC's size, Jamal Pasha and his men ignored the mandated confessional distribution of membership making it possible for a majority of Muslims to be "elected."[48] The council, now having to "conform to military instructions," was nothing but a toothless institution, carrying out orders from Damascus.[49] When the new council's first meeting convened on May 27, 1915, Jamal Pasha tasked his loyal pawn Muhammed Rida Bey to keep a close eye on the AC. Rida Bey had proven himself as the president of the new Ottoman military court in 'Aley, which under his management had become a fierce instrument of Ottoman oppression. Having almost complete control, Rida Bey answered to no one but Jamal Pasha.[50]

All the while political activists outside the empire continued to agitate. Assuming an imminent French invasion of the Lebanese coast, the émigré community in Cairo began organizing a volunteer force. One of the leading men behind these efforts was the journalist Salim al-Najjar, who was being cheered on by Georges-Picot. Najjar enlisted some 3,000 men within only three weeks. The men, however, never left Cairo, since French officials refused to back an uprising. The Entente's lack of enthusiasm and fears that even rumor of rebellion could endanger families back home halted the recruitment effort.[51] Syrian émigrés in Cairo were not the only ones to trying organize; in the United States, the Lebanon League of Progress visited the French embassy in Washington. The committee notified the ambassador of their desire to gain independence for Lebanon from Ottoman rule. Looking to France for help, the men claimed that if they were given adequate transportation, weapons, and ammunition, thousands of volunteers would be ready to take up arms against the Ottomans. Nobody listened to the men in New York.[52] In Europe, Syrian émigré and political activist Shukri Ghanim, agitated from the French capital.⁵³ He promised the French foreign minister up to 15,000 men who were willing to support a French invasion. Weapons and ammunition, he argued, could be sent easily through the harbor in Junieh, north of Beirut, a shortsighted suggestion that did not anticipate the disruption of maritime traffic. No one took Ghanim's idea seriously.⁵⁴ Still the political overtures and plotting bred distrust and skepticism. The anti-Ottoman sentiments and attempts to mobilize in Mount Lebanon and among some members of the Lebanese émigré communities in Cairo, Paris, and New York made the Ottoman leadership further question the loyalty of their Lebanese subjects.

Hearing rumors and reports of possible dissent, Jamal Pasha, having established a military presence and marginalized secular leaders, dealt with the *mutasarrif* Kouyoumdjian Pasha. With only nominal power and as an Armenian feeling "physically threatened by Jamal's henchmen," Kouyoumdjian put in his resignation.⁵⁵ When in June 1915 Jamal Pasha finally granted Kouyoumdjian's wish to leave his position, the local papers announced that the *mutasarrif* was going on vacation. Halim Bey, a man said to have been without vision and leadership skills, stepped in temporarily. No one seemed to believe that Kouyoumdjian Pasha would return; he had had too many disagreements with the military commander. The German consul Mutius was pleased. He saw Kouyoumdjian Pasha as "incapable" and deemed his resignation no loss. To convince the local population of the benefits of a centralized Turkish regime, Mutius urged the appointment of a man with "vision and skills."⁵⁶ The Ottoman interior minister appointed 'Ali Munif Bey.

It was a controversial choice. 'Ali Munif Bey was a Muslim. Maronite clerics, in particular, took offense. How was a Muslim going to head the administration? The appointment clearly was a breach of the 1860 agreement. And he did not even speak Arabic. Mutius reported, "They see in him an enemy, who will make it his mission to eliminate the previously all-powerful influence from the clerics."⁵⁷ Upon his arrival in September 1915, 'Ali Munif Bey had a speech read on his behalf, wherein he promised unspecified reforms. Most important, he announced the end of Mount Lebanon's special privileges while pledging the maintenance of military exemptions and the district's independent financial structure. The speech ended with an important point. The new governor expected in return for reforms and charity the loyal and faithful attachment of the Lebanese to the Ottoman state.[58]

When in June 1916 Jamal Pasha permanently dissolved the AC, power was consolidated in the hands of 'Ali Munif Bey, who would work closely with military commander Muhammed Rida Bey. For Jamal Pasha this meant he could conduct Mount Lebanon's affairs through a "single puppet."[59] But starvation worsened, in particular in the Kisrawan district, under 'Ali Munif Bey. The German consul accused the governor of having "displayed an astonishing amount of indifference to the suffering of the population under his rule." Instead of resolving food shortages, 'Ali Munif Bey spent time in Beirut in the company of women and at the gambling tables. He was known to throw elaborate parties, contributing to people's doubts about the "compassion and sympathy of those in high position." While 'Ali Munif Bey is said to have attempted to secure grain shipments for his district, Mutius dismissed it as a "hopeless endeavor" and lamented the fact that the new *mutasarrif* never gained the locals' full support.[60] The dismissal of the AC and the new governor's failure to feed the mountain benefited the Maronite Church.

Politics of Appeasement and Neutrality: The Maronite Church and the Ottoman State

Increasing Ottoman surveillance, the government's public display of power, and widespread dismissal of inconvenient officials meant that securing food supplies would be difficult if not impossible without consent from the government or would have to be done in secret. Cordial relations with state officials, even if only on the surface, were vital, as any chances at provisions were increasingly linked to access to state power. The realization that religious officials were not immune to persecution and that the church's traditional external patrons were not ready to come to Mount Lebanon's aid in any significant way made courting the Ottomans ever more important.

The Persecution of Defiant Clerics

Religious leaders and outspoken clerics were targets of the Ottomans' no-dissent policy. For example, the Syriac bishop, thirty-five of his clergy, and the Greek Catholic bishop of Acre were condemned to death. The Greek

Catholic bishops of Baalbek, Tripoli, and Damascus were exiled to Adana. Others experienced daily harassment or were called before an Ottoman military court in 'Aley.[61] Jamal Pasha accused Maronite priest Yusuf al-Huwayyik, who was caught carrying an incriminating letter, of treason and ordered his arrest and finally his execution on March 22, 1915.[62] Beirut's Maronite bishop Butrus Shibli was summoned by 'Azmi Bey and forced to resign from his post.[63] The military court then sentenced him to exile in Adana, where he was held in a Jesuit monastery guarded by Ottoman soldiers. The bishop died in exile.[64]

Despite the patriarch's public assurances of loyalty, the military authorities continuously investigated him, trying to find reasons to arrest him. When the Parisian *Le Matin* (The morning) published an article claiming the patriarch had promised 5,000 armed men to aid French forces should they decide to invade Mount Lebanon, Jamal Pasha immediately demanded an investigation. While the inquiries turned up nothing, the patriarch came under close surveillance. In April 1915, Muhammed Rida Bey summoned Huwayyik to the military court in 'Aley. The patriarch's adviser, Yusuf al-Hakim, wrote in his account of the war that he eventually was able to discourage Muhammed Rida Bey from arresting the patriarch. Such a move, he apparently told Rida Bey, would cause unrest. 'Azmi Bey suspected Huwayyik of carrying out French espionage. Informing Jamal Pasha of the treachery, 'Azmi Bey demanded the patriarch's exile. Jamal Pasha's response was measured, knowing that any such arrest would agitate the population and might result in having to send more troops.

Mother France's Hesitant Love

French officials clearly articulated their government's unwillingness to militarily intervene on the church's behalf this time. After the outbreak of war in Europe, a number of secular and religious Maronite leaders declared their allegiance to France. Some community members were convinced of an imminent French invasion of the coastal regions of Syria with the goal of helping them realize their "aspirations for independence."[65] Georges-Picot did little to dispel the rumors. The French consul indeed saw a great opportunity since, according to him, no more than 2,000 soldiers were necessary to take over Mount Lebanon. Besides the mountain being a refuge for draft dodgers, some of its inhabitants volunteered to spy, and others, to fight for the Entente powers.[66] According to the consul's report, a group of an estimated 30,000 to 35,000 Lebanese were ready to defend the privileges of the mountain.[67]

With this assurance, some Maronite leaders began gathering contributions for the French Red Cross and informed Georges-Picot "of the desire of Maronites to enlist in the French army." Others sought direct involvement from the Entente by asking for weapons, ammunition, and the assistance of British and French soldiers in a rebellion against the Ottomans. The response was negative. French officials repeatedly dismissed the "opening of yet another front" as impossible and expressed fears of even a "limited intervention by the allies" possibly "inciting a general massacre."[68] The British consul general urged the Maronites not to challenge the Ottoman army by themselves and not to be caught up in false hopes of French or Russian aid. However, Georges-Picot continued his scheming. He approached the Greek consul general in Beirut, asking him to supply arms to the Maronites.[69] Eventually a delegation traveled to Greece to negotiate a possible weapons transfer. The Greek prime minister, Eleftherios Venizelos, listened to the men and promised to supply them with "3,000–4,000 rifles with ammunition." His condition, however, was that any action taken against the Ottomans had to be in coordination with the French. While the French foreign ministry did not object to Greeks supplying arms, it restated that there would not be any direct involvement of French troops. The British government warned the weapons would not be enough, and it was an extremely dangerous game to encourage any militant actions against the Ottomans,[70] especially since the European powers were not in a position to step in should the Ottoman military retaliate. Still defiant, the Lebanese arranged for the weapons to be shipped to Cyprus. It was only when the French foreign minister declared that France under no circumstances would be engaged on a Syrian front that the plan was completely abandoned. What happened to the weapons is unclear.

Georges-Picot's suggestions and requests were ignored in Europe. The French foreign minister still did not see any benefit in engaging the Ottomans in the Levant; instead, he prioritized France's engagement in the European trenches. But Georges-Picot did not give up so easily and kept intimating France's readiness to invade should the Ottomans declare war. Once the Ottomans entered the war, all diplomatic personnel from belligerent powers, including Georges-Picot, had to leave the empire. He moved to Egypt and continued his intrigue from there, promising émigré Maronites "the tricolor would fly over Syria and Mount Lebanon" in no time.[71]

For the duration of the war French policy, however, remained clear: There would be no weapons or military intervention on behalf of the Lebanese. At the same time French officials were eager not to alienate their Maronite clients. In 1916, the French foreign ministry, now under Aristide Briand, proclaimed that "the government of the republic shares the anxieties of the Syrians and the Lebanese and it will not forget the suffering imposed on them by the Young Turks."[72] A different avenue of support had to be found. French officials in Paris and Cairo agreed any action had to be secret and limited to sending food and medical supplies through neutral powers. They would work with the American ambassador in Istanbul to procure permission to ship material relief into Syria. Briand viewed this strategy as beneficial no matter what the response in the capital. "In case [the Ottomans] refuse," he wrote in a letter to the French ambassador in Rome, "we can further exploit the attitude that would render the Turks odious among the native Christians and Muslims for not allowing our generous intervention on their behalf." It would imply a CUP plan to starve out its own people. Since the ambassador was in close contact with Maronite clergy visiting the Vatican, Briand tasked him to make known France's "efforts to help the Maronites, to whom we are bound."[73] French officials here sought to lay the foundation for respect and loyalty in the aftermath of war through the discussion of provisioning schemes.

In December 1916, the French war ministry decided to form a volunteer unit dubbed the Legion d'Orient. It was stationed in Cyprus, and the men were trained to assist the Franco-British efforts led by General Edmund Allenby.[74] Besides Armenian volunteers (mainly men evacuated from Musa Dagh), some men and funds came from the Syro-Lebanese diaspora. Two new organizations, both founded in 1917, the Paris Comité central syrien (Syrian Central Committee, CCS) in Paris and the New York–based League for the Liberation of Lebanon and Syria, were eager to recruit men for this effort. France supported the CCS and even sent two of its members to South

America to advertise and raise funds for the Legion d'Orient. The CCS was met with great enthusiasm in Brazil and came away with substantial monetary donations. The diaspora in Argentina was less convinced of the benefits of such contributions. The legion was put into action at the end of 1917, but the participation of Syro-Lebanese recruits was minimal. Only five hundred Syrians had been recruited into the legion between 1916 and 1918. About 4,000 Armenians made up the majority.[75] Even with the legion trained and ready for engagement, the French military command was hesitant to send the men into battle, fearing Ottoman reprisals against civilians. Finally, in July 1918, the legion, including a company of Syro-Lebanese, joined Allenby's troops in Palestine. In general, France's promises translated into only limited help, so access to Jamal Pasha and his goodwill became arguably the most important avenue to food.

Courting the State:
The Patriarch and the Commander

Maronite religious leadership from the beginning of the war had employed caution in dealing with the state's authorities. Trying to get in front of possible suspicions, the patriarch had issued a statement in support of the Ottoman government on November 12, 1914.[76] Under much pressure from the authorities, he repeatedly advised his followers in public to maintain "harmony and tranquillity" among themselves and in relations with other sects. It was vital, he urged, for them to remember that they grew up "in the bosom of the Ottoman nation. Her love imprinted on our hearts for many generations." To avoid any misunderstanding, the patriarch ordered priests to be examples of loyal Ottoman citizens and demanded no one should discuss political issues in public. Instead, he called on his followers not to forget those defending the country. And as a sign of the church's allegiance, he instructed his priests to collect donations for Ottoman soldiers from their parishes and say special prayers in their churches on behalf of the Ottoman war effort. Whether anyone followed the directive is unclear, but a public effort of Maronite leadership to erase doubts over its commitment to the Ottoman state is clearly visible in the sources.[77]

While certainly not fond of Jamal Pasha, the patriarch generally made sure not to alienate government officials. For example, he did not publicly blame the Ottoman state or its representatives for starvation in Mount Lebanon. Instead, he strategically linked his people's suffering to the community's own spiritual decay. Communal letters issued by the patriarch and other high church officials and read during church services are examples. The letters were an outward presentation of the church's self-blame. Herein the clerics attribute the war and famine to human sins and the neglect of religious duties, the desertion of worship and ritual. Discussions of the overall lack of grain, rising costs of transportation, hoarding, and confiscations, all of which could be blamed on the Entente blockade, the failures of the Ottoman authorities, and the insatiable appetite of its military, were completely avoided.

Both the causes of and solutions to material devastation were internal to the Maronite community. To appease God and to end the suffering, church leaders called for a return of those who had strayed from their religion and its commandments. Increasing prayers and providing communities who were abandoned by their priests with religious services were sure ways to guarantee the community's salvation. The leadership strategically combined material distributions with prayer, services, hearing of confessions, and absolutions. Repentance, prayer, and regular participation in the religious ritual, the priests reiterated repeatedly in their reports, would be the only way to survive. Indeed, the call for material relief was always—if not subordinated—accompanied by the appeal for "spiritual relief," the comfort of souls and in the very desperate cases preparations for the afterlife. Every Maronite had the moral duty to offer assistance according to his or her ability, spiritually or materially.[78] The church's official correspondence naturally did not cite political ambitions but religious obligation as a motivating factor, based on neighborly love. The famine was a clear opportunity to reassert religious leadership in the mountain without publicly denouncing Ottoman rule.[79]

When Jamal Pasha invited Huwayyik for a meeting in the summer of 1915, the patriarch, having declined earlier invitations, complied. Although their relationship had been tense, the meeting apparently was courteous and respectful. While the German consul was perturbed by the platitudes and, in his eyes obvious, insincerities uttered by the patriarch,[80] Jamal Pasha "received and sent off" the patriarch "with honours."[81] The men met again on a number of occasions.⁸² Huwayyik's strategy paid off to some extent. The outcome of these meetings generally was a *promise* of food to Mount Lebanon. For example, during meetings in May 1916, the patriarch yet again articulated his people's need for food. According to the patriarch's secretary, Father Bulus 'Aql, Jamal Pasha responded by promising the patriarch large and regular shipments of grain. The *Near East* published a report that the community was "presented with twenty tons of corn for the distribution among the poor."⁸³ Wheat was supposed to arrive and be distributed on May 13 or 14.⁸⁴ The shipment benefited not only the Maronites but other Christian orders as well. For example, the Paulists of Harissa, who often felt forgotten by their powerful neighbor, received 2 *qintar* (1,026 kilograms) of wheat allocated by the Maronite patriarch. The allowance was seen as an expression of the patriarch's appreciation of Paulists' efforts in feeding the poor.⁸⁵ They only had to retrieve it from the rail station.

By 1917, Ottoman troops were stretched thin, and desertion was an ever-growing problem. Maintaining good relations with the patriarch increasingly was in Jamal's best interest. Much to the dismay of 'Azmi Bey, Jamal Pasha decided to meet the patriarch yet again. We don't know exactly what happened during the meeting, which took place in early July 1917. Did the patriarch assent to sign yet another statement of loyalty? Did he agree to exonerate the Ottomans from having caused the starvation in Mount Lebanon? Or did Jamal Pasha receive note from the highest church authorities that arresting the patriarch was unacceptable?⁸⁶ What is clear is that the patriarch remained in his position and a promise of food was made. According to Jamal Pasha himself, he promised 300,000 kilograms of wheat to Mount Lebanon in 1917.⁸⁷ It remains unclear if he actually sent the entire amount. Reports of unreliable shipments suggest that usually not all the promised wheat and flour arrived. The account of Fritz Grobba suggests that 200,000 kilograms of grain, meaning not the entire promised amount, arrived at the Maronite church in 1917.⁸⁸ A list of distributions of wheat among the various Maronite bishoprics confirms the "government's *ihsan*" of wheat to the church. A document titled *First List*—indicating that more wheat would be expected—recorded the names of priests in the various districts and the amount they received as "charity from the government."⁸⁹ The priests of St. Paul noted that Jamal Pasha gave Lebanon free wheat, not two but three times. For them this was an indication of the Maronite patriarch's easy access to government aid. The question was whether he was taking full advantage of his connection. The Ottomans' assertion of power was a clear opportunity for the Maronite Church to increase its standing in the mountain district.

While it was then possible to dismiss the AC and expel foreigners, the state was careful not to crack down too hard on the church's leadership, perhaps fearing a complete alienation of Christian Lebanese from the state. This left room for the patriarch—although politically handicapped—to engage in a politics of benevolence that would guarantee him the loyalty of at least some of his flock. While the Maronite patriarch publicly declared his allegiance to the Ottoman state, an act that would no doubt alienate the church from a dominant Francophile Maronite elite, food and feeding in a time of scarcity was an essential element in expanding the authority of the clergy in the eyes of the general public. In secret, the church was still hoping its external allies would come to the rescue—if not with weapons, then with money.

In a Quest for Money:
Loans, Lands, and Foreign Donations

Some wheat came as state *ihsan*, but most of it had to be purchased through government channels. Procuring the necessary cash funds was yet another obstacle. The patriarchate's officials instructed the superiors of monasteries, schools, and religious endowments to negotiate sales contracts with the government to secure funds, even if it would mean large-scale debt.[90] With a budget and plan in place, institutions' leaders could appeal for funds from the archdiocese's treasury at Bkirki. Money, however, would be forthcoming only if all resources were exhausted and everything had been done to procure funding. The patriarch's instructions about how to negotiate mortgages and land sales were vague and at times raised harsh critiques. For example, the secretary of the neighboring Paulist monastery wrote: "Yes, the patriarch wrote an official letter to all the monasteries to help the poor. Even to mortgage their fields on their own, and some monasteries did this." But the archdiocese did not sell its golden chalices, nor did it sell any of its large fields or borrow enough money to give charity as it should have.[91] There are, however, some accounts that speak to the contrary.

According to an account in the Cairo press, Huwayyik sold part of the church's property to two Beirut merchants for 20,000 Ottoman liras, a significant, although probably exaggerated amount of money. The income, according to eyewitnesses, was used to distribute money and food among the poor and needy of Mount Lebanon.[92] Besides selling properties, it is said, the church borrowed money and at times sold properties to pay off some of its creditors. In April 1917, Tannuri informed the patriarch that under the current conditions it was decided that an orchard belonging to the archdiocese, located along the coast of Beirut near Burj Hammud, would be sold to satisfy some creditors who had given their final request for payment.[93] While a preliminary survey of the records and the press suggests the church did sell tracts of land to finance relief, the scope of sales remains unclear. More research is needed.

Money was a continuous problem. According to Tannuri, relief work in the monasteries continued "even under the heavy burden of increasing debts."[94] At St. Anthony's aid work had depleted the treasury, but the institution's superior was able to continue this work with the help of funds supplied by the archdiocese until the end of the war. After 1916, the archdiocese agreed to finance aid work at institutions that were unable to come up with necessary funds. There is no doubt that smaller Christian orders in Mount Lebanon had a much more difficult time dealing with the disproportional debts resulting from their relief efforts, which affected their ability to distribute regular aid. According to the financial records of the Paulist monastery, the order had acquired a debt of 15,000 Egyptian pounds. This was a very large sum for a small and relatively young order, which had been founded only ten years earlier. Moreover, the money had been borrowed at exorbitant interest rates, ranging from 20 to 30 percent.[95]

The properties of religious groups were targets of the Ottoman administration from the beginning of the war. Most missionary institutions of enemy powers were shut down and their properties confiscated. In Beirut, some religious benevolent societies, if not closed down, were harassed with higher taxes. Even neutral and respected Americans constantly worried about the fate of their community's properties. It seemed no property was safe. The Maronite patriarch applied for a sultanic *firman* (decree) to "protect himself from martial inquisitions and his church's property from expropriation by the military authorities."⁹⁶ This *firman*, while guaranteeing the survival of the church in Mount Lebanon, meant alienating some of the Lebanese. It was an act of submission to the Ottomans for the first time in the church's history.⁹⁷ The Ottoman government finally issued the *firman* in January 1916, coinciding with the beginning of an organized relief effort in the mountains.⁹⁸

Neither a simple tightening of the belt nor mortgaging lands was enough or even the most desirable solution. When the situation grew desperate in the winter of 1916, the patriarch needed cash to purchase grain, and he needed it fast. Although he had relatively cordial relations with the Ottoman military leadership, the patriarch's first instinct was to turn to the community's longtime patron, France. He solicited the help of Egypt's Maronite bishop Yusuf Darian. Huwayyik instructed Darian to appeal to the French government to provide the church with cash to feed famine victims. On November 13, 1916, Darian sent a letter to the French army general Albert Trabaud, stationed on the island Arwad off the Syrian coast.⁹⁹ Darian requested a loan from the French government for 1 million francs in exchange for a lien on church properties. The French authorities heeded the patriarch's request and considered the appropriate steps. In fact, French authorities had tasked Trabaud to draw up a plan to aid the Lebanese by providing subsidies to the patriarch in July 1916. The French foreign minister, Briand, favored sending funds to the patriarch as long as the money was used to buy grain. Everyone involved thought this campaign to be risky. There was no guarantee that the transaction could be kept secret, putting those involved in danger. There was some disagreement: some French officials approved the secret transfer of requested funds; others suggested a piecemeal transmission.¹⁰⁰ Sending smaller amounts, some argued, would facilitate immediate relief and was unlikely to raise suspicion. If the transfer was successful and the patriarch used the funds in an efficient and satisfying manner, more cash would be forthcoming and the same route might even be used to transfer funds that had been collected by the Syrian diaspora in Egypt.

In October 1916, the Cairo correspondent of the British bulletin the *Near East* reported, "It is highly gratifying to learn that the work done by the various relief committees formed by Syrians abroad has surpassed all expectations." Apparently by this time, the number of diaspora relief committees was somewhere "in the few hundreds," and the subscriptions "raised by them have attained a very considerable amount."[101] One of the most active émigré communities was the one living in Cairo and Alexandria formed in the spring of 1916.[102] The Syrian Relief Committee in Cairo worked "with unabated energy." At the very first meeting in Cairo, the committee subscribed 6,500 Egyptian pounds.[103] Drawing together religious leaders from across sects, the committee assured the Egyptian authorities that it was a nonsectarian and apolitical undertaking. Having procured the support of religious leaders, the committee rendered total control to them.[104] A special Central Committee was formed to keep in touch with committees outside Egypt.[105]

Indicting the Ottoman government, or even simply criticizing it, was a risky business. The charge would be treason, which carried a death sentence, even in absentia. Those outside the Ottoman realm possibly risked the persecution of their families or the larger community. A warning was circulated in the international press that "political references and allusions to the war or phrases capable of being construed as such by the Turkish authorities, furnish the latter with excuses for taking the addressees as hostages to the interior."[106] Messages broadcast in the Egyptian press reassured the public and potential donors "that the aim and field of action of the committee and its branches is purely humanitarian." Neutrality was crucial. If any member of the Syrian diaspora was involved in politics, the committee warned he did so in his personal capacity and the committee would immediately distance itself from that person. Indeed, if one of committee's administrative members meddled in religious or political affairs, it would be grounds for his resignation. Moreover, the committee assured Egyptian state officials that they would be informed of any money sent to Syria and Lebanon. The committee's public announcements continued to emphasize its purely charitable intentions. It was to ameliorate human suffering. Promising that it would function within the legal premises of the Egyptian state, the committee guaranteed complete transparency of its actions.

At the same time, eyewitness accounts and letters transmitting stories of the horrors back home were published in the Egyptian press, emphasizing that families back home faced an existential crisis. For example, the winter of 1916 was recorded as ruining families and severing kinship bonds in the homeland. Hunger apparently drove people to madness. This *delirio de fome* (madness of hunger) impelled the widow of Ibrahim Wazan Shaʿib to do the unthinkable.[107] In the days of mid-November 1916, Ibrahim had lain tossing in his bed, suffering from nausea and diarrhea, symptoms indicating that he had eaten something poisonous. When he died, he left behind his wife and children. The widow and all of her neighbors were convinced that Ibrahim had died from eating flour stretched with some toxic ingredients distributed by the government. Her husband dead, perhaps fearing her death or in a desperate gamble to save a child's life, the widow was reported to have sold her seven-year-old daughter for a *rotl* of pure flour. "Hunger led to madness and madness led the mother to devour her baby."[108]

That the widow's story was published at least twice and on two different continents speaks to the powerful symbolism of her suffering, which was used to motivate empathy and highlight the disproportional anguish of women (and children) and the end of the Lebanese family. I first read the account in Cairo's *al-Muqattam*, a publication of the Syrian émigré community in Egypt. The story was to inspire community members to donate funds to famine victims. However, this was not the first time the widow's story was told. As far as it is possible to tell, her story initially had appeared in *al-Hawi*, an Arabic newspaper published in Argentina, a paper best described as a weekly clerical publication. Both publications were products of émigré communities. *Al-Hawi*'s editor, Yusuf Milhim Shaʿiya, who went by the name of José M. Chaia, was a Maronite who left Mount Lebanon to settle in South America. The editors of *al-Muqattam* lived in Egypt, which now was under the control of the Entente forces. The former maintained connections to the Maronite patriarch in Bkirki, Mount Lebanon, a relationship that implies his political sentiments most likely being, if not anti-Ottoman, at least critical of the regime.[109] Many in the Cairene Syrian émigré community, reading and writing for *al-Muqattam*, had escaped the hardships in their homeland. Consequently, the community was not only sympathetic to the Entente's war efforts but eager to inform the world of the misery back home. In the end, who originally told the widow's story is lost in the international stream of news. Whether it is true is impossible to know, but it clearly was useful for both editors as they attempted to paint a picture of their homeland in distress.¹¹⁰ It was an attempt to urge the diaspora to save its national family.

The authors often relied on the power of abstractions in their attempts to solicit humanitarian and/or military interventions. In the spring of 1916, Syro-Lebanese émigré papers repeatedly stated, "The death roll in the Lebanon had attained the appalling figure of 80,000."¹¹¹ Its utility, or shock value, was put to the test with none other than the president of the United States, Woodrow Wilson. In May 1916, a delegation of émigré journalists sent a letter to the president, notifying him of a telegram that had arrived from Egypt in the editorial office of the *Daily Mirror* in New York. The telegram simply stated: "Famine Lebanon. Eighty Thousand Died."¹¹² The journalists, in the true spirit of their profession, assured Wilson that they had been skeptical. The telegram, after all, had no signature, and "that eighty thousand victims should succumb in Mount Lebanon out of a population of half a million or less looked impossible." Only after other telegrams and letters followed from different sources confirming the number was the figure taken to be a credible fact. A death count of this magnitude surely would convince the president "in the name of humanity to use [his] best and humane offices to prevent the extermination of a helpless nation and alleviate the suffering of a needy people."¹¹³

In July 1917, the figure is raised to 200,000 in the *Egyptian Mail*. Here the number apparently was to be a corrective to "the official statement published by the Turkish government," which estimated the deaths of "natives of Lebanon" to be 150,000. The author notes, "It is understood that that is considerably below the real figures."¹¹⁴ In September 1917, the report of "an intrepid Syrian" who had fled that "unhappy country" reiterates the more conservative "official" 150,000 death count ("10 per cent died from disease and the remainder of starvation").¹¹⁵ The numbers were, and still are, impossible to verify. But people died at an extraordinary rate, and the estimates echoed around the globe. How is one to imagine 80,000, 150,000, or even 200,000 dead? And more important, how can one do nothing in light of such a travesty? Many responded by opening their pocketbooks.

Sending the money to Syria, however, was not so easy. Neutral powers, such as the United States, were considered a possible avenue. The Greek

Catholic archbishop Macarios Saba and the Maronite archbishop Yusuf Darian, both residing in Egypt, submitted a two-part dispatch to the American government representative in Cairo, Paul Knabenshue. The first part was an account of the suffering in Lebanon, leading to a request for the American government to negotiate and perhaps even facilitate the shipment of aid to the region. This included materials purchased with the funds of the Cairo relief committee. It was a telegram of agony, describing the situation in crudest form: "Suffering people still alive indescribable and reduced to extremity eating leaves and roots and even decaying flesh."[116] The two clergymen did not mention whom they thought was responsible for the mass starvation. The second unsigned dispatch from the same men cited here as in the original, however, left little doubt:

> Distress in Syria particularly in the Lebanon is not due to natural war conditions but to the sinister political design on the part of the Turkish Government to exterminate by starvation Christian population. Eyewitnesses report that a military cordon prevents entry of food into the Lebanon. Food confiscated by Turkish Government without excuse military necessity.[117]

Darian's political affinities with France forged his sentiments and his willingness to place blame. Darian had close connections to French officials in Cairo and Alexandria and was "assisted financially by the Quai d'Orsay." He was part of the French government's plan to create an image of benevolence through relief. Apparently, the French government financed a trip by the archbishop to New York so that he could promote the French position of a postwar Greater Syria to the Syro-Lebanese community there.[118] France's support of Darian's request for American help in shipping the aid collected in Egypt fit well into its strategy of presenting a willingness to aid, without military intervention. Here, too, it did not matter whether the result was successful, as blame could be placed on American incompetency or Ottoman resistance. When it was clear the aid collected in Egypt could not be shipped via American steamer, since American aid ships were blocked from entering the Syrian ports, Darian suggested routing it via the island of Arwad, a suggestion that was approached with great caution by French officials, who felt uneasy about the transfer of funds.

In general, the church's relationship with France was both an asset and a liability. On the one hand, it meant possible access to money and goods, if it was possible to keep the transactions secret, and a history of France's willingness to intervene on behalf of its Maronite clients may have deterred the Ottomans from disbanding the church. On the other hand, the close relationship repeatedly served as an excuse to arrest, exile, and execute some of its members. The dangers and possibilities had to be carefully weighed, and courting the state for access to food was no doubt the safer option.

Conclusion

Despite all endeavors, the situation grew desperate. In a letter dated May 1, 1918, Ignatius Al-Tannuri confirmed that "our brothers in humanity and the sons of our religion are drinking from the cup filled with starvation."[119] Nevertheless, the church's attempts in coordination with smaller religious communities had a significant impact. For some the efforts even meant survival. As the *mudir* of the district Ghosta put it in a letter, "The work of the Paulists in Harissa was of immediate help to many poor of its surrounding villages, and if it had not been for their effort a great many more would have perished from hunger."[120] Indeed, in the remote northern districts, the poor and starving relied mainly on the local Maronite church for food and/or money. The church's institutional network was an important vehicle to distribute government *ihsan*, which would have the potential of cultivating pro-government sentiments. Moreover, the generally conservative attitude of the church, visible in the prewar period, made it a more acceptable ally than the alternative power holder in the mountain district—the secular, reform-minded elite that spoke through the AC.

The relationship between the church and the government, however, was complicated by the church's long-standing relationship with France. The religious leadership treaded with caution, and ever-increasing need for government grain forced the patriarch to publicly court the Ottoman government and avoid any open dealings with France. Any correspondence with French officials was conducted secretly and through the Maronite bishop in Egypt. When dealings became known, others would take the fall for it, leaving Huwayyik untouchable. Regardless of the church's motivations, feeding the poor and selling wheat to the wealthier people of the community certainly generated allegiance to the institution and safeguarded, if not further solidified, its position. The strategy of the church to combine prayer with food could leave little doubt in the recipients' minds who was filling their empty stomachs. The war opened an opportunity for the church to assert its power, and the politics of provisioning in Mount Lebanon would have one clear, albeit seemingly unlikely, beneficiary: the Maronite Church.

Figure 6. Turk [i.e., Turkish] Hospital Tent Interior. Ottoman medical officials disinfecting patients. Source: The American Colony (Jerusalem), G. Eric and Edith Matson Photograph Collection, Library of Congress Prints and Photographs Division, Washington, D.C.

{ CHAPTER 5 }

RATS, LICE, AND MICROBES

The Struggle against Infectious Diseases

When Ahmed Dandan, a worker at the mill in Antelias, a suburb of Beirut, woke up on the morning of September 26, 1915, he felt terribly sick.[1] He was sweating and shivering, and his head felt like it was about to burst into pieces. Instead of going to work and ignoring the aches as he normally would, he hurried to see a doctor. The physician examined Ahmed and concluded the miller had contracted a "simple fever," the cure for which would be lots of rest and fluids. Six days later Ahmed's daughter woke up with symptoms similar to her father's. In addition to the fever, the young woman exhibited a painfully throbbing swollen gland on her thigh. The family took her to the same doctor, who quickly connected the two incidents. Fearing it was worse than a simple fever, he reported the family to the health and sanitation authorities in Beirut. The director of health and the supervising physician of the Vilayet of Beirut drove out to the suburb to inspect the Dandans' home. After a close examination of the daughter and a bacteriological screening of blood and tissue from her swollen gland, the two medical officers decided that her condition could be nothing else but a type of plague.[2]

Immediate action was needed. The director of health called a meeting, which was attended by Governor 'Azmi Bey, Beirut's municipal health officials, and physicians from the city and its suburbs. What could be done? The best solution, the men decided, was to quarantine the house of those infected and ensure the proper treatment and close supervision of the sick.

Once the medical officers learned of large numbers of dead mice and rats in and around the mill, there was no doubt; it clearly was the plague. It had been transferred from the rodents to Ahmed and his daughter. Faced with potential disaster, the authorities immediately extended the quarantine to the entire area of Antelias. This was a controversial move. The suburban business community complained it was not practical to close down the entire town and it would disrupt their work. The bickering stirred up much resentment among the town's residents, so authorities lifted the quarantine only a few days later. The mill remained quarantined. Some officials suggested demolishing the building to eliminate the deadly microbes.[3] Meanwhile, rumors of a cordon sanitaire to be imposed on Beirut spread among the public. The threat of a quarantine line around the city with its potential restrictions on the movement of people and vital goods such as wheat, which already was reduced to a trickle, caused great fear. Any further obstruction to access to the city would throw many more families into starvation. To preclude public unrest, health officials announced in the local press, "NO CORDON on Beirut." The authorities, in larger letters, swore to be taking the matter seriously, and the two infected persons were recovering and would be released from isolation within two to three days.[4]

The story of Ahmed Dandan and his family is exemplary of a battle fought against an imperceptible opponent capable of an attack impossible to keep at bay with guns and bullets. Isolating the sick was one method of fighting the spread of infectious diseases. But lice and bacteria invaded bodies, linens, clothes, and homes. "Disinfectors" hauled mobile steam ovens from town to town to eradicate the visible and invisible threats. Knocking on the doors of frightened families, uniformed men collected infested materials in large sacks. One by one, via pitchfork, dresses and sheets were fed into the ovens. Once inside the iron cauldron, hot steam would singe the lice and suffocate cholera bacilli. The message was clear. Health officials would not simply stand by as mice, lice, and microbes moved from house to house, body to body, and intestine to intestine.

Rarely do we read about famines without diseases being mentioned. Famine scholars argue that hunger inevitably works in tandem with diseases.[5] And it has been shown that infectious diseases tread on the heels of starvation, causing many more famine deaths than malnutrition or starvation.[6] Two processes tend to be at play. First, the lack of food reduces the body's biological resistance, causing a heightened susceptibility to diseases.[7] Second, social processes related to famine, like population movement and breakdown of sanitary conditions, make it easier for communicable diseases to spread.[8] In more recent African famines, for example, it was not starvation and hunger-related diseases but epidemics of communicable diseases like typhus and cholera that caused mass deaths. In the Lebanese case, communicable diseases combined with "total war" and famine formed a deadly and relentless trio both on the battlefront and the home front. On June 3, 1916, the Jesuit priest Louis Cheikho, one of Beirut's leading intellectuals, described it in this way: "Voilà, donc le *trio* complet 'a peste, fame et bello' [So here is the complete *trio*: pestilence, famine, and war]."[9] Of course, there is no direct causal link between the triad. Their connection is tenuous considering the simple fact that there may be wars without epidemics and epidemics without war, famines without wars and wars without famine. Yet both World War I and the famine contributed to an environment that would be vulnerable to outbreaks of epidemics, generating what might best be described as a four-year epidemic emergency. During the famine war, people died of starvation *and* disease.

War, famine, and diseases, in this case, were intimately entangled. It is impossible to think about coping capabilities and politics of provisioning without considering the struggle against microbes and bacteria. The fight defined much of the wartime agenda of local officials and municipal officers in both Beirut and Mount Lebanon. Many of the administrative concerns were not only front-page news but also subject to politics of health provisioning and state intervention. This chapter analyzes the works of a public health and sanitation administration that was rooted in nineteenth-century urban transformations and the transnational circulation of medical knowledge and was consolidated, strengthened, and, most important, militarized during the war to facilitate a forceful top-down intervention. The study of disease in wartime Beirut and Mount Lebanon is complicated because there are no reliable statistics of infections or disease-related mortalities. Eyewitness accounts; admissions records of the hospital associated with the SPC; a unique study commissioned by one of the wartime governors of Mount Lebanon, Ismaʻil Haqqi Bey, including a report by the provincial director of health, Husni Bey Muhyi ad-Din; some fragmented reports sent by the governor to Istanbul;

and public health announcements of the Beirut and Mount Lebanon health directorates, however, disclose various disease-specific prophylactic measures suggested, ordered, and in some cases implemented.[10] They are most useful in exposing the politics of sanitizing spaces and citizens. As in earlier periods, the assurance of healthy Ottoman citizens was a matter of preserving the honor and legitimacy of the state and enhanced the prestige of those in charge.[11]

The crises of total war, the chapter argues, accelerated the consolidation of a preexisting health regime and interventionist policies focused on making sick bodies a public concern to be reported, isolated, and disinfected. The acute war emergency pushed imperial and local agents to boost their efforts in fighting infectious diseases, some of which had been eradicated previously but had resurfaced. The upsurge of diseases enabled, if not demanded, social and administrative changes resulting in the strengthening of a bureaucratic hierarchy of health and public sanitation for the surveillance and regulation of personal and communal hygienic behaviors.[12] The organization of medical care and social provisions in turn altered citizens' interaction with local agents of the state. Municipal authorities increasingly intervened in the daily lives of Beirut's inhabitants, prescribing preventive measures that demanded new behaviors regarding sanitation. Civilians' enclosure into an institutional framework of health and sanitation, public education campaigns, discussions of health and disease in the general press, and the presence of cleaning battalions and surveying health officials all defined significant parts of everyday life on the home front. Unfortunately, the sources seldom address civilian responses to state measures, and stories like those of Ahmed Dandan are rare. A close reading of existing sources, however, reveals a general distrust of health authorities among civilians. Constant warnings against disobedience and punitive threats indicate that the process of creating "sanitary citizens" did not go unchallenged.[13]

The Ottoman authorities were eager to assert power in the city; sanitation and public health, like food provision, was an arena where intervention could be marketed as positive. Health was an equally contested space. 'Abd al-Qadir Qabbani's speech on the occasion of the inauguration of the municipal hospital years earlier in 1898 is illustrative:

> We do thank the founders of these [foreign] hospitals for their services to humanity, albeit we deem it necessary for the patient to be under the custody

of his own mother [the municipality] and under the medical supervision of his own people for the sake of establishing permanent amicability between the people and the exalted Ottoman State. This hospital will—God willing—render a humanitarian [*al-insāniyya*] and a national [*al-milliyya*] service at the same time.[14]

The war was an opportunity to consolidate the people under the custody of the "mother," the municipality and the state. State officials did so by confiscating existing foreign institutions and prohibiting the creation of new ones without its consent. A law published in October 1914 outlined that "foreign, private, philanthropic, religious and educational societies and associations [would be prohibited] to found wholly new sanitary establishments independently of the authorities." The existing foreign sanitary institutions were now subject to state regulations, in particular, rules and regulations issued by the general sanitary department. This included the submission of a list of physicians, along with their specialties and qualifications. Foreign sanitary establishments would be subject to inspection, "just as Ottoman schools and foundations of the same nature" were. In addition, the sanitary establishments were "required to comply with and obey all warnings and directions made to them by the inspector."[15] Besides the German hospital, the only foreign medical institutions the Ottomans did not confiscate were those of the Americans. Ottoman officials, however, closely monitored them.

War, Famine, Disease: Inevitable Boon Companions?

World War I in Greater Syria amplified the adverse effects of climatic and sanitary conditions, altering living conditions and throwing the relationship between humans and microorganisms off balance.[16] Recognizing the power of infectious diseases in generating change, a handful of scholars have examined the Ottoman military's struggle and experiences with diseases on the various battlefronts.[17] There is little to no research, however, on what George Cahen has referred to as *l'autre guerre* (the other war), a war fought on the Ottoman Empire's public health front.[18] The goal was to protect civilians from the menace of cholera, plague, malaria, and especially typhus.

Infectious diseases wreaked havoc on the Ottoman battlefronts, and an Ottoman soldier was seven times more likely to die of disease than of battle wounds.[19] Since the Ottoman fronts were located on the peripheries of the empire, the movement of conscripts over large stretches of territory meant that diseases were at times carried across the entire span of Greater Syria.[20] An inadequate infrastructure amplified the problem.[21] Packed into whatever trains were available, Ottoman troops carried with them disease-infected lice, mosquitoes, and microbes. Dirty bodies, uniforms, and even the upholstery of overcrowded passenger cars made ideal breeding grounds, especially in the winter.[22] In freight cars, common soldiers—sixty at a time—were crammed together in unsanitary conditions and over long stretches of time; many never reached their destinations.[23]

Civilians felt the effects. Crowded trains, now fueled with wood instead of coal, made more frequent stops, providing soldiers with ample opportunity to mix with civilians and share lice, germs, and bacteria. The poor conditions in the army, as soldiers were underpaid, undernourished, and lacked medical care and adequate equipment and clothing, caused frequent desertions.[24] Deserters roamed the countryside, hid out in villages, and at times turned into brigands. An eyewitness wrote that "the military was in trouble and all of the soldiers are running away. . . . Sometimes the escaping soldiers were grabbing from the people the only food they had."[25] In the meantime, these renegade soldiers introduced annoying escorts such as typhus-infected body lice into the most remote corners of Mount Lebanon.[26]

It was not only Russia that saw "a whole empire walking";[27] refugees fleeing from violence and massive state-organized deportations meant people and diseases on the move.[28] Armenians, in particular, who had survived the death marches from Anatolia, were concentrated in makeshift camps wherein starvation and unsanitary conditions facilitated the spread of diseases. This was particularly true in Aleppo and the desert camps in Deir Zor. Local economic migrants trying to escape the famine in the coastal areas posed another, albeit smaller, problem. The wheat-producing plateau of the Hauran, for example, was one destination for Mount Lebanon's impoverished inhabitants in desperate search of food and work. Here these economic refugees turned what was known as the "great wheat land" into a typhus-infected nightmare.

Malnutrition caused by persistent hunger in Beirut and Mount Lebanon created a favorable environment for the spread of diseases, as its slow destruction of the body aided the microbes' assault.[29] A starving body at the point of acute deprivation would have an impaired immune system, making the body vulnerable to diseases. For example, reporting from the Lebanese village of 'Abeih, an eyewitness recounted malaria's effect as "especially terrible, as the people were too weak to withstand the constantly returning fever."[30] The overall deterioration of food quality, changes in ingredients, and eating unfamiliar food provided by relief agencies promoted digestive diseases such as typhoid and cholera.[31]

"The 'Other' War": Staffing and Organizing Medical Trenches on the Home Front

Beirut in the nineteenth and early twentieth centuries witnessed significant transformations of its public health and sanitation administration, as foreign, imperial, and local officials introduced new hygienic practices and scientific cures. Changes at times came in direct response to warfare and/or famine, but not always. The goal, in either case, was to provide tools, technologies, and infrastructure to control and observe diseases and create a stable health environment.[32] The Beirut municipality took on many of these responsibilities, and while things were far from perfect in the city, no serious efforts had been made toward dealing with issues of health and sanitation in the rural areas. In Mount Lebanon, despite the Ottoman *mutasarrif*'s appointments of local physicians to supervise health affairs in the aftermath of the 1860 civil strife and the existence of two military hospitals and a few small American and British clinics, little had been done to organize a health program before 1914.[33]

The Balkan Wars' high disease mortality highlighted many of the persistent difficulties in dealing with communicable diseases affecting soldiers and civilians in times of war. A directive, published in April 1914, sought to remedy some of the flaws. The Regulation for Communicable Diseases included detailed guidelines outlining who was responsible for informing the authorities in case of an outbreak, how infected persons would be treated, what preventive measures should be taken, and calling for the formation of a health commission at the first sign of a possible epidemic.[34] This systematic approach was based on prior experiences and was put to the test and adjusted based on need during World War I.[35]

On December 8, 1914, the Ottoman provincial health director in Beirut demanded all practicing physicians, pharmacists, dentists, and midwives to bring their diplomas and identity cards to the municipal health office for registration.[36] The goal was to compile a list of available medical personnel for conscription into the military.[37] The Ottoman war ministry, as part of post-Balkan military reforms, had drafted a law describing all civilian doctors, pharmacists, and dentists between the ages of twenty and forty-five as eligible to serve in the army.[38] The age range was expanded after October 1915, when men older than forty-five, deemed in good health, could be commissioned to serve.[39] While men from Mount Lebanon were exempt from general conscription, pharmacists and physicians were not.

The Ottoman health director used the beginning of the war as an opportunity to take an inventory and regulate medical services in the city. He immediately instructed the Beirut municipality to reorganize its public health administration and urged the drafting of new directives aimed at controlling the cleanliness of public places and regulating social behavior. Local police, he demanded, were to enforce the directives. On December 15, 1914, the Beirut municipal council announced the appointments of whom it thought to be the most competent men to the wartime health administration and carefully delegated responsibilities to these medical experts. In coordination with the provincial health director, the council appointed Drs. 'Abd al-Rahman al-Unsi and Malkunian to oversee forensic medicine and the overall medical condition in the city. Dr. Najib al-Ardati became the municipal health inspector. Charged with surveying all aspects of public health, he was to report any problems to the president of the Beirut municipality and the Ottoman health directorate.[40] The municipal authorities, fearing the presence of soldiers would lead to a rise in venereal diseases, made sure to appoint a principal surveyor of syphilis, gonorrhea, and the women they held responsible for spreading them. Venereal disease was a problem in the bustling port city even before the war; an 1895 report of the French Medical Faculty listed syphilis as the second most commonly treated disease in Beirut's hospital and clinics.[41] By 1913, Beirut's prostitutes mostly worked in brothels in the Sayfi quarter close to the harbor.[42] Sexually transmitted diseases, according to Husni Bey's report, increased among lower classes during the war, since the rising cost of living forced many of them to engage in "reprehensible actions and fornications."[43] This, however, does not mean these diseases were not also common among middle-class Beirutis and Lebanese.[44] In general, the war increased attention to venereal diseases, and the health directorate reiterated the necessity of controlling prostitutes' bodies in the name of public health.[45] Consequently, Dr. Kamal Effendi received orders to inspect Beirut's "public women" twice a week and assure the treatment of those infected. All physicians in the city were now liable, under severe penalty, to procure the names of possible sources from their infected male patients and issue monthly reports to the municipality and the health directorate.[46]

Three months later, when the first Suez Campaign was in full swing, Jamal Pasha added to the already-existing health administration. He ordered the creation of a commission, made up of a senior military officer, the president of the municipality, the chief physician of the military unit, and the chief municipal doctor.[47] The commission had complete control over matters of health and merged civilian and military powers into one body, inadvertently expanding Jamal Pasha's control by proxy into the city. The blending of military personnel and civilians trickled down to lower levels; the municipality, health commission, and provincial health director employed common soldiers—stationed in Beirut—in urban sanitation projects, where they worked alongside civilians to clean the city.

The General Assembly (GA), organized by Ottoman governor 'Azmi Bey at the end of 1915, also took up public health and sanitation.[48] The GA, made up of thirty-two delegates from all districts of the Beirut province, was to discuss local wartime conditions and provide possible solutions to the most pressing issues.[49] The opening statement of the GA's president assured those present of "the importance of public health of our nation and country," setting the agenda for the years to come. A key concern was the decline in births and infant mortality. The council blamed the decline of healthy children on the "unfortunate consequence of the increase in the rate of certain diseases among parents." Given the dwindling numbers of physicians due to military service and limitations in providing adequate treatment, the council argued for prophylactic measures against all infectious diseases. Public health hence would be its priority as "long as the war continues."[50]

In Mount Lebanon, the appointment of 'Ali Munif Bey as the *mutasarrif* at the end of 1915 marked the beginning of a more organized public health administration. While he was generally seen as careless and even impotent in his efforts to feed his people, the governor's reputation related to health services benefited from the appointment of Husni Bey Muhyi ad-Din, who assumed the post of director of health in February 1916.[51] Under the new director, the military hospital in Baabda was renovated, and three, albeit small, new hospitals were built, with twenty beds each. He also set up a laboratory staffed by a bacteriologist. Husni Bey expanded and systematized the public health administration in the mountains; he appointed a head physician and a number of traveling doctors, whom he supervised directly. He rented a building to store the health department's assets and records, hired physicians for each district of the mountain, and paid them a salary of 1,000 piasters per month.[52] To facilitate the health department's work, the governor divided Mount Lebanon into twenty-three health districts—each with a head physician, health official, and a midwife—and supplied them with the necessary medical equipment. The monthly expenses, deaths, and births were recorded in special registers to facilitate systematic childhood vaccinations for smallpox and cholera.

Who Is Left to Serve?
Manning the Civilian Health Campaign

The conscription of civilian doctors into the army left the home front in despair.[53] Bayard Dodge blamed the ineffectiveness in treating malaria in 'Abeih on the fact that "all of the doctors of the district had gone off to serve in the military hospitals."[54] Even medical and pharmaceutical students were recruited into the army.[55] Physicians were constantly asked to report to the authorities, but the calls were met with resistance. For example, the court published a list of eight physicians who had failed to report to the recruitment office in January 1915. Giving the men ten days to appear, the court announced that no-shows would be tried as deserters and their properties and money confiscated.[56] In June 1915, Beirut's supervising physician, Fuad Hamdi, again ordered all Ottoman physicians regardless of age to report to the health administration, bringing with them their medical license, identity card, and, in case they were exempt from serving in the military, the paperwork to prove it. Despite the repeated mandate to report to the authorities, many medical professionals had not done so. Some had vanished in the mountains. Hamdi required all physicians registered in Beirut to report within five days to undergo a physical examination; otherwise, they would be brought in by force and punished.[57] They would either have to enter the military as a common soldier rather than the customary rank of officer or would be convicted as deserters, meaning a possible death sentence. The military court's rulings in most cases were prison sentences and confiscation of properties.[58] Despite significant penalties and to the frustration of the public health officials, doctors continued to dodge the orders of the recruitment office. To remedy the shortage of working physicians in the city, the remaining doctors extended their hours, advertised their work, and at times took over their colleagues' offices.[59] For example, Dr. Salim Jalakh advertised that he would take on new patients, would hold an open clinic at his house every afternoon from one to four, and was ready to respond at any other time if necessary.[60] The municipality took charge by ordering all remaining doctors to volunteer fifteen hours every week for the municipal health office, significantly increasing its services to the poor of the city.

Making Sanitary Citizens: Education and Regulations

The war was a great shock to the public health systems in all belligerent countries. In the European capitals, the hospitals were almost immediately flooded with wounded and mutilated men. Too far removed from the battlefronts, hospital staff in Beirut saw few battle injuries. The president of SPC, Howard Bliss, reported that despite his offer to treat wounded soldiers free of charge in the college hospital, the admissions were mainly local victims of disease.[61] Civilians infected with malaria, cholera, typhoid fever, plague, and typhus filled the hospital's beds. The increased threat of infectious diseases shifted civilian and military health officials' focus to disease prevention. The goal was to create an environment free of disease, based on a negative definition of individual and communal health. The priorities were, first, efficiency in action and, second, the ease and comfort "in feeling—absence of pain—well-being," meaning that perfect health was the absence of diseases.[62]

In both the city and the mountains, disease prevention was to follow three steps: official notification, isolation, and disinfection. The Regulation

Map 3. Ottoman soup kitchens and disinfection stations.
Source: Developed from a rare Ottoman map. The original is held at BOA, Istanbul, Turkey. Ref. No. DH.I.UM. EK 84/9.

for Communicable Diseases, republished in the Beirut press in March 1915, mandated that all cases of specified diseases be reported within twenty-four hours to town or district sanitary authorities.[63] Medical attendants, heads of families or the oldest relative in the home, nurses, midwives, owners of rental property and shops, janitors or porters for apartment houses, managers of hotels and lodging houses, religious leaders, and the washers of the dead all now had the responsibility to report illnesses. Failure to report was punishable. As part of the project the Ottoman authorities set up disinfection stations along major roads and in some villages and towns. What exactly the process of disinfection involved in these stations is unclear. But the effort shows the urgency state official assigned to curbing the spread of disease among both soldiers and civilians. A sick empire after all could not win a war. Moreover, it is interesting that at times disinfection stations were housed in the same complex as soup kitchens, highlighting that health and food, disease and famine were inseparable problems.[64]

The health administration prescribed sanitary behaviors and routines, urging individuals to exhibit certain types of self-discipline. The authorities and medical experts knew the system relied primarily on informed and knowledgeable citizens. Medical experts in the region, like the SPC's William Thomson Van Dyck, proposed health as not merely the adaptation of a living organism to external conditions but the *conditioned* adaptability of an organism, as a whole, to an ever-varying environment. Health was not a static condition. Education and behavioral adjustments were essential in producing perfect health. Teaching civilians and soldiers the symptoms and causes of circulating diseases quickly became the top priority.[65] The public needed to be infused with an intimate knowledge of threatening diseases. Officials argued in local papers for everyone to know each disease's natural history, its sources and modes of infection, symptoms, and periods of incubation and infectivity. Educating the public was a practice proven successful in nearly eliminating smallpox and cholera as threats. Health officials thus initiated an education campaign targeting the individual's behavior. The public discourse displayed urgency for the need to forge individuals who saw their body, health, and disease in terms of medical epistemologies. The desired citizen was one who adopted hygienic practices ("disciplining their own bodies"), recognized symptoms, saw the obvious dangers of epidemics if not treated, knew the medical landscape of the city, and recognized the monopoly of the expert in defining disease prevention and treatment.[66] Most important, it would be the citizens who placed the well-being of the community ahead of personal attachment to infected persons, since isolation and quarantine often removed family members from their homes.

The military and civilian health and sanitation agencies began informing the public about typhus, cholera, typhoid, and malaria. Science journals like *al-Muqtataf* (Anthology) designated space for discussions of infectious diseases. The emphasis was on prophylaxis, which—as the articles point out—was much easier than treating disease.[67] The journal's primary audience, however, was medical experts, and its scientific descriptions and medical jargon made it inaccessible to the general public. To reach a broader audience, both the provincial and municipal health directorates published "advice" pieces in the local press to raise public awareness. These articles were meant for average readers and listeners; the authors—all trained medical experts—systematically avoided any medical jargon and limited themselves to the basics. Exemplary of advice journalism is an article from March 15, 1915, published in *al-Ittihad al-'Uthmani*, titled "Military Fever." Following a bout of typhus, its author, the Ottoman health director of the Vilayet of Beirut, urged "that the people must understand how the sickness is transmitted." Everyone needed to be "woken up to the seriousness of this disease." It was imperative, he wrote, to teach all people to protect themselves from body lice, the source of infection.

Members of the health commission and the municipal health department were prolific authors and diligent educators. But for the education project to be successful, it needed to move beyond print media because the majority of people in their districts were illiterate. The provincial health directorate ordered all available scientists and town officials to teach about infectious diseases in religious gathering places, markets, and other public places through lectures, publicly posted announcements, and organized meetings. The goal was to put everyone on highest alert.

Foreign medical experts contributed to the health and sanitation debates and the educational campaign. Before the war, a network of international medical experts shared their discoveries in journals, which were circulated across national borders. The international scientific communication networks were interrupted during the war, but at times embassies of neutral powers facilitated the exchange of information about new medical discoveries and potential cures.[68] It is unclear whether embassies in Beirut distributed educational pamphlets, but the experiences of German and Austrian medical experts and those of neutral powers were likely disseminated in the empire,[69] especially given that military sanitary reforms had been drawn up and implemented under the guidance of the German general Liman von Sanders, who arrived in Istanbul in late 1913 and was appointed inspector general to the Ottoman army.[70]

The faculty of SPC's medical school was eager to instruct a new generation of physicians and their students on the importance of hygiene of the body, home, city, and community. The predominance of diseases provided, according to the annual president's report, unusually good opportunities for their study of "especially typhus in the hospitals and clinics," the findings of which would then be shared with colleagues and passed on to the public.[71] In 1916, William Thompson Van Dyck published a bound volume of his lectures on hygiene. His intentions were to teach beyond the classroom. He thought this could be facilitated through his many students who volunteered in local soup kitchens and orphanages.

The Predicament of an Unfamiliar Threat: Typhus

Typhus was the greatest challenge. Although it was known in the region—an outbreak was reported in 1898—typhus was never widespread before the war.[72] The first serious outbreak was reported in the spring of 1915. By the winter of 1916, it had spread quickly in the district.[73] According to Mount Lebanon's health director, there was not one village or subdistrict without typhus.[74] The effects of typhus were continuously lamented. According to Jesuit priest Louis Cheikho it ravaged Beirut.[75] In 1917, Edward Nickoley pointed out that the situation continued to be devastating, as "typhus has been exceedingly bad. People have died in large numbers."[76] Statistics, although incomplete, sent by the *mutasarrif* of Mount Lebanon to Istanbul throughout 1917, confirm Nickoley's assertion. The report recorded 2,424 people as suffering from typhus in the months of March, April, and May. Thereafter, the number of infections declined; however, typhus remained the most notorious disease in all districts of Mount Lebanon from March to

December 1917.[77] Other less common diseases were typhoid, smallpox, dysentery, relapsing fever, measles, croup, cholera, and malaria.[78] Husni Bey, in a published report, estimated that 2.5 per thousand people had contracted typhus during the war, meaning that—with prewar population estimates ranging from 400,000 to 630,000—the number of typhus-infected persons would have been between 10,000 and 16,000. This number, although no more than a rough estimate since neither the report nor population numbers can claim accuracy, would in any case have been devastating in an area with limited medical infrastructure.[79]

A problem in the mountains was the unstoppable movement of the typhus-infected poor, who on the verge of starvation stumbled from place to place in search of food. The poor, in the health director's words, were the prey of this deadly disease.[80] In the city, the authorities warned citizens to avoid congested tramways, prisons, and hospitals, as these generally crowded places bred diseases. While typhus found easy game among the poor, it also affected the middle and upper classes. Edward Nickoley wrote,

> Our own community has had several cases, fortunately none fatal. Dorman, Chesbrough, Mrs. March and half a dozen students were all ill. Miss Shepherd has just come out of the hospital and Miss La Grange at Tripoli is down with it now. We were exposed to the disease everywhere. The body lice, which carry the disease, may be picked up at any time and in any place. We find them in our recitation rooms after a class has gone. Some of the students have brought them in their clothes. The latest discovery is that the beasts cling to flies and are carried about by them, another reason for swatting the fly. But you see there is no way of avoiding infection. The only thing to do is keep clean and well, this reducing the danger to the minimum, both of being exposed and of contracting the disease when bitten.[81]

The greatest difficulty in the fight against typhus was ignorance.[82] It was not a local sickness, and civilians were unfamiliar with, if not completely oblivious to, its symptoms and causes.[83] For example, a Beirut banker mentioned that "we did not know it before the war."[84] Unfortunately, medical experts and physicians also had very little experience with the disease. An eyewitness, who contracted typhus while walking the streets, complained of physicians' unfamiliarity with its modes of transmission as well as possible methods of prevention and cure.[85] The disease was referred to by different names, adding to the confusion. The public announcements in the press most often referred to it as military fever, whereas Husni Bey referred to it as freckle or spotted fever (referring to rashes that might accompany the disease).[86] At times, it was referred to as exanthematic typhus fever, lice fever, or army fever. The difference between typhus and typhoid fever was unclear to most.[87] Often even doctors were unable to distinguish between the two. On May 6, 1915, Beirut's supervising physician, Fuad Hamdi, clarified that typhus was much worse than typhoid. It was, in his words, a fever of the brain (as it was accompanied by severe headaches) rather than an intestinal fever. He relied on the publications from the health director, Hasan Bey Al-Asir, and the head physician of the municipality, 'Abd al-Rahman al-Unsi, both of whom had encountered typhus in Egypt and had written detailed treatises on it in the years leading up to the war.[88]

Cleanliness as Weapon: Soap, Water, and Bodily Hygiene

Second to typhus, cholera was the most frequently discussed disease in the press, in particular in the papers of the mountain districts. While cholera was more prominent in interior cities such as Damascus and Aleppo, it also made an appearance in the coastal cities.[89] Historically, Beirutis fled to the rural regions at the first rumors of cholera. But wartime food shortages in the mountain districts and the fact that the mountain was not exempt from outbreaks made it no longer the perfect escape. At times waterborne diseases like typhoid and cholera appeared first in the mountains and spread into the city.[90] In the mountain villages, most drinking water came from wells that could easily be contaminated and were more difficult to control and regulate. The use of potentially contaminated animal manure or human excrement as fertilizers in fields, gardens, and orchards meant that disease-carrying bacilli would easily seep into the groundwater.[91] On June 7, 1917, the editors of Mount Lebanon's official paper, *Lubnan* (Lebanon), made cholera front-page news. The focus here, as for typhus, was to inform the public about its transmission and symptoms and teach the best precautionary measures. The health director insisted that "perfect cleanliness is the best protection from cholera."[92]

The propagation of cleanliness was one thing, but its practical execution was a challenge on the most basic level. A soap shortage precluded adequate and proper bodily hygiene. The soap shortage in part was due to the blockade of imports, including sodium hydroxide, an essential component in soap fabrication, and the poor olive harvests in 1915 and 1916.[93] The cost of olive oil had doubled and stifled soap production.[94] By 1916, the price of soap had increased eightfold, making it affordable only to the wealthier classes. But cleanliness was the key in avoiding cholera and typhoid and, as Nickoley wrote, the "only preventive against typhus" since it would keep lice from multiplying. When there is "no soap and there is no fuel," Nickoley wrote, people were simply unable "to keep their clothes and their bodies clean."[95] Bayard Dodge warned that the "natural result" of the rising cost of soap was "dirt and disease" everywhere.[96]

The surveillance and inspection of water sources and swift government action at times were successful at reducing cholera. A report published in the *Lancet*, based on fragmented Ottoman records, highlights the lower cholera numbers in Beirut than in interior cities. From May 19, 1916, to February 14, 1917, there were only 64 cases of cholera in Beirut, resulting in 31 deaths; in interior cities such as in Aleppo, there were 2,020 infected and 1,203 deaths; in the environs of Damascus, 1,594 were infected and 713 deaths. Mount Lebanon counted 287 infected and 129 deaths.[97] The higher level of cholera in the interior cities, like the typhus epidemics, was the result of larger refugee populations living in unsanitary conditions and more frequent troop movement through these towns. The deaths from cholera in Mount Lebanon seem to have declined in 1917. The governor's statistics sent to Istanbul account for nine cholera mortalities from June to November.[98] Husni Bey, in his published account, ascribed the relatively small number of cholera cases to swift efforts that the administration set in motion at the first sign of illness.[99] But Husni Bey was obviously interested in reporting successes.

Inoculating the Public: Smallpox, Serums, and Syringes

By late 1915, the Beirut provincial GA expended some of its budget on public health. Much of its money would be spent on vaccinations.[100] Mandatory vaccination was a key preventive measure employed by the health commission. Through the Ministry of Health, the military issued circulars ordering all soldiers to be immunized against cholera, typhoid fever, and smallpox. The vaccination of civilians was dealt with locally. Smallpox, for example, triggered systematic vaccination campaigns in both Beirut and Mount Lebanon. The disease, endemic to the region, had caused much devastation in the past, but it had virtually disappeared; no smallpox outbreak was recorded after the turn of the century until 1915.[101] Its intermittent disappearance can be attributed to vaccinations. The first state-sponsored documented vaccination campaign in Beirut took place in 1861. A number of campaigns, organized by the municipality, in coordination with the central Ottoman Public Health Council, followed. Eventually medical experts insisted on childhood vaccination.[102] Vaccinations were made obligatory and heavy fines imposed on parents who refused or neglected to have their children inoculated. The municipality expanded its program by mandating school vaccinations, opening six vaccination posts in different parts of the city and soliciting the help of private physicians. By 1905, almost all Beirutis had been vaccinated,[103] but there must have been a lapse in implementation thereafter.

When smallpox reentered the region in early 1915, the Beirut municipality devised an elaborate vaccination campaign. After outbreaks were reported in Sidon, Damascus, and Beirut, the municipal health department set up vaccination stations. As in European capitals, poster campaigns and public press announcements accompanied the effort. The health commission warned people that vaccination was mandatory. Employees of schools, shops, manufacturing businesses, and other public places or offices who had already been exposed to smallpox and were thus immune were to obtain a certificate from their doctors. Everyone else had to undergo immunization within a month and carry a certificate attesting to their immunity. It seems that a single physician serviced the municipal vaccination stations. The health director published the vaccination locations and times in the press and posted them in public places. In the neighborhood of Ras Beirut the vaccination station was in the police station and was open during the afternoon. In addition, the municipality distributed free bovine serum to be used to vaccinate against smallpox to every hospital, school, company, and doctor, mandating a list of those vaccinated be submitted to the health department.[104] Some vaccines for smallpox, cholera, and typhoid fever were imported, but significant quantities were prepared in Istanbul, especially after the Ministry of Health expanded the number of laboratories to meet rising demands.

Wartime public announcements and constant reminders in the press of hours and location of vaccination stations revealed a new urgency in the face of smallpox. When cases were reported in April 1915, a headline in the local papers read in large letters: "Smallpox: To the People and Inhabitants of Beirut!" The article confirmed rumors that a Beirut physician had spotted smallpox cases in Beirut's Qarantina district during a routine inspection. The doctor found four brothers near the church of Mar Mikhail whose faces were marked with pox. In compliance with the Regulation of Communicable Diseases, he informed the municipality and began vaccinating the quarter's inhabitants who had not been exposed or vaccinated.[105] Faced with the threat of a smallpox epidemic, the municipal health directorate reminded the city's inhabitants of the directives included in the Regulation for Communicable Diseases, in particular its first paragraph, mandating the reporting of any infectious disease. Failure to report any suspicious illnesses would be met with harsh punishment of a monetary fine up to 15 Ottoman liras or imprisonment ranging from twenty-four hours to a month.[106]

Smallpox continuously resurfaced, to the frustration of Fuad Hamdi. Hamdi was an adamant advocate of vaccinations. For him the failure to implement childhood vaccinations had caused this crisis. In countries where everyone was vaccinated, he argued, smallpox was no longer a problem. He did not blame the people for being suspicious of vaccinations because they were not accustomed to the practice. The answer to his rhetorical question "Why is it that smallpox is not eliminated?" was that the Ottoman state did not "know the value of life." In what he referred to as civilized countries, the life of the individual was honored, but "we don't know how valuable every person is in our country."[107] This failure, according to Hamdi, was at the heart of the Ottoman disintegration and the already significant wartime losses. And when he compared the damage the disease had done to the Ottoman army (his exaggerated figure of 40,000 dead) to its effects on the German military, which he argued had not lost one man under the age of forty to this disease, vaccination seemed to be the magic bullet.[108] Unsurprisingly, Ottoman officials did not respond kindly to this accusation. During the meeting of 'Azmi Bey's GA, its president fired back, saying that municipalities were ill equipped to deal with complex public health issues and "that local organization of public health was detrimental" to the well-being of the cities. It was the fault of local incompetence, not a lack of care from the state. According to its meeting minutes, the GA then used some of its yearly budget to hire a number of health officers to help vaccinate people. The officers, the men boast, vaccinated "more than a 100 people" in a couple of months in the different vaccination stations set up in Beirut.[109] The work it seems was further expanded in the years that followed, in particular in Mount Lebanon.

Husni Bey eventually described a vigorous vaccination campaign in the mountains that included returning to villages multiple times to make sure everyone was vaccinated.[110] The number of vaccinated individuals increased, and Husni Bey noted that 88,973 persons had been vaccinated in his district by December 1917.[111] The available records from the Ottoman governor confirm the scale of the vaccination campaign. According to these reports, his health administration administered 57,900 vaccinations between March and November.[112] But still it seems no one was eager to be vaccinated, and the inoculation often did not work after its first administration.[113] What is visible, however, is the great effort from the side of health officials to expand disease immunity.

Creating Healthy Spaces:
Isolation, Inspections, and New Infrastructure

The public education and vaccination campaign focused on personal hygiene and the individual's body. To improve the health of the community as a whole, the sanitation commission devised a strategy of surveillance, inspections, and infrastructural improvements. The commission was to meet twice a week to discuss conditions in the city. Its evaluations and suggestions were based on daily inspections of all "public shops, streets, water places, depots, jails, public baths and grocery shops" carried out by the municipal health director and his staff.[114] At the heart of all suggested preventive and curative instructions was a clear separation of the sick from the healthy. The practice of isolation was not new. Benoît Boyer, a professor of therapeutics and hygiene at the French Medical Faculty, had already "proposed planning measures aimed to separate the 'healthy' from the 'foul' in the name of 'public welfare'" prior to the war.[115] Now with increased urgency, the committee mandated the isolation of the city's disease-infected poor. All those infected should be removed from private homes and placed in public facilities, hospitals, and clinics. The municipality offered free medical examinations and care in the Ottoman hospital so that family members would not hesitate to report their sick out of financial concerns.[116] While hospitalization was meant to be voluntary, the directive's language suggested that there was little choice. In response to the protest of some upper-class community members, who saw hospitals as dangerous breeding grounds for disease, the municipal health director was forced to make a clarifying statement in a local newspaper.[117] He wrote that admittance to the city's hospital was voluntary, while suggesting it was still the best option for those unable to properly take care of their sick.

Despite the great need, Ottoman officials were selective in who would take care of the sick. For example, abbreviated admission records of the hospital associated with the Greek Orthodox Society of St. George suggests a general contraction of hospital services.[118] In 1914, the hospital staff treated 28,132 people. In 1917, the number of patients decreased to 3,263. Despite the government's desire for poor civilians to be treated in hospitals, the municipal and Ottoman authorities did not extend any financial help to St. George, which would have assured additional hospital beds in the city. No direct reasons are given for the drastic decline in admissions, but shortages of physicians, pharmacists, and medical supplies surely were among them. Another reason might have been an overall fear of infectious disease. Beirut's papers suggested that crowded conditions made hospitals unsafe places. The fear was so prominent that wealthy community members continuously resisted the orders of the provincial health directorate to send infected persons to the city's hospitals. But perhaps most important was the Ottoman authorities' insistence on taking responsibility for the health of the population. The admittance records of the SPC's hospital also show a decrease in treated persons, which supports this possibility.[119] Instead of making sure to maintain the hospital, as in the case of St. George, the Ottomans undermined its work by increasing property taxes.

In general, the limited number of hospitals; shortage of medical personnel; closure and confiscation of existing hospitals, missionary hospices, and clinics; and restrictions on building new ones made hospitalization an inadequate solution. Beirut had only six hospitals in 1914, all of which were smaller than those in the European capitals.[120] Beirut's hospitals and clinics, like those in

Germany, were a mixture of public and private enterprises that combined held only a few hundred beds. In response to shortages and complaints, the committee advised wealthier families with extra room in their homes to isolate their sick and dying persons from the rest of the family. Infected family members should be separated both physically and socially, as food and drink were not to be shared. Interactions between the sick and the healthy—the crossing of the divide—were to be avoided and, if necessary, strictly controlled. One should not eat in the same room as the sick person because flies could transmit the bacillus from the infected person onto the food, nor should one share any food, drink, or cigarette with an infected person. The infected person should be placed under the supervision of a doctor, isolated, and eat and drink only from designated dishes that should be washed in boiling water. The feces of the sick should be mixed with water and Lysol—which could be purchased at the pharmacy—and left standing for an hour before dumping it in a hole far away from any well and then covered with dirt.

The isolation of the sick was thought essential to the creation of healthy spaces, and officials accused everyone who crossed the divide of immoral behavior. The medical experts singled out women, in particular, as polluting the community and the home. Fuad Hamdi scolded women for "flocking" to the clinics for unnecessary social visits. Women, in his eyes, did not respect the boundaries between the sick and the healthy and were transmitters of disease since they went out on visits and carried the bacteria home in their gowns and then transmitted them to their children and husbands.[121] Not only the physically sick were confined to particular places but also those who were "morally" deviant. In June 1915 the police chief ordered that all brothels should hang red gas lamps from their doors to clearly mark places of immorality.[122] The divide between healthy and sick, moral and immoral, became ever more distinct throughout the war.

Improving Communal Health:
Ordering Water and Waste Management

The higher frequency of waterborne diseases, mainly cholera, typhoid fever, and dysentery, resulted in a close inspection of water sources and monitoring of water consumption. Methods of dealing with infected wells predated the war. For example, following a deadly typhoid outbreak in 1895, Benoît

Boyer had suggested sealing all the city's water wells. Little or nothing, however, was done.[123] The idea was revived during the war. Husni Bey's report lamented that the frequent contamination of water remained an unsolved problem. His assessment of public health in Mount Lebanon began with an evaluation of water distribution in the region. He complained that many villages still relied on easily contaminated wells for their drinking water. In many of the coastal villages, people used cisterns for their water supply. In 75 percent of these villages, malaria was a recurrent problem in the fall months, when the water level would run low and containers turned into breeding grounds for mosquitoes. The health director urged people to drink little water and boil it before consumption or cleaning their bodies or food items. Beer, wine, coffee, and tea were deemed safe beverages.[124]

Diseased human waste was another source of possible water and food contamination. At times bacteriological exams of the water supply prevented outbreaks.[125] For example, in 1916, health inspectors found a military encampment set up too close to a spring, possibly causing it to be contaminated with typhoid bacteria. A bacteriological exam confirmed the fears of the authorities.[126] Public toilets, in particular, were a great concern to health officials. In early 1915, Beirut's health officials outlawed public urination and prohibited drinking from wells too close to toilet pits or from wells otherwise deemed unsafe.[127] In May 1915, landlords were given ten days to build toilets in their houses and make sure that filtered water would arrive at the premises.[128] Given the financial burden and the short time allotted for the improvements, many property owners ignored the orders. Senior military officers granted an extension but warned them not to ignore the orders. Anyone who did would be brought in front of the sanitary commission, fined, and still would have to build a toilet.[129] The health commission used the increase in waterborne diseases to propel the toilet into the private realm. The project was difficult; press accounts and penalties suggest that even months later the public toilet issue was not solved to the public health officials' satisfaction. A sewage overflow from one of the public toilets caused the health commission to figure that if they could not be done away with, they should at least be fixed. The solution was to have public toilets dug into the ground, as was the case in "superior or developed countries," done for the sake of public health and public morality.[130]

Public unsanitary behavior was an urgent issue, clearly indicated in so-called advice articles, as their tone suggested them to be much more than just friendly advice. The government's advice health bulletins included warnings that neglecting or not following sanitary suggestions would result in strict punishment. Regulations such as the prohibition against urinating in public or throwing garbage or dirty water in the alleys of the city were backed by punitive measures ranging from monetary fines to exile. The municipality instructed store owners and homeowners to place a closed bin at the threshold of their buildings to collect garbage. A municipal cleaning crew would then regularly collect the trash.[131] Violating the orders of the health protection commission could result in monetary fines or imprisonment from one week to a month, and, in severe cases, even exile.[132]

The health commission, in its public hygiene pursuit, often targeted the residences of the poor. On one occasion, the Beirut municipal officers gave the lower classes ten days to improve the appearance and cleanliness of their dwellings and surroundings. If they failed to meet the standards, the executive agents of the city's health government would seal off their homes.[133] We cannot say whether these warnings translated into action. But the intent was clear: the regulations were to order domestic and public spaces.

Rooting Out the Causes: Lice, Mosquitoes, and All Sorts of Dirt

The previous strategies were specific to waterborne diseases; preventing the spread of typhus demanded an entirely different strategy. Just before the onset of the war, scientists had discovered that infected body lice transmitted typhus. The disease's causative bacteria were unknown until 1916, and an effective vaccine was developed only after the war.[134] The only effective way of dealing with the disease was to eradicate its vector: the body louse. International medical experts had invented various systems of "delousing" (*Entlausung*). In Mount Lebanon, Husni Bey introduced fumigation and disinfection. He invented movable steam ovens, thirty of which were distributed in the mountain's designated health district. The wood-powered ovens produced steam that was directed over infected clothes and linens, suffocating the lice. Infected households had to send their bedding and clothes to the health directorate's cleaning station, where they would be fumigated. If no steam ovens were available, people were advised to iron their clothes, especially the seams.[135]

Sulfur fumigations of entire homes, practiced during the Second Balkan War, were unsuccessful in eliminating all the lice. However, Husni Bey—knowing that his movable steam ovens were not enough to service his entire district—continued to order sulfur fumigation, arguing it to be still a good alternative. It just had to be done correctly.[136] In Beirut, the municipal health director focused on publicizing preventive measures. Lice were found, the director warned, only on people who did not care for their personal hygiene, entered dirty baths, or worked in crowded places.[137] He advised Beirutis to keep their hair short, to avoid congested spaces, not to mix with soldiers who visited their shops and homes, not to enter or work in places infected with lice, and to frequently check and wash their clothing and bodies. If one became infected and washing did not help, he recommended a head wrap dipped in kerosene or oil for an hour. In any case, he encouraged everyone to keep a tin of naphthalene in his or her pockets and dust the skin around the neck, ankles, and wrists with it to keep lice at bay.

Malaria, endemic to the region, also had to be combated by rooting out its causes. Local physicians were well informed about malaria and knew how to avoid it. Husni Bey, for example, mentioned that sleeping under nets could easily avert infection. Unfortunately, few people did so. Prior to the war, mass malaria epidemics were generally prevented through quinine treatment.[138] The naval blockade, however, had depleted quinine supplies, and malaria deaths rose into the thousands.[139] Nabih Sha'ab, a well-known physician from the southern town of Sidon confirmed the increase of malaria cases in his district. When a particularly harsh outbreak of malaria was reported at the end of the summer of 1916, little could be done to distribute medicine. Beirut's "pharmacies were swamped with orders for Epsom salt and quinine" that could hardly be filled.[140] The municipality and the military authorities did their best to scrape up whatever quinine tablets could be found, and they had some success moving the infected persons to the hospital in the quarantine quarter of the city. An eyewitness recounted the German government providing some medical supplies in 1917, including quinine tablets, somewhat reducing fatalities.[141] The dwindling number of pharmacists posed yet another obvious problem. The few remaining pharmacies had limited opening hours, and some greedy pharmacists took advantage of the situation by overcharging their customers. The health commission stepped in by mandating a rotating schedule for the pharmacies and fixing the price of prescriptions. The idea was to ensure at least one open pharmacy at any time and to make sure no more than 11 piasters could be charged. It is impossible to say if this regulation made a significant difference in practice.

The municipal authorities focused their efforts on rooting out the causes, and government ordinances illustrate a concerted effort to eliminate dirt, mud, and stagnant water. The military authorities dispatched a cleaning battalion, made up of thirty soldiers equipped with shovels, cards, buckets, lime, and so forth, to clean the streets and markets of animal dung, stagnant water, and mud and to disinfect public toilets. As the military authorities, the health directorate, and the Beirut municipality decided on work assignments, some SPC staff members suggested employing poor and starving men to clean the city. The municipality welcomed the idea and set up street-sweeping crews made up of the city's poor. The Beirut municipality partially paid for the efforts, and additional funds were transferred by the American Red Cross to pay a small salary to eighty street cleaners.[142]

Finally, the military authorities and the Ottoman governor of Beirut set in motion large-scale infrastructural improvements. Officials justified these projects as improving sanitation and eliminating places that were associated with breeding diseases and stood in the way of a healthy city. Crowded markets and the residences of the poor, in particular, had to be eliminated. 'Azmi Bey was eager to improve the city's image. He argued for the repair of Beirut's streets, which would eliminate mud and stagnant water, to be paid for by raising taxes. He sold the project to the public as a twofold blessing: it would result in better streets and employ hundreds of workers, guaranteeing their survival.[143] A more controversial project was the construction of two boulevards, each fifteen meters wide, spanning the entire city. The previous governor had launched the project, and 'Azmi Bey took it up with great zeal. French hygienists and Beirut notables had proposed a similar project before the war, but the "chronic impecuniosity of the municipality" and the "difficulties in procuring loans had apparently stood in the way."[144]

The war was an opportune moment, and "by a strange irony of fate, these two streets have been opened up at a time of great economic distress for

Figure 7. Beirut, Ancient Street Architecture, Demolished 1915. Source: The Fouad Debbas Collection / Sursock Museum, Beirut, Lebanon. Ref. No. TFDC/CPA/Sarrafian/2/7717.

Beyrout."¹⁴⁵ The governor took advantage of the low price of labor and "the present conditions which simplified the putting through of public enterprises."¹⁴⁶ Observers noted it was "precisely because of this distress that such work has at last been undertaken."¹⁴⁷ The far greater power assigned to the office of the Ottoman governor—under martial law—meant projects like these could easily be pushed ahead, even if the public opposed them. Jamal Pasha, who had made improving the infrastructure of Greater Syria part of his policies, supported the measure.¹⁴⁸ The groundbreaking took place on April 7, 1915, in the presence of religious leaders, senior government officials, and city dignitaries.¹⁴⁹ To carry out the project, the government confiscated shops, homes, and warehouses standing in the way of this Ottoman vision of urban modernity. The owners and inhabitants of properties marked for demolition had three days to evacuate. Eventually 140 stores and 90 buildings were destroyed.¹⁵⁰ No one paid attention to the locals' protests. Instead, the project was sold to the public as a charitable project, as it employed and fed some of the most desperate people in the city.

Conclusion

Historians of the Ottoman Empire have shown late nineteenth-century public health efforts as exhibiting the beginnings of a hierarchical health administration. Local and state officials no longer simply relied on quarantine measures but attempted to keep their cities and towns clean through daily street cleaning; inspection of markets, stores, and places for food storage; and infrastructural improvements. In the aftermath of the Balkan Wars of 1912–1913, the Ottoman state absorbed many of these practices into the legal framework of the state. During the Great War, public health and sanitation became an increasingly interventionist, organized, and militant effort. State and local authorities worked together to create disease-free spaces and cautious, disciplined, and clean subjects. Still, the process of creating sanitary citizens, villages, and cities was thorny, particularly given the lack of the most basic hygienic and medical supplies, the resistance of people to advice of the health commission, and property confiscations and improvements.

In contrast to food, the benefits of health provisions carried out by government intervention in private homes and legislated changes to everyone's daily routines were, it seems, not immediately clear to its recipients. Increasing regulations forged a new social reality by inhibiting free movement, directing individuals' behavior, mandating the turnover of infected family members, and issuing advice that was patronizing and militant in tone. Those who failed to obey the health commission's orders were unsanitary subjects, and their bodies and residences "were subject to deprivatization," meaning that the authorities could inspect their homes, stores, and bodies at will and impose punishments. For Beirutis this was not completely new, but it was certainly more rigid and demanding, and for the rural inhabitants of Mount Lebanon it was unprecedented. Whereas the provisioning of food had the potential to fashion new loyalties based on who fed whom, the invasive nature of health provisioning made it a less competitive political space. The state needed local knowledge, the trust that locals had invested in their own physicians, and the local health administrators needed the power of the military command to back up their work. The state worked in society. And it was through the combined insistence of local municipal agencies and actors and the state that the provisioning of health facilitated a growing and increasingly militant state intervention in the daily life of civilians on the home front. There was nothing to gain but everything to lose.

Figure 8. Jamal Pasha's Visit to Syrian Protestant College, 1917. Source: American University of Beirut / Library Archives.

{ CHAPTER 6 }

LOCAL RELIEF INITIATIVES
Civil Society, Women, and the State

Sometime in early 1917, Ahmad Mukhtar Bayhum entered the house of his good friend Salim 'Ali Salam in Beirut's Msbaiteh district. It was not his usual visit filled with political discussions and, by now, perhaps sugarless cups of strong coffee. Rather, Bayhum came to see one of the daughters of the household, 'Anbara Salam. Many years later, 'Anbara recounted Bayhum asking her to give a speech at a meeting to be held in the house of the president of the municipality, 'Umar Da'uq, that same afternoon. The occasion was Jamal Pasha's visit to Beirut. The military commander had expressed interest in supporting local Arab women in organizing relief work for Beirut's starving women and children. The young woman, surprised and worried, remembered asking herself, "Could I possibly stand up and make a speech before Jamal the Butcher?" She wondered, "What was I supposed to say: Thank you for all the oppression and brutality against my people?" Uncomfortable with the idea, she begged Bayhum to excuse her, saying, "It is more than my nerves can bear." Bayhum responded by telling her that he was conveying the wishes of none other than the Ottoman governor 'Azmi Bey, who had saved her father from the gallows. He urged her to consider how government-supported relief work in the city "might save hundreds of women and children from certain death." He implored her to put any personal feelings aside, since her descriptions of the all-pervading suffering would greatly affect the military commander. Having seen how "death opened its jaws to swallow the starving who were dying in the streets, with cries of Hungry! Hungry!," 'Anbara, "dejected and browbeaten," gave in. Arriving at Daʻuq's house, she was ushered into the inner hall to join Beirut's most prominent women. The men—both civilian and military officials—waited in the outer hall for Jamal Pasha. When he entered, 'Anbara felt the earth "heaving beneath her feet" and "a shiver run down her spine." Here was the man who in her eyes could be blamed for all the suffering that surrounded her. Time passed in a blur, and moments later she stood before the room and delivered her speech "with repressed emotions almost bursting with rage."

After 'Anbara concluded, Jamal Pasha stood and announced his plan to sponsor relief work, including two new refugee shelters and a workshop for poor women. Beirut's leading women were to run the day-to-day business of these institutions with the government's financial and logistical support. Jamal Pasha then asked to meet 'Anbara, who had obviously made an impression. Surprised that she did not speak a word of Turkish, he suggested she call on his friend Halide Edip, who was visiting Beirut. Halide could teach 'Anbara the language of the state. In return, 'Anbara should teach Arabic to the Turkish feminist. Unwilling to learn what she considered the language of her enemy, even years later, or to engage with anyone too close to the pasha, 'Anbara apparently responded, "Our primary duty now in those days of war is relief work. We have stopped our studies in order to pursue that goal."[1] The young woman's encounter with the pasha highlights the politics of provisioning as a gendered process wherein the boundaries between the state and civil society were blurred.

First, it is clear from 'Anbara's memoir that the Ottomans' strategic assertion of power reached beyond official administrative bodies like the municipality into the benevolent space of civil society. Indeed, 'Azmi Bey and Jamal Pasha extended state power deep into the capillaries of society. Since legitimacy, in general, depends less on abstract principles or even the approval of those governed than on the confirmation of alternative authorities, the support of powerful social actors within a given community was essential.[2] Local elites were important legitimizing voices who could solidify or undermine the state representatives' legitimacy through confirmatory statements and social actions. However, in regard to leaders of philanthropic organizations that stood at the heart of prewar communal support, this was a tricky business. Before the war, local elites worked diligently to establish a new kind of charitable organization (jamʻiyya khrayriyya). These organizations were closely linked to religious communities but generally directed by lay elites. Their goal was to provide for the indigent of their city, quarter, neighborhood, or religious group. By the turn of the century, local elites and foreign missionaries dominated philanthropic activities in Beirut, expanding beyond traditional distributive charity. Through their work, including feeding, housing, clothing, and educating the poor, prewar civil society organizations solidified the power positions of secular elites in the city. The organizations themselves became alternative centers of power. Hence, their wartime actions, the continued provision of the destitute, even if claimed to be apolitical, neutral, or pro-government, could easily be perceived as emasculating the "father" state. Their work implicitly discredited the state representatives in their ability to provide for the state's subjects. Instead of securing their support, state officials challenged the local elites' monopoly over charity both as individuals and as leading members of local philanthropic organizations. The implicit goal was to disrupt patron-client relations characterized by a mutually beneficial bond based on giving and receiving. Any interruption in charitable giving would undermine this relationship, and where the patron failed, the state would step in. Now the patron only had to fail! Jamal Pasha and the Ottoman governor did their best to make that happen, hoping their reward would be trust, loyalty, and some stability in the provincial capital.[3]

The state's active strategy was to marginalize competing agents of provisioning. This chapter highlights the wartime experience of Beirut's philanthropic organizations, focusing on al-Maqasid, the Greek Orthodox Benevolent Society, the Society of St. George, and the Greek Catholic Charity Association. From the organizations' financial accounts, it is evident that the state sought to directly or indirectly incapacitate male-dominated local charitable organizations. At times the government denied its support, raising taxes; at other times it simply closed them down, confiscating the attached properties. Only those associations headed by CUP loyalists and by friends or acquaintances of the governor in particular could continue their work. But even with the blessing of the Ottoman authorities, their abilities to organize local war relief faced grave challenges, as donations decreased and their leaders left the country. The inability of male elites, whether due to government interference or wartime exigencies, to maintain their provisionary institutions contributed to what Elizabeth Thompson has called a "crisis of paternity."[4]

The Ottomans' strategy relied on a gendered understanding of the political, evident in the encouragement of female participation in state-sponsored relief efforts. On the one hand, the insistence on and sponsorship of female campaigns indicate an Ottoman dismissal of Arab women as serious threats to the legitimacy of their regime. On the other hand, to undermine elite (family) politics, Ottoman officials sought to draw women into the circle of the father state through volunteer work with the state-supported Syrian Ladies' Association (Jam'iyyat al-Sayyidat al-Suriyya) in Beirut and Society for Aiding the Poor (Jam'iyyat 'Awn al-Faqir) in some parts of Mount Lebanon.[5] The outcome, I argue, resembles what has been referred to as the war paradox. Historian Geoff Eley asserts that while a militarization of public life, meaning state intervention, including censorship, martial law, increased surveillance, and restrictions on movement, severely limited independent activities outside the purview of the authorities, the war opened a space for new voices. Total wartime mobilization legitimized the voices of those individuals or groups who consented or at least pretended to agree with national war aims and policies.[6] The recruitment of women into relief efforts closely associated with a patriotic discourse and government patronage, I argue, boosted Lebanese women's political self-confidence and instigated a politicization process that was not easily reversed after the war. This is not to say that women were not politically active prior to the war, nor were they uncritical of the regime. But as the account of 'Anbara Salam highlights, their participation in government-supported war relief situated them, albeit unwillingly, "into the consensus."[7] This should not come as a surprise. Scholars have cited World War I, in general, as a watershed moment for women, not only in terms of their entry, whether temporary or permanent, into the workforce but also in terms of female political emancipation. For Beiruti elite women, in particular, their contributions to the war effort formed the basis to legitimize their political expressions and rights claims in the postwar period.

Financing Benevolence in Times of War

Charitable giving in Beirut was not triggered by the famine; instead, it was and is an integral part of religious piety for both Muslim and Christian communities in the city.[8] The *jam'iyya* (society or association) of the mid-nineteenth century represented a move from local religious institutions overseeing charitable works to organized associations and societies committed to deliver aid to and raise public awareness of the plight of the deprived and destitute.[9] Beirut's urban elites founded associations dedicated to medical care, education, burials, and subsistence of the poor.[10] These charitable organizations' primary intent, besides curing physical illness, was to deal with larger social problems in an organized fashion, for example, by educating the children of the urban poor free of charge. It was a form of practical philanthropy. This, of course, is not to say that practical philanthropy displaced distributive charity as a practice. All organizations distributed material charity intended to help individuals survive a day at a time.[11] It also does not mean that earlier religious or state charity did not also include practices aimed at effecting long-term change in a person's capability to survive and perhaps even strive. What is important here is that distributive charity, in general, forges a continuous relationship between the recipient and the giver. Practical philanthropy, instead, aims to break this relationship by making the individual self-reliant and a "useful" contributor to society.

Beirut's charitable associations were "purely local initiatives" independent of the Ottoman state or its intervention. Some associations publicly insisted on their nonsectarian benevolence. In practice, their work was less inclusive. The Society of St. George, for example, pledged to provide free services to the city's sick regardless of sectarian affiliation.[12] A close look at the society's records, however, reveals that aid was mainly distributed to Orthodox Beirutis.[13] The same was true for the al-Maqasid and the Greek Orthodox Benevolent Society. Moreover, the social demographics of these lay voluntary organizations' leadership and the correlation of donations with religious holidays and ceremonies indicate not only their continuous sectarian characteristics but also a continued reliance on religious obligatory charity.[14] Other societies, like the Greek Catholic Charity Association, publicly expressed their goal as helping their own community's poor in Beirut and elsewhere.[15] What they all had in common was that their distributions were based on need. Aid was neither a right nor a defined entitlement allocated by the Ottoman state.[16]

The war presented a number of significant challenges. Most important, it affected the organizations' ability to maintain a steady income. Beirut's volunteer associations' income came almost exclusively from rental income, donations, and membership dues.[17] According to available financial records, their benevolent work was well financed before the war. Donations were particularly high in 1914. For example, the Society of St. George received donations amounting to 43,349 piasters from private individuals that year. The incoming funds were recorded either as charity collected on feast days and regular Sunday sermons or as donations expressing gratitude for the safe return from travel, a marriage, or a birth. Prominent Greek Orthodox families, such as the Sursocks, Trads, and Sam'ans, made the largest contributions. For example, the president of the society, Yusuf Bey Sursock, donated the largest amount (1,177.30 piasters) in 1914.[18] Community members often included the organization in their wills. The income from estates made up some of the largest contributions.[19] The society's hospital, for instance, received 11,038 piasters from the estate of the wife of Jurji Habib Trad.[20] The average donation, however, was much smaller, generally 20 to 30 piasters. Large donations from prominent families were not only exceptional but also hint at the community leaders' significant disposable wealth and the communal obligations associated with it.

The war disrupted the money flow, forcing the Society of St. George to significantly scale down its services despite the growing need for medical care.[21] The society's work in the first year of the war was saved by a large surplus (64,889.75 piasters), which it carried over into 1915. This surplus kept the hospital's doors open, despite the 83 percent decline in donations (only 7,474.20 piasters) and a 50 percent reduction in the income from the payments of wealthy patients in 1915.[22] The society's net income (not counting the budget surplus from the previous year) was only half that of the previous year's.[23] Donations to the Greek Orthodox Benevolent Society also steadily decreased. Its individual donations were comparable to those of the Society of St. George, as they reached 43,566.20 piasters, making up about 25 percent of its income in 1914. In 1915, donations shrank by 60 percent, an additional 17 percent in 1916, and ceased completely in 1917–1918.[24] Even bequests from estates, which in the case of the Society of St. George had replaced individual donations as the main income source, were few and significantly smaller than in prewar years.[25] Tuition payments from the society's six schools and donations collected during church services also steadily dropped.[26] For the Greek Catholic Charity Association, a society servicing a significantly smaller community, a similar pattern emerges. Here, too, 1914 was an extraordinarily good year, as the association's income from donations and memberships combined totaled 22,607.55 piasters, accounting for approximately 35 percent of the association's income.[27] In the following years, donations and membership dues decreased by more than half, from 27,768.15 piasters in 1915 to 10,678 in 1917.[28]

Besides donations, active participation and membership dues declined rapidly.[29] For both Greek Orthodox societies, subscriptions were zero by the end of the war. The yearly membership dues for the Society of St. George were 109 piasters, easily affordable for a wealthy family. Being a member, however, mandated active participation in its daily business. Even before the war, only a few men were either allowed or willing to make this commitment. In 1914, the society had fifteen paying members. Only five remained in 1916.[30] In 1917, no membership dues are recorded as income, but a couple of the original members continued to contribute. Yusuf Bey Sursock is a good example. No longer on the membership list after 1914, his name remained on the donor list. He donated 5,625 piasters as *ihsan* in 1917. Membership in the Greek Catholic Charity Association declined as well. Many of its wealthy members, it seems, had left the city, some had died, and others simply stopped attending meetings.[31] The association was unable to elect a new governing body between 1915 and the end of the war. Consequently, the committee elected in 1913–1915, with Nahla 'Awdah as its president, was never replaced. The committee tried to maintain its work but had to do so on a much-reduced scale.[32]

Fund-raising became increasingly difficult. In the years leading up to the war, voluntary associations organized public fund-raising events such as lotteries, concerts, movie nights, and balls. The Society of St. George organized a well-attended charity event, bringing in 18,859 piasters in 1915.[33] However, this was the last such event noted in the records. Overall, the war, although it did not eliminate fundraising events, meant fewer were arranged, especially after 1915.

Governmental Plays and Pays: Property Confiscations and Higher Taxes

Beirut's philanthropic societies, in addition to donations, memberships, and bequests, relied heavily on income from rental properties, registered as religious endowment (*waqf*).[34] Surprisingly perhaps, the Society of St. George's financial records account for a doubling in rents from 23,701 piasters in 1914 to 46,089 in 1918. The additional income came from properties purchased between 1916 and 1918.³⁵ It seems that the organization's leadership acted on good investment opportunities, using the accumulated prewar surplus. War exigencies pushed many people to sell their properties at low prices. The purchases immediately translated into a significant alternative source of income, as rents flowed into the society's coffers. However, the Society of St. George was an exception. For example, rents accounted for 42 percent of the Greek Orthodox Benevolent Society's income.³⁶ Its 1913–1914 budget accounted for 71,854 piasters in rental income. It is reduced to 41,210 piasters in 1914–1915 and 27,435.35 in 1915–1916.³⁷ The reason for this difference is unclear; one possible explanation could be property sales or wartime confiscations of the society's properties. The latter was not unusual.

The Ottoman governor's urban planning scheme, which relied on confiscations and forced sales, affected the Greek Catholic Charity Association in particular. When it was founded, Beirut's Greek Catholic Church leadership registered all of the church's properties as *waqf* properties in the organization's name. The Beirut diocese retained only those properties directly attached to the physical building of the bishopric. Most of the endowments were lands and buildings leased based on old rental agreements. The periodic rent increase was subject to government approval and improvements made to the properties.³⁸ The income to the association from rental properties was 36,473.25 piasters in 1914 and 21,201.05 in 1915.³⁹ The association's records show municipal confiscations of its most important income properties as the reason for the fall in rental revenues.

When in April 1915, the Beirut municipality began its urban renovation project, everyone knew any building along the two main streets would be demolished.⁴⁰ In the process, a commission estimated a property's value, taking into account its structure, attached land, and rental income. Everyone complained that the estimated value generally was much lower than the real worth. The city's authorities were to compensate the owners with special bonds, redeemable after a year. No one trusted the bonds because the municipality had a rather sketchy financial record, including its bankruptcy in 1913. Many Beirutis, much to the frustration of the governor, tried to avoid the usurpation of their property by simply not showing up at the municipal office to register their claims.⁴¹ Others took the bonds and then sold them at a loss of up to 55 percent.⁴² People's losses were staggering, especially since the money cashed in would often be used to purchase food and other necessities rather than invested. By December 1915, buildings worth 750,000 Ottoman liras were demolished, most of which were located in the city's business district. Many smaller businesses, now facing a shortage of rental properties and exorbitant rents, had to close shop.

The municipality appropriated fifteen properties belonging to the Greek Catholic Charity Association. Ten of the properties were religious endowments donated in the previous century, and five had been purchased from donations to the poor to increase the predictable income of the association.[43] Some of its most profitable real estate, located in the Suq al-Barzarakan, was confiscated.[44] In addition, it lost one of its largest stores in the Suq al-Attarin,[45] a store in the Suq al-Haddadin, a storehouse in the wheat port, two storehouses attached to the Khan al-Babir, six stores in the Khan 'Abdl-Salam, and three stores in the tanning district.[46] Consequently, the association's rental income plummeted well below prewar levels. And even more troubling, the suspect character of municipal bonds was confirmed: the association did not receive a single piaster from the municipality. Only after long negotiations with the French Mandate government did it receive compensation for lost properties in the 1930s. Trying to make up for the losses in rents, and given the growing number of people in need, the organization's leading members began to knock persistently on benefactors' doors, soliciting extra donations.[47] Their efforts failed, and donations continued to slump.

Arguably, the greatest stress on Beirut's philanthropic societies, besides property confiscations, was the state's heightened demand for taxes. Not surprisingly, the Ottoman government continuously increased taxes to finance its military campaigns, including taxes on private institutions. In January 1916, the property tax increased to 15 percent. According to press reports, the state not only required heavy taxes for the use of schools, hospitals, and land but also abrogated any previous agreements and exemptions.[48] For the Society of St. George this meant that its obligations to the state rose exponentially. In 1914, the taxes increased from 1,565.35 piasters to 4,035 and in 1916 to 16,565.15. Of course, some of the increase can be blamed on the purchase of a large property in 1916, adding to the overall tax assessment.[49]

The overall decrease in income and simultaneous increase in expenses limited nongovernmental organizations' ability to distribute charity.[50] Aid to the community rendered by the Greek Catholic Charity Association fell from 59,184.70 piasters in 1914 to 17,986 in 1917.[51] The association was forced to temporarily stop cash distributions to the poor in the autumn of 1916 because all its income from subscriptions and rent had to be used to pay taxes. The Greek Orthodox Benevolent Society's cash distributions also shrank considerably, from 13,813.05 piasters in 1914–1915 to 3,962.20 in 1916–1917.[52] The reduction in aid to the poor in the case of the Society of St. George is not as obvious. But from the decrease in the operating costs of the society's hospital by 50 percent and its salary payment, it can be deduced that free medical services to the community declined. At the same time, the Society of St. George responded to the most important emergency in the city, food shortages, and began to provide provisions to the poor. The organization invested in building an oven in 1916, and in the following years, expenses for subsistence were added to its everyday expenditures.[53]

Christian philanthropic organizations, although not outlawed or confiscated wholesale by the Ottomans, were progressively limited in their abilities to help poor Beirutis. Whereas both the Greek Orthodox Benevolent Society and the Greek Catholic Charity Association lost much of their income from rents and donations, the Society of St. George not only was able to purchase new properties, increasing its income to pay mounting taxes, but also to shift its work according to need. Although these Christian volunteer organizations for the most part continued to hand out money and food, their financial records indicate a sharp drop in the overall scope of nongovernmental distributive charity. At the same time the urban authorities created alternatives through rationing and distribution of food and government-run medical services. As a result, it is likely that more and more Beirutis turned to government-sponsored charity. For urban elites this posed a clear threat to their social position as benevolent actors and patrons of the community and, in turn, to their political power.

Power Politics and the Social Demographics of Urban Philanthropy

Being associated with or, even better, heading a private philanthropic association linked to religious leaders and establishments significantly bolstered the status of wealthy men. By being an active member of such a society, a wealthy patron fulfilled two of his important obligations: philanthropy and piety. Running a benevolent scheme might also cover up some less desirable political maneuverings in which a man of means might be engaged.[54] The fact that Beirut's charitable organizations were linked to religious authorities, with leadership positions sometimes occupied by clerics, meant that a lay patron could make "moral appeals to his supporters."[55] Keeping their society's doors open would solidify the urban elites' social position, especially as need increased exponentially. Comparing the leadership of those societies that continued to distribute aid, even if limited, with those that were shut down is telling. The ability to function and maintain one's position in the city's benevolent landscape was reliant on one's relations with the Ottoman authorities. Families who had close relationships with the governors and Jamal Pasha himself or whose patriarchs were ready to play a game of accommodative politics benefited from the war chaos.

A particularly interesting example is the Sursock family, whose wartime maneuvering illustrates an intricate web of political, personal, and patron-client hierarchies underlying Beirut society.[56] One's position in these hierarchies determined access to food, supplies and, ultimately, survival. Throughout the nineteenth century, the Sursock family consolidated its social status as a leading Beiruti family, securing considerable power and wealth as large landowners and international traders.[57] The family's impressive homes lined an entire street, named after itself, in the mainly Christian district of Ashrafieh. The Sursocks made their money by bidding on and winning state concessions. Their investments included local building projects, such as roadwork and the expansion of the Beirut port. This secured them the support of local clients, who reaped the benefits of urban improvements and increased employment opportunities.[58] As part of Beirut's commercial elite, the family's participation in municipal, provincial, and state politics was a given. For example, Alfred Bey Sursock was the secretary of the Ottoman embassy in Paris in the early twentieth century, allowing him to cultivate relationships with high-ranking Ottoman and French officials. The most significant connection, in terms of guaranteeing the family's political and socioeconomic position during the war, was with locally stationed Ottoman officials. It is well known that the CUP was eager to court wealthy urban notables, such as Yusuf and Michel Sursock, to strengthen its position prior to the war.[59]

While Michel Sursock was a member of the Beirut Reform Society, his actions indicate that his allegiance was primarily to guarantee his personal and family wealth. For example, in June 1914, the CUP government granted the Hula Lake land concession to him and 'Umar Bayhum.[60] In turn, Sursock offered his political loyalty, which proved to his advantage during the war. Members of the Sursock family also befriended the Ottoman provincial governor 'Azmi Bey, who became a frequent visitor to the Sursock mansion. Jamal Pasha as well was no stranger to the Sursock home. Antun Yamin remarked on wealthy Christian and Muslim families vying for the attention and goodwill of CUP officials, "showering them with gifts and invitations"; among those who catered to the Ottomans he listed the Sursocks.[61]

The Sursocks' connection to the Ottoman authorities in the city, their overall accommodating politics, and the fact that Jamal Pasha appointed Michel Sursock, an elected deputy in the Ottoman parliament in 1914, as head of grain collection and distribution in Beirut and Mount Lebanon in 1917, drew critique during and after the war. The Sursock family, rumors had it, were war profiteers. To many Lebanese the family's involvement with the Ottoman authorities was treason, which had contributed to the material deprivation of the city. The records leave little doubt that certain family members took advantage of their relationship with the authorities and the general circumstances of the war to expand their economic and social positions. Alfred Bey Sursock, for example, sought permission from the Ottoman authorities to build a horse track in Beirut. He almost immediately was given the go-ahead, helped by the fact that his close associate 'Azmi Bey was very fond of horse racing.

Why would anyone build a racetrack in the midst of famine and war? It turned out that this business investment, or at least the way it was framed, fit well into the Ottomans' development and "charitable" plan for Beirut and Jamal Pasha's overall plan for the cities of Greater Syria.[62] Marketing his project as an urban improvement measure, Alfred Bey Sursock argued that the racetrack, like street repairs and cleaning sponsored by the municipality and the American Red Cross, would provide work for the poor. And it did. According to a carefully crafted narrative of the family archive, Sursock employed four prominent engineers and a supervisor. A man named Ibrahim Hosni was in charge of the bread oven, baking the daily rations

Figure 9. Beirut, the Race Track from the Grand Stand. Source: The American Colony (Jerusalem), G. Eric and Edith Matson Photograph Collection, Library of Congress Prints and Photographs Division, Washington, D.C..

for an undefined number of workers. Alfred Bey apparently asked permission from his friend 'Azmi Bey to supply not only his employees but also their entire families. Each worker was paid 25 piasters per day and given a ration of about 300 grams of bread. The foreman received double that. Employment at the construction site guaranteed exemption from the military service. "And thanks to this," the family archivist wrote, "hundreds of families were spared the vicissitudes of the war."[63] Whether or not it was hundreds of families is unclear, since no detailed records of the building project are available, but it certainly guaranteed the survival of some.[64] But this is not the whole story.

The Sursock family was also involved in both Greek Orthodox volunteer organizations. This might have contributed to the fact that neither was shut down by the authorities. The Society of St. George, with Yusuf Bey Sursock as its president, survived the war intact although it did reduce its medical services. The society even added new properties and began organized food distributions. Besides contributing to the society's leadership talents, the

Sursocks continued to donate significant amounts, Yusuf Bey being one of the most prominent donors, throughout the war.[65] The society also received a substantial bequest from Catherine Sursock's estate. Some of the family's immovable properties even were registered as *waqf* to benefit the society.[66] The family's involvement in the Greek Orthodox Benevolent Society seems to have been limited to financial contributions.[67] Moreover, family members made sure to donate at public functions, in the presence of the Ottoman authorities. For example, Yusuf Bey Sursock donated one hundred sacks of flour to be distributed to the poor during a fund-raising event in November 1914. The Ottoman governor praised him as an example of good citizenship.[68]

As close associates of Ottoman officials, the family did not seem to present an outright threat to the legitimacy of the state. And the family, despite much criticism, was able to continue to service at least some of its clients and partially legitimize its position in the city. The family's good economic and political relations benefited only *its* clients, ultimately adding to unequal distribution of aid and creating distinct hierarchies of survival. Marco Van Leeuwen has argued that poor relief confirms the "proper place of the poor in a static and hierarchical society."[69] While I would argue against the characterization of Beirut's society as static, it was no doubt a hierarchical one. Being the recipient of food, money, work, or shelter placed individuals in a position of submission that would be difficult to undo, especially considering the extreme shortages. However, if the patron failed to give, that hierarchical order was upset or at the very least open to revisions and challenges. Charity was, and is generally, more often than not motivated by individual or collective self-interest.

The wartime fate of the Muslim charitable society al-Maqasid highlights a contrasting experience. Almost immediately upon his arrival in the province, Jamal Pasha sought to politically sideline the society's leadership by shutting it down. Before the war, the scion of the Sunni Salam family, Salim 'Ali Salam, was one of the society's most, if not the most, important patron. Salam too had prospered as a Beirut merchant.[70] The Salams were relative newcomers to the Beirut scene of notables but had risen to prominence, not least because of 'Ali Salam's work with al-Maqasid. Membership in and, even better, leadership of the association had political currency and allowed Salam, as its long-term president, to consolidate his power position in the city. In the early twentieth century, Salam directly challenged his competitor Ahmad Mukhtar Bayhum, showcasing his increasing power within the Sunni community. The point of contention was the community's choice of a Sunni delegate to the newly established Ottoman parliament and the appointment of a new mufti for Beirut in 1908. Both Salam and Bayhum were members of al-Maqasid, and their quarrel at times completely immobilized the organization. Once Salam became the president of the organization in 1909, solidifying his position, he made sure to court Bayhum, who became his closest political ally.[71] At the heart of Salam's mission was education. He and others founded two schools for girls and two for boys. Historians have described Salam as a strong-willed man who seldom compromised, citing his appointment of non-Muslims as the headmasters of two al-Maqasid schools because they were the most qualified for the job. This was an unpopular decision with the rest of the organization's leadership. According to the historian Kamal Salibi, "It was typical of Abu 'Ali [Salim 'Ali Salam] to act against strong objections." Salam's resignation from the provincial administrative council when Istanbul rejected the Beirut reform plan is yet another example.[72]

Salam's uncompromising character, it seems, put him repeatedly into precarious situations with the CUP and certainly did not endear him to Jamal Pasha. The war was an opportune moment for the Ottoman governor to suspend the work of al-Maqasid and place its institutions under state supervision. While I was unable to gain access to the archives of the organization itself, the secondary literature suggests that the society ceased all aid work by the end of 1914.[73] Although some historians suggest that the organization continued to exist despite Ottoman interference, it is unclear to what extent it carried on its work. The reason for the absorption of al-Maqasid and not that of the Society of St. George was, I believe, its leadership's political involvement in the Arab reform movement and its unwillingness to change course. Salam's political activities and his position in al-Maqasid meant that he was particularly visible to the Ottomans. Salam was a devoted Ottoman citizen and, not unlike many of his contemporaries, argued for reforms under the umbrella of the empire. Indeed, he helped found the Beirut Reform Society to, according to his memoirs, contain growing Arab nationalist aspirations and keep them "from running wild."[74] He portrayed himself as neither having sided with the younger men who eagerly joined the Decentralization Party in Egypt, which argued for independence from the sultan, nor as having been infatuated with particularist aspirations of Christian nationalists, advocating for an independent Mount Lebanon under the tutelage of France. He presented the Reform Society as his solution to bring both these groups together.[75] Before the war Salam, as a member of the Reform Society, the provincial AC, the Beirut municipality, the president of al-Maqasid, and one of the Arab deputies from the Beirut province in the Ottoman parliament, continuously lobbied for reforms.

While the liberal government under Beirut's governor, Kamil Pasha, entertained reform proposals from the Beirut Reform Society, the CUP military coup on January 23, 1913, marked a change in attitude. When the newly CUP-appointed governor, Abu Bakr Hazim Bey, arrived in Beirut, he summoned Salam and told him that reforms would be forthcoming but counseled patience. Salam and his colleagues decided not to wait. Instead, they sent their list of demands to Istanbul as they had planned. In a show of resistance, Salam refused to accept the renewal of his position on the province's AC.[76] Then Salam and fellow merchants resigned from the Beirut Chamber of Commerce, forcing its dissolution, and organized a boycott of the municipal elections, forcing the governor to make extra-electoral appointments. The reformers made running the daily affairs of the city and the province an administrative nightmare. The governor took revenge by closing down the Beirut Reform Society, which triggered a citywide general strike that only Salim 'Ali Salam and his friends could end. The leaders of the Reform Society went from shop owner to shop owner, urging them to reopen. It was clear that Salam was one of the most powerful men in the city.

By 1914, Arabists were perceived as a real threat to the integrity of the empire. A CUP official's report dated March 1914 alerted Istanbul of the Arabists' connection to foreign powers and their separatist desires. The report's author suggested a carrot-and-stick approach in dealing with the opposition. Some of them should be given government positions, and others "should be punished moderately, and the rest should be subjected to what the author calls persuasion."[77] The perception of Arabs "as self-seekers" among the Turkish elite was instrumental in shaping this approach. CUP officials, including Jamal Pasha, thought the men could easily be bought in return for prestigious posts in the government. He believed bribing Arabists to be necessary for the CUP's political line to be accepted among them. Intolerant of what he thought to be a "deceitful" opposition, he had little doubt that Arabists could be bought.[78] Upon his arrival in the province, he invited some of the more receptive opposition and gave them money. Not long thereafter, however, he began arresting Arabists, executing some, and exiling others. The central government for the most part approved of this apparently preconceived plan, which would be the basis for "Jamal Pasha's reign of terror."[79]

Salim 'Ali Salam was on Jamal Pasha's watch list. In the winter of 1914, Jamal Pasha summoned Salam to Damascus. The first meeting set the tone of their relationship, and not in a positive way, at least according to Salam. The tension between the two eventually appears to have contributed to the end of al-Maqasid. In his memoirs, Salam reported of taking the opportunity to advocate for the release of Nakhla Pasha Mutran and Asad Bey Haydar, whom Jamal had accused of conspiring against the regime and sympathizing with France. Writing in the postwar period and with the intent of countering criticism against him, Salam's memoirs are critical of Jamal Pasha. It is impossible to tell exactly what is true and what is invented for political reasons. But according to his memoirs, Salam told the Pasha that "it was politically advisable to have them released on bail."[80] Jamal Pasha would have none of it and instead made sure everyone knew who was in charge. From then on, it seems Salam tried to strategically avoid Jamal Pasha, which, while a good choice in theory, was not so easy in practice. The years of Salam's leadership in the reform movement could not be erased overnight. Although he rejected participating in any anti-Ottoman scheme, he continued to meet with individuals opposing the CUP regime. After another wave of arrests, Salam was summoned to testify before the military court in 'Aley. Salam insisted that he refused to testify but also was unable to convince anyone of the men's innocence. Convictions and executions followed. Of course, his postwar memoir would emphasize his opposition to the regime. He knew that an uncompromising anti-Ottoman politics, while dangerous during the war, would be beneficial in the context of postwar politics.

Salam recounted every encounter with Jamal Pasha as hostile in an attempt to position himself as a selfless reformer who challenged the legitimacy of the Ottoman regime. For example, after yet another uncomfortable meeting with Jamal Pasha in 1915, Beirut's chief of police is said to have knocked on Salam's door. The message: the fate of some political prisoners once again depended on Salam's testimony.[81] The police had come to arrest him. Salam spent the following days in solitary confinement in the 'Aley prison. Jamal Pasha himself interrogated him. Was the Beirut Society linked to the Decentralization Party in Cairo? It was not. Was there a plan of establishing an Arab state? "I know nothing about it" was Salam's recorded response. But he could not waste a chance to remind his readers that he was a reformer interested in the collective good of the community. Salam presented himself as saying, "If, however, you wish to open the subject of reforms, I am fully prepared to discuss it."[82] This apparently left the pasha furious, but Salam was sent home. It is impossible to know whether the military command could not prove Salam's engagement in any antistate dealings or if it was a calculated move to not stir up public resentment. It was rumored that 'Azmi Bey himself urged Jamal Pasha to release Salam to avoid public unrest. Salam's friends and acquaintances were not so lucky. Only a couple of days later, another group of Arab reformers, friends and political associates of Salam, were executed. Salam and Jamal Pasha had a third encounter in 1916, in the wake of executions of Arab leaders in Damascus. The conversation, according to Salam, took a similar course. He apparently brought up the notion of reforms, and the pasha turned away in anger.[83] Salam no doubt exaggerated his resistance and resolute insistence on reforms. In light of the execution of many of his friends and acquaintances, he most probably sought to redeem himself and reestablish his credibility as leader of his community. Salam represented himself as a defiant man of principles. It was, I believe, a calculated political move, especially since by then accusations of Salam profiteering from the war were publicized. He had good connections to Aleppo, and his family no doubt ate throughout the war. And his cordial relationship with 'Azmi Bey had not gone unnoticed.

It is difficult to estimate the real extent of Salam's contentious attitude. But so much is clear: Jamal Pasha must have felt threatened by Salam's power potential in the city and audacious insistence on reforms, and he clearly was annoyed by his ability to avoid giving incriminating testimony.

The commander's public order to close the philanthropic society signaled to the community that those who had cared for their needs in the past were now impotent. It would be the state, or the pasha himself, to which one had to look for care. Salam no longer stood at the helm of charitable giving to the poor of his community, a fact that he tried to remedy in his own account of the war.

The Alternative: Female Volunteerism

While Jamal Pasha and 'Azmi Bey worked to exclude some of the leading male elites from nongovernmental charity work and some preexisting philanthropic societies associated with religious groups saw their donations and therefore their abilities to aid those in need decline, the two encouraged a state-supported alternative, the Syrian Ladies' Association. This particular volunteer organization was not linked to one specific religious organization, it was financially supported by the government, and women staffed its leadership. Beginning in the spring of 1915, the association began to organize charitable work in Beirut. Led by upper-class women from all sects who worked through a number of committees, the association coordinated relief efforts in different neighborhoods. The privileging of female volunteerism through the Syrian Ladies' Association, I believe, illustrates the state's view of women as apolitical subjects. The Ottoman leadership in Beirut clearly saw female distribution of food, work, and shelter as unthreatening and incapable of inspiring divergent allegiances. This stood in contrast to the potentially "dangerous" charitable activities of men. The Syrian Ladies' Association became a substitute for the work of local male leaders and foreign philanthropists, both of which Jamal Pasha and 'Azmi Bey viewed with suspicion.

Scholars have evaluated women's experience of World War I mainly through the lens of their entrance into male jobs, their work as medical professionals on the front, and their contributions to the war effort as a vehicle to increased equality. The war's importance in accelerating women's entrance into the public sphere and making important gains in terms of political and social equality, whether permanent or temporary, cannot be neglected.[84] The literature on Ottoman women's wartime experience remains limited and generally has picked up the discussions of patriotic feminism and female emancipation initiated by gender historians of the European theater of war.[85] It is interesting to note the literature's tendency to separate women's philanthropic activities (defined as apolitical) from feminist activities (political). This is an artificial and flawed separation, since philanthropy clearly cannot be conceived "as an essentially unconcerned, uninterested purely apolitical field."[86]

The earliest work paying attention to Ottoman women during World War I is the account of Turkish journalist and eyewitness Ahmed Emin Yalman. Yalman, highlighting the entrance of Muslim Ottoman women into the workforce, argued for the emancipatory power of war.[87] Only decades later, Turkish feminist writers took up this argument, showcasing women's war work, which had been marginalized in the national memory. Deniz Kandiyoti's work describes women's wartime contributions as patriotic feminism and as part of a longer history of Turkish state feminism.[88] More recently, Yavuz Selim Karakışla has questioned Yalman's overly simple assertion that women's entry into the workforce meant emancipation, especially since, unlike in the European context, there was no real industrial labor shortage in the Ottoman Empire.[89] Thus, Ottoman Muslim women entered the wartime workforce in smaller numbers than their European counterparts.

Regardless, female labor is key to understanding Ottoman women's experiences of war. For example, women increasingly became subjects of state policies through the Society for Employment of Ottoman Women, women's war brigades, and the distribution of allowances to wives and widows of soldiers. In 1917, Minister of War Enver Pasha and his wife set up the Society for Employment of Ottoman Women, which mainly dealt with women whose husbands were conscripted into the military. The society's goal was not only to seek employment for women and teach them skills so they could earn their own living but also to mobilize women for the war effort. In July 1917, Enver oversaw the organization of women workers' brigades attached to the First Ottoman Army in Istanbul. The women were volunteers who, in exchange for working in agriculture or in road construction, received a salary, clothing, and shelter.[90] Through this and other projects, women encountered the state more frequently as they became the subject of its policies and regulations and more often entered into negotiations with government officials over their rights and privileges.[91]

The impact of the war on the home front in general and on the lives of women in particular differed according to class, ethnic group, and geography.[92] In the Arab provinces, women also became subject to state policies. Jamal Pasha organized women workers' brigades to labor in the agricultural regions of the Bekaa and Adana. In exchange, the Turkish press reported, women were supposedly given all they needed to sustain their families. The program was praised as a new step in women's progress instigated by Jamal.[93] Moreover, Jamal and his close advisers encouraged and financially supported urban elite women in organizing workshops for women in Beirut, which is the focus here.[94]

Faced with massive male conscription, food shortages, and an Ottoman crackdown on male opposition leaders, Arab women founded the Arab Girl's Awakening Society (al-Jam'iyyat Yaqzat al-Fatat al-'Arabiyya).[95] Besides advocating for female education, the society openly opposed all foreign intervention, including Turkish rule. The obvious political spirit of early female wartime social engagement was either entirely lost on the Ottomans or dismissed as inconsequential. For example, while women staged demonstrations against the regime mainly to demand bread, at least one woman was executed for political reasons. Rather than bar female opposition, the Ottoman authorities, it seems, appropriated the Arab Girl's Awakening Society's momentum and channeled women's participation in the public sphere into wartime relief.[96]

Government patronage of nonsectarian women's relief projects began in February 1915. The Beirut press announced that some of the "leading ladies" had organized the Syrian Ladies' Association "under the patronage of the wives" of Beirut's and Mount Lebanon's governors, 'Azmi Bey and Ohannes Kouyoumdjian Pasha, respectively.[97] Besides the governors' wives, the leading ladies came from important Beirut families. In the western—mainly Muslim—neighborhoods, the Bayhum women dominated. Najla Bayhum, with the help of the wife of 'Abdl Hamid Ghandur as the treasurer, was in charge of refugees. The wife of Ahmad Mukhtar Bayhum ran the second committee, the role of which is unclear. The young 'Adila Bayhum ran a third committee in charge of various workshops. As we have seen, 'Azmi Bey had successfully sidelined Ahmad Mukhtar Bayhum, the patriarch of the household, from municipal politics. At the same time, the governor had no problem approaching the Bayhum women as well as the wives and daughters of other influential families of Beirut to take the lead in wartime relief. 'Anbara Salam, the daughter of Salim 'Ali Salam, was also recruited despite her father's shaky relationship with the Ottoman authorities. 'Anbara Salam relates in her memoir that she only grudgingly accepted the assignment. She was critical of the Ottomans, and with good reason. Her would-be fiancé 'Abd al-Ghani al-'Uraysi was one of the men accused of treason and hung by order of Jamal Pasha. According to 'Anbara, the Christian women of East Beirut ran two shelters and a workshop, but we do not have detailed accounts of who was active in these committees or about the extent of their work.[98] A great part of the work seemed to have been funded by donations from the community, and the government made up the deficit.

The first report of any organized efforts coordinated and arranged by the Syrian Ladies' Association was dated March 22, 1915. Unlike any other private charity association, the Syrian Ladies' Association was guaranteed the state's financial backing and enjoyed the unconditional support of 'Azmi Bey. Beirut resident Bayard Dodge described the governor's effort in an unofficial report: "When he ['Azmi Bey] forbade the Americans helping his people he himself organized some of the wealthy ladies of higher circles of society and started many public charities. He arranged for nearly thirteen hundred children and women to live in hospices or to work in industrial centers."[99] To jump-start the project, 'Azmi Bey commissioned sewing work and placed 100 Ottoman liras at the disposal of the women.[100] The governor was intimately involved in the work and often came to inspect the various relief sites. To fill the order, the committee employed young women and set up temporary work stations in local schools. Small salaries were paid based on skills and productivity; for every one hundred bags sewn workers would each receive 7 piasters, about the cost of 2.5 kilograms of flour in 1915.[101] For every shirt or men's undergarment manufactured, the women earned two and a half coins—about 0.80 piasters.[102] Although the work was initiated with the state's financial support, the committee tirelessly collected private contributions in the form of bedding, clothes, kitchenware, food, and money. In April 1915, the association raised 23,615 piasters, of which 17,315 were used to pay the salary of poor women who had sewn 22,000 pieces of clothing for Ottoman soldiers.[103] 'Anbara Salam dated the initiation of the women's relief operations in Beirut to the end of 1917. However, other available sources suggest that the women were at work much earlier. Perhaps the 1917 initiatives were no more than an extension of the work under way since March 1915.

In 1917, the work of Beirut's women received the attention of Jamal Pasha, who insisted on transforming the Syrian Ladies' Association's provisional and makeshift workshops into permanent relief centers "to teach girls and women in the western part of the city various handicrafts."[104] 'Anbara Salam later remembered how shocked the women were when Jamal Pasha summoned them to a meeting in the home of the president of the municipality, 'Umar Da'uq, during which he outlined his project. It included the opening of a workshop and two refugee shelters, one in Muslim West Beirut and a second in the predominantly Christian east.[105] The military commander promised full government support and was prepared to provide "all that was required by way of housing, food, clothing, and so forth."[106] Heeding Jamal Pasha's wishes, West Beirut's women reorganized themselves and opened four refugee centers and two permanent workshops "for women and young girls, where they would be taught various crafts, given food, and paid a symbolic wage for their work."[107] The women eventually found themselves gathering hungry children from the streets or "from houses that had closed their doors, silently suffering from hunger, pain or disease for baths, medical exams, and lessons in crafts and reading."[108]

The women's wartime efforts were significant, and an indirect result, Dodge asserted, was "the encouraging of labor among Mohammedan women."[109] We do not have statistics totaling the number of women employed by the association, but 'Adila Bayhum's workshop alone is said to have employed close to eighteen hundred women. Beirut's women were not entirely new to working outside the home, but now many more young women under the tutelage of Beirut's female elites and the Ottoman authorities "attempted or consented to work."[110] Despite criticism of Beirut's wealthy women as being "unaccustomed to philanthropic work" and never having "thought of doing anything unselfish," the work seemed well organized. And according to Bayard Dodge, the women "gave most of their time and thought to the management of the institution" and proved to "be capable workers and saved hundreds of lives."[111] This war-inspired transformation in gender relations and labor, however, was unique neither to Muslim women nor to women of the Ottoman Empire. It has been widely documented that European and American women entered into employment in higher numbers as well and experienced similar socioeconomic changes during the war. In Greater Syria, as Elizabeth Thompson shows, the war worked to transform "the bourgeois ladies' charities into self-conscious subaltern movements."[112]

The association aimed to impart practical skills with the long-term goal of self-sufficiency. It focused not on distributive charity but on teaching impoverished women skills that would guarantee an income even after the war. Elite women, with the aid of the governor, closed the Ottoman school in the Burj Abu Haydar quarter of the city and transformed it into a workshop where girls and women learned various handicrafts. The work it seems was well organized: the committees assigned skilled instructors to small groups of women, gathered in separate rooms, to teach sewing, embroidery, and knitting. An additional industry established in this particular workshop was carpet weaving—the women hired Armenian master craftsmen, who taught the appropriate techniques and skills. The various products would then be sold to local wealthy families. Besides the workshops, the Beiruti women arranged shelters for poor and starving children.[113] The children were admitted into the shelter after being scrubbed clean, their hair shaved, and having undergone medical examinations. The children were instructed in elementary math and reading. An important aspect of the philanthropic work of the Syrian Ladies' Association and others was that it moved beyond helping the sick, academic education, and distributive charity that had characterized the prewar work in Beirut, seeking to teach practical skills that would provide income and self-sufficiency to the recipients.

In Mount Lebanon, the administrator of the Kura district, Yusuf al-Hakim, had a similar scheme in mind. When he was appointed to this position in 1916, he knew that food shortages were acute in his district. He blamed it on local and state authorities' inability to protect the people from the greedy war profiteers, "who appear in every moment of crisis to get rich." To deal with the situation at hand, he apparently set up committees in every town and village to aid the poor. Here, too, it was women who were to "collect donations and distribute them among the poor." If we can trust Hakim's account of his work, it seemed to help some. He himself described it as so successful that the *mutasarrif* thanked him and sent requests to other districts to establish such work.[114]

Besides the collection and distribution of funds, Hakim established orphanages in the mountains. One he described in detail is the orphanage at Anfeh, which was housed in a local school that had been closed because of the war. He financed his project by appealing to both local philanthropists and the *mutasarrif*. Once he had secured the funds, local "ladies and young women" took over the everyday work at the institution. Hakim described their efforts in dealing with the half-naked people as filled with compassion and "kindness that was similar to that of a mother to their babies and sisters to their little sisters." A local doctor was asked to ensure that the children were healthy. Within a month, the number of children housed in Anfeh exceeded one hundred. This, Hakim noted, was the point when a more secure income was needed, and he hoped for a permanent commitment from the *mutasarrif*. The way he framed his appeal is telling. He warned the governor about what the closure of the orphanage would do to the people's confidence in the compassion of the Ottoman government. It was clear to Hakim, as it was for others, that providing safety and shelter for the most vulnerable members of the community would elevate the officials in the eyes of what was seen to be a suspicious population.[115] The well-known orphanage at Aintoura is another example of an institution set up by the Turkish state representatives in Mount Lebanon.[116]

Conclusion

Only a few studies of World War I have paid attention to local relief efforts.[117] The focus has generally been on international humanitarian efforts, like that of the Red Cross or, in the case of the Middle East, the Near East Relief. What is often forgotten is that these international agencies worked in a crowded field of existing or impromptu local organizations dedicated to servicing those in need. In Beirut and Mount Lebanon, it was a gendered and politically charged field that highlights the work of the state in society. The ability to distribute relief and render charity was not based on one's sect, as it often has been argued, but on position in regard to power and, in this case, gender. Religion was not the determining factor for survival. Access to food was dependent on whether one's patron was willing to accommodate the Ottomans' assertion of power. Government officials actively sidelined male competitors, especially those men who were perceived as continuously challenging the state to implement reforms that would relocate power to the provinces. Others who were willing to compromise, even if only pretending to, or were willing to work on levels below that of state officials were rewarded. The reward included noninterference with their organized charitable ventures, meaning that their position in the social hierarchy of giving and provisioning could potentially be maintained. Of course, they still encountered difficulties generated by wartime exigencies. Out-migration, food shortages, price hikes, and higher taxes, although not independent of state politics, affected the daily activities of the organizations in the city. Ottoman officials made little effort to help private charitable associations overcome these difficulties; indeed, it seems that the officials welcomed the demise of these associations. At the same time, the government actively worked to challenge the order of things in the city to take up its place in the hierarchy of giving. Jamal Pasha and 'Azmi Bey closed the organizations run by those they considered competitors or curbed their power by insisting on additional taxes, while at the same time they moved to support associations they saw as apolitical, such as those of women.

Figure 10. Children Waiting in Front of the 'Abeih Soup Kitchen. Source: American University of Beirut / Library Archives.

{ CHAPTER 7 }

BENEFICIAL BENEVOLENCE

International Wartime Relief Efforts

In the midst of devastation, hunger, and starvation, an unnamed woman climbed the steep mountain paths, hope for life pushing her onward to her destination, the American soup kitchen in Brumana. Alongside her, a small group of children dragged their feet, complaining of hunger and exhaustion. After hours of staggering, pulling, and pushing, the ragged band reached a little brook. There the children collapsed at the side of the water. None of them had eaten a square meal for days, and they cried bitterly, refusing to go on. Squatting and contemplating her course of action, the woman noticed her eldest daughter's old doll. It was the little girl's prized possession and almost all that they had left in the world, a reminder of a different time. A small tear in the doll's body left some bran trickling from its stuffing, something the eyes of a starving person would not overlook. With a mother's wit, the woman emptied the doll of its stuffing. She softened the bran with water and made little cakes in her hands. "It was not much for them to eat, but it was something. Cheered by the taste of wet bran, they went on their journey, until they finally arrived at the soup kitchen tired, but courageous."[1] The woman begged for all her children to be accepted into the shelter, and she herself took on work as a seamstress. Not all families were this fortunate. But arriving at the American soup kitchen meant a meal, if not life, for at least some.

International war relief and American humanitarian work in the eastern Mediterranean during World War I have received much attention in recent years. Keith Watenpaugh has argued that the work of international agencies in former Ottoman territories in the postwar period was instrumental in birthing modern humanitarianism in theory and practice.[2] Shifting the focus to the war and local politics of provisioning, I argue, highlights the messy struggle on the ground that predated and contributed to gradual secularization, professionalization, and bureaucratization of international relief that would mark the interwar period. The spotlight here is directed on war relief rendered by international agents, who had direct experience with the famine's inhumanity and, due to their diplomatic relations with the Ottomans, had continued access to its victims. American and German diplomats and missionaries and German military officials witnessed, recorded, and responded to the local suffering based on their political position in the empire and the international context of World War I.

In general, foreign relief workers and government officials believed humanitarian work as having the great potential of advertising the benevolence and goodwill of their nations to local populations. At the same time, they were equally sensitive to the Ottomans' dismissals and critiques of any aid work as "simply for purposes of propaganda" and of the potential difficulties they could face if their work could be accused of having the slightest hint of a political purpose. Consequently, men like the American philanthropist Bayard Dodge insisted on the separation of humanitarianism and politics. As a long-term resident of Beirut, he expressed his hope that any nonphilanthropic business the United States might have in the region would be kept separate, unless "one may help the other."[3]

The German government overall was a latecomer to the Ottoman Empire. While German missionaries, diplomats, and entrepreneurs were working to expand Germany's presence prior to the war, their influence, especially in Beirut and Mount Lebanon, could not be compared to that of France, Britain, and even Russia. Besides the German consulate in Beirut and a small number of institutions run by German Catholic and Protestant missionaries, a few German merchants and hoteliers had made the city their home. The Turko-German wartime alliance sparked a debate in diplomatic circles about the role of Germany in the Ottoman Empire during and after the war. Among German officials, there was a clear desire to expand their government's influence in the empire. However, opinions about how this was to be accomplished differed significantly. The possibility for distribution of German relief to victims of starvation was entangled in this debate. Initially German government and military officials stationed in Beirut abstained from instigating large-scale relief projects in an attempt to avoid accusations of ulterior colonial motives. Sensitive to the CUP's desires to rid the empire of European paternalism, German officials urged no or small-scale relief work, so as not to irritate their allies. Any suggested efforts were carefully weighed and supported only if Germany could not be accused of meddling in the empire's business. At the same time, officials thought it imperative to establish positive attitudes toward Germany on the ground to benefit their government's imperial and economic ambitions after the war. War relief would help in this regard.

International actors' strategies concerning how and when to engage in relief efforts were also informed by local politics. Both American and German efforts on the ground were subject to internal divisions. Missionaries, educators, diplomats, and military officials had different priorities. In the American case, some acquiesced when Ottoman officials, questioning the effort's neutrality, ordered an end to relief work in Beirut, but others defied the order. Opposition or support among Germans for war relief was based on immediate wartime experiences on the ground versus long-term imperial desires, respectively. This diversity in opinion, at the very least, forces us to question the familiar and overly general interpretations of humanitarian aid as being either purely philanthropic or an imperialist scheme.[4] Instead, humanitarian and political actors were not simply uncomfortable bedfellows; they were more often than not the same person, who had to mediate between local and international desires and humanitarian sentiments.[5]

Organizing and Funding American Relief

Well-organized and well-financed relief efforts during and after World War I played an important role in situating the United States as a benevolent Great Power neither driven by imperialist desires nor covetous of Ottoman resources and lands. Indeed, as Ussama Makdisi writes, "Never has the star of America shone so brightly in the Arab world as it did during the First World War."[6] While internationally after April 1917 this perception was largely attributed to President Woodrow Wilson's promise of self-determination, which stood in stark contrast to European imperial ambitions in the region, American philanthropists' relief efforts were instrumental in painting a similar picture on the local level years earlier. In December 1914, American residents of Beirut inaugurated a concerted relief effort, since "the winter has only fairly begun, but already there is great suffering among not only the very poor but those who have been ordinarily in fair circumstance."[7] A group of American educators, missionaries, and diplomats began to aid those in need through the existing administrative apparatus of the five-year-old chapter of the American Red Cross (ARC) in Beirut.[8] The community set up a committee and elected a local executive body. The American consul Stanley Hollis was elected president; Professor James Alfred Patch from the Syrian Protestant College, vice president; and Charles A. Dana, manager of the American Mission Press, treasurer. Three additional members associated with the SPC were elected to the executive committee: Bayard Dodge, Mary Dale Dorman, and the wife of Harold G. Nelson.[9] The executive committee's initial composition exemplified a cooperative spirit among resident Americans for alleviating hunger.

Funding for the work came from diverse sources. Donations from "numerous friends in Turkey," who were "coming generously forward with their offers of assistance," met some of the need.[10] In late December 1914, the committee organized a large fund-raiser for "the poor people" near the American college.[11] Various college clubs raised money for relief by putting on festivities, often inviting high Ottoman officials.[12] The largest support, however, came from abroad. In late 1914, ARC headquarters in the United States furnished the Beirut chapter with $15,000 donated by American religious organizations, relief societies, and private individuals.[13] For example, the Presbyterian Mission collected $1,136 and sent it to Beirut "for Relief through the Red Cross."[14] Howard Bliss, president of the SPC, solicited funds from wealthy donors such as the Rockefeller family. He wrote to the family's financial adviser, Starr Murphy, describing the devastation in Syria: "Local resources are very small," and while the "well-to-do people of Beirut will do their part in meeting the need, the demands will be much greater than the local supply of funds can meet." "Even with the Red Cross in America donating ten thousand dollars," Bliss warned, "the need in Syria will far exceed the limits of such amount." Bliss urged Murphy to consider including Syria in the "generous aid, which Mr. Rockefeller is extending."[15]

The Rockefellers eventually contributed to the cause and encouraged their wealthy friends to do the same.[16] For two years, the ARC sent money to Beirut, donating a total of $33,641.55.

The ARC provided a start-up fund and the necessary organizational infrastructure, but most of the committee's funds and logistical support came from newly organized societies in the United States. In September 1915, American ambassador Henry Morgenthau issued an urgent appeal to help victims of war and survivors of the systematically organized genocide against Ottoman Christians (mainly Armenians) in Anatolia. In response, a group of American philanthropists formed the Committee for Armenian Relief (later changed to American Committee for Relief in the Near East), bringing together politicians, journalists, and prominent philanthropists from various religious backgrounds, most of whom had personal ties to the Near East.[17] By the end of the year, the men added committees to solicit funds for relief work in Persia, Syria, and Palestine. The Palestine-Syrian Relief Committee immediately organized a fund-raising campaign to mitigate the "distress conditions among the civilian population in Syria."[18] The committee united with the Armenian Relief Committee to become the American Committee for Armenian and Syrian Relief (ACASR) in November 1915.[19] ACASR had the full support of the American government and would work closely with the US State Department and its diplomatic corps in the empire.

Officially, the American government denied any part in relief work in the empire. But in reality, this division of state policies and humanitarian work was a farce. Cleveland Dodge, an industrial magnate, philanthropist, president of ACASR, and father of Bayard Dodge, was President Wilson's close friend and former classmate. He most certainly had the ear of the president. ACASR benefited from this relationship. Wilson opened State Department files for the committee to view information on the situation in the Ottoman Empire, and Secretary of State Robert Lansing was seen continuously intervening on behalf of ACASR nationally and internationally.[20] By fall of 1916, ACASR was collecting and administering much of the relief in the Ottoman Empire, replacing the ARC, which increasingly focused its energy on the European front. The ACASR's fund-raising efforts were impressive. By 1917, it had raised more than $2 million. Taking into account the postwar years, the total funds "collected and administered by ACASR was over 116 million dollars."[21]

Relief Work and Politics of Neutrality

The Beirut executive committee used its funds for two purposes: the organization of a medical expedition to accompany the Ottoman army during the first Suez Campaign and the establishment of local relief committees to deal with the "distress among the civilian population."[22] During one its first meetings, the executive committee decided that it should "offer some assistance to the wounded during the war."[23] It not only offered the Ottoman military command the free treatment of wounded soldiers at the hospital associated with the SPC but also proposed organizing medical services on the Ottoman battlefront. The underlying motive of serving the Ottoman military, despite a guise of neutrality, was to garner the goodwill of the Ottoman state; it was a strategic decision, exemplifying the committee's wartime politics of neutrality. More specifically, since faculty and staff associated with the SPC dominated the committee, its actions were dictated by the college administration's needs and concerns. Its basic dictate: relief work was not to endanger the existence and business of the college. Having witnessed the expulsion of their French, British, and Russian colleagues and the confiscation of their properties, Howard Bliss wrote to Cleveland H. Dodge:

> We can still hardly believe the facts, that the French schools have been confiscated; ... that the proud new and beautiful buildings of the French School of Medicine are being stripped of their equipment and are themselves in the keeping of the Ottoman authorities; that the French Hospital here has likewise been taken over by the Turkish Government![24]

Fearing the same fate, Howard Bliss and Edwin Ward, professor of surgery, presented their offer for a medical relief campaign to the German consul and Beirut's governor, Bekir Sami Bey. The response was positive, but approval had to come from Jamal Pasha himself. Hence, Ward traveled to Damascus to confer with the commander. Ward made three points at the meeting. First, he assured Jamal Pasha that the Beirut ARC committee was ready to provide a group of medical professionals to accompany him to the front. Second, in return he requested permission for three British professors employed by the SPC to remain in the empire.[25] Third, he expressed the desire to have SPC students accompany the mission.[26] Jamal Pasha welcomed the idea, especially since the Ottoman military struggled to provide adequate medical services to its soldiers.[27] He accepted Ward's conditions.

Subsequently, the Beirut committee began organizing the mission. A call for student volunteers resulted in a list of twenty-eight Armenian and Arab senior classmen from the Departments of Medicine, Pharmacy, and Dentistry.[28] The committee voted that all senior "students in Medical and Pharmacy Departments be held for Red Cross work."[29] Faculty members Naimeh Nucho, a pathologist, Atman Saadeh, and Atiyeh volunteered to assist Ward in his role as head surgeon. On January 4, 1915, the committee asked Reverend George C. Doolittle from the American Mission stationed in Sidon to join the expedition as its associate director.[30] Doolittle, with "his knowledge of Arabic and with his long experience as a touring missionary," would be able "to care for the many practical problems that will arise."[31] Four German nurses from the Kaiserswerth Diocese and two graduates from the SPC Nurses Training School, a Miss Akabir and a Miss Nezha, joined

Figure 11. SPC Red Cross Expedition to the Station at Auja al-Hafir, 1915. Source: American University of Beirut / Library Archives.

the mission as well. The last people added were Yusuf Kenen, as the "mission's native agent," and three cooks.³²

The Beirut committee provided tents, beds, medical equipment, surgical supplies, and food.³³ The Ottoman governor issued blankets and mattresses. Some supplies that were not otherwise available—including rice, sugar, and coffee—were purchased from the municipality. Jamal Pasha assured Ward, during the latter's visit to Jerusalem, of the "unstinted support" of the Ottoman military. According to Ward's report of the meeting, the military had access to all possible medical and surgical equipment, and he was promised "transportation, supplies, untrained servants, and armed guards." It even had sugar, wood, petroleum, and soap stored, all commodities that were in short supply on the open market.³⁴ The expedition was eventually equipped with a fully functioning operating tent and supplied with a three-month supply of medicine.³⁵ The day before the mission set out into the desert, the committee, in a public show of American neutrality and commitment to humanitarian causes, set up the tents and equipment on the college ground. "Many people from the city" came to see them.³⁶

The Ottomans, it seems, were not entirely convinced of the purely humanitarian motives of the mission. A high-ranking Ottoman medical staff officer reminded Ward that the mission needed to wear the Red Cross insignia so they would "not be molested," and it was bound to the norms and practices of the International Committee of the Red Cross (ICRC). All personnel had to wear armbands with both the Red Cross and the Red Crescent emblem on them.³⁷ The Red Cross stencil had to be put on all boxes, tents, bundles, and packages. The mission would need to "fly the Red Cross flag, and will be protected in this."³⁸ Absolute neutrality was imperative. To assure the mission's adherence, a Turkish doctor and a scribe were to accompany the Americans and issue reports to the government. A military commander and twenty-five soldiers were assigned as guards for the mission.

Jamal Pasha ordered the American mobile unit to be stationed near the planned battlefront in the Sinai desert, about a "day's ride from Beersheba." The mission's organizers expected their hospital would be "the most important" medical station "in the southern district and would receive all the wounded that could be brought from Akaba and Suez" for treatment and eventual transfer to the government hospital in Beersheeba.³⁹ However, when the expedition returned on March 27, 1915, it had treated only about two hundred patients. Few made it to their station. "Those that escaped the British bullets succumbed to disease and starvation," and others simply got lost in the desert.[40]

The Americans' medical aid on the Ottoman front and in their hospital was motived both by a genuine humanitarian desire to help those in need and local political aspirations aimed at earning favor with the Ottoman authorities. From its conception, the medical mission was framed as contingent on the Ottomans' willingness to fill the SPC's demands. Pressing Jamal Pasha, it was successful in retaining British medical faculty in Beirut and "enabled not a few students—liable to military service—to postpone this service until the end of the year."[41] Yusuf Rawda, a fourth-year medical student, for example, was released from military service to join the Red Cross mission. Overall, the SPC's administration believed the medical missions had fostered a "sympathetic attitude of the army officials" toward the Americans.[42]

German nurses also participated in the mission. The Central Powers' mobilization effort included a general call for nurses to work in field hospitals. The Kaiserswerth deaconesses, who had worked in Beirut since the 1860s as educators, missionaries, and nurses, were eager to join this call. On November 10, 1914, the congregation's administrative center, referred to as the Mutterhaus, in Kaiserswerth received a telegram from Sister Anna Zorn, the head nurse at the Johanniter hospital in Beirut, asking for permission to send a number of her sisters with the Red Cross mission to care for wounded Turkish soldiers. The Mutterhaus agreed as long as they were not needed in the hospital.[43] A lottery decided that Sisters Sophie Wemuke and Luise Hanike would travel to Beersheba accompanied by Sister Lina Knüsermann, who spoke good Turkish. Sister Hanna Mayer was freed from her duties in the Zoar orphanage to join the desert sisters. This was not the only mission. German missionaries continued to volunteer as nurses. For example, in 1916, another delegation of German nurses was sent to Beersheba. Others volunteered locally in a military hospital in 'Aley under the supervision of a German physician. Caring for wounded Ottoman soldiers, the women claimed their way to "at least indirectly serve the Fatherland."[44] The aid campaigns to the battlefronts were international affairs and worked to curry favor with the Ottoman government, but rendering relief to civilians was a much more controversial issue.

Civilian Relief in the City

In January 1915, the Beirut executive committee initiated its civilian relief efforts "to help the pathetic people of the city."[45] Three departments were to address the various needs: employment, distribution of food, and assisting families of Ottoman soldiers in "obtaining from the government the promised allowance for support."[46] The committee investigated local needs, appointed subcommittees (which could include native volunteers), and administered all funds. To facilitate the work, the committee divided the city into twelve "relief districts" and staffed them with native volunteers, supervised by American women from the SPC or Protestant missionary community.[47] All donations were equally distributed among these districts. SPC student volunteers kept track of applications.[48] Five or six of the districts and the employment office for women of the northern city districts were controlled from a large college dormitory building located across the tramline from the college gate.

Word that the Americans were distributing money, food, and work spread in the city. Between the months of January and August 1915, the main office handled about fifteen hundred new applications a month. In February 1915, Dodge reported that in one week about four hundred cases had been dealt with by the relief station near the college and approximately the same number in the relief stations in the city proper.[49] Each day, Dodge wrote, "we see as many women as time allows for, which must average about sixty [per day], for our half of the city alone."[50] At the headquarters, senior committee members checked the applicants' residency and pointed them toward their district's waiting room or sent them to the correct office elsewhere in the city. Generally, student volunteers would stand at the entry holding back the crowd and assist in prescreening the hungry.

To avoid fraud, all applicants were investigated to ensure their need. No one was helped until visited or thoroughly looked into. American female volunteers, assisted by SPC students, scrutinized claims of destitution to record "statistics about the women and give them work or flour, if they deserved."[51] The committee encouraged home visits to ensure the veracity of claims and the appropriate use of money and flour. Moreover, a proactive "investigation committee" staffed exclusively by American women surveyed the city, assessed the conditions of the poor, registered those in desperate need, and distributed flour and medicine.⁵² Generally male students escorted female volunteers, serving as translators and chaperones, as they maneuvered an urban public space that was almost exclusively male. The teams visited homes and determined the actual needs and issued papers, including names and number of dependents, to needy families. These papers could then be presented to their district's distribution center in exchange for money. The methods of the Beirut committee—registering all applicants, investigating their worthiness, and making unannounced follow-up visits—closely resembled practices of late nineteenth-century American scientific philanthropy. The goal was to avoid indiscriminate soup-kitchen charity, which was vulnerable to "the forces of experienced and crafty pauperism." Once the committee realized that "even the very poor people were apt to spend some of their money on tobacco and other luxuries," it began to distribute only flour. In general, the Americans gave a week's portion of flour to destitute families without a wage earner.⁵³

To solve the dilemma between providing Christian obligatory charity and encouraging potential slothfulness and as staunch believers that "a man proved himself exclusively in his vocational work,"⁵⁴ the committee put aid recipients to work whenever possible. Volunteers noted applicants' former occupation and brokered employment. The investigation team worked closely with the employment committee and considered "it advisable, whenever possible, to supply work, rather than food and money."⁵⁵ An article in *al-Ittihad al-'Uthmani* confirmed the Americans' determination to provide work "in case the poor person is able-bodied," paying one or two coins depending on age.⁵⁶ Working with the Beirut municipality, the committee employed male aid recipients to clean the city's streets. It was agreed that a Red Cross volunteer would supervise the crews, and a number of men began "to keep the main street beautifully clean."⁵⁷ The executive committee itself employed a number of women in sewing clothes for the poor, making lace, doing needlework, and making bandages for the hospital expedition.⁵⁸ By February 1915, the American employment office had managed to put about three hundred men and as many women to work for the municipality.⁵⁹ In addition, the SPC employed "Red Cross workers" to lay some terraces on campus.⁶⁰ Cleveland Dodge donated $5,000 to hire workers to improve the campus. The employment committee's plan was to use the funds to employ about two hundred men "to work [one] week on and [one] week off from June to December" with another two hundred working the alternate weeks. The salary was set at $1.50 per week. This way, the committee argued, about four hundred families could be maintained for six months. Important work would be done "for the college at a minimum cost and instead of making paupers out of the poor they will be taught to work. All men to whom work is given will be thoroughly investigated as to their needs."[61] By mid-May, about 560 men were working off and on in the American relief effort.[62]

The humanitarian practices employed by foreign philanthropists on the ground shaped Ottoman civilians' experiences on the home front, forging a new social reality that included the reimagining of urban space and the challenging of traditional forms and institutions of charity. Well financed and organized, it competed with religious institutions and native charitable societies—which faced downturns in donations and difficulties in obtaining supplies—as the main distributor of charity to the poor. A nonstate, foreign agency registered and surveyed Beirutis. It was the Americans who labeled Ottoman civilians as needy, poor, and able-bodied, and divided the city into relief districts according to their vision of the city, at the heart of which was the headquarters of the relief committee near the American college. As a result, the poor and needy would traverse the city along the paths of the resident Americans' understanding of the city.

Local residents and Ottoman officials initially welcomed the work of the American committee. The men and women making up Beirut's American community had lived in the city and the surrounding areas for years, some families like the Dodges and the Blisses for generations. These "foreigners" had deep local connections and were committed to the well-being of the city and its residents. Since the United States had remained neutral until April 1917, the American community "enjoyed the privileges of the most favored nation."[63] Or in the words of Charles Dana, Americans occupied "a most enviable position" in the empire.[64] An article published in *al-Ittihad al-'Uthmani* on January 8, 1915, praised the committee's work as "nothing but another proof offered by the Americans of the pains they are taking in the affairs of the country in which they are living and the effort . . . to render sincere service, free from ulterior motive."[65] Dana was convinced that all Ottoman officials recognized the Americans as "mediators," placing the committees work into what he saw as a "forceful position." As he told the Mission

Board's New York office, American relief work strengthened the mission's relations "with the government" and "with the people and especially with some of the religious sects" who considered the mission a rival and in some cases even an enemy.[66]

Politics of Religion, State, and Colonialism

War relief by the Germans was also debated as a potential "unsuspicious arena" facilitating the entrance of missionaries into the empire to cultivate pro-German sentiments. Aiding those on the verge of starvation would not only guarantee a generally positive attitude toward Germany but would also open the way for the postwar expansion of trade and missionary activities. The abrogation of the capitulation and the Ottomans' alliance with Germans changed the configuration of the missionary presence in the region. While the French had dominated Catholic missionary institutions in both Beirut and Mount Lebanon, their expulsion opened a space for Germans and Americans to step in.[67]

Some German Catholics saw the expulsion of their French counterparts as an opportunity to be seized as fast as possible for "general humanitarian reasons as well as national interest."[68] A report from the foremost German expert and chair of missiology in Münster, Joseph Schmidlin, outlined the hopes of German Catholics. For Schmidlin, the closure of French missionary institutions had opened new possibilities "for both German Orientpolitik *and* Catholic Germany,"[69] and the task was now twofold. First, Germany had to step up and maintain Christian institutions and European cultural influences in the region in general, and more important, make an effort to replace French-dominated Christian influence with a German one. It was in the Germans' general interest to "put an end to the notoriously anti-German French Orient missions."[70] The second task was to expand the influence of German Catholics in the empire in particular. Schmidlin feared the Ottoman authorities would not return confiscated Catholic institutions after the war. A victory of the Central Powers would end French influence in the region, and German diplomatic circles would gain greater influence with the Ottoman government, which could help in expanding the church's work and guarantee the return of Catholic institutions, but now under German supervision. German Catholics worried they would miss out on this opportunity, especially since Ottoman officials generally perceived Germany as a Protestant power. But if all French Catholic institutions would raise the German flag, Schmidlin argued, German Catholicism would overnight be the dominant Christian power in the empire, thereby sidelining the nation's Protestants.[71]

Given Ottoman politics, Schmidlin saw the only way to get a foot in the door was through war relief. He suggested converting French institutions into military hospitals staffed by German missionaries for the duration of the war. Since nurses were in short supply, this would be a great a service to the Ottoman war effort and by extension the German fatherland. Caring for the wounded and sick, Schmidlin calculated, would create sympathies for the Germans during the war and facilitate demands to turn military hospitals into German missionary and educational facilities after the war.[72] He further imagined asking the government to accept German as the second language after Turkish in higher education.

German diplomatic and military staff promptly responded and vehemently argued against any such moves. Such an inquiry with the Ottoman government, they argued, would raise suspicion. The most outspoken opponent to this plan was German ambassador Hans von Wangenheim. The ambassador wrote to the German chancellor that the substitution of German Catholics for French missionaries was not an entirely bad idea, but under the circumstance he strongly advised against it. Requests like these, he argued, would generate mistrust and make postwar negotiations more difficult. He suggested asking German consular staff in the provinces whether military hospitals were needed in their cities.[73] Overall, he was not enthusiastic. The closure of mission institutions was, Wangenheim reminded the chancellor, an outcome of the CUP's desire to eliminate foreign influence in the empire. The CUP saw missionary schools, and not without reason, as a breeding ground for anti-Ottoman sentiments. Hence, the government was eager to replace foreign religious schools with secular national institutions. It would make no sense, he wrote, for the CUP to agree to replace one foreign missionary group with another, no matter how friendly the relations. But he promised to solicit the opinion of German diplomatic staff outside Istanbul. The German consuls of Adana, Haifa, Baghdad, and Beirut all informed Istanbul that either there were enough hospitals or, as it was the case for most, the Ottomans had already turned French institutions into government-run hospitals.⁷⁴ Wangenheim suggested instead pushing German influence and creating pro-German sympathies through local small-scale aid activities. Why not send some German Catholic teachers, who could work in wartime relief and could step in if an opportunity to reopen any of the closed schools arose? The ambassador promised to monitor the developments and ensure the government's goodwill.⁷⁵ Rumors of a plan to substitute German nuns and monks for French ones even without government approval were circulated in anti-German circles. The rumors caused uproar among the CUP, who complained to the ambassador. For Wangenheim, this was proof that any import of foreign staff, even for war relief, had to be handled with caution.

German missionaries who were already on-site, however, were called on to contribute to the war relief. The work of Beirut's Kaiserswerth deaconesses is a good example of the small-scale efforts that were thought to paint a positive picture of the Germans among the empire's inhabitants. The sisters, as the "need and bread shortages among the poor population increased constantly," decided to help in whatever small way they could. Early on in the war, the women baked thirty loaves and distributed them among the poor on Saturdays. They did so for three months, and according to Sister Magda Schönrock, "it helped a great many of the poor."⁷⁶ But as prices rose and access to provisioning became more difficult, Saturday distributions stopped and work turned inward as the sisters took in increasing numbers of orphans in the fall of 1915.⁷⁷

The deaconesses, in general, were on good terms with both Ottoman and German officials. As a result, their work continued uninterrupted. Jamal Pasha visited the Zoar orphanage in January 1917, and the women and children greeted him by hoisting the Ottoman flag, singing, and reciting poems in Turkish. Schönrock in her chronicle of the orphanage described Jamal Pasha as friendly and helpful. He for the most part kept his promise of sending supplies, and foodstuffs continued to trickle in for the war's duration. German military officials assisted by ensuring the goods' safe transport from the train station to the orphanage. Unlike the missionary institution of enemy citizens, the Kaiserswerth work was never questioned or encroached on.⁷⁸ Because the work was unimposing and small scale, not even the most adamant opponent of foreign relief work, 'Azmi Bey, had any concerns. The American efforts, however, attracted the governor's suspicion and anger.

The Tide Turns:
Ottoman Prohibition of American Aid in Beirut

> The state of things excited the compassion of the American missionaries, who formed societies for the distributing of food among the poor and tending the sick; but the authorities actually stopped this work of mercy, saying that they would undertake it themselves. The result was that the death toll from hunger and disease assumed appalling proportions.[79]

Clearly the government's positive attitude toward American relief efforts in Beirut was short-lived. The arrival of 'Azmi Bey marked the change. The new governor saw the Red Cross committee's work, not unlike the work of the municipality, as a direct challenge to Ottoman authority in the city. Any aid to civilians, in the eyes of the governor, was a political act undermining the state's credibility by creating alternative loyalties. These fears perhaps were not unwarranted, given the efficiency of the Americans. Not only did their work stand in stark contrast to the fledgling efforts of the municipality at rationing and market controls but also predated any Ottoman formal civilian food supply policies. In August 1915, the governor suspended all foreign relief work in Beirut. According to Howard Bliss, the governor informed the college administration and the Red Cross committee that "any one desiring to distribute charity could do so openly through the municipality . . . otherwise no distribution could be made."[80]

The governor was serious, and arrests of relief workers, intimidation campaigns, and in some cases exile to Anatolia followed. The same day the governor prohibited relief, Mary Dale Dorman, an employee of the SPC and a Red Cross volunteer, was arrested. Accompanied by two local volunteers, she was making her monthly rounds distributing money on behalf of the ARC to poor women in the neighborhood of Mar Nicolas when she was taken into custody. Police officers took Dorman and her companions to the local station. Confiscating the group's coins, the chief of police informed her of the prohibition of nongovernmental relief. And American, Austrian, and German consulates, he scolded her, had all been notified of this decision.

What was she doing disobeying orders? After a fierce lecture, he released Dorman; as a high-profile member of the foreign community, her arrest no doubt would cause a political scandal. The young men who had helped her, however, were kept in custody. It took the intervention of two senior SPC faculty, James Steward Crawford and Frederick Bliss, with 'Azmi Bey himself to set them free. The governor agreed to release the students but reiterated that charity had to be carried out through the municipality. The executive committee abandoned its publicly displayed work in the city, making sure not to appear disloyal to the Ottoman state.

The executive committee's obedience to the governor's orders can be explained in part by its close link to the SPC. By the end of 1915, SPC employees dominated the Beirut relief committee. The demographics of the committee had a direct effect on decision making concerning its aid efforts. Following orders from the US Department of State prohibiting consular employees from holding office in any Red Cross chapters, Stanley Hollis had resigned as the president of the committee. The committee proceeded to elect SPC faculty members James Alfred Patch and James Steward Crawford as its president and vice president, respectively.[81] As its faculty headed relief work, the college administration meddled with the executive committee's decision making. Hearing the threats and knowing there would be little differentiation between the college and its faculty's actions, the administration urged for relief work to be halted. To the dismay of many of its employees, the college administration pledged political neutrality mainly to preserve its large investments.

American Unofficial Relief: Remittances

The willingness of the SPC to follow 'Azmi Bey's orders caused a split in the relief committee. Presbyterian missionaries, led by Charles Dana, insisted on continuing relief work even if it had to be done in secret. Disobeying Ottoman orders was nothing new to the AMP. In the early months of the war, the AMP distributed money received from Britain to pay the salaries of the Syrian employees of the British missions.[82] Dana had received a list from an unnamed person of "persons connected" to the British mission via an "underground mail route." The salaries were to ensure that the work continued even "under these very trying circumstances." While recognizing the dangers of possibly being accused of aiding the enemy, Dana felt obliged to "assume responsibility" and keep "native workers from starvation."[83] He was also willing to take his chances in regard to assisting American relief efforts. Since the AMP received funds from abroad even when local officials prohibited foreign aid, he thought it imperative to continue relief work. In defiance of the SPC's proposed neutrality, the AMP focused its work instead on facilitating the transfer and distribution of remittances to the poor. The work, besides being forbidden, confronted a great many practical challenges.

By the fall of 1914, remittance transfers had become difficult. The CUP had closed banks and postal services associated to the Entente powers, and Ottoman censors diligently scrutinized private correspondence, effectively blocking the usual channels for money from abroad.[84] Money could still be sent, however, through the AMP and the US State Department, a fact that was widely publicized abroad. With the dual blockade in place, however, the transfer of messages, checks, cash, and money orders relied on the creativity and ingenuity of all involved. Dana, for example, set up an underground mail line.[85] Clandestine mail packages, including duplicates of remittance lists and checks, arrived in Beirut via American cruisers in the early months of the war.[86] His line to the United States relied on total secrecy, and he cautioned the New York office "to make *no* reference in any of your letters to having received mail through the Cruiser." Any mention "might be embarrassing to them as well as to us."[87] No personal letters should accompany the remittances because the government's discovery of an "objectionable" message could put local Syrians in great danger.[88] Private shipments, everyone knew, carried a timestamp. One small mistake could shut the door with a loud thud. In May 1915, it was time for the "big blowup." The Presbyterian Mission's treasurer had sent a letter to Captain Oman of the *North Carolina* through regular mail, carelessly mentioning the underground mail route. Ottoman censors took note, and suddenly the mere presence of American cruisers on the coast was questioned. "The officials here," Dana explicated, maintain "that a great deal of news detrimental to the spirit of the country leaks out through the cruisers." Dana denied these accusations, and the Ottomans eventually backed off.[89]

The few remaining banks charged high fees and exchange rates to process remittances, meaning that money from abroad lost significant value. The

Imperial Ottoman Bank, for example, exhibited "a desire to load down every transaction with high commissions and charges and [was] not accommodating in the matter of exchange."[90] Still much of the money transferred between Istanbul and Beirut went through the Ottoman Imperial Bank.[91] The Ottoman Bank generally was "behaving badly." If not refusing outright to pay out amounts, it disbursed "five pound notes which cannot be used to pay for relief and must be changed at a heavy loss for small money."[92] Only after continuous pressure did the bank agree to pay out the sums in as much small money "as it could spare."[93] According to Dana, the Turkish government had emptied all banks of cash, and paying out funds was sometimes impossible. "The town has been robbed and re-robbed of cash and food until we marvel that the people are able to live."[94] American private companies with branches in the Ottoman Empire, such as Standard Oil and the American Tobacco Company, eventually emerged as alternatives to banks.[95] In the spring of 1915, Standard Oil gave the mission "credit in many parts of the country."[96] As trust built, Standard Oil transferred larger amounts of money at low rates to Dana.[97] Still, there were moments when these private partners were unable to help, and Dana had to resort to risky maneuvers, such as shipping money from Istanbul by overland "parcel post."[98] A glut of currency was yet another concern; purchasing anything in the empire could involve an array of metals and bills. British pounds, French francs, Egyptian gold pieces, Ottoman silver piasters, and gold lira exchanged hands in daily commerce. Everyone living in Beirut and its surroundings was versed in the protocols of exchange. Unfortunately, foreign do-gooders often lacked the same knowledge. Dana was flabbergasted by such ignorance. When one of the foreign agencies sent him $20 gold coins totaling $10,000, he called it "a blunder!" Was it not common knowledge that the gold circulating in the empire was generally of Italian, French, Swiss, Austrian, Russian, and British origins? He eventually shipped the gold to Istanbul, where it was exchanged for unstable and constantly depreciating Ottoman paper currency.[99]

Ottoman officials viewed the distribution of remittances with suspicion just as it saw the ARC's practical relief in the city. Dana voiced his frustration, especially about 'Azmi Bey's disregard of all past customs. Missionaries "have never known such bad treatment."[100] Officials with whom the mission had built friendly relationships over the years were no longer in power, and some had simply disappeared. Among those remaining, even the boldest hesitated to defend even "his best friend under the present conditions."[101] 'Azmi Bey, it seems, mistrusted Dana in particular. The payments made by the AMP, in the eyes of the governor, were an attempt at "purchasing" the loyalties of Ottoman subjects, undermining the credibility of the state.[102] Determined to put an end, just as he done with the ARC work, to the money distributions, the governor cut the AMP off from its mail, staged intimidation campaigns, and charged it with interfering in the business of local banks.[103] Hostilities from the authorities continued to grow, but Dana stubbornly carried on his work even when his "life was one of constant annoyance and danger."[104]

The distribution on the ground relied on a network of locally stationed missionaries and consulate staff and the cooperation of local village officials. The AMP had four main stations in Beirut, Sidon, Tripoli, and Zahle. In coordination with the American consular employees, the staff sorted remittances by districts and dispatched the money to the outlying towns. Receipts were to be returned as proof that the proper person had received the money.[105] While this process was simple on paper, the volunteers faced a number of challenges in practice. Often recipients simply could not be found, and months elapsed between money arriving in Beirut and its reaching people in need. In-person appearance at the distribution stations was mandatory, but the journey could be burdensome due to sickness, old age, or even bad weather.[106] "Remitters" unable to write their relatives' names in the Latin alphabet addressed their envelopes in Arabic.[107] This added confusion, because consular and mission staff transliterated based on their personal preferences, and names were often misspelled. Stanley Hollis, in particular, was bad at spelling local names. He became the subject of jokes among missionaries, who suggested he hire someone "who reads and writes Arabic, who should not get the names so misspelled."[108] Confusion and delays were the everyday at the office; "Hasseb Jamel Eldin Rashed" as spelled in the telegram from Istanbul was "Hassain Djemaldeen Rasheed" according to the correspondence of the Beirut consulate.[109] Not a small difference. The man had to produce additional proof of his person. Albert Haleem of Aberdeen sent funds to his father "Kareem Haleem" in Safed. He never got note of its arrival and worried since his father's name was alternatively spelled Karym, Ceryne, and Cerm.[110] At times, names had changed in the diaspora: Khalil became Julio in Chile; Julio became Khalil in the ancestral village. Wrong addresses or wrongly transliterated addresses caused months of delay. Others had no address at all: "$50 for Abdullah Ghanim, Beirut. He is 5 ½ feet high and must wear glasses on his eyes to see you." Or multiple ones: "$25 for Yusef Azar of Abdilli, Batroun, Beirut, Egypt, Odessa, Lebanon, Kisserwan."[111] Confusion ensued.

The amounts paid out by the AMP, with the help of the American consul, even with prohibition from 'Azmi Bey, were significant. Hollis, spelling mishaps and all, oversaw the disbursement of $378,553.93 in 1,321 payments in the year 1916 alone.[112] The AMP's secretary disbursed approximately $2 million to some 30,000 people in less than a year. Whether the number is correct is impossible to confirm, but sentiments were moved and people rallied to donate money.

> The war conditions in Syria have stirred the hearts of Syrians in America to send relief to relatives and friends who are in need in the home land. Finding that money could be forwarded through the Presbyterian Board of Foreign Missions, they have either called in person or sent through the mails the relief funds. From June 1st to July 7th (as we go to press) the number of such remittances aggregated [was] 714, and the amount which they represented was $143,126.[113]

The Presbyterian Mission did its best to publicize the possibility of sending money to relatives back home. Ads in newspapers in the United States, South America, and Egypt caused money to come "pouring in from all quarters of the globe."[114] In early 1917, the Board of Foreign Missions of the Presbyterian Church accounted for $1,750,988 "remitted by Syrian emigrants, including Lebanese, to their people at home since the beginning of the war."[115] The payments mainly came from individual family members, and the average amount recorded by the Beirut consulate was somewhere between $50 and $100, but amounts as small as $5 were transmitted as well. For some, the money came in the nick of time. "One person to whom we paid $30 which you sent from her son, had been without food for herself and children for three days."[116] These dollars saved her life. Remittances once contributing to the income of families now were a matter of life and death for some. And the AMP was committed to not be intimidated by 'Azmi Bey. Dana distanced himself from the SPC and stepped outside its dedication to neutrality to take advantage of the consulate's neutral and seemingly untouchable position. The Ottoman authorities eventually had enough of Dana, sending him to Istanbul to be tried for his misconduct.

Moving into the Mountains: American Soup Kitchens and Workshops in Mount Lebanon

The ARC committee instead focused its relief efforts on Mount Lebanon.[117] The governor of Mount Lebanon, 'Ali Munif Bey, intimated that he would be grateful if the committee would transfer what he called "the relief machinery that had operated so effectively in Beirut" to his province. The only demand he made was for Americans to work with locally appointed representatives of the Red Crescent. The executive committee elected a joint relief team, including employees from the SPC, the AMP, and a representative of the Red Crescent, a local judge named Muhammed Effendi Izzedine.[118]

The joint committee began by distributing small sums of money to trustworthy individuals, who were to dispense it to the most needy people in their communities. "Honest shopkeepers" received money from the Americans in exchange for giving "food to a few families in abject poverty."[119] Organized food distribution funded by the Americans and administered by a committee of village leaders followed. The village committees registered needy families and assured that every person was given a *rotl* of wheat every two weeks. In the summer of 1916, Bayard Dodge opened a soup kitchen in the mountain village of 'Abeih, and a second one in the neighboring village of Suq al-Gharb.[120] Combined, the two kitchens fed eight hundred people.[121]

The Americans, here too, insisted that everyone who "could do something in return for his or her food" do so. Adult men were employed to build and repair roads. Those who refused to work were dropped from the list. Children were told to collect wood or spin raw wool on hand spindles. Older girls and women spun wool and knitted garments for the winter. Dodge argued,

> It seemed best to encourage self-respecting labor, paying for the same in grain, bread or cooked food. This seemed better than giving help to people like beggars, even though a minimum return of labor was required. Instead of developing the begging instinct by offering free charity, self-respect was maintained by offering labor. As we gradually introduced the change, it was

pathetic to see how far the pauperizing tendency had developed. Some even preferred to beg rather than to bring two pounds of wool weekly or to knit half a pound of wool per week. However the new plan was developed and in the end won its way.[122]

The committee expanded the employment-for-food scheme by organizing large-scale labor projects such as planting grain. Hiring a local Druze sheikh, who was skilled in the mountain's agriculture and willing to help, the committee employed thirty to forty men to plant wheat, barley, beans, tomatoes, millet, and corn. While the financial investment was significant, the harvest fed no fewer than one hundred people. Purchasing a similar amount of grain on the market would have been more expensive. The second industry developed was weaving. Since imported manufactured cloth was hard to find and expensive, local weaving promised to be profitable. After setting up a small weaving room, the committee figured a special expertise that "no American possessed or could easily acquire" was needed, and the high demand for woven

Figure 12. Ploughing the Ground for Corn. Source: American University of Beirut / Library Archives.

cotton cloth necessitated a much larger effort. After receiving its first two orders totaling 480 yards, the volunteers employed a master weaver and paid him a decent living wage "so that he would give his best energy and interest in the management of the industry."[123]

American relief workers also invested in the silk industry. Designating 6,000 Ottoman liras to purchase cocoons, the committee employed six men as buyers. To process the silk thread, the Americans rented three silk factories. Staffed by more than sixty mostly girls and women, the factories worked at full speed, unwinding raw silk. Thereafter the silk was spun by unwinding it onto separate reels according the thread's thickness, bleaching and dyeing it, and then rolling it onto small skeins. For this work, the committee hired thirty young women from more than half a dozen villages. The silk was then to be woven into clothes, which proved to be difficult. Silk weaving required precision and patience. "Many of the weavers came and remained a few days and were dismissed for careless work."[124] Good weavers were hard to find, especially since many master weavers had been conscripted or had died in the famine. In general, the American soup kitchens were buzzing with workers. Raw wool had to be washed and dried before it could be knitted. So every day, a group of men and women left the soup kitchen in the early-morning hours to wash the wool in a stream four miles from the village. Other women sat and hand-fed sheep, stuffing and fattening them, so they could be killed in the autumn. Workmen and stonemasons were on the kitchen's payroll to improve the facilities.

In Brumana a similar project was under way. Local women had begun to organize a soup kitchen in the mountain village. The British dentist Arthur Dray expanded it from feeding a dozen people in 1916 to an establishment employing two hundred or three hundred people to care for twelve hundred destitute souls.[125] Hundreds of people arrived to be fed daily in Brumana from neighboring villages. Each person received tickets for a "number of loaves of bread and a dipper of soup." In time, the Brumana station grew into a large orphanage. Through 1917, the orphanage sheltered more than six hundred children.[126] The children "attended classes, they exercised in out of door play and gymnastic drills and employed their leisure time in industrial occupation." Many of the girls spun wool or knitted dresses for their younger siblings. The boys learned carpentry and masonry. The work at Brumana included teaching skills to those who had none, providing the children with vocational training to assure self-sufficiency and their future contributions to society at large.[127]

America's Entrance into the War and the Fate of Relief Work

American war relief work continued after the United States entered the war. In a telegram sent on April 21, 1917, Interior Minister Talat Pasha instructed the provincial authorities to treat American citizens and institutions "exactly as before the break."[128] The rupture in diplomatic relations was not a state of war. Since Stanley Hollis had to leave Beirut, a Dutch official took over American consular affairs in Beirut, and a Swedish legation took charge of American interests on April 26, 1917. By August 1917, the US government became more cautious, ordering that remittances not exceed $125 per person per month.[129] The goal was to make sure remittances were seen as individual private aid to family members and not an organized government scheme.

Eventually the possibility of transferring money into the empire was nullified by the American government through the "so-called Trading with the Enemy Act (H.R. 4960)." While the State Department challenged the War Trade Board's ruling, it publicly requested ACASR to discontinue the "transmission of all lists, drafts, transfers, or other communications."[130] In practice, the State Department continued to approve ACASR to transmit relief through its agents in the empire, in particular, donations to support soup kitchens. In July 1918, Secretary of State Robert Lansing requested a relaxation of the War Trade Board's limits so he could send a total of $402,800 into the empire: $252,800 to the work of ACASR, $50,000 to individual relief societies for Lebanon villages, and $100,000 to pay out individual remittances to Syrian relatives. "This sum," Lansing argued, was "in the nature of reimbursement for amounts paid out by the various relief committees prior to the recent reductions in monthly allotment."[131] According to the Beirut consular reports kept by Dutch officials, American relief continued even as the international situation grew tense. The American efforts in creating a positive image of the United States, especially the work at the Brumana soup kitchen, did not go unnoticed. German officials, in particular, saw it as a project well worth imitating toward the war's end.

Mothers Do Eat Their Children!
German Last-Minute Relief

Beirut's German consul Gerhard von Mutius was a keen observer, reporting on the famine and often criticizing Ottoman officials. But he stood back and seems to have made little to no effort to engage his government in large-scale aid campaigns until 1918. German officials supported small-scale efforts of resident German missionaries but made no attempt to instigate official war relief or deploy private citizens to do so. Any such move, officials feared, would be perceived as meddling in the internal affairs of the empire and could strain German-Ottoman relations.

A desperate plea for the German government to intervene, however, came from German vice consul Hermann Hoffmann, who was stationed in Tripoli, on February 19, 1918. He reported that for three weeks children between the ages five and eight went missing and could not be found. A few days earlier, a small girl was found wearing the jacket of one of the missing children. After questioning her and carrying out investigations, city officials came upon two women living near the port who had lured children into their home to kill and eat them. One of the women's victims was the six-year-old daughter of a municipal employee. She had been missing for two days, and her father had been searching the countryside for her. The authorities recovered the remains of at least nine children, which the vice consul himself inspected. The women, both physically in bad condition, gave "hunger" as the reason for their actions.

Hoffmann's letter was filled with cruel details, which he admitted seemed unbelievable. He swore, however, to the events' veracity, insisting that they were exemplary of the truly devastating situation in his town. He wrote "that a horrific famine, one that cannot be imagined any worse, is reigning here is no longer a question, and if the Ottoman government does not intervene with forceful measures to end these conditions, we might encounter more such terrible instances." Shortages of foodstuffs in his region, he added, were not a given, and further starvation deaths could be prevented if the "government would finally decide to end the criminal speculation. It was well known where the supplies were, and it is my sacred conviction that the government could force large landowners and speculators with little effort to surrender their supplies."[132]

Moved and shocked by the cruelty of hunger, Hoffmann solicited funds to organize aid. Unprecedented price hikes and inflation meant that private charity given by a handful of humanitarians had declined and could no longer affect any significant changes. Hoffmann had a bit of money and, according to his letter, began to act locally. In the month of February, he had spent 105 Ottoman liras to provide meals for about eighty poor people. His funds, however, were depleted, and he was forced to stop distributions. One could affect much with relatively little money, he told Mutius. But unfortunately, neither the Ottoman government nor wealthy community members had shown great interest in establishing an ordered provisioning scheme for the poor of Tripoli. Hoffmann asked for his account to be forwarded to German chancellor Georg von Hertling with the request that a monthly stipend would be made available from the German public fund to expand the work he had begun on a small scale. Mutius forwarded the letter to Germany and to the German embassy in Istanbul with a note that the governor of Beirut had forwarded 5,000 Ottoman liras "for the distribution to the poor" to Tripoli.[133]

The new German ambassador, Johann Heinrich von Bernstoff, unlike his predecessor, believed in the potential benefits of distributing food. He secured a one-time stipend of 10,000 German marks for Hoffmann in Tripoli and now asked for permission to advertise the money's origins. In Istanbul, where he had publicly financed soup kitchens with German money, this had generated "friends in Turkish circles."[134] Why not do the same in the provinces? Mutius followed Hoffmann's example and requested help to establish a large-scale relief campaign for the poor and starving of Lebanon. Bernstoff was low on money but sent 500 Ottoman liras to Beirut. He knew this would do little to expand relief work, so he presented Mutius's work to the German government, framing it as an excellent measure to promote Germany in the empire. Bernstoff forwarded Mutius's request.

Mutius carefully presented the humanitarian and political benefits relief work could secure. But so far the money spent was just not enough and had done little in forging the reputation of the Germans as friends and helpers of the poor. That it was possible to improve one's standing in the community through relief, he argued, was clearly visible in the American example. The Americans had created a very positive image of the United States due to their "generous relief work" in Beirut. Germans no doubt could do the same. Mutius estimated, based on wartime exchange rates, the price of wheat at about 8 to 10 German marks per kilogram, and a person's need of about

300 grams of bread per day, a total of 80 to 90 German marks was needed to feed a family of five for one month. If the government wanted to assure positive "propaganda for Germany," large amounts of funds were needed. He suggested that since the harvest was near, the price of grain was expected to decrease a bit in the next few weeks. So a quantity of grain (wheat, barley, or corn), enough to feed five hundred people from the worst-affected regions of Lebanon's Kisrawan for six months, should be purchased now. At a daily ration of 200 grams of grain, a monthly supply of 3 tons (or 18 tons for the entire six months) was needed. Based on his experience on the ground, Mutius figured a ton of wheat would cost approximately 250 Ottoman liras, and barley and corn would be a bit cheaper. To purchase the supply for six months, he needed exactly 4,320 Ottoman liras (based on his calculation of an average of 9 marks per kilogram of wheat, he needed 155,520 marks; or $12,960, based on a wartime currency exchange rate of $3 per gold lira). A German company had agreed to store the grain free of charge. Once a month a sixth of the grain would be sent to Junieh and distributed to the poor. To save on transport costs, he would solicit the help of the Yıldırım Army Group, which could provide the necessary trucks. Mutius preferred distributing grain to organizing a soup kitchen. He thought soup kitchens were less effective in making sure that five hundred people would be saved from starvation. And there was no reliable German staff available to prepare daily meals and distribute them. He urged the German officials to act quickly, since the success of his proposal relied on the timely purchase of the grain.[135] And he warned that for real change to be effected, financial support needed to be extensive. Anything short of a successful campaign would further discredit Germany and its officials working in the empire. It would be better to avoid getting involved in the scheme if a full commitment was not made. The decision whether to finance Mutius's work was put to the German chancellor.[136]

In Beirut, a soup kitchen run by German missionaries was already feeding some people. Mutius, eager to expand its reach by getting his government involved, inquired how the work was going, and the missionaries returned a detailed report.[137] It was a small but organized effort. Female missionaries prepared the food in the Johanniter hospital. Since the hospital's kitchen was equipped to cook only for a limited number of people, those deemed needy received stamped wooden tablets, which served as identification. The improvised stamp contained the name of a local doctor, but the report suggested that the stamp should include the words "Deutsche Volksküche" (German Soup Kitchen). Such a stamp would remind charity recipients of the German origins of their benefactors. The work had begun on April 1, 1918, financed with donations from German, Swiss, and Austrian citizens living in Beirut. After purchasing beans, lentils, flour, salt, cracked wheat, onions, oil, and figs, the meal distribution began on April 9, 1918. Estimating a monthly need of 100 Ottoman liras, supplies would feed the current number of poor until September. Meals were made from lentils or beans with some added flour and cracked wheat. Although people were used to eating bread with their meals, the missionaries did not have the funds to bake large amounts of bread.

The soup was "absolutely free," and only the poorest of Beirut, meaning those who were living more or less on the street, received food. Often based on recommendations from her German landsmen, the Johanniter hospital's head nurse determined who would receive food. Fifty to sixty women and children regularly received a meal in the garden of the hospital. Most of the aid recipients were Christian but also included some Jews and a few Muslims. Missionaries closely monitored distributions; only those with the proper wooden tablet were let through the iron gate and had to eat on the premises. The gate was guarded, as there were many more people who wanted to get in. Those inside were not allowed to take their meals away from the premises. There had been instances of the poor selling their ration once on the street. Getting supplies for the kitchen was difficult. Neither Ottoman nor German military officials were particularly helpful. "The German division said it could not give up any provisions and the Turks did not cooperate, as was usual." Only once had General Liman von Sanders, who now commanded the Ottoman army stationed in Syria, provided a cheap supply of lentils and figs. The soup kitchen organizers had no doubt their work was good advertisement for the Germans in the empire. The missionaries and Mutius agreed and introduced their work to the government as positive propaganda to businessmen interested in trade with Syria. Mutius approached a number of German, Austrian, and Hungarian companies to solicit donations so the work could continue past September.[138]

German military officials were still cautious about expanding the work. In a letter to the German ambassador in Istanbul, the chief of the German division of the Yıldırım Army warned that even now it was extraordinarily difficult for the German military to suddenly begin provisioning Arabs, in particular Arab civilians. It would be seen, "and rightly so," he argued, as German intervention and meddling in Ottoman domestic politics. He was not convinced it was a good idea, mainly because failure could reflect badly. For example, the officer thought that 'Azmi Bey "worked hard to ensure grain shipments to Mount Lebanon, but due to the circumstances it was not surprising that only the most necessary was done" because even supplying the military was extremely difficult, "and soldiers were living hand to mouth." This had reflected badly on the governor. Moreover, the governor had prioritized the military and had not "sufficiently considered" the "generally Entente-friendly Lebanon." But how could he, the chief argued, given the administration's difficulty in providing "its own employees with enough food?" Civilians in non-Turkish districts were not a priority. Moreover, it was impossible to move the grain through local offices, since even when it was designated for relief, it would be subject to "unscrupulous speculation." He was not entirely against helping those in need, but he demanded it be done by nongovernmental organizations so that Germany could not be accused of meddling in the domestic politics of the Ottoman state. He suggested that "Lebanon and Beirut can be helped, and at the same time propagate a positive image of the Germans, only if German civil societies would organize small-scale soup kitchens and bread distributions in various locales." The military could then assist, but it could not be front and center. Moreover, the work would have to be done in coordination with the local Ottoman civil administration. Otherwise, it was hopeless, "since suspicion and jealousy over German influence in Arab regions remained a major concern." For the military commander it was impossible to have German officials intervene in the domestic affairs of the empire without damaging the trust invested in them by the Ottoman military and civilian administrations.[139]

The Germans did not escape blame for the starvation in Beirut and Mount Lebanon. Rumors spread of Germans buying all the grain and sending it to Germany. It was not only "Entente-friendly elements" who spread these claims, but Ottoman officials also tried to undermine German influence. People speculated about the German military's role in the famine, since an otherwise "powerful Germany, which dictated its will in all matters, would have forced Turkey to ship enough grain to the Lebanon, or would have at least pushed for permission to import grain to into the Lebanon," if its command cared about Ottoman civilians. Viewing the Americans' work, especially that of Dr. Dray in Brumana, as a perfect example of "the very best propaganda," German military officials wondered if they could arrange for a similar project to save the Germans' reputation.[140] Or since Dray had mentioned his willingness to pass his project into the hands of the Turkish or German government at any time, why not take the offer? Whether Dray was serious or just said this to appease the Ottomans is unclear. The German command saw it as an opportunity to get involved without great expenditure. In the end a compromise was suggested. Since the biggest problem remained transportation, the German command suggested supplying Dray with German trucks. Because this meant working with the enemy, the military commander reminded his government that the German High Command had provided the American committee working in Belgium and northern France with trucks to feed the local populations. So what could be done for the enemy should be done to feed an Allied population.

Germany had sacrificed its citizens' lives and provided millions in gold and materials to the Ottoman campaign in Syria and Palestine, but nothing had been done to ensure "robust propaganda" to raise Germany's reputation among the local population. The military, it was argued, had a duty to take this into consideration. Good relations in the region would ensure the strengthening and growth of Germany's national wealth. A German-Ottoman victory would allow Germany to bolster its presence in the empire, and since local populations would be the consumers of German goods, it was important to create good rapport. The local merchant community, the German military chief asserted, had plenty of money stored away and would be formidable trading partners. For this reason, he said that "we must spread healthy and robust German propaganda to strengthen the German nation."[141]

Conclusion

German and American war relief to civilians in Beirut and Mount Lebanon was subject to Ottoman suspicion and entangled in the international imperialist politics that characterized the early twentieth century. Although cast in apolitical terms, American emergency aid was not apolitical; in fact, it was invariably enmeshed in local and international politics.[142] Ussama Makdisi notes, first, that local Muslim elites tended to question the "intentions and integrity of American missionaries." Second, he cautions that in their "eagerness to craft an American Protestant diplomacy," based on American innocence, neutrality, and lack of imperial ambitions, missionaries and philanthropists obscured the fact that the United States was an expansionist power.[143] Most important for this discussion, relief work, as it was entrapped in international wartime politics, was subject to pragmatic decision making that did not always prioritize humanitarian concerns but furthered American interests. For example, to obtain official permission to remain in the empire and distribute relief, ensure the community's safety and supplies, and avoid confiscation of American properties led people such as Howard Bliss at times to compromise humanitarian work. It was an intricate political game with the main purpose of creating an image of American neutrality. And in this game, local Ottoman government officials largely defined what neutrality meant. Moreover, the American project was inevitably political in its desire to affect social transformation. The majority of relief personnel on the ground and their donors abroad championed top-down social engineering with the goal of tackling societal problems much deeper than the immediate wartime suffering on display. While the Americans faced obstacles in their relief efforts, their work continued and expanded, especially in the tremendous effort asserted on behalf of Armenian survivors of genocide in other parts of the empire. Eventually, relief work contributed to establishing the United States as the benevolent power in the region. The functionality of civilian aid as good publicity for international actors was not lost on the Germans allied with the Ottomans. Germany's imperialist desires included an expansion into the empire, and relief work had the potential to rally trading partners and consumers to the German side. However, as an ally of the Ottoman regime, Germans interfering in the domestic affairs of the Ottoman Empire was a delicate business. It was only toward the end of the war that German diplomatic and military personnel stationed in the empire were willing to discuss projects that would be visibly sponsored by the German government. Moving beyond local small-scale missionary efforts, German officials knew, was not without risk since failure or even marginal success would not be positive propaganda for Germany in the aftermath of the war. The outcome of the war naturally was the deciding factor in determining the long-term benefits of the wartime efforts. For the victors of war, as James Barton, one of the principal architects of relief in the Middle East put it, the work left the "door open for America to participate in the social, economic and moral reconstruction of the Near East."[144]

Figure 13. Martyr's Square, Renato Marino Mazzacurati statue, circa 1960. Source: American University of Beirut / Library Archives.

❨ CONCLUSION ❩

BEIRUT 1919

The Chaos of Memory and Politics

On October first, the year 1918,
A wonderful sight in our village was seen:
Guns popping, flags flying, skyrockets went up:
We were so excited we hardly could sup:
The Turks had all left us, the British were near:
Our troubles were over, we knew peace was here.
Hurrah for the Arab nations—three cheers!
Away with all sorrows and sighing and tears:
The people are happy because they all know
That their Arab nation in freedom may grow.
             Anonymous ten-year old American girl[1]

On Sunday, September 29, 1918, a violent earthquake like "a super-Titanic Dog took the world by the scruff of its neck." It shook Beirut as if to forewarn its inhabitants that great change was on its way.[2] And so it was. The following day the surface of the Beirut–Damascus road was drenched in the blood of Ottoman soldiers. The British field marshal Edmund Allenby's forces had been pushing toward Beirut. With the arrival of enemy forces imminent, Ottoman troops retreated from the coast toward Damascus on September 30, only to be caught by Australian troops and gunned down as they crossed the valley of Nahr al-Bared.[3] Fearing for their lives, Ottoman officials stationed in the provincial capital fled under cover of darkness on October 1, marking the end of the multiethnic empire that had ruled the region for four hundred years.

In the wake of the Ottoman retreat an Arab flag was hoisted in Damascus. Arab troops led by the son of Sharif Husayn, Emir Faisal, with the encouragement and material support of the British, had staged a revolt against the Ottomans in the Arabian Peninsula beginning in June 1916. Faisal's troops, as part of the British offensive, had moved steadily north and entered Damascus on October 3, 1918. In anticipation of Faisal's arrival, Damascene notables had announced an independent Arab government a few days before and cabled the president of the Beirut municipality, 'Umar Da'uq, urging him to follow their lead.[4] Da'uq, according to Salim 'Ali Salam's account, was unsure and sought his counsel. Salam advised him to command Ottoman civilian officials, most notably the current Beirut governor, Isma'il Haqqi Bey, to leave the city. Seizing the opportunity, a well-known Beirut trio made up of Salim 'Ali Salam, Ahmad Mukhtar Bayhum, and Alfred Sursock, accompanied by

Figure 14. Turkish Casualties on the Beirut–Damascus Road. Source: American University of Beirut / Library Archives.

armed guards, paid the governor a visit in the middle of the night. The men, according to Salam, negotiated into the early-morning hours, until one of Salam's sons finally escorted the last Ottoman governor to the city borders at six o'clock. Mount Lebanon's Ottoman governor, Mumtaz Bey, fled from Baabda by car to join the remnants of the Turkish army at the train station in Rayak the same day. In his possession, he had all the money of the mountain district's treasury.[5] Following the swift flight of Ottoman officials, local politicians and notables rushed to stake a claim in whatever would come next.

On October 6, 1918, Bayhum, Salam, and Da'uq followed the example and instructions from Damascus and raised the banner of Arab independence on the Grand Serail in the heart of the city. Shukri Ayyub, who had been dispatched by Faisal, arrived from Damascus the same day and took up his assigned post as the new governor-general of Beirut and Mount Lebanon. After meeting with Salam the following day, Ayyub appointed Habib Pasha al-Sa'ad, a friend of Salam's and former president of Mount Lebanon's AC, as the governor of the adjacent district. Sa'ad readily agreed and swore his allegiance to the new government in Damascus and hoisted the Arab flag in Baabda on October 7. How would these men, largely sidelined during the war, failed patrons of provisioning, some even accused of profiteering, regain their legitimacy? Could they feed the city and its mountains?

The year 1919 would put them to the test; the process of rehabilitation of local leadership was complicated by the fact that there had been only a "brief flirtation" with independence.[6] The day the Arab flag was hoisted, the French fleet entered the port of Beirut. Allenby's troops were not far behind and marched into the city on October 8. Moving on the secret wartime agreement between British colonel Mark Sykes and French diplomat François Georges-Picot from May 1916, the French army command occupied Beirut without much hesitation. And on October 10, French troops paraded through the city, "waving the tricolor flag to the wild acclaim of a throng of Christians," who with this demonstration publicly threw in their lot with, in their eyes, the French liberators, whose benevolent reputation dated back to 1860.[7] The French military command immediately ordered Faisal's men to withdraw together with their flags and ambitions. The British had no objections. And on the night of October 11, a British company entered the Grand Serail and lowered the Sharifian flag. French colonel Philpin de Piépape took over the military command of the city the next morning. His immediate concern, as he telegraphed the French war ministry of his government takeover, was a question that had remained "most urgent": securing supplies "to alleviate the 'horrors' of the famine."[8] Piépape, at least on the surface, made food and famine relief a priority of the occupying power for the months to come. The power to forge ties and establish legitimacy by filling people's stomachs was not lost on the colonial masters to be.

France's Postwar "Benevolence": Cultivating and Narrating Humanitarian Legitimacy

Following the armistice, a group of European politicians and diplomats sat around tables and made it their prerogative to draw a new political map of the former Ottoman territories based on British, French, and Zionist interests. In 1919 Paris, the men determined the region's national futures with a stroke of their pens. The immediate concerns and requests of the region's inhabitants, in the meantime, were buried at the bottom of piles of papers on oak desks in Paris. Local aspirations proved peripheral and were largely ignored in the European decision making. However, 1919 was not only a Parisian year. For Beirut and Mount Lebanon, 1919 was a year of swift changes, hopes, promises, rewards, despair, and disappointments. How did Beirut and Mount Lebanon experience the acclaimed year 1919? And how did the politics of provisioning, so important in the years of famine, translate into the postwar period? Within a few months, a French protectorate took shape amid international negotiations over self-determination, territorial divisions, and reparations and in confrontation and conversation with still-fluid political and national identities. As one Lebanese author notes, the *exit from the war* was a *makhlouta*,[9] or, as Linda Schilcher puts it, "The years at the end of, and immediately following, the war have remained a kind of historic limbo."[10] For international and local actors the ability to assert humanitarian legitimacy was a stabilizing and powerful source to swing loyalties and politics one way or another, or so it seemed.

As the French troops entered Beirut, the famine's material reality, or as Piépape wrote, the "horrors of the famine," were not only an urgent problem but had the great potential of legitimizing the colonialist's intervention. Relief work was the "new crusade," a conquest through people's stomachs.[11]

Total war, as it engulfed the Ottoman provincial home front, had the effect of erasing the possibility of a rights-based politics, which had made headway in both municipal and provincial administrations. Unable to compete with the obvious coercive or nervous power of the state, the benevolent power of provisioning presented itself as an opportunity for various actors to maintain or assert legitimacy. Legitimacy, as suggested by Tilly and others, does not rely simply on people believing the dictates of the state to be right and proper but rather is the outcome of, among other things, the ability to protect a potential group of subjects/citizens. In this case study, the protection from starvation and disease took center stage. As a result, the act of provisioning became the space of politics, wherein power could be gained or lost. The ability to provide, as we have seen, depended on internal and external allegiances and cooperation with those who could facilitate access to food. Patronage, *not* entitlements, dictated the wartime game of power and survival, forestalling a return to rights- and representative-driven politics that had marked the beginning of the century. Wartime interventionist state politics and the empowerment of nonthreatening local allies eventually characterized the politics of provisioning. It was this setup, these rules of the game, that bridged the catastrophic disappearance of the Ottoman state and opened the space for a new powerful agent of provisioning to step into the void. Therein, the power of provisioning facilitated the takeover of yet another imperial regime, and French government officials used and replicated wartime politics of provisioning to establish their neopatrimonial imperial rule of the Lebanese Mandate.

The wartime food debacle had tarnished most Beirut merchants and power players as having failed their communal obligations, impotent in resisting the Ottoman takeover of provisioning; as having privately profiteered; or as having collaborated with the Ottoman government, which also had failed to properly feed its population. It was in this turmoil of questioned legitimacy and intentionality that the French and British occupying forces were to recruit "replacements for the disgraced wartime notability."[12] The colonial power sought to empower men whose political allegiance to France was unquestioned, who had an intimate local knowledge that would facilitate the execution and propagation of French relief operations, and carried little or no baggage of failure.

To begin, Piépape dispatched a mission led by the Catholic priest Father Rémy to Port Said to purchase as many food supplies as possible. Within a few days, according to French reports, the men, with the help of French officials in Egypt, had gathered flour, rice, and dried vegetables worth more than a million francs and shipped the supplies to Beirut. To organize relief, the French military command divided the work into three relief districts: Beirut, Northern Lebanon, and Southern Lebanon. In Beirut, the new military governor of the city, Doizelet, instigated a relief system and appointed Charles Corm, a Jesuit-educated Maronite intellectual to supervise it. Corm is said to have been a dashing young fellow, who, it is rumored, had a passionate love affair with the Swedish actress Greta Garbo later in life. But more important, he was the right person for the job. He was an ardent Francophile familiar with Beirut's prewar charitable scene and municipal politics, and even better, or at least that is what we are told, he had fed people during the war.[13] At the height of the famine, twenty-year-old Charles Corm is said to have traveled across Mount Lebanon to provide much-needed relief. He apparently came up with a way to make a high-caloric sweet paste from dried grapes that could be found in abandoned vineyards. He organized the production and then distributed it among the poor.[14]

French relief operations included three kinds of aid. First was aid to soup kitchens, asylums, hospitals, hospices, and refugee shelters, which received supplies free of charge. Father Rémy coordinated much of this work. The second type was reminiscent of Ottoman wartime relief strategies, "semi-free" relief, which relied on lists and distribution of cards. Registration and proper identification allowed people to purchase subsidized supplies at thirteen distribution centers in the city. A multiconfessional committee of urban notables supervised this work. No Salam, no Bayhum, no Sursock was part of this committee. The third kind was "paid relief," which attempted to curb market speculation by supplying foodstuffs to fifty-five stores that would sell the wares at a fixed price.[15] It was a significant undertaking, and Charles Corm supervised the work of 225 employees and coordinated the spending of 20 million francs on approximately 15,000 tons of foodstuffs.[16]

Firmly establishing relief work in the city, the French drew on local agents for help and, as the Ottomans had done before them, sidelined potential competitors. German troops and consular officials had withdrawn with the Ottomans, and with them German government–sponsored relief came to an end. But not so easily displaced were German missionaries, in particular the female deaconesses who had run small provisioning schemes in the city. It is not that the women could have competed with French humanitarian intervention in Beirut, but their presence seemed to have been a nuisance in the eyes of French officials, especially when after enemy citizens were ordered to evacuate French-occupied zones, some of the German women stayed behind to guard the properties of their mission. At least one of them held on until French officials confiscated all German-owned real estate, just as the Ottomans had done with their enemy's possessions at the beginning of the war.

Discourses of Lebanese Victimhood: Guilty Tyrants, Death, and Starvation

Wartime suffering and postwar ambiguities persuaded many local groups to articulate and lobby for their preferred postwar political constellation. And their differential and at times competing territorial and political desires entered into public discourse over national independence, Mandatory tutelage, and humanitarian aid. Within this *makhlouta*, the famine, its causes, and humanitarian responses had political potency. Local and international agents of wartime provisioning, with their main competitor—the Ottoman state—removed from the scene, used accounts of real and fictitious wartime benevolence to assert political power. A "divisive" discourse of famine was forged.[17] Looking at the first generation of famine narratives, which merge the recollections of wartime political actors, witnesses, journalists, and amateur historians, the ideological prejudices, while at times murky, follow lines with distinct political agendas. This comes as no surprise considering that these accounts were written and published either during the war or shortly thereafter. Therein the famine as an event was either to be mentioned, foregrounded, interpreted, or silenced and hence was subject to the contentious politics of memory and history. It had great political currency for some but could mean political suicide for others. Political ambitions, the need to establish famine guilt, and the aspiration to distance themselves and their communities from being responsible for the suffering dictated authors' inclusion or exclusion of the famine in their postwar accounts.

As the power of provisioning moved to Paris in 1919, the famine and French rescue loomed large in the publications of pro-French-leaning, mostly Christian circles. It turned out that Corm was central not only in implementing relief work but also in advertising it as France's liberation of the Lebanese and a great humanitarian success. The new 1919 journal *La revue phénicienne* (The Phoenician Review) is exemplary of this current. The journal was founded by no other than Charles Corm, who had invited a group of Francophile businesspeople, lawyers, and administrators to contribute to his newest intellectual adventure. According to historians this short-lived, four-issue publication likely received financial help from French officials, such as Robert de Caix, the general secretary of the French high commissioner.[18] It included essays discussing social, political, economic, and historical issues, as well as plays, short stories, and poems, many directly related to the war and the famine.[19] Its discussion of the famine was framed by the "unadulterated francophilism of its writers," whose political agenda may be summarized by the Maronite patriarch Ilias Butrus al-Huwayyik's petition for independent Lebanon in its natural, historical, and geographic borders under the guidance of France at the Paris Peace Conference in August 1919.[20]

The famine was used to highlight the CUP's wartime tyranny and establish the regime's intention to rid the empire of its Christians. One of the authors, Alfred Coury, left little to the imagination regarding who he thought was to blame for the famine: the Turks—who else? And, of course, by extension the Germans were guilty too. In the December 1919 edition of *La revue phénicienne*, Emile Arab described the Lebanese as "an entire population prostrated as victims of Turkish barbarism."[21] Moreover, the Lebanese, according to Arab, were victims of a *systematic* attempt by the regime to rid itself of Lebanese Christians. Characterizing the Turks as "our tyrants,"[22] Corm, under the pseudonym Cedar, recounted that "an entire population was systematically starved by the Turks during the four years of war."[23]

Not everyone believed that the Ottomans were specifically targeting Christians. A number of first-generation authors articulate a transconfessional agony. For example, Najwa al-Qattan cites Antun Yamin, Jirjis al-Maqdisi, and Butrus Khuwairi.[24] Yamin insisted that "Turkish abuses were blind to all social distinctions: the young and old; the sick and the healthy; Christians and Muslims." Maqdisi argued not only for a communal suffering across sects but also across class. The famine was so severe that all but a few people were reduced to a state of "desperate poverty." The war "united Muslims and Christians" in a shared suffering. Khuwairi widens the circle. He was convinced that the CUP not only targeted Armenians and Lebanese but Syrians as well. Indeed, "all Arabs, Muslim and Christians" were on Jamal Pasha's list of people to be eliminated.[25]

At times, authors blamed a single person, Jamal Pasha, for having caused the famine. Postwar Catholic bulletins highlighted Jamal Pasha as "infamous, bloodthirsty," and "known for his cruelty."[26] "The decision to starve Syria," one article claimed, "was taken by a group of people headed by Jamal the governor, assisted by the German general who commanded the Syrian army."[27] Reports and letters sent to the Catholic missions in France were published and distributed to potential donors and patrons and most clearly indicted the Ottomans. For example, a Syrian Lazarist priest writes, "The Turks in the four years of war did nothing to assure the life of its population. On the contrary, they certainly caused the famine that decimated the country."[28] To highlight the regime's intention, authors often recounted the fate of the Lebanese side by side with that of the Armenians, who were the victims of a systematic genocide. Some argued that the Turks, along with the Germans, "adopted a more silent yet no less efficient method" than they did in the case of Armenian Christians.[29] For example, Lebanese writer and émigré activist Khalil Gibran wrote in a letter to his friend Mary Haskell, "My people of Mount Lebanon are perishing from a famine that has been organized by the Turkish government. The same thing that is happening in Armenia is happening in Syria." The Armenians died by the sword and the Lebanese of hunger, both wielded by the hands of the tyrant Turks, he continued.[30] Jamal Pasha replied to these accusation in his postwar memoir: "I say that when you maintain in your books that I intentionally allowed the Christians of Syria to die, you are stating what is pure fiction!"[31] But the Turks did not work alone. Damascus and Aleppo, Charles Corm wrote, "saw their prosperity grow more than ever during the war"; Corm insisted the Lebanese were "hunted by the Turks and betrayed by the Arabs" during the war.[32] Albert Naccache in the December 1919 issue of the *Revue* blamed "the population of the hinterland" for draining the savings of the Lebanese "in the most complete and inhumane" way.[33] Lebanon's political separation from the Arabs, hence, was a necessity.

Securing humanitarian intervention through soliciting empathy and shock was yet another discursive tool: here the famine's horrors dominate. Alfred Coury, based on his own wartime experience, lamented its cruelty. While claiming to avoid the "heart-breaking scenes and the suffering of innocent people, who died of hunger," he nevertheless paints a powerful, albeit broad picture: "The famine transformed villages into cemeteries; mothers buried their children with their hands. For a year, the number of deaths in some regions was such that burials became impossible. Lebanon was nothing more than a charnel house."[34] To drive his point home, he cites the 1917 American Red Cross's estimation of 250,000 dead from starvation. The number, rather than claim any accuracy, serves as a rhetorical device. "How many have died since?" he asked. No one knew, but "whole villages were deserted. In others deprivation and misery were awaiting all of those more resilient people, who had survived." Moreover, in a nod to France's benevolent potential, he wrote that it was a known fact that the French high commissioner, upon his arrival in Beirut, had collected fifteen hundred homeless children in just one day.[35] How could it have come to this?

For Corm and other Christian Lebanese nationalists, the famine was central to their personal history and that of their country. There was little ambiguity concerning Corm's vision of the future. As the owner of the *Revue*, he signed one of the many petitions presented to the inter-Allied commission led by two Americans, Charles R. Crane and Henry C. King. American president Woodrow Wilson had tasked the King-Crane Commission to survey local political desires. Traveling across Greater Syria in the summer of 1919, the commission met with numerous people and received even more petitions. Corm placed his signature on a document drawn up by a group of Beiruti journalists who demanded the establishment of a "Greater Lebanon," with France as its Mandatory power.[36] In the eyes of Christian Lebanese nationalists, like Corm, the new state should be Christian leaning; oriented toward France, which had the power to provision and protect; and separate from an Arab or Syrian state, which had failed or intentionally neglected to care for its people. Their argument for such separation was the cultural and ethnic distinctiveness of the people of Mount Lebanon. The help of France, framed not as a colonial but as a benevolent power, was needed. Lebanese victimhood fit nicely into this request.

Narratives of Victimhood:
Visual and Textual Representations of Suffering

The famine's visual archive expanded the humanitarian narratives aimed at providing shocking facts and soliciting empathy. Viewing the war years through the lens of his camera, Ibrahim Na'um Kan'an, an assistant to the governor of Mount Lebanon, captured what newspaper and journal articles could only hint at: death calling for women and children.[37] The titles of his presumably mostly staged photographs hint at Kan'an's intention to make visible to a future generation the "Excessive Torment." The victims here were mothers and their children. A "little daughter rests her head on the knee of her mother, waiting for her unjust death." Kan'an's mother "bows her head to her children and the torment tears apart her heart."[38] Both textual and visual accounts suggest not even the most intimate bond as that between mother and child could withstand the war of famine.[39] Similar images were put to work in a special edition of the *L'Asie française* (French Asia) in 1922. The bulletin was the sounding board of the Comiteé de l'Asie française (Committee of French Asia), which was one of four committees established between 1890 and 1910 to advertise French colonial expansion.[40] The images,

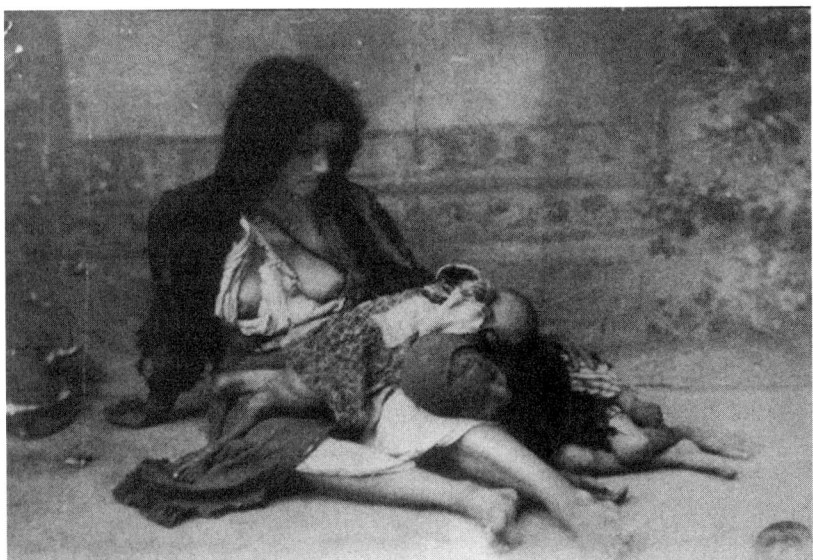

Figure 15. Excessive Torment. Source: Kan'an, *Lubnan fi al-Harb al-Kubra*, 175.

accompanied by eyewitness accounts of the famine and accounts of *successful* French relief efforts, highlight the impotence of Lebanese men, who had disappointed not only their families but also ultimately their country. The *Scene of the Lebanese Famine: In Expectation of Death* lends a visual of the men, who were incapable of living up to their role as providers,[41] helplessly sitting by, as death was pending. This man failed to preserve female dignity and the family.

That the war placed immense pressure on the family as a unit cannot be denied.[42] It was a reality running through many of the sources.[43] Larger numbers of orphans and female heads of household (this was particularly true for Armenian refugees settling in the region) were the symptoms of a crumbling family support system. The absence or impotence of men to provide for their families generated a crisis in familial hierarchies. Men had lost their honor and with it control over their families, as normative gender roles based on male protection and guardianship over women had fallen victim to war and famine.[44] Combined with the failure of urban male patrons, the failure of fathers and husbands "produced a pervasive crisis of paternity."[45]

Figure 16. Scene of the Lebanese Famine: In Expectation of Death. Source: The Fouad Debbas Collection / Sursock Museum, Beirut, Lebanon. Ref. No. TFDC/A187/1882.

The despair among men who were unable to sustain their families or who had simply lost everything apparently caused a surge in male suicides.[46] The result: There was no longer a governing structure in the city or the family.

Narrating the Rescue of the Famine Victim: Liberation and Relief

This visual gendered discourse of suffering was framed by a narrative account of France's postwar famine relief. It elevated France as the legitimate power, the rescuer who had a moral obligation to help this male shadow regain his strength and heal the family. One of the authors in *La revue phénicienne* exclaims, "'It is necessary to aid the city!' This was the primary concern of the French government in Paris." This assertion was not wrong. There was an urgency to relieve the suffering expressed, in the timing of the relief work and also Piépape's telegram. A report on the relief work published in Corm's *Revue* described the relief efforts as working like clockwork, and within eight months he had made assurances that no one in the city would starve. The authors praised the relief operation's success, citing the declining numbers of people considered needy. This was possible "thanks to our government!"[47]

While France was able to establish a new imperial regime, the urgency and success of its provisioning efforts were not uncontested. Counternarratives highlighting the continued contentions in the political field of provisioning emerged. For example, rumors spread of Corm's scheme as perhaps not being as efficient as thought, due to wastage and lazy French officials.[48] Simon Jackson argues that Corm's constant defense of the French relief operations in his journal and to the Beirut press intimates things were probably not going so well. Carla Eddé's account of relief work highlights the power of narration. Her reading of Beirut paper *Lisan al-Hal* in combination with French colonial archives highlights the complex postwar political landscape. The Beirut municipality reemerges as an agent of relief, absent in Corm's account. The visibility of the municipal council here is both a result of Eddé's sources and her project itself. In Eddé's account the French military officials financed soup kitchens, placed them under the supervision of the municipality, and started a fund for the poor with 1,000 Egyptian pounds, a measure that, according to the local press, did little to solve the city's problem.[49] The entrance of French troops and the arrival of thousands of refugees was partially blamed for the worsening of the situation because they placed further pressure on the food supplies.[50] While Corm's account locates the organization of relief firmly in the hands of the French and his own, Eddé argues that the organization was done in conversation with merchants and the municipal council.[51] Furthermore, her sources decried the increasing government intervention in the market and a repression of merchants. *Lisan al-Hal* then forges another narrative based on its editor's political sentiments. Unlike Corm, whose pro-French leanings were unquestioned, *Lisan al-Hal*, a Christian publication, was moderate. Nadine Méouchy sees the paper as representative of voices of merchants and businessmen, and thus the editor, although recognizing Greater Lebanon as a desired outcome, advocated for an economic union with Syria and condemned confessionalism.[52] A subtle anti-French sentiment can be detected in its editor decrying the French military government as irresponsible when signing over the relief operations to the municipality in an attempt to "spare the French budget."[53] In Eddé's reading of *Lisan al-Hal* it was not the French success that decreased the number of recipients from December 1918 to January 1919 but the limited budget of the municipality, a fact that could now be blamed on the colonial government. Simultaneously, price controls and registry of inventory were phased out as well. And in February 1919, a "liberalization" of trade was decreed. Given that shortages persisted, the measure, according to Eddé, was aimed at mollifying the merchant community in the city, who as important and powerful persons were not so easily sidelined after all.

Municipal council members, however, did not entirely let go of the potential of "giving." Beginning in March 1919, knowing that free distribution would eventually come to an end, the council began to make monthly payments to the most destitute of the city. Approximately 150 households were deemed deserving after inspection by the council members or by suggestion of the president of the municipality. The program lasted until the fall of 1920. The majority of recipients were women, widows with children, and families of soldiers who had not returned from the front. Most recipients were Sunni Muslims. The money distributed was not enough to sustain most of these families. Instead, the subsidies were more rewarding for the giver than the receiver. The scheme as narrated in *Lisan al-Hal* and interpreted by Eddé demonstrated the council's autonomy in matters of provisioning from the

Mandatory powers.⁵⁴ Male urban notables, merchants, and council members, who were blamed for the failures of the war period, were not so easily dismissed but continued to work to reassert their power in the city. Their rehabilitation took time, however.

The Political Woman: From Angels of Charity to Outspoken Nationalists

For elite Muslim women the war years were not a failure. Instead, women had stepped in where their male counterparts were unable to function and asserted a political position in the space of provisioning. Their gained confidence, in contrast to the male crisis, is visible in their postwar political activities. Elite Muslim women of Beirut came together in a number of societies and articulated their political desires to the American King-Crane Commission. The women introduced themselves to the commission by alerting them of their agency: "Many westerners imagine oriental women as mere playthings or slaves with no idea of any knowledge or education, but imagination is not reality and what may be said of the few may not be true of the whole."⁵⁵ The women insisted that the "oriental woman" was "now taking an active part in all affairs." Female education, they argued, would raise a new woman aware "of her position in the East, as the mother who commands and is obeyed." Their position in the politics of provisioning was instrumental in adding to the women's self-confidence. The women announced that during the war they had more than ever before taken on responsibilities outside the home, directing "hospices, conducting schools, managing industrial works." To lighten the burdens inflicted by the war, women of all classes had shared in the work. What is most important is that the women saw their new work as "driven by circumstances."⁵⁶

Ibtihaj Kaddourah in her letter to the King-Crane Commission wrote: "The cries of hunger, sight of distress, conditions which have affected us no less than the roaring cannons or the crash of ruins. The sight of thousands in distress dying hopeless has inspired us to strive for better things for our people that in the future they may be better fitted to lead a stronger life."⁵⁷ Helping those in distress, the women felt, had taught them that their actions were essential to the well-being of society. Now it was their responsibility to express their desires for the future. Independence of the nation was equated with the independence of women. Aware of the opportunity and critical nature of the moment, the women saw it as their duty not to remain silent. "We have for the first time disregarded the custom which bars the oriental woman from participating in political affairs in the hope of achieving that liberty and independence upon which our hearts are set."[58]

American womanhood was presented as an ideal, as it, according to the author, did not go to extremes, such as taking women out of their rightful sphere, as mothers, sisters, and wives who direct and lead the family. So independence with guidance and help from the Americans, it was thought, would serve them well. Besides international rhetoric of self-determination propagated in what has been called the "Wilsonian Moment," Americans had proven to be benevolent actors on the ground. Their continued work in the mountains and in the city through the consul and the AMP, as well as private charity distributed by SPC, had positioned America as *the* benevolent power. American wartime neutrality and the fact that foreign missionaries and educators, although clearly part of prewar Ottoman society and politics, stood outside obligatory communal patronage meant that American relief efforts were less likely to be measured by failures. In addition, Ottoman involvement and support of their work in the mountains were submerged beneath the internationalist humanitarian banners of the Red Cross and Red Crescent. The state was not front and center as it was in the failed Ottoman attempts in the city curated by ʿAzmi Bey and others.

The Americans' postwar relief efforts contributed to a vision of the United States as a sensible tutelary power in the eyes of women and others. Members of the American Red Cross committee arrived in Beirut as part of the British occupation forces and ensured that American relief work was immediately restarted in Beirut and expanded in the mountains. Mary Bliss Dodge helped organize a soup kitchen near the college grounds, and the Red Cross started a "huge central cooking plant from which they sent supplies to five or six substations in the city." Bayard Dodge and his wife were in charge of a substation near the college, where they gave out bread and cooked food for about 550 persons every day. Dodge expressed his discomfort with the distribution of food, wishing to add industrial work as had been done in the mountains during the war.[59] According to Dodge, what "the people need now is not easy charity and sentimental sympathy, but hard work and strict justice. Years of despotism and war have demoralized the people, so that what they need most of all is to learn self-respect and to shift for themselves."[60] The Americans, now with the threat of confiscation and expulsion removed, began to promote what was referred to as active citizenship, defined as an individual's economic contribution to the community. This was an ideal in line with the desires of the Beirut elite women. Dodge argued that "pauperizing a land is worse than starving it" and that it was the duty of the men in charge to do everything in their power to make "the people feel some self-respect and teach them the love of work."[61] For Dodge, the benefits from developing industry were not only teaching young men responsibility, developing their skills, and building up their self-respect and confidence but also building in them "the hope for a future generation of honest, efficient businessmen."[62] In practice, the Americans had been educating women in their schools for decades, and wartime relief was coupled with teaching valuable skills, such as carpet weaving. This American role as patron, which had proven to work during the war because it saved people from starvation, was something that women could get on board with. France had after all been absent during the war. Still, full independence was the ideal.

In a desideratum to the King-Crane Commission, the leading members of four Muslim women's societies issued seven demands, which included the political independence of Syria, a rejection of Article 22 of the League of Nations, an objection to any secret treaties concerning Syria, and the immigration of foreign Jews into Palestine. The government was to be constitutional, democratic, and decentralized and led by Faisal and the "Executive Head of the States." This meant that there was no room, according to the letter, for "the establishment of a greater or lesser Lebanon separate from the rest of Syria, and [we] repeat our request that the unity of our country not be broken."[63] The women leading this movement and publicly asserting themselves politically were the same ones who had worked to feed the hungry during the war under the umbrella of the Syrian Ladies' Association. Some, like Ibtihaj Kaddourah, signed the petition as a member of the Arab Girl's Awakening Society. Others, like 'Adila Bayhum, Amina Bayhum, and a Miss Da'uq, signed as the leaders of the Beirut Industry Shelter (Dar al-Sana'at al-Beirutiyyah), which had been established during the war in the house of 'Umar Da'uq. Miss Salam, Miss Ihsan Bayhum, and Fatmeh Nabeer endorsed the petition as leading women of a society concerned with charity for Muslim girls. The majority of signatures were those of the unmarried daughters of Muslim urban notables. Beirut's elite women, as did women in Egypt, made national independence their primary political concern.[64] Women's political rights were not addressed. Instead, participation was based on women's role as mothers, who run family rather than state affairs. This drive to contribute to the new nation was not temporary. Female political activism was expanded under French occupation. Although they continued to be rebuked by their male counterparts, during the French occupation urban women would demand political participation, especially the right to vote.[65]

The women's view of the United States as a potential benevolent Mandatory power was buttressed by Americans continuing to distribute aid and opening and supplying orphanages for Armenian genocide survivors, as well as by Wilson's rhetoric of self-determination. That the Americans had gained legitimacy within the context of provisioning is clear, but why did this not translate into an instituted power position, as it did for France? Both internal and external influences were factors. For example, their longstanding relations with the Maronite community, as an important "other authority," served to confirm the decisions of French government officials.[66] Whereas power theorists of legitimacy more often highlight the internal processes that forge hierarchies of rule, external influences through particular policies put in place in Paris to prove the validity of the French Mandate cannot be ignored when thinking of American positionality in the postwar politics of provisioning.

The Dangers of a Famine Memory: Why Forget the Eaters of Children?

Whereas pro-French, mostly Christian authors and women saw the famine as central to their wartime narratives, others avoided mentioning it.[67] Those men who had either collaborated with the Ottomans, failed as charitable and communal patrons, or, worst of all, been accused of wartime profiteering had to work to reestablish themselves in the aftermath of war. In this case the famine memory was problematic. Beirut urban notables, such as Salim 'Ali Salam and Muhammad Jamal Bayhum, for example, did not dwell on the famine. Instead, the focus of their wartime accounts was their political involvement, their marginalization under the CUP regime, and the public execution of Arab reformers in Beirut and Damascus. Historian Youssef Mouawad believes the absence or marginal mention of the famine in their work occurred partly because mass starvation had affected mainly Christians of Mount Lebanon. Thus, it was natural for non-Christian communities to be less invested in this story. While this might be true to a certain extent, it is more likely that the desire to speak about the famine, the experience of which was not confined to Mount Lebanon, was also linked to postwar political ambitions and wartime activities.[68] For urban notables like Salam, who was in support of an Arab government and an outspoken critic of French intervention, it was not simply lack of interest or an inability to relate to suffering. The Bayhum and Salam families were represented on the Beirut municipal council, in the leadership of local philanthropic organizations, and in Ottoman wartime relief efforts. This meant that some family members were at the center of provisioning politics, at least for part of the war, the story of which includes an overall failure and some not-so-flattering activities, such as profiteering.[69] The causation of famine thus would be a slippery subject to discuss, especially since Salam and Bayhum were eager to take on a leadership role in the post-Ottoman period. The men's political ambitions were exemplified in their rush to take leadership in the celebratory moment of independence following the withdrawal of the Ottomans. Writing about the famine would in one way or another expose failure and perhaps even corruption, effectively disqualifying the authors as able and trustworthy leaders. Resistance to Ottoman rule and communal martyrdom had more political currency for men like Salam. Salam's political allegiances were clear when, as a representative at the Syrian National Congress, he voted against the Faisal-Clemenceau accords in 1920.[70] Highlighting his resistance against Ottoman rule was one way to elevate him as a political leader who would work against foreign rule even when his life was in danger.

The opposition to the accords did not upset only the French but also the Maronite patriarch Huwayyik, who had used his continued wartime connection to France and his, albeit shaky, unremitting role as patron of Mount Lebanon's Maronites, to assert a political voice and power in the postwar political landscape. Huwayyik expressed his dissent in a telegram to the French high commissioner, assuring him the vote of the Syrian Congress was not representative of the desires of the Lebanese people. Instead, he reminded the commissioner that "we trust that the Allies will be just in dealing with the poor Lebanese, who had suffered so much because of their dedication to the Entente cause."[71] The Lebanese had sacrificed.

Huwayyik, as is well known, led a Lebanese delegation to the Paris Peace Conference in 1919 and has been considered by some as the founder of modern Lebanon. But even here some work had to be done in the immediate postwar period to rehabilitate Huwayyik and forge the image of a loyal and capable patron. The discussion over food and famine was central. Huwayyik's power position was not uncontested, as he faced resistance from secular Maronites as well as Muslims and Druze, who in large part were not considered in the wartime provisioning scheme of the church. Postwar accounts acknowledge that secular Maronites criticized the patriarch for his accommodating stance toward Jamal Pasha, a fact that made recalling the famine here too problematic. They "felt the Patriarch had shown weakness" when in 1916 he signed a statement publicly announcing that Jamal Pasha had been treating the population of his district and beyond well, particularly Christians. The church explained this, and other actions of the patriarch that could be perceived as spineless or as pro-Ottoman, as sound political strategy in light of "an existential crisis" that deserved extraordinary measures. For example, in an article in the Jesuit paper *al-Bashir* (The herald) on March 1, 1922,[72] the patriarch's deputy described the famine as a calamity of life and death and praised Huwayyik as a man who only thought of saving his people. Swallowing his pride and humbly bowing to Jamal Pasha, he did not think of himself but of those who were starving. His selflessness made him a perfect communal leader. A large proportion of the Maronite community agreed with this assessment, making Huwayyik the spokesperson of their community. The patriarch's power was buttressed by the Mandate power's assurance of the political prominence of the church.[73] For the Maronite Church and the larger Maronite community the war and the church's role in wartime and postwar politics of provisioning meant both internal and external recognition of political legitimacy. The church was losing power to a secular representative governing body in the mountain district prior to the war, but the war clearly reversed that trend. Jamal Pasha's crackdown on the AC; the continued, albeit at times fledgling, role of the church in provisioning; and the support of its long-standing French ally allowed the church not only to reassert political power but also to descend from the mountain district to pick up the reins of governing the new colonial state with strict supervision of its neopatrimonial patron.

Beyond the 1920s: A Wartime Memory Lost in History and Landscape

Once the political chaos of the 1920s turned into fixed borders, colonial occupation, and, later, independence, the famine disappeared as a prominent historical event altogether. The fact that people experienced the famine differently did not neatly fit into a communal history of the newly forming nation. Because it was a "Pandora's box or a ticking bomb, the question of famine had to be relegated to oblivion."[74] Consequently, the official Lebanese state narrative casts the war and the last years of Ottoman rule as heroic resistance and martyrdom. The everyday experience of the war, dominated by ugly accounts of hunger, starvation, and social collapse, was overshadowed by accounts of nationalism, in which the memory of the execution of Arab reformers, both Christians and Muslims, by Jamal Pasha and the CUP took center stage. Focusing on both the person of Jamal Pasha and the multisectarian martyrs preempted the possibility of exonerating the Turks and blaming Muslims in general.[75]

This change in focus is evident in historical writings. George Antonius's book *The Arab Awakening*, first published in 1938, is an early example of this historiographical shift. While he does account for the famine and its "variety of causes," he argues that underlying any of these was a "deliberate motive." Jamal Pasha gave orders prohibiting or allowing the purchase of grain. Since "whole sections of the population were known to be disaffected" and suspected to be collaborating with the Allies, Jamal applied "the discrimination" (prohibiting food from being shipped into the region) wholesale, indifferent to the consequences.[76] In this, Antonius's explanation of the famine resembles that of earlier Christian, pro-French narratives, which also placed the blame on a premeditated, systematic Turkish policy. However, the famine, covered in a few paragraphs, is not a prominent concern in his book. The emphasis is on burgeoning Arab nationalism during and after the war.[77]

Publishing in the 1950s and 1960s, professional historians of Lebanon either avoided including the famine or briefly mentioned it without discussing its social and economic causes and consequences in any detail. Most authors continue to blame the Ottoman Turks for the suffering. Stephen Longrigg, in 1958, writes:

> The accusations of "deliberate extermination" brought by Lebanese spokesmen and later writers are overstated. It is certain that Turkish malice *as well as* their military exigencies (and sheer inefficiency) was largely to blame in a long-drawn tragedy which cost the Mountain perhaps a fifth of its inhabitants, and Beirut and the coastal towns a large though lesser proportion.[78]

Longrigg rearticulates the content of earlier narratives without taking into account the politics of their production, while mediating intentionality by acknowledging "sheer inefficiency." Philip Hitti mentions World War I as marking the end of the capitulations, the *mutasarrifiyya*, emigration abroad, and the beginning of a broad-based nationalism. Hitti both addresses Jamal Pasha's oppression of individuals and makes him responsible for much of the suffering caused by military conscription, requisitioning, and the use of "crops for troops and trees as fuel for trains and camps," while the Allied blockade "interfered with food, clothing and medical supplies."[79] He hints at local profiteering, but overall Hitti does not dwell on the topic of starvation. The locusts and other environmental factors are absent from his account. Kamal Salibi excludes the famine in his *The Modern History of Lebanon*.[80] If not avoiding the famine, important historical works on Lebanon and Syria tend to summarize its causes and swiftly transition to discussing the Arab Revolt, Sykes-Picot, and the Balfour Declaration.

The physical memory of the famine was also revised. Yusuf Huwayyik's *Deux pleureuses*, which introduced us to the wartime suffering, remained in place under the French Mandate (1923–1946) and into the early years of the new Lebanese Republic. The representation of female suffering, endured and depicted poignantly by Huwayyik's statue, had fit well with the politics of European postwar paternalism charged with Mandates in Greater Syria. However, the gendered discourse of suffering, an expression of a crisis of paternalism, lacked a visualization of brave resistance, a fact that was increasingly voiced in public. The resistance to the statue became physical when a man named Salim Sleem in protest partially destroyed one of the women's faces in broad daylight in September 1948. In his view the statue did not represent the heroic resistance of the Lebanese but reminded everyone of the shame incurred by years of war.[81]

In the spring of 1960, the public's discontent was finally mollified with a new monument. The new statue that ultimately gained approval from the political leadership and continues to be displayed in Beirut's city center, although now riddled with bullet holes from the most recent civil war (1975–1990), was the work of Italian sculptor Renato Marino Mazzacurati (1907–1969). It is an imposing bronze monument, which was installed in a ceremony attended by Lebanese president Fuad Shihab (1902–1973) on May 6. Its theme was the episode of male martyrdom, presented as a heroic moment of resistance.[82] Mazzacurati's monument evoked the themes of Lebanese liberation and freedom. At its center we find Liberty towering victoriously, raising a torch with her right hand, its fire dancing in the wind. Her hair, garments, and body imply forward movement. Dynamic and strong, she stretches her left arm around a smaller yet vigorous and muscular male figure: the Nation. At the feet of this "allegorical pair of Liberty and Nation," and as if thrown to the floor, two young male "martyr" figures struggle against an unseen foe.[83]

The famine, characterized by a slow, lethargic, tired, and most important, passive mode of starvation, was successfully and intentionally silenced in a nationalist discourse of dynamism, courage, and violent emancipation. Its memory was removed, like Huwayyik's *Deux pleureuses*, from public view. And with it the famine's destructive and formative power, which had dominated the everyday wartime experience of all inhabitants of Beirut and Mount Lebanon and forged the political landscape of the nascent state, disappeared into oblivion. It was like Huwayyik's monument hidden away. The *Deux pleureuses*, however, mysteriously reappeared in an "unspecified warehouse" in 2001, recovered by the director of the Nicolas Ibrahim Sursock Museum in Beirut, and has been on display in the museum's garden since 2008.[84] It is no longer true that there are no plaques and no statues to commemorate starvation. Inspired by mysterious recoveries and lingering silence, here the famine's history and memory have been put on display, issuing an urgent call for further evocations.

NOTES

Abbreviations

AUB	American University Beirut, Beirut, Lebanon
AGOP	Archive of the Greek Orthodox Patriarchate, Beirut, Lebanon
Bkirki	Archive of the Maronite Patriarchate, Bkirki, Lebanon
BOA	Başbakanlık Osmanlı Arşiverli [Ottoman State Archive], Istanbul, Turkey
FKS	Fliedner Kultur Stiftung [Fliedner Cultural Foundation], Kaiserswerth, Germany
GCA	Archives of the Greek Catholic Archdiocese, Beirut, Lebanon
GCCA	Greek Catholic Charity Association, Beirut, Lebanon
HI	Hoover Institution, Stanford University, Stanford, CA
LNA	Lebanese National Archive, Beirut, Lebanon
MAE	Ministère des affaires étrangères [French Ministry of Foreign Affairs], Nantes, France
NARA	National Archives and Record Administration, Washington, DC
NEST	Near East School of Theology, Beirut, Lebanon
PA-AA	Politisches Archiv des Auswärtigen Amtes [Political Archive of the Federal Foreign Office], Berlin, Germany
PO	Jesuit Archives Proche-Orient [Jesuit Archive of the Near East], Beirut, Lebanon
StPH	Archives of St. Paul, Harissa, Lebanon
USDS	US Department of State
USEK	Université Saint-Esprit de Kaslik [Holy Spirit University of Kaslik], Kaslik, Junieh, Lebanon
USJ	St. Joseph University, Beirut, Lebanon

Acknowledgments

1. "News from Syria," May 4, 1917, 5.
2. The title of the article was changed midday: see Anne Barnard, Hwaida Saad, and Somini Sengupta, "Starving Syrians in Madaya Are Denied Aid amid Political Jockeying," *New York Times*, January 11, 2016, http://www.nytimes.com/2016/01/11/world/middleeast/syria-starvation-madaya-siege-united-nations.html?_r=0.

Introduction

1. Lebanon gained independence from France in 1943.
2. The square's shape and name have changed a number of times since the nineteenth century. Khalaf, *Heart of Beirut*, 190–191; Volk, *Memorials and Martyrs*, 52–53.
3. Yusuf Huwayyik was the nephew of one of the most powerful political figures in postwar Lebanon, the Maronite patriarch Ilias Butrus al-Huwayyik. Volk, *Memorials and Martyrs*, 67.
4. Al-Hakim, *Bayrut wa-Lubnan* [Beirut and Lebanon], 131.
5. "Syrian and Lebanese News," *Al-Muqattam* [literally "the broken," the name of a range of hills southeast of Cairo], Cairo, September 19, 1916; Edward Nickoley, "Historic Diary," Edward Nickoley Collection, Box 1, File 2, AUB.
6. For mobilization in a Greater Syrian town, see Rida, *Mudhakkirat lil-tarikh* [Memories of history]. For a detailed account of the Ottomans' entry into the war, see Aksakal, *The Ottoman Road to War*.
7. The numbers exclude hundreds of thousands of men and women conscripted into labor battalions. See Aksakal, "The Ottoman Empire," 468.
8. Historians Stephane Audoin-Rouzeau and Annette Becker estimate the war's total casualties of mostly soldiers as around 9 to 10 million. See Audoin-Rouzeau and Becker, *14–18*, 21. Edward J. Erickson estimates Ottoman military casualties at 771,844. See Erickson, *Ordered to Die*, 237–243. Ottoman civilian deaths are approximated as about 2.5 million, with some historians citing numbers closer to 5 million. This includes approximately 1.2 million Ottoman Armenian victims of genocide. Gelvin, *The Israel-Palestine Conflict*, 77.
9. The Ottoman military engaged in five major campaigns: the Caucasus Campaign (1915–1918) against the Russians along the northeastern borders of the empire; the Gallipoli Campaign (1914–1916) against the French and British; the Mesopotamian Campaign (1914–1918) against the British; the campaign against British and Russian troops in northern and western Persia (1914–1918); and the Palestine Campaign against mostly British troops in the Sinai. In addition, the empire fought a number of smaller battles, most notably against Arab forces in the Hejaz region of the Arabian Peninsula (1916–1918).
10. Greater Syria includes the geographic area of today's Jordan, Syria, Lebanon, and Israel and the occupied territories of Palestine.

11. There are no reliable statistics concerning the death toll from the famine. George Antonius estimated that 350,000 people succumbed to famine in Greater Syria. Based on German records, Linda Schilcher argued for the number to be closer to 500,000. Antonius, *The Arab Awakening*, 241; Schilcher, "Famine in Syria," 231; Thompson, *Colonial Citizens*, 27.

12. Beirut's population was about 185,000 in 1914. By 1918 it was reduced to 80,000, according to a letter from Jerome Vuallie, Superior of the Capuchin brothers in Syria, published in the journal *Les missions catholiques* [The Catholic missions], October 10, 1918. Vuaille, "La famine à Beyrouth [The famine in Beirut]," 553.

13. T. Khalidi, "The Arab World," 292.

14. Grayzel, *Women's Identities at War*, 7; Healy, *Vienna*, 5.

15. Nickoley, "Historic Diary."

16. Adivar, *House with Wisteria*, 371.

17. Nickoley, "Historic Diary."

18. "The State of Affairs in Syria and Lebanon," *Al-Muqattam*, October 24, 1916.

19. Unofficial Report from Bayard Dodge to Cleveland Dodge, "Relief Work in Syria during the Period of the War," 1918, Howard Bliss Collection, Box 18, File 3, AUB.

20. Downes, *Targeting Civilians*, 14.

21. The historian Nicholas Ajay interviewed Yusuf Rufa'il in 1964. Ajay, "Mount Lebanon," appendix, 61.

22. Ibid.

23. Stories of cannibalism were and continue to be powerful rhetorical devices exemplifying the complete breakdown of society and family and the real horrors of famine. Najwa al-Qattan points out that a subsection of Ibrahim Kan'an's *Lubnan fi al-Harb*, titled "Eaters of Children's Flesh," was republished by Lebanese historian Wael Hallaq in a volume edited by Khalid al-Lahham under the title *Old Beirut in the Papers of Ibrahim Na'um Kan'an* in the 1990s. See Kan'an, *Lubnan fi al-Harb al-Kubra* [Lebanon during the Great War], 167–169; Wael Hallaq, "Social Life in Beirut," 127–135; Al-Qattan,"When Mothers Ate Their Children," 724.

24. Al-Qattan, "When Mothers Ate Their Children," 724; also see Fawaz, *Land of Aching Hearts*, 115.

25. Al-Qattan, "When Mothers Ate Their Children," 724.

26. Thompson, *Colonial Citizens*, 15.

27. Ó Gráda, *Famine*, 68.

28. Quoted in al-Qattan, "Fragments of Wartime Memory," 135.

29. Khalaf, *Heart of Beirut*, 191; Volk, *Memorials and Martyrs*, 69.

30. Lebanese minister Muhieddine al-Nsouli was an outspoken critic of Huwayyik's statue. Volk, *Memorials and Martyrs*, 67–69.

31. Morgenthau, *Ambassador Morgenthau's Story*, 172.

32. Çiçek, *War and State Formation*, 2, 7.

33. Morgenthau, *Ambassador Morgenthau's Story*, 174.
34. Tauber, *The Arab Movements*, 28; Volk, *Memorials and Martyrs*, 41.
35. One of the first scholarly works that addressed the memory of World War I in the region was Farschid, Kropp, and Dähne, *The First World War as Remembered*.
36. Furayha, *Qabl an Ansa* [Before I forget], 49.
37. By "popular memory" I mean a memory that is articulated in the course of casual conversations and interviews.
38. The historiography of the Armenian genocide looms large here. See, for example, Suny, *"They Can Live in the Desert"*; Kévorkian, *The Armenian Genocide*; for Syria, see Thompson, *Colonial Citizens*; al-Qattan, "When Mothers Ate Their Children."
39. Mukherjee, *Hungry Bengal*, 1.
40. Farge, *The Allure of the Archives*, 44.
41. R. Khalidi, *The Origins of Arab Nationalism*; Kayalı, *Arabs and Young Turks*; Jacobson, "Negotiating Ottomanism"; Kayalı, "Wartime Regional and Imperial integration"; Çiçek, *War and State Formation*.
42. Notable exceptions are Watenpaugh, *Bread from Stones*; and Jacobson, *From Empire to Empire*. For a more general account of famine and humanitarian relief, see Edkins, "Legality with a Vengeance."
43. Tanielian, "Politics of Wartime Relief," 70.
44. Letter from Bayard Dodge to unknown relative (Bub), January 21, 1915, Bayard Dodge Collection, Box 6, File 4, AUB.
45. Gill, "The Rational Administration of Compassion," 12.
46. Bourdieu, "The Social Space," 723.
47. Abigail Jacobson's *From Empire to Empire* partially tells the history of Jerusalem through this lens.
48. Antonius, *The Arab Awakening*; McKale, *War by Revolution*.
49. Fromkin, *A Peace to End All Peace*.
50. Schneer, *The Balfour Declaration*.
51. There are some notable exceptions to this usual trend. See Morrow, *The Great War*.
52. Letter to Bayard Dodge to unknown relative (Bub), January 21,1915, Bayard Dodge Collection, Box 6, File 4, AUB.
53. The concept of "total war" is derived from General Erich Ludendorrff's statement that "total war meant total mobilization of all human and material resources for unlimited warfare under the total control of a military dictatorship." Chickering and Förster, *Great War, Total War*, 7.
54. Historians Stig Förster and Roger Chickering have edited multiple volumes exploring the term's history and utility. See Chickering and Förster, *The Shadows of Total War*; Chickering and Förster, *Great War, Total War*; Boemeke, Chickering, and Förster, *Anticipating Total War*.

55. Ernst Jünger, lieutenant in the German army and World War I veteran, coined the term *totale Mobilmachung* (total mobilization). See Kitchen, Miller, and Rowe, *Other Combatants*, xxv.

56. Chickering, *The Great War*, 159.

57. Healy, *Vienna*, 3.

58. The erasure of the division did not follow a linear trajectory. Throughout the nineteenth century, European diplomats and politicians were eager to strengthen the line between soldiers and civilians in warfare, codifying attacks on civilians as war crimes. Downes, *Targeting Civilians*, 1.

59. Chickering, "Total War," 16; Chickering, *The Great War*, 159.

60. In John Morrow's imperial history of the war, *The Great War*, the Ottoman home front simply does not exist. For examples of an effort to include non-European actors and societies, see Fogarty, *Race and War in France*; Samson, *World War I in Africa*; Liebau et al., *The World in World Wars*; Kitchen, Miller and Rowe, *Other Combatants, Other Fronts*. The centennial of World War I sparked the desire to rewrite the war's history as a global or transnational conflict. This opened the arena for historians of the Ottoman Empire and the Middle East to contribute to a growing, more inclusive historiography and to challenge the peripheralization of the empire. For example, the 2014 Istanbul conference "Not All Quiet on the Ottoman Front" invited scholars of the Great War from eighty countries to symbolically and intellectually provincialize Europe by viewing the war through the Ottoman experience.

61. The Ottoman victory at Gallipoli was instrumental in framing Mustafa Kemal as a national hero. The loss at Sarikamish has served to blame the CUP leadership for its reckless actions that led to the end of the empire.

62. The exception is a twenty-seven-volume official Ottoman military history commissioned by the Turkish General Staff in the 1930s. Because the volumes are almost impossible to obtain within and outside Turkey, historians have been unable to examine their content and reliability. See Erickson, "Turkish Official Military Histories," 190–198.

63. Aksakal, "The Ottoman Empire," 463–465.

64. Migdal, *State in Society*.

65. C. Tilly, "War Making," 171.

66. Ibid.

67. Hunt, *The Nervous State*, 8.

68. In *War and State Formation*, Talha Çiçek frames Jamal Pasha's policies in the context of state formation and larger Ottoman imperial centralization policies. See also Kayalı, "Wartime Regional and Imperial Integration," 295.

69. Çiçek, *War and State Formation*, 17.

70. Rabinow and Rose, "Biopower Today," 200; Çiçek, *War and State Formation*, 16–19.

71. C. Tilly, "War Making," 181.
72. Barnett, *Empire of Humanity*, 23.
73. Rabinow and Rose, "Biopower Today," 200.
74. Hunt, *The Nervous State*, 8.
75. Mitchell, "Limits of the State," 82.
76. Midgal, *State in Society*, 63.
77. Mitchell, "Limits of the State," 82.
78. Midgal, *State in Society*, 49.
79. Rabinow and Rose, "Biopower Today," 203.
80. Watts and Bohle, "Hunger," 118.
81. Midgal, *State in Society*, 52.
82. Hanssen, *Fin de Siècle Beirut*; Sharif, *Imperial Norms*; Fawaz, *Merchants and Migrants*.
83. Naguib and Okkenhaug, *Interpreting Welfare*, 2.
84. Beşikçi, *The Ottoman Mobilization*, 8.
85. Eley, "War and the Twentieth-Century State," 155–174.
86. Rabinow and Rose, "Biopower Today," 200.
87. Jacobson, *From Empire to Empire*, 23.
88. Singer, "Politics of Benevolence," 230.
89. Maksudyan, "Being Saved to Serve," 48.
90. Ibid.
91. Midgal, *State in Society*, 52.
92. Jacobson, *From Empire to Empire*, 23; For an account of postwar humanitarian relief in the eastern Mediterranean see Watenpaugh, *Bread from Stones*.
93. Acknowledging the difficulties, Chickering's "total history" is narrowly focused on the German city of Freiburg between 1914 and 1918. Chickering, *The Great War*, 159.
94. The SPC was renamed American University of Beirut (AUB) on November 18, 1920.
95. Howard Bliss, "*51st Annual Report of the Syrian Protestant College* (1917)," AUB.
96. Such headlines can be found in Arabic-language papers across the globe, for example, *Al-Salam* [literally, Peace or Soundness] (Argentina), originals of which are held at USJ in Beirut, *Al-Muqattam* (Egypt), and *Mirat al-Gharb* [Mirror of the West] (United States).
97. Samuel, *Theatres of Memory*, 443–444.
98. Ibid.
99. Eley, "War and the Twentieth-Century State," 156.
100. Frederick Bliss, "Retrospect: (1914–1919)," Howard Bliss Collection, Box 17, File 2, AUB, 12.
101. Healy, *Vienna*, 15.

Chapter 1: A City and Its Mountain

1. Nellie Miller-Mann to her family, September 25, 1921, in Mann, *Letters from Syria*, 19.
2. Nellie Miller Mann to her sister, October 2, 1921, in ibid., 20.
3. Baufort, *Egyptian Sepulchres*, 103.
4. Historically, scholars have described famine as an unavoidable curse of nature that maintains the equilibrium between population and resources. Thomas R. Malthus (1766–1834) famously argued that famine occurs when a population has outgrown the earth's capacity to produce subsistence. See Malthus, *Essay on the Principle of Population*, 56. This Malthusian explanation remained influential well into the twentieth century. See Gritzner, *Feeding a Hungry World*, 22; Ehrlich, *The Population Bomb*. Since the 1980s, scholars of Africa and South Asia have successfully challenged Malthus's theory, proving famine to be a man-made disaster. The Ottoman Empire's history with famine provides another strong case against Malthus. For example, while the empire's population doubled in the nineteenth century, famines decreased. An increase in economic opportunities and mobility mediated population growth. Famines, of course, did not completely disappear. The Ottoman historian Özge Ertem, for example, has written an excellent study of previously unexamined famines in central Anatolia (1873–1875) and in eastern Anatolia (1879–1881). Ertem, "Eating the Last Seed," i.
5. Ibn Khaldun is said to have been the first to use the Arabic term *maja'a*. See Allouche, *Mamluk Economics*, 11.
6. Ibn Khaldun, *The Muqaddimah* [Introduction], 249.
7. Chapra, "Islamic Economics."
8. Taqi ad-Din al-Maqrizi served as the market supervisor under the Circassian Mamluk regime in Egypt. Al-Maqrizi drew on Khaldun's theory to explain the economic catastrophe leading to a famine in fifteenth-century Egypt. Like al-Maqrizi, Ibn Taghribirdi focused on governmental failures. In his example, people were unable to purchase food because of high prices (not the absolute absence of food) and oppressive taxes. The result was a decline in peasants' productivity, resulting in grain shortages, which were amplified by the debasement of currency. The interpretational framework of these fifteenth-century men of letters, albeit couched in religious rhetoric, may be seen as an early precursor to Amartya Sen's entitlement theory. Allouche, *Mamluk Economics*, 3.
9. Ibid., 11.
10. Sen, *Poverty and Famines*. Among the many works that built on Sen's example was Alamgir, *Famine in South Asia*; For critiques of Sen, see Rangasami, "Failure of Exchange Entitlements," 1457; Ertem, "Eating the Last Seed," 14.
11. Sen, *Poverty and Famines*, 1.
12. Watts, *Silent Violence*, lxx.
13. Ibid.
14. Solnit, *A Paradise Built in Hell*, 3.

15. Watts and Bohle, "Hunger," 118.
16. Ibid.
17. Following the example of Healy, *Vienna*, 11.
18. Independence movements include, for example, the Greek War of Independence (1821–1832), the Egyptian occupation of Syria (1831–1841), the Crimean War (1853–1856), the Russo-Turkish War (1877–1878), the Italian-Turkish War (1911–1912), and the Balkan Wars (1912–1913).
19. Deringil, "They Live in a State of Nomadism," 311.
20. Makdisi, "Corrupting the Sublime Sultanate," 193.
21. Suny, *"They Can Live in the Desert,"* 7.
22. Controlling much of the land and tax collections, elite families dominated specific areas in the mountains. The Janbulat family ruled the Shuf, and the Khazin family presided over the Kisrawan. Makdisi, "Corrupting the Sublime Sultanate," 186; for a detailed history of this period, also see Traboulsi, *A History*, 5–23.
23. In resistance, the commoners demanded an end to exploitation and administrative reforms, including the formation of a representative council. Traboulsi, *A History*, 12–13.
24. Ibid.
25. The treaty outlawed monopoly economies in the empire, lowered and fixed import and export duties, and reduced the amount of taxes paid as part of internal trade.
26. Fahmy, *All the Pasha's Men*, 291.
27. Ibid.
28. Beirut and Mount Lebanon were not unique in this vulnerability-producing shift. The geographer Michael Watts argues for a similar intensification of commodity production driven by colonial occupation in Nigeria. Reducing peasants' subsistence farming, British colonial policies also undermined peasants' abilities to deal with climatic stress, making it impossible to avoid famine. Watts, *Silent Violence*, lvii.
29. Traboulsi, *A History*, 53.
30. Fawaz, *Merchants and Migrants*, 102.
31. Economic historian Charles Issawi estimates a population growth from 6,000 inhabitants in 1800, to 10,000 in 1840, 60,000 in 1860, 100,000 in 1890, and approximately 150,000 in 1914. Issawi, *The Fertile Crescent*, 28; Fawaz, *Land of Aching Hearts*, 35.
32. Zachs, *The Making of a Syrian Identity*, 44.
33. Fawaz, *Merchants and Migrants*, 44.
34. For a detailed discussion of Beirut's shifting demographics, see ibid., 51.
35. Ibid., 62.
36. Pamuk, "The Ottoman Economy," 112.
37. In 1910, the import value was estimated at $25,595,000, which declined to $15,980,000 in 1912 and rose again in 1913 to $20,390,700. Exports showed a steady decline beginning in 1910. Stanley Hollis, *Trade and Commerce at Beirut, Syria, for the Year 1914 and January 1915*, File 610, Vol. 187, Record Group (RG) 84, NARA.

38. Stanley Hollis, *Trade and Industry of Syria, September 3, 1915*, File 610, Vol. 187, RG 84, NARA.
39. Hollis, *Trade and Commerce at Beirut, Syria*.
40. Hollis, "Commerce and Industries of Syria," 1610.
41. Ibid., 1605; Fawaz, *Merchants and Migrants*, 63.
42. Khater, *Inventing Home*, 27.
43. Ibid., 65.
44. Pamuk, *A Monetary History*, 209.
45. Khater, *Inventing Home*, 202n50.
46. Hollis, *Trade and Commerce at Beirut, Syria*.
47. Ibid.
48. Khater, *Inventing Home*, 19–47.
49. Fawaz, *Merchants and Migrants*, 63–66.
50. Hollis, *Trade and Commerce at Beirut, Syria*.
51. Lebanese out-migration began in the late eighteenth century when about 4,000 Syrian urban elites settled in Cairo and Alexandria. Philipp, *The Syrians in Egypt*, 11.
52. The majority of migrants were young, lower-class, single men. Although out-migration was not exclusively male, the norm seemed to be that women stayed put, running the households and filling in for their husbands and fathers wherever needed. Women's increasing presence outside the home, as was the case elsewhere, challenged preexisting family structures and internal politics and, according to Khater, "strained the gender 'contract' to its breaking point." Khater, "Queen of the House?," 274; Naff, "Lebanese Immigration," 141–145.
53. Emigrants have been estimated at 10,000 in 1909, 20,000 in 1911, 25,000 in 1912, and 30,000 in 1913. Issawi, "The Historical Background," 31; Naff, "Lebanese Immigration," 141–145.
54. Ajay, "Mount Lebanon," 300.
55. Haqqi, *Lubnan* [Lebanon], 472.
56. In 1913, one bank alone had paid more than $2.5 million in remittances from South America. Stanley Hollis, *Trade and Industry of Syria*.
57. Grobba, *Die Getreidewirtschaft Syriens* [The grain economy of Syria], 13.
58. Ajay, "Mount Lebanon," 302.
59. Hollis, "Commerce and Industries of Syria," 1605.
60. Kassir, *Beirut*, 135.
61. High travel expenses discouraged visitors from America; to facilitate trade, the American consul at Beirut organized the American-Syrian Chamber of Commerce, which was charged with advertising American companies and products in Greater Syria.
62. Hollis, "Construction Work in Turkey," 505.
63. Khater, *Inventing Home*, 116.

64. One French franc equaled approximately $5.16. The construction of the Beirut–Damascus road alone cost its French investors 4.2 million francs, or about $800,000. See Hanssen, *Fin de Siècle Beirut*, 10; For a conversion table, see Pamuk, *A Monetary History*, 209.

65. The Beirut–Damascus railway was built and operated by a French company under a concession purchased from the Ottoman state. But even with such development, there was still no railway connection between Istanbul and the Arab provinces as late as 1912.

66. Forder, "Damascus, the Pearl of the Desert," 63.

67. Hollis, "Commerce and Industries of Syria," 1605.

68. Özdemir, *The Ottoman Army*, 28; Townshend, *Desert Hell*, 15.

69. Hourani, "Ottoman Reform," 87.

70. Gelvin, *The Modern Middle East*, 19.

71. Hathaway, *The Arab Lands*, 80; Gelvin, "The 'Politics of Notables' Forty Years After."

72. R. Khalidi, "Ottomanism and Arabism," 63.

73. Traboulsi, *A History*, 13.

74. The Ottomans, in a controversial move, appointed Bashir Milhim Qasim (Bashir III) as the new emir of Mount Lebanon. The emir's reign, a short eighteen months, was marked by tensions between Druze, who were disillusioned with the Shihabi regime, and loyal Maronites. Traboulsi, *A History*, 22–23, 48–49; Hakim, *The Origins*, 13.

75. The remaining 31 percent were 22 percent Christians and 9 percent Muslims. Fawaz, *Merchants and Migrants*, 23; Kassir, *Beirut*, 71; Ziser, *Lebanon*, 4; Makdisi, "Corrupting the Sublime Sultanate," 193–194; Traboulsi, *A History*, 15.

76. Van Leeuwen, "The Political Emancipation," 7; Makdisi, *The Culture of Sectarianism*, 68.

77. Hakim, *The Origins*, 19; Fawaz, *Merchants and Migrants*, 23.

78. Salibi, *House of Many Mansions*, 15–16; Hakim, *The Origins*, 39.

79. Gelvin, *Modern Middle East*, 72–89.

80. For property and land reforms, see Doumani, *Rediscovering Palestine*; Islamoğlu, *Constituting Modernity*; Mundy and Saumarez Smith, *Governing Property*; for the debate, see Deringil, "They Live in a State of Nomadism," 311–342; Jacobson, *From Empire to Empire*, 17.

81. Deringil, *The Well-Protected Domains*, 9–10.

82. Makdisi, "Corrupting the Sublime Sultanate," 194.

83. Hitti, *Lebanon in History*, 399.

84. Makdisi, "Corrupting the Sublime Sultanate," 196.

85. For example, prior to the election of Bulus Mas'ad (a commoner) as the patriarch in 1854, the *muqata'ji* families held the monopoly over the appointments to the patriarchal seat. Hakim, *The Origins*, 19.

86. Ibid., 20.

87. As reported by the French consul to Lebanon in 1881. See ibid.

88. Hitti, *Lebanon in History*, 436.

89. Locally collected taxes were the basis of the mountain's yearly budget. Only the surplus was sent to Istanbul, and the Ottoman treasury made up any deficits. Salibi, *Modern History of Lebanon*, 110.

90. Spagnolo, "Mount Lebanon," 149.

91. The elections took place in two stages. Villagers elected a local representative, who after being confirmed by the *mutasarrif*, proceeded to elect council members. The council, after some revisions, was to be made up of four Maronites, three Druze, two Greek Orthodox, one Greek Catholic, one Sunni, and one Shiite Muslim. Arkalı, *The Long Peace*, 184.

92. Salibi, *Modern History of Lebanon*, 109.

93. One point of contention was a later-revised legal provision assigning equal representative shares to Maronites and religious groups, despite the Maronites' demographic majority. Hakim, *The Origins*, 164.

94. Arkalı, *The Long Peace*, 184; Hakim, *The Origins*, 122–123.

95. Arkalı, *The Long Peace*, 136; Hakim, *The Origins*, 167.

96. Hanssen, *Fin de Siècle Beirut*, 7–8.

97. Ibid., 39.

98. The government in Istanbul appointed the heads of each of these departments. Mundy and Saumarez Smith, *Governing Property*, 44.

99. Kassir, *Beirut*, 133.

100. The first municipality was established in Istanbul (Pera and Galata) in 1858. See Baer, "The Beginning of Municipal Government." Under the Egyptian occupation of Greater Syria an urban council created new departments of public health and commerce as well as a police force. See Kassir, *Beirut*, 102–103.

101. Urban reforms as part of the Tanzimat restructuring have been addressed by only a handful of scholars. See Lafi, "Mediterranean Connections"; Rosenthal, "Foreigners and Municipal Reform"; Rosenthal, "Urban Elites." For Beirut, see Hanssen, *Fin de Siècle Beirut*; Davie, *Beyrouth* [Beirut]; Sehnaoui, *L'occidentalisation de la vie quotidienne à Beyrouth* [The Westernization of everyday life in Beirut]. One of the most important new studies is Malek Sharif's *Imperial Norms*.

102. Kechriotis, "Protecting the City's Interest," 210.

103. For more details, see Hanssen, *Fin de Siècle Beirut*, 150–162; Hanssen, "Origins of the Municipal Council," 148–151; Pamuk, *Monetary History*, 209.

104. Sharif, *Imperial Norms*, passim.

105. Hanssen, *Fin de Siècle Beirut*, 84–110.

106. The tax was set at 100 piasters per month. By 1880, only 724 individuals out of about 100,000 were eligible to run for positions in the municipality. Ibid., 64. For a conversion table, see Pamuk, *Monetary History*, 209.

107. Hanssen, "Origins of the Municipal Council," 149.
108. Kaufman, *Reviving Phoenicia*, 56.
109. Ibid.
110. Salibi, "Beirut under the Young Turks," 205.
111. Çiçek, *War and State Formation*, 40–41.
112. Traboulsi, *A History*, 48.
113. For the various strands of this group's political ideologies, see Hakim, *The Origins*, 157.
114. The AC also lobbied for a port on the Lebanese coast so that the mountain could directly benefit from international trade. However, a powerful lobby of Beirut and French merchants, who feared it would reduce commerce at the Beirut port, objected to the measure.
115. Hakim, *The Origins*, 163–164.
116. Ibid., 168.
117. Mundy and Saumarez Smith, *Governing Property*, 44.
118. Hathaway, *The Arab Lands*, 80.
119. Midgal, *State in Society*, 63.
120. Hanssen, *Fin de Siècle Beirut*, 74.
121. Singer, "Serving Up Charity," 481–482.
122. Ener, *Managing Egypt's Poor*, 20.
123. Barnett, *Empire of Humanity*, 49.
124. Pollard, "Egyptian by Association," 241.
125. Cole, "Al-Tahtawi on Poverty," 229.
126. Examining the emergence of such volunteer associations in Egypt, the historian Lisa Pollard describes the initial associations as combining elements of guilds and Sufi lodges. Pollard, "Egyptian by Association," 243.
127. Ibid., 241–242.
128. For example, the Education Society (Jam'iyyat al-Tahdhib) was founded in 1845. Ibrahim al-Yaziji, Butrus al-Bustani, and Mikha'il Mashaqqa founded the Syrian Society of Arts and Science (Jam'iyyat al-Suriyya lil-Iktisab al-'Ulum wa al-Funun) in 1847, which was renamed the Syrian Scientific Society (al-Jam'iyyat al-'Ilmiyya al-Suriyya) in 1852. Elshakry, *Reading Darwin in Arabic*, 48–49.
129. There are no systematic studies of local nongovernmental philanthropic activities before or during the war. The existing works are organizational histories of single associations, and most of these accounts gloss over the war years as a period of reduced or discontinued communal work. See Kabkab, *Jam'iyyat al-khayriyya* [Charitable Society]; Kabkab, *Jam'iyyat al-Mursalin al-Bulusiyyin* [Missionary Society of St. Paul]; Slim, *The Greek Orthodox "Waqf"*; Davie, *Atlas historique* [Historical atlas]; Shibaru, *Jam'iyyat al-Maqasid* [Society of Al-Maqasid].
130. The Protestant British Syrian Mission, American Board for Foreign Missions,

and the Free School of Scotland began educating girls and instructing a female cadre of teachers in the early 1820s. Catholics understood the potential influence of the Protestant missions and sent their own female missionaries. Others, like the German Protestant Kaiserswerth deaconesses, joined the mission field after the war of 1860. Hauser, *German Religious Women*, 208–214; Ajay, "Mount Lebanon," 97; Jessup, *Fifty-Three Years*, 53.

131. Sultan Abdul Hamid II promulgated the Law for Public Education. Hauser, *German Religious Women*, 265.

132. Ibid., 257.

133. One of the driving forces behind the project was Labiba Jakhshan, who was educated in the foreign mission schools herself. Ibid., 263–264.

134. Watts and Bohle, "Spaces of Vulnerabilities," 44.

135. Watts and Bohle, "Hunger," 117.

136. Bourdieu, *The Logic of Practice*, 68.

Chapter 2: Wartime Famine

1. Whiting, "Jerusalem's Locust Plague," 533.

2. "The terrible plague of locusts in Palestine, March–June 1915. Locusts stealing in like thieves through window," The American Colony (Jerusalem), G. Eric and Edith Matson Photograph Collection, Library of Congress Prints and Photographs Division, Washington, DC.

3. Whiting here refers to Joel 2:9 in the Old Testament.

4. For newspaper articles, see "Plague of Locusts, like That of Biblical Times, Grips the Holy Land To-day," *San Francisco Chronicle*, November 17, 1915; "Remarkable Details from American Consul on Palestine Locust Plague," *New York Times*, November 21, 1915.

5. Lewis Larsson was the head photographer of the American Colony in Jerusalem.

6. Jamal Pasha appointed the agricultural scientist and Jewish émigré Aaron Aaronsohn as the inspector-in-chief of a new locust eradication program in 1915. Anderson, *Lawrence in Arabia*, 109.

7. Whiting, "Jerusalem's Locust Plague," 513. Frequent and recurring locust attacks were reported in Istanbul, Izmir, Aleppo, and Urfa during the war. Ayalon, *Natural Disasters*, 205.

8. Letter from Bayard Dodge to an unknown relative (Bub), April 14, 1915, Bayard Dodge Collection, Box 6, File 4, AUB.

9. Ibid.

10. McGilvary, *The Dawn*, 179.

11. The locust as divine punishment appeared both in the Bible and the Qur'an as one of God's punishments of the Egyptians. See Qur'an (Surat al-'A'raf 7:133).

12. McGilvary, *The Dawn*, 180.

13. See Tamari, *Year of the Locust*; Foster, "The 1915 Locust Attack."

14. Tamari, *Year of the Locust*, 107; Tamari, "The Short Life of Private Ihsan," 30.

15. Ayalon, *Natural Disasters*, 12.

16. As part of formulating an early-warning system, scholars have identified climate-produced famine regions. Greater Syria is located in a drought-induced famine belt. Devereux, *Theories of Famine*, 46.

17. Ajay, "Mount Lebanon," 335.

18. "Syria Suffers Drought," *Washington Post*, June 27, 1915.

19. *Report of the German Consul on the State of Sericulture in Lebanon*, June 5, 1916, Beirut 10, PA-AA.

20. Ayalon, *Natural Disasters*, 13.

21. Ibid.

22. The large body of historical literature on food production, distribution, and consumption originated with the French Annales school of the 1950s. In recent years, historians and anthropologists have framed eating increasingly as a process of cultural creation. Wallach, *How America Eats*, xii.

23. Ibid.

24. Tanielian, "Food and Nutrition."

25. Ó Gráda, *Eating People Is Wrong*, 1, 40.

26. Ibid., 39.

27. Mukherjee, *Hungry Bengal*, 7.

28. Prewar Ottoman foreign debt, according to economic historian Şevket Pamuk, accounted for 60 percent of the Ottoman gross domestic product (GDP). Servicing these loans took much of the yearly income of the empire. The CUP continued to pay the debt owed to Germany but declared a moratorium on all other debt payments. Pamuk, "The Ottoman Economy," 114.

29. Gelvin, *The Modern Middle East*, 113.

30. Communiqué from François Georges-Picot to Théophile Delcassé, October 3, 1914, *Guerre 1914–1918, Turquie*, Doc. 121, MAE.

31. Makdisi, *The Culture of Sectarianism*.

32. Haddad, "The City, the Coast," 146.

33. Jacobson, *From Empire to Empire*, 10.

34. Report from Jamal Pasha to Talat Pasha, December 12, 1914, BOA, Dahiliye Nezareti, Şifre Kalemi (Ministry of the Interior's Cipher Office; hereafter DH. ŞFR), 453/28, cited in Çiçek, *War and State Formation*, 95. Also see Schilcher, "Famine in Syria," 236.

35. Communiqué from Enver Pasha to the Interior Ministry, October 26, 1914, BOA, Dahiliye Nezareti Kalem-i Umumi (Ministry of the Interior's General Office; hereafter DH.UEM.KLU), 4/11 cited in Williams, "Economy, Environment, and Famine," 152.

36. Report from Gerhard von Mutius to German Consulate in Istanbul, May 1, 1915, Türkei 177, Bd. 11, PA-AA; letter from A. Defrance to Théophile Delcassé, April 24, 1915, *Guerre 1914–1918, Turquie*, Doc. 138, MAE.

37. Letter from the agent of the Archipelago American Steamship Company to Stanley Hollis in Beirut, January 29, 1915, File 624, Vol. 187, RG 84, NARA.

38. Letter from Stanley Hollis to Henry Morgenthau, February 10, 1915, File 624, Vol. 187, RG 84, NARA.

39. Telegram, Henry Morgenthau to Stanley Hollis, February 1, 1915, File 624, Vol. 187, RG 84, NARA.

40. Letter from the agent of the Archipelago American Steamship Company to Stanley Hollis in Beirut, January 29, 1915, File 624, Vol. 187, RG 84, NARA.

41. Letter from Henry Morgenthau to Stanley Hollis, March 9, 1915, File 624, Vol. 187, RG 84, NARA.

42. Letter from Henry Morgenthau to Wheeling Corrugating Company in New York City, January 4, 1916, File 610, Vol. 187, RG 84, NARA.

43. Strachan, *Financing the First World War*, 112.

44. McGilvary, *The Dawn*, 59.

45. Strachan, *Financing the First World War*, 112.

46. Letter from Stanley Hollis to Robert P. Lewis, March 5, 1915, File 610, Vol. 187, RG 84, NARA.

47. Schilcher, "Famine in Syria," 243.

48. Kramer, "Blockade," 462.

49. Vincent, *The Politics of Hunger*, 29.

50. Ó Gráda, *Famine*, 229.

51. While Kramer's German case study makes international comparisons, it neglects to mention the blockade's effects on the Ottoman Empire and the famine in Syria. Kramer, "Blockade," 462.

52. Schilcher, "Famine in Syria," 235.

53. Kramer, "Blockade," 462.

54. Ira Harris, *Commercial Report from the Year Ending 1914, Tripoli-Syria*, File 610, Vol. 187, RG 84, NARA. For military operations, see Ajay, "Mount Lebanon," 196.

55. Letter from Stanley Hollis to the Secretary of State in Washington, May 5, 1915, File 610, Vol. 187, RG 84, NARA.

56. Letter from Stanley Hollis to the editor of *Dun's Review*, September 29, 1915, File 610, Vol. 187, RG 84, NARA.

57. At the beginning of the war, the Ottomans packed up the customhouse's archives and took them into the interior. Stanley Hollis, *Trade and Commerce at Beirut, Syria, for the Year 1914 and January 1915*, File 610, Vol. 187, RG 84, NARA.

58. Ibid.

59. Ruppin, *Syrien als Wirtschaftsgebiet* [Syria as an economic zone], 246.

60. *Report of the German Consul to Beirut on the State of Sericulture in Lebanon*, June 5, 1916, Beirut, Bd. 10, PA-AA.

61. Hollis, *Trade and Commerce at Beirut, Syria*.

62. Haqqi, *Lubnan*, 389–390.

63. Letter from Stanley Hollis to the Secretary of State in Washington, June 8, 1915, File 620, Vol. 187, RG 84, NARA.

64. Pamuk, "The Ottoman Economy," 118.

65. Hollis, *Trade and Commerce at Beirut, Syria*.

66. Letter from Stanley Hollis to the Secretary of State in Washington, May 5, 1915, File 610, Vol. 187, RG 84, NARA.

67. Stanley Hollis, "Supplement to Commerce Reports," September 30, 1915, File 600, Vol. 187, RG 84, NARA.

68. Bayard Dodge, *Report of the Soup Kitchens in 'Abeih and Souk al-Gharb*, Howard Bliss Collection, Box 18, File 3, AUB; letter from A. Defrance to Théophile Delcasseé, April 24, 1915, *Guerre 1914–1918, Turquie*, Doc. 138, MAE.

69. Al-Qissis, *Lubnan fi al-harb* [Lebanon during the war], 407.

70. Although sugar and coffee were considered luxury goods, their prewar consumption was not limited to the wealthy. Indeed, all social classes consumed baked sweets during religious holidays and family celebrations. Many of the most prominent families continued to throw elaborate parties See "The Calamities in Syria," *Al-Muqattam*, March 31, 1916; "The Conditions in Beirut," *Al-Salam*, July 26, 1915; "Prices of Necessities," *Al-Ittihad al-'Uthmani* [Ottoman union], December 3, 1914.

71. Interview with Yusuf Nakhle and Archibald Crawford conducted by Nicholas Ajay, 1964. Published in Ajay, "Mount Lebanon," appendix, 95–97.

72. McGilvary, *The Dawn*, 64.

73. Stanley Hollis, "Supplement to Commerce Reports."

74. In 1913, the excess was about 76,000 tons. Grobba, *Getreidewirtschaft*, 11.

75. Linda Schilcher describes Grobba as a German relief worker. See Schilcher, "Famine in Syria," 235. Her description obscures the fact that he was an agent of the German government and fought with the German military on the Ottoman front. After the war, he was sent to Afghanistan to represent the German government and later became ambassador to Iraq and Saudi Arabia.

76. Letter from Ira Harris to Stanley Hollis, February 1, 1915, File 610, Vol. 187, RG 84, NARA.

77. Williams, "Economy, Environment, and Famine," 153.

78. "The Situation," *Al-Muqattam*, November 4, 1915.

79. "Les martyrs en Armenie et en Syrie [The martyrs in Armenia and in Syria]," 90–91.

80. Letter from Howard Bliss to Caleb F. Gates, April 25, 1918, Howard Bliss Collection, Box 10, File 1, AUB.

81. Winter, "Paris, London, Berlin," 10.

82. Ibid.

83. Grobba, *Getreidewirtschaften*, 19.

84. Adivar, *House with Wisteria*, 322.

85. Letter from A. Defrance to Théophile Delcassé, April 24, 1915, *Guerre 1914–1918, Turquie*, Doc. 138, MAE.

86. Stanley Hollis, *Trade and Industry of Syria, September 3, 1915*, File 610, Vol. 187, RG 84, NARA.

87. Hollis, *Trade and Commerce at Beirut, Syria*.

88. Dodge, *Report of the Soup Kitchens*.

89. Before the war, a railway car could be hired for about 20 Ottoman liras; in 1914, it cost 60. Grobba, *Getreidewirtschaft*, 18.

90. Schilcher, "Famine in Syria," 237; Kouyoumdjian, *Le Liban* [Lebanon], 137.

91. Grobba, *Getreidewirtschaft*, 18.

92. As stated by a Greek Orthodox refugee from Aleppo. "The Situation," *Al-Muqattam*, November 4, 1915.

93. Çiçek, *War and State Formation*, 239.

94. Ruppin, *Syrien als Wirtschaftsgebiet*, 312.

95. Dodge, *Report of the Soup Kitchens*.

96. Grobba, *Getreidewirtschaft*, 16.

97. A report by Reverend William S. Nelson, "Chaos Reported in Every Field," *Courier Journal*, September 24, 1914.

98. Kouyoumdjian, *Le Liban*, 74.

99. Edward Nickoley, "Historic Diary," February 12, 1917; letter from Howard Bliss to Kiazim Bey, May 29, 1917, Howard Bliss Collection, Box 1, File 1, AUB.

100. Nickoley, "Historic Diary."

101. Letter from Bayard Dodge to Cleveland H. Dodge, December 2, 1914, Bayard Dodge Collection, Box 6, File 3, AUB.

102. Pamuk, "The Ottoman Economy," 120; letter from Howard Bliss to Kiazim Bey, May 29, 1917, Howard Bliss Collection, Box 1, File 1, AUB.

103. "Carriage hire has quadrupled, and as much as £12 has been paid for a drive from Beyrout to Tripoli." "News from Syria," April 28, 1916, 701; "The Calamities in Syria," *Al-Muqattam*, March 31, 1916.

104. Schilcher, "Famine in Syria," 235.

105. The title of the section references the 1941 American war comedy starring Jimmy Durante and Jane Wyman.

106. Rida, *Mudhakkirat lil-tarikh*, 34–35.

107. Zürcher, "The Ottoman Conscription System," 79–94. For a comprehensive history of conscription in the Middle East and Central Asia, see Zürcher, *Arming the State*.

108. The Ottomans introduced a conscription system well before 1914, but universal conscription remained a utopian ideal due to inadequate infrastructure, religious and class biases, and the exemption fees that, abolished on paper, stayed in place. Beşikçi, *Ottoman Mobilization*, 67, 94.

109. The first round of conscription under the newly reformed system was issued on May 17, 1914, for all men born in 1894. Shaw, *The Ottoman Empire*, 131–136; Akın, "War, Women, and the State," 17.

110. "The Blockade," *Weekly Irish Times*, August 15, 1914.

111. Letter from François Georges-Picot to Gaston Doumergue, *Guerre 1914–1918, Turquie*, Doc. 103, MAE.

112. Ibid.

113. Beşikçi, *Ottoman Mobilization*, 103; Akın, "The Ottoman Home Front," 12; Shaw, *The Ottoman Empire*, 115, 121–123; Zürcher, "The Ottoman Conscription System," 451.

114. The term *safar barlik* was used first at the end of the nineteenth century, referring to the travel of recruits—mainly by foot—to the Ottoman fronts. See Hanna, "The First World War," 300; Al-Qattan, "Safarbarlik," 163–173.

115. McGilvary, *The Dawn*, 54–56.

116. Grobba, *Getreidewirtschaft*, 11.

117. Hanna, "The First World War," 304.

118. Letter from Bayard Dodge to Grace Dodge, August 20, 1914, Bayard Dodge Collection, Box 6, File 3, AUB.

119. "The Blockade," *Weekly Irish Times*, August 15, 1914.

120. Çiçek, *War and State Formation*, 94.

121. Letter from Stewart Crawford to Stanley Hollis, August 31, 1915, File 370, Vol. 187, RG 84, NARA.

122. For the total numbers of conscripted men, see Shaw, *Ottoman Empire*, 148.

123. "The Blockade," *Weekly Irish Times*, August 15, 1914.

124. Women, non-Muslims (officially until 1856 and in practice until 1909), residents of Mecca and Medina, religious functionaries and religious students, and some professional groups were exempted. Zürcher, "The Ottoman Conscription System," 79–94.

125. A government decree published in *Journale de Beyrouth* (Beirut journal) in the spring of 1917 demanded military exemption taxes to be paid in kind. Any of the following provisions would purchase a year of freedom: "4,000 kg of wheat, 4,550 kg of barley, 4,000 kg of potato, 5,150 kg of lentils, 3,200 kg of dry peas, 3,320 kg of bulgur, 4,300 kg of durrha [sorghum], 8,000 kg of berseem [clover]." Also see Çiçek, *War and State Formation*, 253.

126. Beşikçi, *Ottoman Mobilization*, 112.

127. Grobba, *Getreidewirtschaft*, 13.

128. Letter from Bayard Dodge to Cleveland H. Dodge, December 2, 1914, Bayard Dodge Collection, Box 6, File 3, AUB.

129. McGilvary, *The Dawn*, 56.

130. A *dunum* is approximately 900 square meters. Grobba carefully examined the given numbers, taking into account the differences in territories included from year to year. He includes a detailed discussion of his methodology. Grobba, *Getreidewirstchaft*, 1–20.

131. Grobba argues that the relatively small drop occurred because peasants still had plenty of seed grain from the previous year. Ibid.

132. Çiçek mentions that the Ottoman authorities, as did everyone else, thought the war would be short and thus mobilized without considering long-term difficulties. Çiçek, *War and State Formation*, 234.

133. Zürcher, "The Ottoman Conscription System," 443.

134. For a more detailed discussion, see Akın, "The Ottoman Home Front," 107.

135. Ajay, "Mount Lebanon," 161.

136. Letter from Gerhard von Mutius to German Consulate in Istanbul, May 1, 1915, Türkei 177, Bd. 11, PA-AA.

137. Ajay, "Mount Lebanon," 161–165.

138. Yalman, *Turkey in the World War*, 106; "The Abolition of the Capitulations: Consternation at Beirut," *Irish Times*, October 7, 1914; "Turkish Plunder under the Guise of War Needs," *Nashville American*, November 7, 1914.

139. Letter from Gerhard von Mutius to German Consulate in Istanbul, May 1, 1915, Türkei 177, Bd. 11, PA-AA.

140. Yalman, *Turkey in the World War*, 106.

141. According to Akın, the Ottoman authorities were not ignorant of the widespread abuses and, after amending the law, imposed punishments to curb abuses, but it seemed to no avail. Akın, "The Ottoman Home Front," 81.

142. Letter from Stanley Hollis to Mercer P. Moseley, March 17, 1915, File 610, Vol. 187, RG 84, NARA.

143. "Chaos Reported in Every Field," *Courier Journal*, September 24, 1914.

144. "Turkish Plunder under the Guise of War Needs," *Nashville American*, November 7, 1914.

145. Djemal [Jamal] Pasha, *Erinnerungen* [Memories], 202.

146. Ajay, "Mount Lebanon," 313.

147. Akın, "The Ottoman Home Front," 99.

148. Letter from Gerhard von Mutius to German Consulate in Istanbul, May 1, 1915, Türkei 177, Bd. 11, PA-AA.

149. Ajay, "Mount Lebanon," 304.

150. Hoskins, "In Syria," 550.

151. Grobba, *Getreidewirtschaft*, 9.

152. The study relies on a small number of privately held accounting records. Sa'id, "Tatawwur [Evolution]," 374–375.

153. Ibid.

154. Ajay, "Mount Lebanon," 305–306.

155. Khater, *Inventing Home*, 27.

156. Sa'id, "Tatawwur," 391.

157. Ibid.

158. Hoskins, "In Syria," 500.
159. Edkins, *Whose Hunger?*, 43–67.
160. Quoted in Ó Gráda and Eriksson, *Ireland's Great Famine*, 20.
161. Remoulière, "L'oeuvre du ravitaillement [The work of provisioning]," 56.
162. Letter from François Lahoud to R. P. Delore, May 28, 1919, in *Les missions catholiques* 51, no. 2621 (August 29, 1919): 411.
163. Al-Hakim, *Bayrut wa-Lubnan*, 249–259.
164. Quoted in Fawaz, *Land of Aching Hearts*, 124.
165. Ibid., 122.
166. Schilcher, "Famine in Syria," 249.
167. Fawaz, *Land of Aching Hearts*, 123.
168. Nickoley, "Historic Diary."
169. Letter from Gerhard von Mutius to Theobald von Bethmann-Hollweg, July 20, 1916, Türkei 177, Bd. 12, PA-AA.
170. Ó Gráda, *Eating People Is Wrong*, 39.
171. Devereux, *Theories of Famine*, 148.
172. Sewell, *Logics of History*, 197–198.
173. Ayalon, *Natural Disasters*, 3.
174. Arnold, *Famine*, 7.

Chapter 3: The Politics of Food

1. "The Flour Issue," *Al-Ittihad al-'Uthmani*, November 14, 1914; Ajay, "Mount Lebanon," 351; Parts of this chapter have been published in the International Journal for Middle East Studies. See Tanielian, "Feeding the City."
2. How widespread these attacks on the bakeries were cannot be established from this account. "The Flour Issue," *Al-Ittihad al-'Uthmani*, November 21, 1914.
3. Grobba, *Getreidewirtschaft*, 18; Schilcher, "Famine in Syria," 237–238.
4. Ajay, "Mount Lebanon," 351.
5. "The President of the Municipality in Damascus," *Al-Ittihad al-'Uthmani*, November 17, 1914.
6. "Flour," *Al-Ittihad al-'Uthmani*, November 20, 1914.
7. Although the shipment was the result of a combined effort of the Ottoman governor, the Beirut municipality, and merchants, the paper credited the president of the municipality, Ahmad Mukhtar Bayhum, for its success. Ibid.
8. Winter, "Paris, London, Berlin," 8.
9. Jacobson, *From Empire to Empire*, 23.
10. Hanssen, *Fin de Siècle Beirut*, 161.
11. "The Flour Issue," *Al-Ittihad al-'Uthmani*, November 21, 1914; Ajay, "Mount Lebanon," 354.
12. "The Flour Issue," *Al-Ittihad al-'Uthmani*, November 21, 1914.

13. Ibid.
14. Hanssen, "The Origins of the Municipal Council," 149.
15. Grobba, *Getreidewirtschaft*, 18.
16. "Ten Thousand Liras for Wheat," *Al-Ittihad al-'Uthmani*, November 23, 1914.
17. Ibid.
18. "The Wheat Issue," *Al-Ittihad al-'Uthmani*, April 20, 1915.
19. Letter from Gerhard von Mutius to German Consulate in Istanbul, May 1, 1915, Türkei 177, Bd. 11, PA–AA.
20. Williams, "Economy, Environment, and Famine," 153.
21. "The Prices of Necessities," *Al-Ittihad al-'Uthmani*, December 3, 1914.
22. Ibid. For a discussion of the economic situation in Damascus and Aleppo and the initial supply problems in Beirut, also see Williams, "Economy, Environment, and Famine," 150–162.
23. Furayha, *Qabla an Ansa*, 45; Ziadeh, "A First-Person Account," 266.
24. Faroqhi, *Towns and Townsmen*, 58, 132, 221.
25. Yıldırım, "Bread and Empire," 252.
26. Sharif, *Imperial Norms*, 58.
27. Hanssen, *Fin de Siècle Beirut*, 150; Hanssen, "The Origins of the Municipal Council," 149.
28. "Prices of Necessities," *Al-Ittihad al-'Uthmani*, December 4; "Beirut Municipality," *Al-Ittihad al-'Uthmani*, December 6, 1914.
29. For example, the Cairo papers report that wheat prices rose from about 15 piasters per *rotl* in July 1916 to about 40 piasters in November 1916. "Syrian and Lebanese News," *Al-Muqattam*, July 18, 1916.
30. "The Famine in Syria and Lebanon," *Al-Muqattam*, November 22, 1916.
31. Grobba, *Getreidewirtschaft*, 35.
32. *Sijil al-Joumiyya* [Daily register] 1 (1903–1930), November 25, 1916, StPH.
33. Ibid., April 13, 1916, StPH.
34. I thank Şevket Pamuk for pointing out to me the purchasing power of unskilled labor.
35. Grobba, *Getreidewirtschaft*, 24.
36. Also see Hanssen, "From Social Status."
37. Yusuf 'Abdallah Susa, "Beirut and Its Basic Needs: An Open Letter to His Excellency the Vali of Beirut," *Al-Ittihad al-'Uthmani*, December 7, 1914.
38. The French press during World War I issued similar appeals to the moral obligation of communal sacrifice. Robert, "The Image of the Profiteer," 104.
39. T. Khalidi, "The Arab World," 289.
40. Williams," Economy, Environment, and Famine," 153.
41. Letter from Gerhard von Mutius to German Consulate in Istanbul, May 1, 1915, Bd. 11, PA-AA.

42. Paul Rabinow describes the *dispositif* as "a device whose purpose was control and management." Rabinow, *Anthropos Today*, 50; Foucault, *Security, Territory, Population*, 31.
43. Hanssen, *Fin de Siècle Beirut*, 6.
44. R. Khalidi, "Ottomanism and Arabism," 53.
45. *Al-Ittihad al-'Uthmani*, November 21, 1914; December 10, 1914; January 9, 1915; April 11, 1915.
46. *Lubnan* [Lebanon], November 11, 1914. A copy of this paper can be found on microfilm at the Lebanese National Archive (LNA). According to an article in Cairo's *al-Muqattam*, only three Beirut papers still operated under the close scrutiny of authorities by the middle of 1916: *al-Akhbar* (News), *al-Balagh* (Communication), and *al-Haqiqa* (Truth). "News from Syria and Lebanon," *Al-Muqattam*, April 8, 1916.
47. Salibi, "Beirut under the Young Turks," 205; Tauber, *The Arab Movements*, 5.
48. Hanssen, *Fin de Siècle Beirut*, 78; Kassir, *Beirut*, 241.
49. Kassir, *Beirut*, 240.
50. For a more detailed account, see Salibi, "Beirut under the Young Turks," 207.
51. 'Abd al-Ghani al-'Uraysi was an outspoken Arabist. His editorials were often harsh critiques of the Turkish nationalism espoused by the CUP. See R. Khalidi, "The 1912 Election Campaign," 466.
52. Tauber, *The Emergence*, 143.
53. Tauber, *The Arab Movements*, 49–50.
54. Ibid., 44–45.
55. An act of treachery committed by a member of the Decentralization Party, Muhammad al-Shanti, exposed the actions of the reformers. Yamin, *Lubnan fi al-Harb*, 52–53; Tauber, *The Arab Movements*, 44–45.
56. Letter from Gerhard von Mutius to Theobald von Bethmann-Hollweg, March 8, 1916, Türkei 177, Bd. 12, PA-AA.
57. "The Flour Issue," *Al-Ittihad al-'Uthmani*, November 21, 1914.
58. Hanssen, *Fin de Siècle Beirut*, 157.
59. Kassir, *Beirut*, 204.
60. Fawaz, *Merchants and Migrants*, 96–97.
61. Bayhum sold the company only a couple of years later to a French entrepreneur who built the Beirut–Damascus road. Hanssen, *Fin de Siècle Beirut*, 95.
62. Ibid., 146–147.
63. Ibid., 154.
64. Sharif, *Imperial Norms*, 141.
65. Hanssen, *Fin de Siècle Beirut*, 160.
66. Kassir, *Beirut*, 242.
67. "Beirut and Its Basic Needs," *Al-Ittihad al-'Uthmani*, December 7, 1914.
68. "Commercial Activities in Beirut," *Al-Ittihad al-'Uthmani*, December 8, 1914.
69. "Flour," *Al-Ittihad al-'Uthmani*, April 9, 1915.

70. Habash, *Al-Jihad Lubnan* [Lebanon's struggle], 82.

71. "15 Municipal Sergeants," *Al-Ittihad al-'Uthmani*, November 25, 1914; for an elaboration on the role of municipal sergeants, see Salibi, "Beirut under the Young Turks," 201.

72. Kanaʻan, *Lubnan fi al-Harb*, 201.

73. Ibid., 106.

74. Historically, bitter vetch was consumed only as a last resort in times of great starvation. Grobba, *Getreidewirtschaft*, 36.

75. McGilvary, *The Dawn*, 205; "Syria during [the Month] of March," *al-Muqattam*, March 30, 1916.

76. Habash, *Al-Jihad Lubnan*, 97.

77. "Flour," *Al-Ittihad al-'Uthmani*, April 9, 1915.

78. See Qur'an, Surat al-Baqarah (2:179); "In Punishment There Is Life," *al-Ittihad al-'Uthmani*, March 31, 1915.

79. "The Vali's Attention to the Flour Issue," *Al-Ittihad al-'Uthmani*, March 31, 1915.

80. "Flour," *Al-Ittihad al-'Uthmani*, April 9, 1915.

81. "Wheat in Lebanon," *Al-Ittihad al-'Uthmani*, April 13, 1915.

82. Jamal Pasha to Talat Pasha, August 10, 1915, DH.ŞFR. 483/63, BOA, cited in Çiçek, *War and State Formation*, 23n. 121.

83. Salam, *Mudhakkirat* [Memoirs], 188.

84. Quoted in Ajay, "Mount Lebanon," 356.

85. "How to Distribute Flour?," *Al-Ittihad al-'Uthmani*, June 8, 1915.

86. "Syria and the Lebanon," January 26, 1917, 292.

87. Letter from Stanley Hollis to William Jennings Bryan, April 21, 1915, Records of the Department of State: Relating to Internal Affairs of Turkey, 1910–29, RG 59, 867.48/126, NARA.

88. Edward Nickoley, "Historic Diary, 1917," Edward Nickoley Collection, Box 1, File 2, AUB.

89. "The State of Syria," July 15, 1915, 303.

90. Whether the story is true or the author's narrative device to convey the chaotic and desperate situation in the city is unclear. See Kanʻan, *Lubnan fi al-Harb*, 156.

91. "The State of Agriculture," *Al-Salam*, May 9, 1916.

92. Grobba, *Getreidewirtschaft*, 18.

93. Letter from Howard Bliss to American Consul of Beirut Stanley Hollis, August 17, 1915, Missionaries, Box 2, File 1, AUB.

94. Eddé, *Beyrouth* [Beirut], 40.

95. *Bayrut Vilayet-i meclis umumisinin 1330 senesi ictimaʻında itiḥaz eylediği mükarirat* [Resolutions That Beirut General Assembly Adopted during Its Assembly/Meeting in the Year of 1330]. I thank Jens Hanssen for sharing this report with me.

96. Hanssen, *Fin de Siècle Beirut*, 80–81. For the economic survey, see Bahjat and Tamimi, *Wilayat Bayrut*.

97. *Bayrut Vilayet-i meclis umumisinin 1330 senesi ictima'ında itiḥaz eylediği mükarirat.*

98. Schilcher, "Famine in Syria," 237–238.

99. 'Ali Munif Bey replaced Ohannes Kouyoumdjian Pasha as the *mutasarrif* of Mount Lebanon in 1915.

100. Ajay, "Mount Lebanon," 352; Schilcher, "Famine in Syria," 237.

101. Grobba, *Getreidewirtschaft*, 19.

102. Çiçek, *War and State Formation*, 239.

103. Claude-Jacques Herbert in the 1750s and A. R. J. Turgot in the 1760s also promoted a free-market economy as alleviating famine. Ó Gráda, *Famine*, 13.

104. In May 1917, Ottoman authorities renamed the Office the General Directorate of Provisioning and placed it under the direction of Kemal Bey, who replaced the German-trained personnel with men loyal to him. German observers soon complained that the new provisioning scheme was aimed at enriching a small circle of Ottoman officials. And there was money to be made; the war ministry assigned a budget of 500,000 Ottoman liras to feed the provinces of the empire. Grobba, *Getreidwirstchaft*, 166.

105. Ibid., 22.

106. Taxes were rendered to the state in kind and in peacetime consisted of a tenth of the harvest.

107. The original draft of the law was published on July 25, 1916 (*Takvim-i Vekayi* [Calendar of events] Nr. 2598). The law was amended at least four times: September 7, 1916 (Nr. 2643); September 11, 1916 (Nr. 2643); November 7, 1916 (Nr. 2598); and December 13, 1916 (Nr. 2701) and amended on October 24, 1916 (Nr. 2690), as published in Grobba, *Getreidewirtschaft*, 22–23, 165–166.

108. Pamuk, "The Ottoman Economy," 123.

109. See *Takvim-i Vekayi* Nr. 2628 (September 11, 1916), in Grobba, *Getreidewirtschaft*, 166.

110. "Syrian News," *Al-Muqattam*, October 24, 1916.

111. Sen, *Poverty and Famines*, 80; Tilly, "Food Entitlement," 47–50; Also see Ó Gráda, "Adam Smith and Amartya Sen."

112. The interior minister had direct control over the commission, which was made up of all the members of the General Directorate of Provisioning, the undersecretary to the minister of trade, the director of the Ottoman Bank, and additional persons appointed by the minister of the interior. Grobba, *Getreidewirtschaft*, 166; Akın, "The Ottoman Home Front," 112.

113. These were led by the highest appointed Ottoman official and seated with members of the local governing bodies and chambers of commerce, the local military commander, and the director of the Ottoman Bank. Akın, "The Ottoman Home Front," 111.

114. Grobba, *Getreidewirtschaft*, 24.

115. In April 1917, the central authorities adjusted the districts. Only Jamal Pasha's zone did not change. For an account of provisioning of areas outside Greater Syria, see Akın, "The Ottoman Home Front," 112–120.

116. Schilcher, "Famine in Syria," 242.

117. Grobba, *Getreidewirtschaft*, 66.

118. Jamal Pasha assigned Tripoli's Mustafa 'Izzadin to Hama and Jerusalem merchant Albert Antebi to the grain-producing areas of Palestine. 'Izzadin was to deliver 60,000 tons and Antebi 20,000 tons. Grobba, *Getreidewirtschaft*, 24.

119. Ibid., 23–24.

120. The Ottoman government introduced paper currency at the outset of the war. Due to high inflation it quickly lost value. At the height of the famine, its worth plummeted by 75 percent.

121. Pamuk, "The Ottoman Economy," 124.

122. Scott, *Weapons of the Weak*, xvii.

123. Wiegand, *Halbmond im Letzten Viertel* (Half moon in the last quarter).

124. The Compulsory Cultivation Law was first announced on September 18, 1916 (*Takvim-i Vekayi* Nr. 2656), but it was not put into effect until April 3, 1917. See Grobba, *Getreidewirtschaft*, 174.

125. The Ministries of the Interior, Finance, Justice, Commerce, and Agriculture were charged with the implementation of this law. Ibid.

126. The organizations listed included trading companies, civil society associations, and subsidiary chapters of the Red Crescent. *Takvim-i Vekayi* Nr. 2656 (September 18, 1916). Ibid.

127. The amount of land to be cultivated by farmers who owned a set of male oxen or horses was 45 *dunums* and for a female pair, 35 *dunums*, according to the Ordinance on the Implementation of the Compulsory Cultivation Law, published on April 3, 1917. Ibid., 174.

128. Article 10, Ordinance on the Implementation of the Compulsory Cultivation Law. Ibid., 176.

129. A similar development may be seen in Germany. Davis, *Home Fires Burning*, 2.

130. Agamben, *What Is an Apparatus?*, 2.

Chapter 4: Prayers and Patrons

1. "Report of Father Louis and Father Butrus," November 22, 1917, Hoyek 77, Doc. 51, Bkirki.

2. Ibid.

3. Ibid.

4. *Sijil al-Joumiyya* [Daily register] 1 (1903–1930), August 8, 1916, StPH.

5. Ibid., December 1916.

6. Ibid., November 25, 1915.

7. Ibid., January 1916.
8. Ibid., March 6, 1916.
9. Ibid. December 1916.
10. "Total List of the Greek Catholic Sect in the Villages Associated to the Monastery of Mar Sema'an," *Al-Mutran [Bishop] Ignatius Suwaya* (1919), GCA.
11. "Syria and the Lebanon," 245.
12. "Census of Church Membership," *Al-Mutran Ignatius Suwaya* (1919), GCA.
13. "Report of Father Louis and Father Butrus," November 22, 1917, Hoyek 77, Doc. 51, Bkirki.
14. *Sijil al-Joumiyya* 1 (1903–1930), March 13, 1916, StPH.
15. Azzi, *Buhuth* [Research], 295.
16. "Proclamation of the Maronite Archbishop of Beirut," *Ittihad al-'Uthmani*, November 23, 1914.
17. See Azzi, *Buhuth*, 296.
18. Ibid.
19. Ibid., 293.
20. *Sijil al-Joumiyya* 1 (1903–1930), January 1916, StPH.
21. See, for example, *Sijil Beit Shabab* [Register of Beit Shabab], Record Number APCE-1215, Manuscript No.1, USEK.
22. See Azzi, *Buhuth*, 296.
23. *Sijil al-Joumiyya* 1 (1903–1930), January 1916, StPH.
24. Kabkab, *Jam'iyyat al-Mursalin al-Bulusiyyin*, 213.
25. The Paulists were initially not included in the committee. The convents were Deir el-Kerim (Maronite), Zumar (Armenian), Shirfe (Syriac), Nsbieh (Maronite), Ain Waraqa (Maronite), Mar Chalita (Maronite), and Deir Mar Bulus (Roman Catholic). Ibid.
26. Ibid.
27. *Sijil al-Joumiyya* 1 (1903–1930), March 12, 1916, StPH.
28. Kabkab, *Jam'iyyat al-Mursalin al-Bulusiyyin*, 214.
29. Letter from Georges-Picot to Théophile Delcassé, October 7, 1914, *Guerre 1914–1918, Turquie*, Doc. 123, MAE.
30. Çiçek, *War and State Formation*, 93.
31. McGilvary, *The Dawn*, 45–46.
32. Ajay, "Mount Lebanon," 102.
33. Çiçek, *War and State Formation*, 93.
34. The Syro-Lebanese community in Egypt counted close to a hundred thousand individuals and as a whole has been characterized as educated, ambitious, dominating in commerce, and generally wealthier than the average Egyptian community. Syro-Lebanese émigrés even owned six of the eleven Egyptian newspapers. Tauber, *The Arab Movements*, 12; Jackson, "Diaspora Politics," 168–171.

35. "France and Syria," *Mirat al-Gharb*, January 14, 1915.

36. Before the war a small Ottoman cavalry squadron of forty to fifty men, under the direct control of the Ottoman governor, was stationed in Beit ad-Din, the summer seat of the *mutasarrif*. The governor controlled a local militia of twelve hundred men. Ajay, "Mount Lebanon," 32.

37. Ibid., 35.

38. Quoted in ibid., 37.

39. Quoted in ibid., 38.

40. Ibid.

41. Ibid., 36.

42. Ibid., 217.

43. *Ittihad al-'Uthmani*, January 1, 8, and 10, 1915; March 12, 24, and 25, 1915. See also Ajay, "Mount Lebanon," 219.

44. "The Lebanese Administrative Council," *Ittihad al-'Uthmani*, January 24, 1915.

45. Ajay, "Mount Lebanon," 221.

46. Letter from Gerhard von Mutius to Istanbul, May 15, 1915, Türkei 177, Bd. 12, PA-AA.

47. Letter from A. Defrance to Théophile Delcassé, April 24, 1915, *Guerre 1914–1918, Turquie*, Doc. 138, MAE.

48. "The State of Syria," 303.

49. "News of the Lebanon," 321.

50. Colonel Rida Bey replaced the more lenient Tahsin Bey as president of the tribunal. Tauber, *The Arab Movements*, 63.

51. Ibid., 13–19.

52. The Syrian community in Canada approached its government in early 1915, expressing their wish to join the Entente forces. Ibid., 11–13.

53. Maronite Lebanese Khrayrallah Krayrallah founded the Comité libanais de Paris in 1912. Letter from Shukri Ghanem to Théophile Delcassé, November 30, 1914, *Guerre 1914–1918, Turquie*, MAE.

54. A letter dispatched to the Decentralization's branches in Lebanon listed available funds and manpower. Jamal Pasha's men discovered this communiqué among papers hidden in the French consulate. Tauber, *The Arab Movements*, 16.

55. Thompson, *Justice Interrupted*, 118.

56. Letter from Gerhard von Mutius to Theobald von Bethmann-Hollweg, June 19, 1915, Türkei 177, Bd. 12, PA-AA.

57. Ibid., October 2, 1915, Türkei 177, Bd. 12, PA-AA.

58. Ibid.

59. Ajay, "Mount Lebanon," 222.

60. Letter from Gerhard von Mutius to Theobald von Bethman Hollweg, July 20, 1916, Türkei 177, Bd. 12, PA-AA.

61. "News of Syria," 317.

62. Letter from A. Defrance to Théophile Delcassé, April 24, 1915, *Guerre 1914–1918, Turquie*, Doc. 138, MAE.

63. The German consul named Butrus Shibli as among the most dangerous clerics, who could pose a serious threat to the regime. See Letter from Gerhard von Mutius to Theobald von Bethmann-Hollweg, June 19, 1915, Türkei 177, Bd. 12, PA-AA.

64. "Syrian and Lebanese News," *Al-Muqattam*, October 3, 1916. For a more detailed account of Butrus Shibli, see Kanaʻan, *Bayrut*, 170.

65. Tauber, *The Arab Movements*, 11.

66. See, for example, the illustrious story of Beshara Buwari, recounted in Fawaz, *Land of Aching Hearts*, 148–160, based on al-Buwari, *Arbaʻ sinin al-harb* [Four years of the war].

67. Report by Georges-Picot reproduced in a letter by Théophile Delcassé to A. Defrance, November 5, 1914, *Guerre 1914–1918, Turquie*, Doc. 147, MAE.

68. Letter from Aristide Briand to Camille Barrère, June 20, 1916, *Guerre 1914–1918, Turquie*, Doc. 141, MAE.

69. The Greeks, according to Picot, agreed to supply some weapons and ammunition. For more details, see Tauber, *The Arab Movements*, 11.

70. Note from the British Ambassador in Paris to the French Foreign Ministry, December 18, 1914, *Guerre 1914–1918, Turquie*, MAE.

71. Tauber, *The Arab Movements*, 11.

72. Letter from Aristide Briand to Camille Barrère, June 20, 1916, *Guerre 1914–1918, Turquie*, Doc. 141, MAE.

73. Ibid.

74. Edmund Allenby led the Egyptian Expeditionary Force during the Sinai and Palestine Campaign, successfully occupying Palestine at the end of 1917.

75. There was much complaint about the Syro-Lebanese volunteers since they apparently lacked the will to go to battle and overall discipline. By October 1917, only 263 Syrians had joined the legion, which was stationed in Cyprus. Jackson, "Diaspora Politics," 171–172.

76. It would be published under "Announcement of the Patriarch" in *Ittihad al-'Uthmani* on December 2.

77. "Proclamation of the Maronite Archbishop of Beirut," *Ittihad al-'Uthmani*, November 23, 1914.

78. Ibid.

79. Azzi, *Buhuth*, 299.

80. Letter from Gerhard von Mutius to Theobald von Bethmann-Hollweg, July 19, 1915, Türkei 177, Bd. 12, PA-AA.

81. "For the Relief of Distress in Syria," 199.

82. In Beirut on July 31, 1915, December 1915, and May 1916, and in the mountain

town of Bhamdun in July 1917. See for example, "Local News," *Ittihad al-'Uthmani*, July 31, 1915; "The Maronite Patriarch and Jamal Pasha," *al-Muqattam*, December 18, 1915.

83. "For the Relief of Distress in Syria," 199.

84. *Sijil al-Joumiyya* 1 (1903–1930), May 1916, StPH.

85. Copy of the original letter published in Kabkab, *Jam'iyyat al-Mursalin al-Bulusiyyin*, 214.

86. Ajay, "Mount Lebanon," 246.

87. Djemal Pasha, *Erinnerungen*, 288.

88. Grobba, *Getreidewirtschaft*, 36.

89. The total amount of wheat distributed was 840 *rotl*, amounting to roughly 2 tons. Hoyek 31, Doc. 29, November 22, 1917, Bkirki.

90. Hoyek 31, Doc. 25, November 5, 1917, Bkirki.

91. *Sijil al-Joumiyya* 1 (1903–1930), September 1916, StPH.

92. "Syrian and Lebanese News: Maronite Patriarch Mortgages Properties of the Patriarchy," *Al-Muqattam*, October 3, 1916.

93. Letter from Ighnatius Al-Tannuri to Ilias Butrus Al-Huwayyik, April 11, 1917, Hoyek 77, Bkirki.

94. Letter from Ighnatius Al-Tannuri to Ilias Butrus Al-Huwayyik, May 1, 1918, Hoyek 77, Bkirki.

95. See Kabkab, *Jam'iyyat al-Mursalin al-Bulusiyyin*, 213.

96. Historically, the Maronite Church had functioned outside the realm of Ottoman supervision. While other religious groups, for example, were obliged to submit the results of their internal elections to Istanbul for approval, the Maronites answered only to the pope. Arkalı, *The Long Peace*, 174.

97. Ajay, "Mount Lebanon," 244.

98. McCallum, *The Christian Religious Leadership*, 63.

99. Letter from Aristide Briand to Jean Jules Jusserand, July 4, 1916, *Guerre 1914–1918, Turquie*, Doc. 401, MAE.

100. Letter from Yusuf Darian to Albert Trabaud, November 13, 1916, *Guerre 1914–1918, Turquie*, Doc. 4198–4200, MAE. Also see Ajay, "Political Intrigue," passim.

101. "Help for Syria," 4.

102. Community leaders blamed the late start of their aid effort on the international focus on Belgium, which had dominated the Egyptian papers, spurred by British propaganda efforts against Germany.

103. "For the Relief of Distress in Syria," 199; "Famine in Syria," *al-Muqattam*, July 10; "Appeal for Aid to Lebanon and Syria," *al-Muqattam*, June 9, 1916.

104. This included Sheikh al-Islam; the local representatives of the Coptic, Greek Orthodox, Maronite, and Greek Catholic Churches; the head rabbi of Egypt's Jewish community; American missionaries; and the leaders of the Protestant Church in Jerusalem and Egypt. Subcommittees, similarly constituted, were formed to collect funds

outside Cairo and Alexandria. "Famine in Syria," *al-Muqattam*, July 10; "Appeal for Aid to Lebanon and Syria," *al-Muqattam*, June 9, 1916.

105. Syrians living in Manchester appointed a provisional committee to act as a branch of the Syrian Relief Fund in Cairo. During the first meeting those present were able to collect subscriptions amounting to 1,000 Egyptian pounds. "Distress in Syria," 227.

106. "Letter to Syrians," *The Scotsman*, January 18, 1915.

107. Nancy Scheper-Hughes uses the term *delirio de fome* (madness from hunger) to discuss what becomes of love when lives are dominated by hunger. Scheper-Hughes, *Death without Weeping*, 132–133.

108. "The Famine in Lebanon and Syria," *Al-Muqattam*, November 22, 1916.

109. Yusuf Milhim Sha'iya founded the paper in 1912. The exact date when it ceased publication is unknown, but it seems to have had a short run as an émigré publication. *Al-Hawi* (Buenos Aires), the Maronite archives at Bkirki, include prewar correspondence between Yusuf Milhim Sha'iya and the patriarch. I thank Stacy Fahrenthold for sharing with me her discovery of letters between the two men.

110. The war was instrumental in shaping Syrian activism in the diaspora. Stacy Fahrenthold has shown how the brutal regime of Jamal Pasha not only triggered local resistance but also affected actions in the diaspora. Fahrenthold, "Sound Minds in Sound Bodies," 263.

111. The number became a convenient shorthand for suffering. Salim Effendi Sarkis, the editor of the Egyptian paper *al-Mushir*, published the number, calling for donations. It was further cited in the Argentinian Arab-language paper *al-Salam* and Egypt's *al-Muqattam* in May 1916; *Near East* on June 9, 1916; and in the Arabic journal *al-Mustakbal* (The future) in Paris. Also see Sefi, "The Plight of Syria," 175.

112. One of the undersigned was Na'um Mukarzal, a Maronite journalist who had immigrated to the United States in 1890. He founded the Lebanese League of Revival in 1911, an organization that would eventually advocate for an independent Greater Lebanon.

113. Delegates of the Syrian-Lebanonian Associated Press (New York) to Woodrow Wilson (Washington, DC), May 31, 1916, Records of the Department of State Relating to Internal Affairs of Turkey, 1910–29, RG 59, 867.48/301, NARA.

114. An article from the *Egyptian Mail*, cited in "Conditions in Syria," 254.

115. "The Position in Syria," 365.

116. This is the original wording of the telegram. Telegram from Macarios Saba and Yusuf Darian to Paul Knabenshue, May 29, 1916, Records of the Department of State Relating to Internal Affairs of Turkey, 1910–29, RG 59, 867.48/291, NARA.

117. Correspondence from Paul Knabenshue to Robert Lansing includes the complaint of Darian and Saba. Letter from Paul Knabenshue to Robert Lansing, May 29, 1916, Records of the Department of State Relating to Internal Affairs of Turkey, 1910–29, RG 59, 867.48/293, NARA.

118. Kaufman, *Reviving Phoenicia*, 70.

119. Letter from Ighnatius Al-Tannuri to Ilias Butrus Al-Huwayyik, May 1, 1918, Hoyek 77, Bkirki.

120. Copy of the original letter published in Kabkab, *Jam'iyyat al-Mursalin al-Bulusiyyin*, 217.

Chapter 5: Rats, Lice, and Microbes

1. "No Cordon on Beirut," *Al-Ittihad al-'Uthmani*, October 6, 1915.

2. The plague had continued to be a threat in the region until the mid-nineteenth century, and a few cases were reported in Beirut during World War I.

3. "No Cordon on Beirut," *Al-Ittihad al-'Uthmani*, October 6, 1915; "Syrian and Lebanese News," *al-Muqattam*, March 1, 1916.

4. "No Cordon on Beirut," *Al-Ittihad al-'Uthmani*, October 6, 1915.

5. Mokyr and Ó Gráda, "Famine Disease," 1–3.

6. De Waal, *Famine That Kills*, 25.

7. Devereux, "Sen's Entitlement Approach," 251.

8. Ibid., 252.

9. Louis Cheikho began to teach at the Université St-Joseph in Beirut in 1894. He spent the war years trying to protect the Jesuit order's library and its archives from Ottoman confiscation. "Diary of Father Louis Cheikho," 149, PO.

10. Appointed governor of Mount Lebanon in May 1916, Isma'il Haqqi Bey commissioned a social, economic, historical, and geopolitical study of Mount Lebanon, which is still considered one of the most important scholarly projects of the time. The final report was printed in Beirut in 1918. See Kaufman, *Reviving Phoenicia*, 34–37; Haqqi, Lubnan, 643–666.

11. Sharif, *Imperial Norms*, 191.

12. Similar processes were at play in Europe. See Rollet, "The 'Other War' I," 421.

13. Briggs, "Why Nation-States," 288.

14. Quoted in Sharif, *Imperial Norms*, 192.

15. Ministry of Education Law, Howard Bliss Collection, Box 16, File 3, AUB.

16. Özdemir, *The Ottoman Army*, 4.

17. Dağlar, *War, Epidemics and Medicine*; Özdemir, *The Ottoman Army*; Erickson, *Ordered to Die*; Woodward, *Hell in the Holy Land*.

18. Cahen, "L'autre guerre" [The other war], cited in Rollet, "The 'Other War' I," 421.

19. Zürcher, "The Ottoman Conscription System," 437–449.

20. Hourani, *A History*, 314.

21. Zürcher, "Between Death and Desertion," 245.

22. Ajay, "Mount Lebanon," 413.

23. For example, see Zürcher, "Between Death and Desertion," 245.

24. By the end of the war, the number of deserters was four times that of soldiers on the front. Zürcher, "The Ottoman Conscription System," 79–94.

25. *Sijil al-Joumiyya* 1(1903–1930), May 19, 1918, StPH.

26. Zürcher, "Between Death and Desertion," 245.

27. Gatrell, *A Whole Empire Walking*.

28. Sanborn, "Unsettling the Empire," 290–324.

29. The biological effects of famine cannot be ignored, as both acute starvation and chronic malnutrition render the body more vulnerable. Zurbrigg, "Hunger," 16.

30. Bayard Dodge, *Report of the Soup Kitchens in 'Abeih and Souk al-Gharb*, Howard Bliss Collection, Box 18, File 3, AUB.

31. The famine victims' bodies' reaction to unfamiliar foods is a common problem when providing aid. Devereux, *Theories of Famine*, 16.

32. Briggs, "Why Nation-States," 288.

33. By 1848, military hospitals were built in "every quarter of the Turkish empire." Mount Lebanon's two hospitals were in Baabda and Beit ad-Din. "State of Medical Education in Turkey," 233.

34. Dağlar, *War, Epidemics and Medicine*, 122.

35. Regulations on the Infectious Disease and Epidemics consisted of sixty-five articles detailing treatment and prevention. Ibid.

36. "From the Director of Health," *Al-Ittihad al-'Uthmani*, December 8, 1914.

37. Özdemir, *The Ottoman Army*, 26.

38. The head physician at the military hospital began teaching the proper care for battle wounds to all registered physicians early in the war. "Official Announcement," *Al-Ittihad al-'Uthmani*, November 20, 1914.

39. The Law on the Liabilities of Physicians, published on July 20, 1914, outlined the logistics of emergency (wartime) recruitment of physicians. Dağlar, *War, Epidemics and Medicine*, 122. For age increases, see "Local News," *Al-Ittihad al-'Uthmani*, October 7, 1915.

40. "From the Beirut Municipality," *Al-Ittihad al-'Uthmani*, December 15, 1914.

41. Malaria was number one. Khouri, *La médecine au Liban* [Medicine in Lebanon], 230.

42. Historical records concerning the location of the red-light district are vague, and it seems that Beirut brothels constantly moved. Khalaf, *Heart of Beirut*, 211; Hanssen, *Fin de Siècle Beirut*, 210.

43. Haqqi, *Lubnan*, 654.

44. British diplomatic records named Beirut as one of the empire's cities with the highest rate of venereal diseases. Zürcher, "Between Death and Desertion," 245.

45. Compulsory medical inspection of prostitutes was introduced in the Ottoman Empire in the early 1880s. Demirci and Somel, "Women's Bodies," 381.

46. "From the Beirut Municipality," *Al-Ittihad al-'Uthmani*, December 15, 1914.

47. "Communicable Diseases," *Al-Ittihad al-'Uthmani*, March 30, 1915.

48. *Bayrut Vilayet-I meclis umumisinin 1330 senesi ictima'ında itihaz eylediği mükarirat.*

49. Jens Hanssen highlights the role of this committee in bringing together notables from the outlying districts and introducing them to Beirut politics. Another outcome of the assembly was the survey of the Beirut province by Rafiq Bey al-Tamimi and Bahjat Bey. Hanssen, *Fin de Siècle Beirut*, 80.

50. *Bayrut Vilayet-I meclis umumisinin 1330 senesi ictima'ında itihaz eylediği mükarirat.*

51. Haqqi, *Lubnan*, 661.

52. Ajay, "Mount Lebanon," 458.

53. "From the Health Directorate," *Al-Ittihad al-'Uthmani*, March 15, 1915. For doctor-patient ratios in the European context, see Proctor, *Civilians in a World at War*, 160.

54. Dodge, *Report of the Soup Kitchens*.

55. While first-year medical students in Ottoman institutions were exempt from service in the army, medical students of the American Medical School in Beirut in their first or second year were conscripted. Letter from Howard Bliss to Shukri Bey (Minister of Education), June 29, 1916, Howard Bliss Collection, Box 16, File 5, AUB.

56. "Doctors Are Fleeing," *Al-Ittihad al-'Uthmani*, January 17, 1915.

57. "Local News," *Al-Ittihad al-'Uthmani*, June 7, 1915.

58. "From the Medical Headquarters," *Al-Ittihad al-'Uthmani*, October 28, 1915.

59. For example, Ahmed al-Tunisi, whose assigned district was the Qarantina quarter, held additional daily office hours in the pharmacy of Mohamed Masbah Effendi al-Jamal, located in an adjacent quarter. "Doctor Sharif Ahmed Tunisi," *Al-Ittihad al-'Uthmani*, February 27, 1915.

60. Ibid.

61. Howard Bliss, *Forty-Ninth Annual Report of the Syrian Protestant College to the Board of Trustees 1916–1917*, AUB, 14.

62. Van Dyck, *Syllabus of Lectures on Hygiene*, 3.

63. "Communicable Diseases," *Al-Ittihad al-'Uthmani*, March 30, 1915.

64. I thank Zackary Foster and Nick Danforth for alerting me to the map of Ottoman soup kitchens and disinfection stations and sharing their insights, as well as Tugce Kayaal for helping procure a copy of the original.

65. This was a priority not only in the Ottoman Empire. Weindling, "The First World War," 234.

66. Anthropologist Charles Briggs has called this a sanitary *citizen*. Briggs, "Why Nation-States," 288.

67. For example, in August 1915, an article specifically clarifies the difference between typhus and typhoid. "Typhoid Fever," 181.

68. Physicians advertised their knowledge and application of the latest methods used in European hospitals to cure venereal diseases. Dr. Samah Fakhouri, for example, announced that he would conduct blood tests for venereal diseases and promised that his practice employed the latest scientific methods. "Doctor Samah Fakhouri," *Al-Ittihad al-'Uthmani*, June 7, 1915.

69. Weindling, "The First World War," 228.

70. Tanielian, "Disease and Public Health," 2.

71. Howard Bliss, *Fiftieth Annual Report of the Syrian Protestant College to the Board of Trustees 1916–1917*, AUB.

72. The admittance records of the SPC's hospital show no typhus cases before 1915. Ajay, "Mount Lebanon," appendix, 167.

73. Kana'an, *Bayrut*, 168; McGilvary, *The Dawn*, 186.

74. Haqqi, *Lubnan*, 659.

75. "Diary of Father Louis Cheikho," 149.

76. Edward Nickoley, "Historic Diary, February 1917," Edward Nickoley Collection, Box 1, File 2, AUB.

77. A number of reports about infectious diseases in Mount Lebanon for the months of March through December 1917 were sent from the province's governor to Istanbul. These can be found at the Basbakanlik Osmanli Arsiverli (BOA) in Istanbul, Turkey. See archival notations DH.I.UM.EK. 84/9/14–16 for occurrences of disease; for a breakdown of diseases according to smaller districts showing typhus as a problem in all of them, see DH.I.UM.EK. 85/9/7.

78. The central Matn and Shuf districts and the town of Zahle were most affected. Haqqi, *Lubnan*, 658.

79. Husni Bey's report has to be read with caution. His system of registering diseases, death, and births was in its infancy, and government-appointed physicians had little practical experience. Ibid.

80. Ibid.

81. Nickoley, "Historic Diary."

82. Habash, *Al-Jihad Lubnan*, 113.

83. Husni Bey distinguished "local diseases" known and common before November 1914 that increased during the war, such as malaria and typhoid fever, from known diseases, such as plague and cholera, which were reduced if not eliminated prior to the war but now reappeared. Haqqi, *Lubnan*, 649.

84. See Ajay, "Mount Lebanon," appendix, 47.

85. Ibid.

86. Haqqi, *Lubnan*, 658.

87. Another disease that was completely unknown was relapsing fever. "Typhus Fever," *Al-Ittihad al-'Uthmani*, May 6, 1915.

88. Ibid.

89. Cholera most often occurred along lines of troop and refugee movements. On May 15, 1916, Father Louis Cheikho reported: "Cholera broke out in Aleppo ten days ago, and created great havoc in the city and this year will be especially bad due to the miserable state of the population." "Diary of Father Louis Cheikho," 148; also see Clemow, "Cholera in Turkey," 1215.

90. On May 21, 1916, cholera cases were reported in Mount Lebanon and about three weeks later in Beirut on June 10.

91. Fawaz, *Merchants and Migrants*, 37.

92. The Lebanese official gazette *Lubnan* (Lebanon) is available at the Lebanese National Archive (LNA) on microfilm. "Cholera," *Lubnan*, June 7 and 12, 1917.

93. See Ajay, "Mount Lebanon," appendix, 52.

94. For a discussion of soap production, see Doumani, *Rediscovering Palestine*.

95. Nickoley, "Historic Diary."

96. Bayard Dodge, "Relief Work in Syria during the Period of the War: (A Brief and Unofficial Account)," Howard Bliss Collection, Box 18, File 3, AUB.

97. Clemow, "Cholera in Turkey," 1213.

98. For reports of mortalities for the province of Mount Lebanon from June to November 1917, see DH.I.UM.EK. 84/9/9–10, BOA.

99. Haqqi, *Lubnan*, 657.

100. *Bayrut Vilayet-I meclis umumisinin 1330 senesi ictima'ında itiḫaz eylediği mükarirat.*

101. Earliest forms of smallpox inoculations were practiced in India, China, and later in the Ottoman Empire. English physician Edward Jenner first discovered a vaccine in the late eighteenth century. For a history of smallpox, see Tucker, *Scourge*.

102. Istanbul had its first documented campaign in 1840. Sharif, *Imperial Norms*, 197–208.

103. Ibid., 204.

104. "Smallpox Vaccinations," *Al-Ittihad al-'Uthmani*, January 21, 1915.

105. "Smallpox," *Al-Ittihad al-'Uthmani*, April 2, 1915.

106. Ibid.

107. "Why Has the Sickness of Smallpox Not Been Destroyed?," *Al-Ittihad al-'Uthmani*, July 29, 1915.

108. Ibid.

109. *Bayrut Vilayet-I meclis umumisinin 1330 senesi ictima'ında itiḫaz eylediği mükarirat.*

110. Haqqi, *Lubnan*, 657.

111. Ibid., 665.

112. For reports of the Ottoman governor's count of vaccinations in Mount Lebanon from March to November 1917, see DH.I.UM EK. 89/9/12–13, BOA.

113. The success rate for vaccinations after only one administration was somewhere between 45 and 55 percent. See ibid.

114. "Communicable Diseases," *Al-Ittihad al-'Uthmani*, March 30, 1915; Ajay, "Mount Lebanon," 459.

115. Hanssen, *Fin de Siècle Beirut*, 128–129.

116. The French Medical Faculty was confiscated and renamed the Ottoman hospital. "The French Hospital in Beirut," *Al-Ittihad al-'Uthmani*, December 2, 1914.

117. "To Sick Persons," *Ittihad al-'Uthmani*, May 23, 1915.

118. Unfortunately, the number of admissions is available only for 1914 and 1917. *Report of the Society of St. George*, File BEY 170, AGOP.

119. In 1914 the hospital admitted 2,098 patients; in 1915, only 680. The number increased to 796 in 1916 and 1,001 in 1917 and returned to a prewar level in 1918. Ajay, "Mount Lebanon," appendix, 166.

120. For example, the public health department in Paris was in charge of a hospital system with more than 30,000 beds. Rollet, "The 'Other War' I," 423.

121. "From the Health Commission," *Al-Ittihad al-'Uthmani*, May 21, 1915.

122. Ibid., June 7, 1915.

123. Benoît Boyer advocated expanding Beirut Water Company's spring-water piping systems and eliminating wells altogether. Khouri, *La médecine au Liban*, 228.

124. "Cholera," *Lubnan*, June 7 and 12, 1917.

125. Haqqi, *Lubnan*, 644.

126. Ibid., 652.

127. "Communicable Diseases," *Al-Ittihad al-'Uthmani*, March 30, 1915.

128. "From the Health Commission," *Al-Ittihad al-'Uthmani*, May 28, 1915.

129. Ibid., June 12, 1915.

130. "Public Toilets," *Al-Ittihad al-'Uthmani*, September 18, 1915.

131. "From the Municipality," *Ittihad al-'Uthmani*, May 11, 1915.

132. "Local News," *Ittihad al-'Uthmani*, January 21, 1915.

133. "Public Cleanliness," *Al-Ittihad al-'Uthmani*, November 3, 1915.

134. Charles Nicolle, director of the Pasteur Institute in Tunis, discovered that body lice transmit typhus in 1909. Howard T. Ricketts and Russell M. Wilder in 1910, as well as John F. Anderson and Joseph Goldberger in 1912, confirmed his findings. In 1916, Rocha Lima, a Brazilian bacteriologist, discovered the disease's causative agent to be the bacterium *Rickettsia prowazekii*. The zoologist Rudolf Weigl invented a vaccine against typhus in the interwar period. See Weindling, "The First World War," 227–228.

135. "Typhus Fever," *Al-Ittihad al-'Uthmani*, May 20, 1915.

136. The proper sulfur fumigation of homes was described in detail, including the necessary amount of the chemical to be burned per cubic meter. Ibid., May 20, 1915.

137. Ibid., May 21, 1915.

138. Khouri, *La médecine au Liban*, 230.

139. Kana'an, *Bayrut*, 169.

140. Ajay, "Mount Lebanon," 420.

141. Ibid.

142. Letter from Bayard Dodge to Cleveland Dodge, May 2, 1915, Bayard Dodge Collection, Box 6, File 4, AUB.

143. "Repair of Roads," *Al-Ittihad al-'Uthmani*, July 20, 1915.

144. "News from Syria," January 7, 1916, 260.

145. Ibid.

146. Letter from Howard Bliss to Cleveland Dodge, October 30, 1915, Howard Bliss Collection, Box 10, File 1, AUB.

147. "News from Syria," January 7, 1916, 260.

148. Kayalı, "Wartime Regional and Imperial Integration," 296.

149. "Celebration of the Opening of the Two Streets," *Al-Ittihad al-'Uthmani*, April 7, 1915.

150. Kana'an, *Bayrut*, 144.

Chapter 6: Local Relief Initiatives

1. The memoir of 'Anbara Salam Khalidi was published in Arabic by Dar al-Nahar (Beirut) in 1973 as *Jawlah fi l-dhikrayat bayna Lubnan wa-Filastin* [Journey of memories between Lebanon and Palestine]. Tarif Khalidi has recently published an English translation of the text. See A. Khalidi, *The Memoirs of an Early Arab Feminist*, 68–70.

2. C. Tilly, "War Making," 181.

3. For similar challenges to civil society organization in the European capitals, see Bonzon, "Transfer Payment and Social Policy," 302.

4. Thompson, *Colonial Citizens*, 16.

5. Al-Hakim, *Bayrut wa-Lubnan*, 257.

6. Eley, "War and the Twentieth-Century State," 155.

7. Ibid.

8. For more on charity in the Middle East, see Bonner, Ener, and Singer, *Poverty and Charity*.

9. Ener, *Managing Egypt's Poor*, 51.

10. Pollard, "Egyptian by Association," 241–242.

11. For example, the Greek Orthodox Benevolent Society focused on educating poor children and provided material assistance in the form of cash payments.

12. *Report of the Society of St. George*, File BEY 170, AGOP.

13. The governing bodies of these organizations generally were a mix of secular urban notables, intellectuals, and religious leaders. Michael Johnson highlights this demographic for al-Maqasid. Johnson, "Factional Politics in Lebanon," 57–58.

14. *Report of the Society of St. George*.

15. Help was at times extended to Damascus and Alexandria. Kabkab, *Jam'iyyat al-khrayriyya*, 50, 120.

16. This is not to say that there was no effort by the state to engage in relief for the poor.

17. Greek Orthodox societies received some donations from the Russian consulate, but most of their income came from local benefactors. *Report of the Society of St. George*.

18. Ibid.

19. For example, income from the estate of Philip Thabet was 2,177.20 piasters; and from Jurji Yusuf Sursock, 2,718.20 piasters. Ibid.

20. The Trad family was and is one of the key Greek Orthodox families in Beirut. One of its most prominent members, Petro Trad, fled Beirut during the war to escape an indictment for treason by the Ottoman military court. Traboulsi, *A History of Modern Lebanon*, 84–85.

21. Significantly, fewer patients received care in the hospital in 1917 than in 1914. *Report of the Society of St. George*.

22. The clinic income in 1914 was 382 piasters, and in 1917, it was 6,350 piasters, with no income noted for 1918 and 1919. Ibid.

23. The budget surplus from 1914 was 64,889.75 piasters, added to the now lesser income. The total available funds in 1915 were 119,523.15 piasters (about 20,000 less than the previous year). Ibid.

24. *Report of the Work of the Greek-Orthodox Benevolent Society*, File BEY 223, AGOP.

25. The total income from estates for the Greek Orthodox Benevolent Society: 23,037 piasters in 1914–1915; 5,714.10 in 1915–1916; 16,207.20 in 1916–1917; and 1,225.00 in 1917–1918. Ibid.

26. Income from tuition was cut in half from 1913–1914 to 1917–1918. It is unclear whether the decrease was due to fewer enrollments or if students were exempt from tuition payments. Ibid.

27. The Greek Catholic Charity Association's total income was 64,713.20 piasters in 1914. Kabkab, *Jam'iyyat al-khrayriyya*, 137.

28. Ibid., 139.

29. *Report of the Society of St. George*.

30. The total income from membership dues was 1,499 piasters in 1914 and only 717 in 1916. Ibid.

31. "Meeting Minutes of the Greek-Catholic Charity Association (1915–1923)," *Sijil* [Register], no. 2, GCCA.

32. Only the representative in charge of the poor, the treasurer, and the registrar were replaced during the war. Kabkab, *Jam'iyyat al-khrayriyya*, 114–116.

33. *Report of the Society of St. George*.

34. For a discussion of *waqf* properties, see Slim, *The Greek Orthodox "Waqf"*; Van Leeuwen, *Notables and Clergy in Mount Lebanon*.

35. The financial records show property purchases for 28,070 piasters in 1916 and 30,454 in 1918. *Report of the Society of St. George*.

36. *Report of the Work of the Greek Orthodox Benevolent Society*.

37. The income levels to around 40,000 piasters for the remainder of the war. Ibid.

38. The maintenance and improvements of properties were a significant part of the daily dealings of the organization.

39. After 1915, the income fluctuated between 35,000 and 40,000 piasters. See Kabkab, *Jam'iyyat al-khrayriyya*, 139.

40. "Celebration of the Opening of the Two Streets," *Al-Ittihad al-'Uthmani*, April 7, 1915.

41. Ibid.

42. *Report of the Deutsche-Palästina Bank for the Year 1915*, Türkei 177, Bd. 13, PA-AA.

43. These properties were storage rooms and stores. Kabkab, *Jam'iyyat al-khrayriyya*, 125.

44. The market was located near the eastern wall of the Amir Munzur Mosque and near the Shams ad-Din Mosque, and stores there typically specialized in fabrics and sewing tools. Hallaq, *Bayrut al-Mahrusah* [Beirut al-Mahrusah], 34–36.

45. Suq al-Attarin was situated west of the Great Umari Mosque, in the center of Beirut, and specialized in herbs and home remedies as well as perfumes. Ibid.

46. "Meeting Minutes of the Greek-Catholic Charity Association (1915–1923)."

47. Kabkab, *Jam'iyyat al-khrayriyya*, 46.

48. "About Beirut and Lebanon," *Al-Salam*, April 18, 1916.

49. *Report of the Society of St. George.*

50. See Kabkab, *Jam'iyyat al-khrayriyya*, 137.

51. Ibid., 141.

52. The Greek Orthodox Benevolent Society's taxes rose from 9,042.25 piasters in 1914 (including past-due payments from 1913) to 16,728.25 in 1916, to 18,429.25 in 1917. *Report of the Work of the Greek-Orthodox Benevolent Society.*

53. *Report of the Society of St. George.*

54. Johnson, "Factional Politics in Lebanon," 58.

55. Ibid.

56. See Quilty, "Bridging the Dichotomy," 108–110; Traboulsi, *History of Modern Lebanon*, 22, 59.

57. The Sursocks were the agents of the international trade company Lascaridi and Company in the late nineteenth century.

58. See Quilty, "Bridging the Dichotomy," 108–110; Hanssen, *Fin de Siècle Beirut*, 88.

59. Özveren, "Beirut," 494.

60. Quilty, "Bridging the Dichotomy," 103.

61. As quoted in Fawaz, *Land of Aching Hearts*, 124.

62. Kayalı, "Wartime Regional and Imperial Integration."

63. "Texte retrouvé dans les archives de Lady Yvonne Sursock Cochrane: Champ de Courses-Residence des Pins [Text found in the archives of Lady Yvonne Sursock: Racetrack-Pine residence]," Sursock Family Archive.

64. A paper provided to me by Yvonne Sursock Cochrane reports that Alfred Bey bought wheat from Palestine and transported it to Beirut, where it was stored in his

home. Every day some of it was distributed to the families of workers employed by the family. Whether he sold wheat as well is unclear from the text. Ibid.

65. Yusuf Bey Sursock donated 2,177 piasters in 1914 and 5,625 in 1917. *Report of the Society of St. George*.

66. *Report of the Work of the Greek Orthodox Benevolent Society*.

67. Ibid.

68. "Celebration," *Al-Ittihad al-'Uthmani*, November 22, 1914.

69. Quoted in Maksudyan, "Being Saved to Serve," 47.

70. Fawaz, *Land of Aching Hearts*, 125.

71. Salibi, "Beirut under the Young Turks," 203.

72. Ibid.

73. Officially, the organization was unable to function. But the society was able to reopen with little difficulty at the end of 1918, which suggests that its leadership remained in close contact and its institutional structure was less damaged than one would expect. However, although I believe that the organization was never fully abandoned, no proof exists. Shibaru, *Jam'iyyat al-Maqasid*.

74. Salibi, "Beirut under the Young Turks," 204.

75. Ibid.

76. Ibid., 207.

77. Çiçek, *War and State Formation*, 42.

78. Ibid., 43.

79. Ibid., 45.

80. Salibi, "Beirut under the Young Turks," 212.

81. Ibid., 213.

82. Salam, quoted in ibid., 214.

83. Ibid., 215.

84. The debate over whether or not the economic, social, and political gains of women outlived the immediate war experience has been a subject of debate. For a discussion of the war's emancipatory powers, see Kent, *Making Peace*. Some scholars argue that women's emancipation was limited and temporary, and their experiences depended on class and race. Daniel, *The War from Within*; Greenwald, *Women, War and Work*.

85. Kandiyoti, *Women, Islam, and the State*, 28.

86. Maksudyan, "This Time Women as Well Got Involved in Politics!," 108.

87. Karakışla, *Women, War and Work*, 21.

88. Kandiyoti, *Women, Islam, and the State*, 29.

89. Karakışla cites as the reason the ready supply of non-Muslim men. Karakışla, *Women, War and Work*, 40.

90. Ibid., 101.

91. Akın, "The Ottoman Home Front," 124.

92. Ibid.

93. "L'agriculture et les femmes" [Agriculture and women], 4.

94. The Young Turk period (1908–1918) witnessed the formation of a number of women's associations, many of which focused on philanthropy and drew their membership from upper-middle-class women. In prewar Beirut, upper-class women mainly engaged in philanthropic enterprises as individuals.

95. Thompson, *Colonial Citizens*, 95.

96. Ibid., 26.

97. Ajay, "Mount Lebanon," 510.

98. A. Khalidi, *Jawlah fi al-Dhikrayat*, 69.

99. Bayard Dodge, "Relief Work in Syria," Howard Bliss Collection, Box 18, File 3, AUB; Ajay, "Mount Lebanon," 510–511.

100. Unfortunately, we do not know whether 'Azmi Bey gave the money in gold or in paper currency. The difference would have been significant, as paper currency fast decreased in value. *Al-Ittihad al-'Uthmani*, March 22, 1915.

101. The bags were to be used as sandbags during the Suez Campaign. See McGilvary, *The Dawn*, 172.

102. "Syrian Ladies' Association," *Al-Ittihad al-'Uthmani*, March 22, 1915.

103. "Charitable Association," *Al-Ittihad al-'Uthmani*, April 9, 1915.

104. A. Khalidi, *Jawlah fi al-Dhikrayat*, 69.

105. Thompson, *Colonial Citizens*, 95.

106. A. Khalidi, *Jawlah fi al-Dhikrayat*, 69.

107. "Syrian Ladies' Association," *Al-Ittihad al-'Uthmani*, March 22, 1915; A. Khalidi, *Jawlah fi al-Dhikrayat*, 69.

108. Jamal Pasha put Salma Sayigh and the Turkish feminist Halide Edib in charge of orphanages. See Thompson, *Colonial Citizens*, 95.

109. Ibid.

110. Bayard Dodge, *Report of the Soup Kitchens in 'Abeih and Souk al-Gharb*, Howard Bliss Collection, Box 18, File 3, AUB; Dodge, "Relief Work in Syria."

111. Dodge, "Relief Work in Syria."

112. Thompson, *Colonial Citizens*, 95.

113. Ibid.

114. Al-Hakim, *Bayrut wa-Lubnan*, 257–259.

115. Ibid.

116. See Panian, *Goodbye, Antoura*.

117. Roger Chickering's study of the wartime German city of Freiburg pays attention to local philanthropic activities during the war. See Chickering, *The Great War*.

Chapter 7: Beneficial Benevolence

1. Bayard Dodge, "Relief Work in Syria during the Period of the War," Howard Bliss Collection, Box 18, File 3, AUB.

2. Watenpaugh, *Bread from Stones*.

3. Letter from Bayard Dodge to Cleveland H. Dodge, March 16, 1919, Bayard Dodge Collection, Box 7, File 1, AUB.

4. Rosenberg, "Missions to the World," 256.

5. Rieff, *A Bed for the Night*, 61–64.

6. Makdisi, *Faith Misplaced*, 3.

7. Letter from Howard Bliss to Starr Murphy, December 30, 1914, Missionaries, Box 2, File 1, AUB.

8. Established in 1909, the Beirut chapter was the first national chapter outside the United States. McGilvary, *The Dawn*, 83.

9. Mary Dale Dorman was the granddaughter of the SPC's founder Daniel Bliss.

10. Letter from Margaret McGilvary to Headquarters of the ARC in New York, January 1, 1915, AUB Missionaries, Box 7, File 2, AUB.

11. Letter from Bayard Dodge to his mother, December 28, 1914, Bayard Dodge Collection, Box 6, File 3, AUB.

12. Letter from Bayard Dodge to his aunt, January 28, 1915, Bayard Dodge Collection, Box 6, File 3, AUB.

13. McGilvary, *The Dawn*, 86.

14. Letter from Charles Dana to New York Treasurer of the AMP, Russell Carter, May 3, 1915, Letters to the NY Treasurer: 1914–1916, NEST Special Collection.

15. John D. Rockefeller hired Starr Murphy as the family's lawyer and financial adviser in 1904. The Rockefellers donated $20,000 to the Committee on Armenian Atrocities. Letter from Howard Bliss to Starr J. Murphy, December 30, 1914, AUB Missionaries, Box 2, File 1, AUB.

16. An Egyptian relief commission noted that the "Rockefeller Institute of Charity will double each award made at this opportunity." "Commission to Aid the Victims of the Famine in Syria," *Al-Muqattam*, September 23, 1916.

17. For a complete list of members and their backgrounds, see Barton, *Story of Near East Relief*, 4.

18. Ibid., 5.

19. Watenpaugh, *Bread from Stones*, 51.

20. Barton, *Story of Near East Relief*, xii.

21. Makdisi, *Faith Misplaced*, 120.

22. Howard Bliss, *Forty-Ninth Annual Report of the Syrian Protestant College to the Board of Trustees 1916–1917*, 18, AUB; letter from Charles Dana to Russell Carter, February 23, 1915, Letters to the NY Treasurer: 1914–1916, NEST Special Collection.

23. "Minutes of the Syrian Protestant College Sub-Committee for the Red Cross Mission," December 1914, Missionaries, Box 2, File 2, AUB.

24. Letter from Howard Bliss to Cleveland H. Dodge, November 28, 1914, Bayard Dodge Collection, Box 6, File 3, AUB.

25. See the correspondence between the college administration and Jamal Pasha in the Howard Bliss Collection, Box 17, File 1, AUB.

26. "Minutes of the Syrian Protestant College Sub-Committee for the Red Cross Mission," January 11, 1915.

27. Tanielian, "Disease and Public Health."

28. For student volunteers, see "Minutes of the Syrian Protestant College Sub-Committee for the Red Cross Mission," December 1914.

29. Ibid., January 2 and 10, 1915.

30. "Faculty Minutes," January 4, 1915, Minutes of the Faculty, 1867–1920, AUB.

31. Letter from Howard Bliss to Franklin Hoskins (clerk of the American Mission in Syria), January 13, 1915, Missionaries, Box 2, File 1, AUB.

32. Howard Bliss, *Forty-Ninth Annual Report of the Syrian Protestant College*, AUB, 18.

33. "Minutes of the Syrian Protestant College Sub-Committee for the Red Cross Mission," January 2, 1915. For a detailed list of expenses, including salaries, see "Faculty Minutes," January 12 and 26, 1915.

34. Letter from Edwin Ward to Howard Bliss, "Report from Jerusalem," January 2–5, 1915, Missionaries, Box 2, File 1, AUB.

35. McGilvary, *The Dawn*, 87.

36. Howard Bliss, *Forty-Ninth Annual Report of the Syrian Protestant College*, AUB, 18.

37. "Minutes of the Syrian Protestant College Sub-Committee for the Red Cross Mission," January 2, 1915.

38. Edwin Ward, "Report on the Mission," December 31, 1914, Missionaries, Box 2, File 1, AUB.

39. Letter from Bayard Dodge to Bub, January 21, 1915, Bayard Dodge Collection, Box 6, File 4, AUB.

40. McGilvary, *The Dawn*, 88.

41. The permission was granted, but their stay continued to be disputed. See the correspondence between the college administration and Jamal Pasha in the Howard Bliss Collection, Box 17, File 1, AUB.

42. Howard Bliss, *Fiftieth Annual Report of the Syrian Protestant College to the Board of Trustees 1916–1917*, AUB, 20.

43. Letter from Luise Hanich to the Kaiserswerth Mutterhaus, April 1, 1915, Box 237, Folder: Lazarettpflege 1914–1916, FKS.

44. Ibid.

45. The committee bought corn for poor widows and destitute families in Beirut. Letter from Bayard Dodge to Grace Dodge, December 21, 1914, Bayard Dodge Collection, Box 6, File 3, AUB.

46. Robert B. Reed headed the employment department for men, and Anna Jessup took care of women in need of work. McGilvary, *The Dawn*, 85.

47. Letter from Margaret McGilvary to unknown recipient, January 1915, Missionaries, Box 2, File 1, AUB; letter from Bayard Dodge to unknown recipient, January 21, 1915, Bayard Dodge Collection, Box 6, File 4, AUB.

48. Letter from Charles Dana to Russell Carter, April 27, 1915, Letters to the NY Treasurer: 1914–1916, NEST Special Collection.

49. Letter from Bayard Dodge to Grace Dodge, February 5, 1915, Bayard Dodge Collections, Box 6, File 4, AUB.

50. Letter from Bayard Dodge to Cleveland H. Dodge, January 21, 1915, Bayard Dodge Collection, Box 6, File 4, AUB.

51. Letter Margaret McGilvary to unknown recipient, January 1915, Missionaries, Box 2, File 1, AUB.

52. Ibid.

53. McGilvary, *The Dawn*, 89.

54. Weber, *Sociology of Religion*, 220–223.

55. Letter from Margaret McGilvary to unknown recipient, January 1915, Missionaries, Box 2, File 1, AUB.

56. "A Venerable Project," *Al-Ittihad al-'Uthmani*, January 14, 1915.

57. Letter from Bayard Dodge to Grace Dodge, February 5, 1915, Bayard Dodge Collection, Box 6, File 4, AUB.

58. Letter from Bayard Dodge to Bub, January 21, 1915, in ibid.

59. Letter from Bayard Dodge to Grace Dodge, February 5, 1915, in ibid.

60. Letter from Bayard Dodge to Bub, January 21, 1915, in ibid.

61. Letter from Bayard Dodge to Cleveland H. Dodge, May 2, 1915, in ibid.

62. Letter from Bayard Dodge to unknown recipient, May 15, 1915, in ibid.

63. McGilvary, *The Dawn*, 82.

64. Letter from Charles Dana to Russell Carter, February 23, 1915, Letters to the NY Treasurer: 1914–1916, NEST Special Collection.

65. "The American College and the Red Crescent Society," *Al-Ittihad al-'Uthmani*, January 8, 1915.

66. Letter from Charles Dana to Russell Carter, February 23, 1915, Letters to the NY Treasurer: 1914–1916, NEST Special Collection.

67. "Catholic Missions and Education in Turkey and the German Catholics," Türkei 175, Bd. 36, PA-AA.

68. Ibid.

69. Joseph Schmidlin, "Memorandum: Concerning the Retrieval of French Missionary Institutions," n.d., Türkei 175, Bd. 36, PA-AA; Müller, "The Legacy of Joseph Schmidlin," 109–113.

70. Schmidlin, "Memorandum: Concerning the Retrieval."

71. Ibid.

72. Schmidlin provided a detailed list of closed Catholic institutions and suggested that if at all possible the same Catholic order would step in, meaning German Jesuits would take over St. Joseph University. Ibid.

73. Letter from Hans von Wangenheim to Theobald von Bethmann-Hollweg, February 4, 1915, Türkei 175, Bd. 36, PA-AA.

74. Ibid., February 17 and 23, 1915.

75. Telegram from Hans von Wangenheim to Theobald von Bethmann-Hollweg, December 1914, Türkei 175, Bd. 36, PA-AA.

76. Magda Schönrock, "Chronik des Waisenhauses Zoar in Beirut [Chronicle of the Zoar Orphanage in Beirut] 1914–1929," Box 239, File 2, FKS.

77. The number of orphans increased from fifty-five to one hundred in the fall of 1915. Ibid.

78. Ibid.

79. "News from Syria, a Terrible Record," 341.

80. Letter from Howard Bliss to Stanley Hollis, August 17, 1915, Missionaries, Box 2, File 1, AUB.

81. McGilvary, *The Dawn*, 85.

82. Letter from Charles Dana to Russell Carter, November 18, 1914, Letters to the NY Treasurer: 1914–1916, NEST Special Collection.

83. Ibid.

84. "The Abolition of the Capitulations: Consternation at Beirut," *Irish Times*, October 7, 1914; letter from Charles Dana to Russell Carter, October 1, 1914, and December 14, 1914, Letters to the NY Treasurer: 1914–1916, NEST Special Collection.

85. Letter from Charles Dana to Russell Carter, January 19, 1915, Letters to the NY Treasurer: 1914–1916, NEST Special Collection.

86. Ibid., March 9 and 30, 1915.

87. Ibid., February 3, 1915.

88. Ibid., March 19, 1915.

89. Ibid., May 20, 1915.

90. For details on banks in the Ottoman Empire, see Ruppin, *Syrien als Wirtschaftsgebiet*, 353.

91. "Report of the Ottoman Imperial Bank," September 27, 1916, RG 84, Vol. 169, File 310, NARA.

92. Letter from Stanley Hollis to Henry Morgenthau, April 4, 1916, in ibid.

93. Letter from Philip Hoffman to Stanley Hollis, April 12, 1916, in ibid.

94. Letter from Charles Dana to Russell Carter, November 18, 1915, Letters to the NY Treasurer: 1914–1916, NEST Special Collection.

95. Ibid., November 9, 1914.

96. Ibid., May 13, 1915.

97. Ibid., June 14, 1915.

98. Letter from Stanley Hollis to Henry Morgenthau, March 16, 1916, RG 84, Vol. 169, File 310, NARA.

99. Letter from Charles Dana to Russell Carter, January 30, 1915, Letters to the NY Treasurer: 1914–1916, NEST Special Collection.

100. Ibid., June 23, 1915.

101. Ibid.

102. Ibid.

103. McGilvary, *The Dawn*, 108.

104. Ibid., 83.

105. Letter from George Young to Stanley Hollis, December 9, 1915, RG 89, Vol. 162, File 310, NARA.

106. Letter from Stanley Hollis to William S. Nelson, January 11, 1917, RG 89, Vol. 168, File 310, NARA.

107. Letter from Abram Elkus to Stanley Hollis, February 15, 1917, RG 84, Vol. 162, File 310, NARA.

108. Letter from Wega S. Little to Stanley Hollis, October, 20, 1915, in ibid.

109. Letter from Stanley Hollis to Henry Morgenthau, October 14, 1915, in ibid.

110. Letter from Lamont to Royal Johnson, January 10, 1917, RG 84, Vol. 168, File 310, NARA.

111. Woman's Foreign Missionary Societies of the Presbyterian Church, "Editorial Notes," 146.

112. From the reports sent by Stanley Hollis to Henry Morgenthau throughout 1916. See RG 84, Vol. 169, NARA.

113. Hoskins, "In Syria," 552.

114. McGilvary, *The Dawn*, 120.

115. "Relief for Syria," 364.

116. Letter from Charles Dana to Russell Carter, March 9, 1915, Letters to the NY Treasurer: 1914–1916, NEST Special Collection.

117. Dana often complained about his limited funds. Ibid., May 6, 1915.

118. McGilvary, *The Dawn*, 92.

119. Bayard Dodge, *Report of the Soup Kitchens in 'Abeih and Souk al-Gharb*, Howard Bliss Collection, Box 18, File 3, AUB.

120. 'Abeih is located in the Shuf district about fifteen kilometers from Beirut, adjacent to the Beirut–Damascus road.

121. Letter from Bayard Dodge to Cleveland H. Dodge, October 5, 1918, Bayard Dodge Collection, Box 7, File 1, AUB.

122. Dodge, *Report of the Soup Kitchens*.

123. Ibid.

124. Ibid.

125. McGilvary, *The Dawn*, 222.

126. Bayard Dodge, "Relief Work in Syria during the Period of the War," Howard Bliss Collection, Box 18, File 3, AUB.

127. McGilvary, *The Dawn*, 35, 226, 227.

128. Letter from Abram Elkus to Robert Lansing, June 10, 1917, Papers Relating to the Foreign Relations of the United States, 1917, Supplement 1: The World War, USDS.

129. Letter from Robert Lansing to ACASR, August 24, 1917, in ibid.

130. Letter from Robert Lansing to ACASR Office New York, October 16, 1917, in ibid.

131. Letter from Frank L. Polk to War Trade Board, July 22, 1918, in ibid.

132. Letter from Philip Hoffmann to Gerhard von Mutius, February 19, 1918, Türkei 177, Bd. 16, PA-AA.

133. Letter from Gerhard von Mutius to Georg von Hertling, March 1, 1918, in ibid.

134. Letter from Johann Heinrich von Bernstorff to Georg von Hertling, April 12, 1918, in ibid.

135. Letter from Gerhard von Mutius to Johann Heinrich von Bernstorff, June 30, 1918, in ibid.

136. Letter from Johann Heinrich von Bernstorff to Georg von Hertling, August 6, 1918, in ibid.

137. Unsigned report, June 22, 1918, in ibid.

138. Ibid.

139. Report from Chief of the German Division to Johann Heinrich von Bernstorff, May 15, 1918, in ibid.

140. Letter from Chief of the Secret Field Police to Johann Heinrich von Bernstoff, May 11, 1918, in ibid.

141. Ibid.

142. Makdisi, *Faith Misplaced*, 251.

143. Ibid., 124.

144. Barton, *Story of Near East*, xiii.

Conclusion

1. Cortas, *A World I Loved*, 12.

2. Frederick Bliss, "Retrospect: (1914–1919)," Howard Bliss Collection, Box 17, File 2, AUB. Eyewitnesses into the 1980s continued to remember the earthquake as signaling the end of the Ottoman Empire. See Hanna, "The First World War," 307.

3. "Turkish Casualties on Beirut Damascus Road," AUB Libraries Online Exhibits, accessed April 24, 2017, http://www.aub.edu.lb/ulibraries/asc/online-exhibits/exhibits/show/wwi/item/238.

4. For details, see Gelvin, *Divided Loyalties*, 25–26.

5. Al-Hakim, *Bayrut wa-Lubnan*, 293.

6. Kassir, *Beirut*, 251.

7. Ibid., 247.

8. Telegram from Philpin Piépape to the Minister of War, October 12, 1918, *E-Levant 1918–1940, Turquie*, MAE.

9. *Makhlouta*, from the Arabic verb *khalt*, "to mix or scramble," may be best translated here as "uncertain chaos." Letter from an anonymous Lebanese to Joseph Delore, May 28, 1919, published in *Les missions catholiques*, no. 2621 (1919): 316.

10. Schilcher, "Famine in Syria," 232.

11. "La famine au Liban et l'assistance française aux Libanais pendant la Grande Guerre (1915–19)" [The famine in Lebanon and French assistance during the Great War (1915–19)], *L'Asie française* [French Asia], supplement (February 1922): 9.

12. Jackson, "Compassion and Connections," 65.

13. Ibid., 66.

14. Fawaz, *Land of Aching Hearts*, 124, 123, 324n23.

15. Jackson, "Compassion and Connections," 65–67.

16. Thompson, *Colonial Citizens*, 60.

17. Mouawad, "Grande Guerre" [The Great War], 28.

18. Kaufman, "Tell Us Our History," 4.

19. Kaufman, *Reviving Phoenicia*, 93.

20. Ibid., 85.

21. Emile Arab was a close associate of Corm and lecturer at the St. Joseph University in Beirut. Arab, "Au coeur de la commission americaine" [At the heart of the American Commission], 83.

22. Corm, "L'ombre s'entend" [The shadow is heard], 11.

23. Charles Corm as Cedar, "L'impression d'un jeune phénicien" [The impressions of a young Phoenician], 31.

24. Yamin, *Lubnan fi al-harb*; Maqdisi, *A'zam Harb* [The greatest war]; Khuwairi, *Al-Rihla al-Suriyya* [Travels in Syria].

25. Al-Qattan, "Historicising Hunger," 123–126.

26. A letter from the Secretary General of the Archdiocese of Beirut T. H. Malouf published in *Les missions catholiques*. Malouf, "Les souffrances du Liban" [Lebanon's sufferings], 603.

27. "La syrie martyre" [Syrian martyrdom], 192.

28. From the report of the Lazarist priest Heudre, *Les missions catholiques*, no. 2613 (July 4, 1919): 316.

29. "Les martyrs en Armenie et en Syrie," 90–91.

30. Mouawad, "Grande Guerre," 28.

31. Djemal Pasha, *Erinnerungen*, 204.

32. Corm, "L'ombre s'entend sur la montagne," 11.

33. Naccache, "L'industrie de la villégiature au Liban" [The tourism industry in Lebanon], 212.

34. Coury [Khoury], "Le martyre du Liban" [The martyrdom of Lebanon], 226.
35. Ibid.
36. Kaufman, "Tell Us Our History," 24n11.
37. Kan'an, *Bayrut*, 158–167.
38. Ibid.
39. Kelleher, *The Feminization of Famine*, 2–11.
40. White, *The Emergence*, 134.
41. "La famine au Liban," 3–14.
42. Mina, *Fragments of Memory*.
43. Famine scholars note breakdown of traditional social bonds as one of the symptoms of famine. Devereux, *Theories of Famine*, 14–15.
44. Thompson, *Colonial Citizens*, 38.
45. Ibid., 19.
46. Fawaz, *Land of Aching Hearts*, 114.
47. Remoulière, "L'oeuvre du ravitaillement," 55–57.
48. Jackson, "Compassion and Connection," 68.
49. Eddé, *Beyrouth*, 65.
50. Ibid., 64.
51. Ibid., 65.
52. Méouchy, "Les nationalists arabes" [The Arab nationalists], 118.
53. Eddé, *Beyrouth*, 66.
54. Ibid.
55. Letter from Ibtihaj Kaddourah to the King-Crane Commission, July 5, 1919, Donald M. Brodie Miscellaneous Papers, 1919–1941, Box 1, File 3, HI.
56. Ibid.
57. Ibid.
58. Ibid.
59. Letter from Bayard Dodge to Cleveland H. Dodge, December 21, 1918, Bayard Dodge Collection, Box 7, File 1, AUB.
60. Letter from Bayard Dodge to his mother, January 13, 1919, in ibid.
61. Bayard Dodge, *Report of the Soup Kitchens in 'Abeih and Souk al-Gharb*, Howard Bliss Collection, Box 18, File 3, AUB.
62. Ibid.
63. Petition from Muslim Women of Beirut, July 8, 1919, Albert H. Lybyer Papers, 1876–1949, Box 16, File 3, University of Illinois at Urbana-Champaign, University Archive, Digital Publisher: Oberlin College Archives, Ohio.
64. Ibid.
65. For a discussion of the women's movement during the Mandate period, see Thompson, *Colonial Citizens*.
66. Tilly, "War Making and State Making," 181.

67. Mouawad, "Grande Guerre," 28.

68. Malouf, "Les souffrances du Liban," 602.

69. Fawaz, *Land of Aching Hearts*, 123.

70. The Faisal-Clemenceau accords secured France's full control over Lebanon.

71. Telegram from Ilias Butrus al-Huwayyik to Henri Gouraud, March 10, 1920, Mandats, Beyrouth, Secrétariat Général, MAE.

72. Walker, "Clericist Catholic Authors," 240.

73. For more on the postwar political maneuvering of the Maronite Church, see Walker, "The Role of Ilyas Butrus al-Huwayyik."

74. Mouawad, "Grande Guerre," 28.

75. For a more detailed discussion of the politics of memory in Lebanon, see Zachs, "Transformations of a Memory."

76. Antonius, *The Arab Awakening*, 201.

77. Also see Tibawi, *A Modern History*, 246–247.

78. Longrigg, *Syria and Lebanon*, 48–49.

79. Hitti, *A Short History*, 216.

80. Salibi mentions the 1915 political executions in the context of his discussion of Arab and Lebanese nationalism. The everyday wartime suffering of ordinary people is absent from his account. Salibi, *The Modern History*, 159.

81. See Volk, *Memorials and Martyrs*, 67.

82. For example, Yussef Ibrahim Yazbek's description of the execution and defiance of the martyrs in *The Conference of Martyrs: The Conference That Spread National Aspiration and Dragged Its Members to the Gallows* became the basis for Lebanese history textbooks. Volk, *Memorials and Martyrs*, 41.

83. Ibid., 27.

84. Ibid., 69.

BIBLIOGRAPHY

Adivar, Halide Edib. *House with Wisteria: Memoirs of Halide Edib*. Charlottesville, VA: Leopolis Press, 2003.

Agamben, Giorgio. *What Is an Apparatus? And Other Essays*. Stanford, CA: Stanford University Press, 2009.

"L'agriculture et les femmes" [Agriculture and women]. *Iktisadiyat mecmuasi* [Journal of economics] 54 (1917): 4.

Ajay, Nicholas Z. "Mount Lebanon and the Wilayah of Beirut, 1914–1918: The War Years." PhD diss., Georgetown University, 1973.

———. "Political Intrigue and Suppression in Lebanon during World War I." *International Journal of Middle Eastern Studies* 5 (1974): 140–160.

Akın, Yiğit. "The Ottoman Home Front during World War I: Everyday Politics, Society and Culture." PhD diss., Ohio State University, 2011.

———. "War, Women, and the State: The Politics of Sacrifice in the Ottoman Empire during the First World War." *Journal of Women's History* 26 (Fall 2014): 12–35.

Aksakal, Mustafa. "The Ottoman Empire." In *The Cambridge History of the First World War*, vol. 1, *Global War*, edited by Jay Winter, 459–478. Cambridge: Cambridge University Press, 2014.

———. *The Ottoman Road to War in 1914: The Ottoman Empire and the First World War*. New York: Cambridge University Press, 2008.

Alamgir, Mohiuddin. *Famine in South Asia: Political Economy of Mass Starvation*. Cambridge, MA: Oelgeschlager, Gunn & Hain, 1980.

Allouche, Adel. *Mamluk Economics: A Study and Translation of Al-Maqrizi's Ighathah*. Salt Lake City: University of Utah Press, 1994.

Anderson, Scott. *Lawrence in Arabia: War, Deceit, Imperial Folly and the Making of the Modern Middle East.* New York: Doubleday, 2013.
Antonius, George. *The Arab Awakening: The Story of the Arab National Movement.* New York: Capricorn Books, 1965.
Arab, Emile. "Au coeur de la commission americaine" [At the heart of the American Commission]. *La revue phénicienne* [The Phoenician review] 1, no. 6 (1919): 183–186.
Arkalı, Engin Deniz. *The Long Peace: Ottoman Lebanon, 1861–1920.* Berkeley: University of California Press, 1993.
Arnold, David. *Famine: Social Crisis and Historical Change.* Oxford: Blackwell, 1988.
Audoin-Rouzeau, Stephane, and Annette Becker, eds. *14–18: Understanding the Great War.* New York: Hill & Wang, 2002.
Ayalon, Yaron. *Natural Disasters in the Ottoman Empire: Plague, Famine, and Other Misfortunes.* New York: Cambridge University Press, 2014.
Azzi, Ellie. *Buhuth Muhada ila l-Abati Bulus Na'man* [Research dedicated to Bulus Na'am]. Junieh, Lebanon: Al-Matba'a al-Bulisiyya, 2008.
Baer, Gabriel. "The Beginning of Municipal Government." *Middle Eastern Studies* 4 (1969): 118–140.
Bahjat, Muhammed, and Muhammed Rafiq Tamimi. *Wilayat Bayrut 1915–1916* [Beirut province, 1915–1916]. 2 vols. Beirut: Lahad Khater, 1987.
Barnett, Michael N. *Empire of Humanity: A History of Humanitarianism.* Ithaca, NY: Cornell University Press, 2011.
Barton, James L. *Story of Near East Relief (1915–1930): An Interpretation.* New York: Macmillan, 1930.
Baufort, Emily A. *Egyptian Sepulchres and Syrian Shrines, including a Visit to Palmyra.* London: Macmillan, 1874.
Bayrut Vilayet-i meclis umumisinin 1330 senesi ictima'ında itihaz eylediği mükarirat [Resolutions that the Beirut General Assembly adopted during its assembly/meeting in the year of 1330]. Beirut: n.p. 1915.
Beşikçi, Mehmet. *The Ottoman Mobilization of Manpower in the First World War: Between Voluntarism and Resistance.* Leiden, Netherlands: Brill, 2012.
Boemeke, Manfred F., Roger Chickering, and Stig Förster, eds. *Anticipating Total War: The German and American Experiences, 1871–1914.* Washington, DC: German Historical Institute, 1999.
Bonner, Michael David, Mine Ener, and Amy Singer, eds. *Poverty and Charity in Middle Eastern Contexts.* Albany: State University of New York Press, 2003.
Bonzon, Thierry. "Transfer Payment and Social Policy." In *Capital Cities at War: Paris, London, Berlin 1914–1919*, edited by Jay Winter and Jean-Louis Robert, 286–302. Cambridge: Cambridge University Press, 1997.
Bourdieu, Pierre. *The Logic of Practice.* Translated by Richard Nice. Stanford, CA: Stanford University Press, 1990.

———. "The Social Space and the Genesis of Groups." *Theory and Society* 14, no. 6 (1985): 723–744.
Briggs, Charles L. "Why Nation-States and Journalists Can't Tell People to Be Healthy: Power and Pragmatic Miscalculations in Public Discourses of Health." *Medical Anthropology Quarterly* 17 (2003): 287–321.
al-Buwari, Bishara. *Arba' Sinin al-Harb* [Four years of the war]. New York: Al-Huda Newspaper Publications, 1926.
Chapra, M. "Islamic Economics: What It Is and How It Developed." *EH.Net Encyclopedia*, edited by Robert Whaples. Accessed May 18, 2011. http://eh.net/encyclopedia/islamic-economics-what-it-is-and-how-it-developed/.
Chickering, Roger. *The Great War and Urban Life in Germany: Freiburg, 1914–1918*. Cambridge: Cambridge University Press, 2007.
Chickering, Roger, and Stig Förster, eds. *Great War, Total War: Combat and Mobilization on the Western Front, 1914–1918*. Washington, DC: German Historical Institute, 2000.
———. *The Shadows of Total War in Europe, East Asia, and the United States, 1919–1939*. Washington, DC: German Historical Institute, 2003.
———. "Total War: The Use and Abuse of a Concept." In *Anticipating Total War: The German and American Experiences, 1871–1914*, edited by Manfred F. Boemeke, Roger Chickering, and Stig Förster, 13–28. Cambridge: Cambridge University Press, 1999.
Çiçek, Talha, ed. *Syria in World War I: Politics, Economy, and Society*. London: Routledge, Taylor & Francis, 2016.
———. *War and State Formation in Syria: Cemal Pasha's Governorate during World War I, 1914–17*. Abingdon, UK: Routledge, 2014.
Clemow, F. G. "Cholera in Turkey, etc., since 1914." *Lancet* (December 11, 1920): 1215–1216.
Cole, Juan. "Al-Tahtawi on Poverty and Welfare." In *Poverty and Charity in Middle Eastern Contexts*, edited by Michael David Bonner and Mine Ener, 223–238. Albany: State University of New York Press, 2003.
"Conditions in Syria." *Near East* 13, no. 325 (1917): 254.
Corm, Charles. "L'ombre s'entend sur la montagne" [The shadow is heard on the mountain]. *La revue phénicienne* 1, no. 1 (1919): 11–13.
———. [Cedar]. "L'impression d'un jeune phénicien d'aujourd'hui" [The impressions of a young Phoenician of today]. *La revue phénicienne* 1, no. 1 (1919): 30–33.
Cortas, Wadad Makdisi. *A World I Loved*. New York: Nation Books, 2009.
Coury [Khoury], Alfred "Le martyre du Liban" [The martyrdom of Lebanon]. *La revue phénicienne* 1, no.6 (December 1919): 226–235.
Dağlar, Oya. *War, Epidemics and Medicine in the Late Ottoman Empire (1912–1918)*. Haarlem, Netherlands: Sota, 2008.
Daniel, Ute. *The War from Within: German Working-Class Women in the First World War*. Oxford: Berg, 1997.

Davie, May. *Atlas historique des orthodoxes de Beyrouth et du Mont Liban 1800–1940* [Historical atlas of the orthodox of Beirut and Mount Lebanon 1800–1940]. Tripoli, Lebanon: n.p., 1999.

———. *Beyrouth et ses faubourgs (1840–1940): Une interprétation inachevée* [Beirut and its suburbs (1840–1940): A preliminary interpretation]. Beirut: Presses de l'Ifpo, 1996.

Davis, Belinda. *Home Fires Burning: Food, Politics, and Everyday Life in World War I Berlin*. Chapel Hill: University of North Carolina Press, 2000.

Demirci, Tuba, and Selçuk Akşin Somel. "Women's Bodies, Demography, and Public Health: Abortion Policy and Perspectives in the Ottoman Empire of the Nineteenth Century." *Journal of the History of Sexuality* 17 (2008): 327–340.

Deringil, Selim. "'They Live in a State of Nomadism and Savagery': The Late Ottoman Empire and the Post-colonial Debate." In *Comparative Studies in Society and History* 45, no. 2 (2003): 311–342.

———. *The Well-Protected Domains: Ideology and the Legitimation of Power in the Ottoman Empire, 1876–1909*. London: I. B. Tauris, 1998.

Devereux, Stephen. "Sen's Entitlement Approach: Critiques and Counter Critiques." *Oxford Development Studies* 29, no. 3 (2001): 245–263.

———. *Theories of Famine*. New York: Harvester Wheatsheaf, 1993.

De Waal, Alexander. *Famine That Kills: Darfur, Sudan*. Oxford: Oxford University Press, 2005.

"Distress in Syria." *Near East* 11, no. 270 (1916): 227.

Djemal [Jamal] Pasha. *Erinnerungen eines Türkischen Staatsmannes* [Memories of a Turkish statesman]. Munich: Drei MaskenVerlag, 1922.

Doumani, Beshara. *Rediscovering Palestine: Merchants and Peasants in Jabal Nablus, 1700–1900*. Berkeley: University of California Press, 1995.

Downes, Alexander B. *Targeting Civilians in War*. Ithaca, NY: Cornell University Press, 2008.

Eddé, Carla. *Beyrouth: Naissance d'une capital 1918–1924* [Beirut: Birth of a capital 1918–1924]. Beirut: Sindbad, 2009.

Edkins, Jenny. "Legality with a Vengeance: Famine and Humanitarian Relief in 'Complex Emergencies.'" *Journal of International Studies* 25 (1996): 547–575.

———. *Whose Hunger? Concepts of Famine, Practices of Aid*. Minneapolis: University of Minnesota Press, 2000.

Ehrlich, Paul R. *The Population Bomb*. San Francisco: Sierra Club, 1969.

Eley, Geoff. "War and the Twentieth-Century State." *Daedalus* 124 (1995): 155–174.

Elshakry, Marwa. *Reading Darwin in Arabic, 1860–1950*. Chicago: University of Chicago Press, 2013.

Ener, Mine. *Managing Egypt's Poor and the Politics of Benevolence, 1800–1952*. Princeton, NJ: Princeton University Press, 2003.

Erickson, Edward J. *Ordered to Die: A History of the Ottoman Army in the First World War*. Westport, CT: Greenwood Press, 2001.

———. "The Turkish Official Military Histories of the First World War: A Bibliographic Essay." *Middle Eastern Studies* 39, no. 3 (2003): 190–198.

Ertem, Özge. "Eating the Last Seed: Famine, Empire, Survival and Order in Ottoman Anatolia in the Late Nineteenth Century." PhD diss., European University Institute, 2012.

Fahmy, Khaled. *All the Pasha's Men: Mehmed Ali, His Army, and the Making of Modern Egypt*. Cambridge: Cambridge University Press, 1997.

Fahrenthold, Stacy. "Sound Minds in Sound Bodies: Transnational Philanthropy and Patriotic Masculinity in Al-Nadi al-Homsi and Syrian Brazil, 1920–32." *International Journal of Middle East Studies* 46, no. 2 (2014): 259–283.

"La famine au Liban et l'assistance française aux Libanais pendant la Grande Guerre (1915–19)" [The famine in Lebanon and French assistance during the Great War (1915–19)]. *L'Asie française* [French Asia], supplement (February 1922): 9.

Farge, Arlette. *The Allure of the Archives*. Translated by Thomas Scott-Railton. New Haven, CT: Yale University Press, 2013.

Faroqhi, Suraiya. *Towns and Townsmen in Ottoman Anatolia: Trade, Crafts, and Food Production in an Urban Setting, 1520–1650*. Cambridge: Cambridge University Press, 1984.

Farschid, Olaf, Manfred Kropp, and Stephan Dähne, eds. *The First World War as Remembered in the Countries of the Eastern Mediterranean*. Beirut: Orient-Institut, 2006.

Fawaz, Leila Tarazi. *A Land of Aching Hearts: The Middle East in the Great War*. Cambridge, MA: Harvard University Press, 2014.

———. *Merchants and Migrants in Nineteenth-Century Beirut*. Cambridge, MA: Harvard University Press, 1983.

Fogarty, Richard Standish. *Race and War in France: Colonial Subjects in the French Army, 1914–1918*. Baltimore: Johns Hopkins University Press, 2008.

"For the Relief of Distress in Syria." *Near East* 11, no. 269 (1916): 199.

Forder, Archibald. "Damascus, the Pearl of the Desert." *National Geographic* 22, no. 1 (1911): 62–82.

Foster, Zachary. "The 1915 Locust Attack in Syria and Palestine and Its Role in the Famine during the First World War." *Middle Eastern Studies* 50 (2014): 370–394.

Foucault, Michel. *Security, Territory, Population: Lectures at the Collège de France, 1977–78*. Basingstoke, UK: Palgrave Macmillan, 2007.

Foucault, Michel, Graham Burchell, Colin Gordon, and Peter Miller. *The Foucault Effect: Studies in Governmentality: With Two Lectures by and an Interview with Michel Foucault*. London: Harvester Wheatsheaf, 1991.

Fromkin, David. *A Peace to End All Peace: The Fall of the Ottoman Empire and the Creation of the Modern Middle East*. New York: H. Holt, 2001.

Furayha, Anis. *Qabl an Ansa* [Before I forget]. Beirut: Dar al-Nahar, 1979.

Gatrell, Peter. *A Whole Empire Walking*. Bloomington: Indiana University Press, 1999.
Gelvin, James L. *Divided Loyalties: Nationalism and Mass Politics in Syria at the Close of Empire*. Berkeley: University of California Press, 1998.
———. *The Israel-Palestine Conflict: One Hundred Years of War*. New York: Cambridge University Press, 2014.
———. *The Modern Middle East: A History*. New York: Oxford University Press, 2005.
———. "The 'Politics of Notables' Forty Years After." *Middle East Studies Association Bulletin* 40, no. 1 (2006): 19–29.
Gill, Rebecca. "'The Rational Administration of Compassion': The Origins of British Relief in War." *Le mouvement social* [The social movement] 227, no. 1 (2009): 9–26.
Grayzel, Susan R. *Women's Identities at War: Gender, Motherhood, and Politics in Britain and France during the First World War*. Chapel Hill: University of North Carolina Press, 1999.
Greenwald, Maurine Weiner. *Women, War, and Work: The Impact of World War I on Women Workers in the United States*. Westport, CT: Greenwood Press, 1985.
Gritzner, Charles F. *Feeding a Hungry World*. New York: Infobase Publishing, 2010.
Grobba, Fritz. *Die Getreidewirtschaft Syriens und Palästinas seit Beginn des Weltkrieges* [The grain economy of Syria and Palestine since the beginning of the World War]. Hanover, Germany: H. Lafaire, 1923.
Habash, Yusuf. *Al-Jihad Lubnan* [Lebanon's struggle]. Beirut: n.p., 1920.
Haddad, Mahmoud. "The City, the Coast, the Mountain, and the Hinterland: Beirut's Commercial and Political Rivalries in the 19th and Early 20th Century." In *The Syrian Land: Processes of Integration and Fragmentation: Bilad al-Sham from the 18th to the 20th Century*, edited by Thomas Philipp and Birgit Schäbler, 129–153. Stuttgart: F. Steiner, 1998.
Hakim, Carol. *The Origins of the Lebanese National Idea, 1840–1920*. Berkeley: University of California Press, 2013.
Al-Hakim, Yusuf. *Bayrut wa-Lubnan fi 'Ahd al-'Uthman* [Beirut and Lebanon during the Ottoman period]. Beirut: al-Matba'a al-Kathulikiyya, 1964.
Hallaq, Wael. "Social Life in Beirut." In *Bayrut fi al-Dhakira al-Sha'biyya* [Beirut in popular memory], edited by Khalid al-Lahham, 5:124–137. Beirut: Sharikat al-Zawaya, 1992.
Hanna, Abdallah. "The First World War according to the Memoirs of 'Commoners' in Bilad al-Sham." In *The World in the World Wars: Experiences, Perceptions and Perspectives from Africa and Asia*, edited by Katrin Bromer, Heike Liebau, Katherina Lange, Dyala Hamzah, and Ravi Ahuja, 299–313. Leiden, Netherlands: Brill, 2010.
Hanssen, Jens. *Fin de Siècle Beirut: The Making of an Ottoman Provincial Capital*. Oxford: Oxford University Press, 2005.
———. "From Social Status to Intellectual Activity: Some Prosopographical Observations on the Municipal Council in Beirut, 1868–1908." In *From the Syrian Land to*

the States of Syria and Lebanon, edited by Thomas Philipp and Christoph Schumann, 59–76. Würzburg, Germany: Ergon, 2004.

———. "The Origins of the Municipal Council in Beirut, 1860–1908." In *Municipalités méditerranéennes: Les réformes urbaines ottomanes au miroir d'une histoire comparée (Moyen-Orient, Maghreb, Europe méridionale)* [Mediterranean municipalities: Ottoman urban reforms in a comparative perspective (Middle East, North Africa, Southern Europe)], edited by Nora Lafi, 139–175. Berlin: K. Schwarz, 2005.

Haqqi, Isma'il, ed. *Lubnan: Mabahith 'Ilmiyya wa Ijtima'iyya* [Lebanon: Scientific and social studies]. 1918. Reprint. Beirut: n.p., 1968.

Hathaway, Jane. *The Arab Lands under Ottoman Rule, 1516–1800*. New York: Longman, 2008.

Hauser, Julia. *German Religious Women in Late Ottoman Beirut: Competing Missions*. Leiden, Netherlands: Brill, 2015.

Healy, Maureen. *Vienna and the Fall of the Habsburg Empire: Total War and Everyday Life in World War I*. Cambridge: Cambridge University Press, 2004.

"Help for Syria." *Near East* 12, no. 287 (1916): 4.

Hitti, Philip K. *Lebanon in History: From the Earliest Times to the Present*. London: Macmillan, 1967.

———. *A Short History of Lebanon*. London: Macmillan, 1965.

Hollis, Stanley. "Commerce and Industries of Syria." In *Daily Consular and Trade Reports*, no. 229, 1601–1611. Washington, DC: The Bureau of Foreign and Domestic Commerce and Department of Commerce and Labor, 1912.

———. "Construction Work in Turkey." In *Daily Consular and Trade Reports*, no. 103, 505–506. Washington, DC: Department of Commerce and Labor, Bureau of Manufactures, 1911.

Hoskins, F. E. "In Syria." *Assembly Herald* 21, no. 8 (1915): 550–552.

Hourani, Albert. *A History of the Arab Peoples*. Cambridge, MA: Belknap Press of Harvard University Press, 1991.

———. "Ottoman Reform and the Politics of Notables." In *The Modern Middle East*, edited by Albert Hourani, Phillip S. Khoury, and Mary C. Wilson, 83–110. Berkeley: University of California Press, 1993.

Hunt, Nancy Rose. *The Nervous State: Violence, Remedies, and Reverie in Colonial Congo*. Durham, NC: Duke University Press, 2016.

Ibn Khaldun. *The Muqaddimah; An Introduction to History*. Translated by Franz Rosenthal. New York: Pantheon Books, 1958.

İslamoğlu, Huri. *Constituting Modernity: Private Property in the East and West*. London: I. B. Tauris, 2004.

Issawi, Charles Philip. *The Fertile Crescent, 1800–1914: A Documentary Economic History*. New York: Oxford University Press, 1988.

———. "The Historical Background of Lebanese Emigration, 1800–1914." In *Lebanese in the World: A Century of Emigration*, edited by Albert Hourani and Nadim Shehadi, 13–32. London: I. B. Tauris and Centre for Lebanese Studies, 1992.

Jackson, Simon. "Compassion and Connections: Feeding Beirut and Assembling Mandate Rule in 1919." In *The Routledge Handbook of the History of the Middle East Mandate*, edited by Cyrus Schayegh and Andrew Arsan, 62–75. New York: Routledge, 2015.

———. "Diaspora Politics and Developmental Empire: The Syro-Lebanese at the League of Nations." *Arab Studies Journal* 21 (2013): 166–190.

Jacobson, Abigail. *From Empire to Empire: Jerusalem between Ottoman and British Rule*. Syracuse, NY: Syracuse University Press, 2011.

———. "Negotiating Ottomanism in Times of War: Jerusalem during World War I through the Eyes of a Local Muslim Resident." *International Journal of Middle East Studies* 40 (2008): 69–88.

Jessup, Henry Harris. *Fifty-Three Years in Syria*. New York: Fleming H. Revell, 1910.

Johnson, Michael. "Factional Politics in Lebanon: The Case of the 'Islamic Society of Benevolent Intentions' (Al-Maqasid) in Beirut." *Middle Eastern Studies* 41 (1978): 56–75.

Kabkab, Wisam Bisharah. *Jam'iyyat al-Khayriyya lil-Ta'ifa al-Rum al-Kathulik fi Bayrut (1883–1983)* [Charitable society of the Greek Catholic sect in Beirut (1883–1983)]. Beirut: n.p. 1983.

———. *Jam'iyyat al-Mursalin al-Bulusiyyin* [Missionary Society of St. Paul]. Beirut: Al-Maktabah al-Bulusiyya, 1987.

Kana'an, Ibrahim Na'um. *Lubnan fi al-Harb al-Kubra: 1914–1918* [Lebanon during the Great War: 1914–1918]. Beirut: Mu'assasat 'Asi, 1974.

Kandiyoti, Deniz. *Women, Islam, and the State*. Philadelphia: Temple University Press, 1991.

Karakışla, Yavuz Selim. *Women, War and Work in the Ottoman Empire: Society for the Employment of Ottoman Muslim Women, 1916–1923*. Istanbul: Osmanli Bankasi Arsiv ve Arastırma Merkezi, 2005.

Kassir, Samir. *Beirut*. Berkeley: University of California Press, 2010.

Kaufman, Asher. *Reviving Phoenicia: The Search for Identity in Lebanon*. London: I. B. Tauris, 2004.

———. "'Tell Us Our History': Charles Corm, Mount Lebanon and Lebanese Nationalism." *Middle Eastern Studies* 40, no. 3 (2004): 1–28.

Kayalı, Hasan. *Arabs and Young Turks: Ottomanism, Arabism, and Islamism in the Ottoman Empire, 1908–1918*. Berkeley: University of California Press, 1997.

———. "Wartime Regional and Imperial Integration of Greater Syria during World War I." In *The Syrian Land: Processes of Integration and Fragmentation: Bilad al-Sham from the 18th to the 20th Century*, edited by Thomas Philipp and Birgit Schäbler, 295–306. Stuttgart: F. Steiner, 1998.

Kechriotis, Vangelis. "Protecting the City's Interest: The Greek Orthodox and the

Conflict between Municipal and *Vilayet* Authorities in Izmir (Smyrna) in the Second Constitutional Period." *Mediterranean Historical Review* 24, no. 2 (2009): 207–221.

Kelleher, Margaret. *The Feminization of Famine: Expressions of the Inexpressible?* Cork, Ireland: Cork University Press, 1997.

Kent, Susan Kingsley. *Making Peace: The Reconstruction of Gender in Interwar Britain.* Princeton, NJ: Princeton University Press, 1993.

Kévorkian, Raymond H. *The Armenian Genocide: A Complete History.* London: I. B. Tauris, 2011.

Khalaf, Samir. *Heart of Beirut: Reclaiming the Bourj.* London: Saqi, 2006.

Khalidi, 'Anbara Salam. *Jawlah fi al-Dhikrayat bayna Lubnan wa-Filastin* [Journey of memories between Lebanon and Palestine]. Beirut: Dar al-Nahar, 1973.

———. *The Memoirs of an Early Arab Feminist: The Life and Activism of Anbara Salam Khalidi.* Translated by Tarif Khalidi. London: Pluto Press, 2013.

Khalidi, Rashid. "The 1912 Election Campaign in the Cities of Bilad Al-Sham." *International Journal of Middle East Studies* 16, no. 4 (1984): 461–474.

———. *The Origins of Arab Nationalism.* New York: Columbia University Press, 1991.

———. "Ottomanism and Arabism in Syria before 1914: A Reassessment." In *The Origins of Arab Nationalism*, edited by Rashid Khalidi, 50–72. New York: Columbia University Press, 1991.

Khalidi, Tarif. "The Arab World." In *The Great World Wars 1914–45: The People's Experience*, edited by John Bourne, Peter Liddle, and Ian Whitefield, 2:291–308. London: HarperCollins, 2001.

Khater, Akram Fouad. *Inventing Home; Emigration, Gender, and the Middle Class in Lebanon, 1870–1920.* Berkeley: University of California Press, 2001.

———. "'Queen of the House?': Making Immigrant Lebanese Families in the Mahjar." In *Family History in the Middle East: Household, Property, and Gender*, edited by Beshara Doumani, 271–300. Albany: State University of New York Press, 2003.

Khouri, Robert M. *La médecine au Liban: De la Phénicie jusqu'à nos jours* [Medicine in Lebanon: From Phoenicia to the present day]. Beirut: Éditions ABCD, 1986.

Khuwairi, Butrus. *Al-Rihla al-Suriyya fi al-Harb al-'Ummumiyya, 1916: Akhtar wa-Ahwal wa A'ajib* [Travels in Syria during the World War, 1916: Dangers, horrors, and strange happenings]. Edited by Yusuf Tuma al-Bustani. Cairo: Al-Matba'a al-Yusufiyya, 1921.

Kitchen, James E., Alisa Miller, and Laura Rowe, eds. *Other Combatants, Other Fronts: Competing Histories of the First World War.* Newcastle upon Tyne: Cambridge Scholars, 2011.

Kouyoumdjian, Ohannes Pasha. *Le Liban à la veille et au début de la guerre: Mémoires d'un gouverneur, 1913–1915* [Lebanon immediately before and at the beginning of the war: The memories of a governor, 1913–1915]. Paris: Centre d'histoire arménienne contemporaine, 2003.

Kramer, Alan. "Blockade and Economic Warfare." In *The Cambridge History of the First World War*, vol.2, *The State*, edited by J. M. Winter, 460–489. Cambridge: Cambridge University Press, 2013.

Lafi, Nora. "Mediterranean Connections: The Circulation of Municipal Knowledge and Practices during the Ottoman Reforms, c. 1830–1910." In *Another Global City: Historical Explorations into the Transnational Municipal Moment, 1850–2000*, edited by Pierre-Yves Saunier and Shane Ewen, 35–50. New York: Palgrave Macmillan, 2008.

Liebau, Heike, Katrin Bromer, Katherina Lange, Dyala Hamzah, and Ravi Ahuja, eds. *The World in World Wars: Experiences, Perceptions and Perspectives from Africa and Asia*. Leiden, Netherlands: Brill, 2010.

Longrigg, Stephen. *Syria and Lebanon under French Mandate*. London: Oxford University Press, 1958.

Makdisi, Ussama Samir. "Corrupting the Sublime Sultanate: The Revolt of Tanyus Shahin in Nineteenth-Century Ottoman Lebanon." *Comparative Studies in Society and History* 42 (2000): 180–208.

———. *The Culture of Sectarianism: Community, History, and Violence in Nineteenth-Century Ottoman Lebanon*. Berkeley: University of California Press, 2000.

———. *Faith Misplaced: The Broken Promise of U.S.-Arab Relations: 1820–2001*. New York: Public Affairs, 2010.

Maksudyan, Nazan. "'Being Saved to Serve': Armenian Orphans of 1894–1896 and Interested Relief in Missionary Orphanages." *Turcica* 2, no. 2 (2010): 47–88.

———. "'This Time Women as Well Got Involved in Politics!': Nineteenth Century Ottoman Women's Organizations and Political Agency." In *Women and the City, Women in the City: A Gendered Perspective on Ottoman Urban History*, edited by Nazan Maksudyan, 107–135. New York: Berghahn Books, 2014.

Malouf, Th. "Les souffrances du Liban pendant la guerre" [Lebanon's sufferings during the war]. *Les missions catholiques* [The Catholic missions] 51, no. 2637 (1919): 603–604.

Malthus, Thomas. *An Essay on the Principle of Population: Text, Sources and Background, Criticism*. Toronto: George J. McLeod, 1976.

Al-Maqdisi, Jirjis. *A'zam Harb fi al-Tarikh* [The greatest war in history]. Beirut: al-Matba'a al-'Ilmiyya, 1918.

"Les martyrs en Armenie et en Syrie" [The martyrs in Armenia and in Syria]. *Oeuvre des écoles d'Orient* [The work of the schools of the Orient], no. 330 (October 1916): 90–91.

McCallum, Fiona. *The Christian Religious Leadership in the Middle East: The Political Role of the Patriarch*. Lewiston, NY: Edwin Mellen Press, 2010.

McGilvary, Margaret. *The Dawn of a New Era in Syria*. New York: Fleming H. Revell, 1920.

McKale, Donald M. *War by Revolution: Germany and Great Britain in the Middle East in the Era of World War I*. Kent, OH: Kent State University Press, 1998.

Méouchy, Nadine. "Les nationalists arabes de la premiere génération en Syrie: 1918–1928: Une génération méconnue" [The first generation of Arab nationalists in Syria: 1918–1928: A little-known generation]. Bulletin d'études orientales [Bulletin of Oriental studies] 47 (1995): 109–128.

Migdal, Joel S. *State in Society: Studying How States and Societies Transform and Constitute One Another*. Cambridge: Cambridge University Press, 2001.

Miller-Mann, Nellie. *Letters from Syria 1921–1923: A Response to the Armenian Tragedy*. N.p., 2012.

Mina, Hanna. *Fragments of Memory: A Story of a Syrian Family*. Translated by Olive Kenny and Lorne Kenny. Austin: University of Texas Press, 1993.

Mitchell, Timothy. "The Limits of the State: Beyond Statist Approaches and Their Critics." *American Political Science Review* 85, no. 1 (1991): 77–96.

Mokyr, Joel, and Cormac Ó Gráda. "Famine Disease and Famine Mortality: Lessons from Ireland 1845–1850." In *Famine Demography: Perspectives from the Past and Present*, edited by Tim Dyson and Cormac Ó Gráda, 19–43. Oxford: Oxford University Press, 2002.

Morgenthau, Henry. *Ambassador Morgenthau's Story*. Garden City, NY: Doubleday, Page, 1918.

Morrow, John. *The Great War: An Imperial History*. New York: Routledge, 2004.

Mouawad, Youssef. "Grande Guerre et grande famine" [Great war and great famine]. *Lebanus* 7, no. 1 (2004): 12–29.

Mukherjee, Janam. *Hungry Bengal: War, Famine and the End of Empire*. London: Hurst, 2015.

Müller, Karl. "The Legacy of Joseph Schmidlin." *International Bulletin of Mission Research* 4, no. 3 (1980): 109–113.

Mundy, Martha, and Richard Saumarez Smith. *Governing Property, Making the Modern State: Law Administration and Production in Ottoman Syria*. London: I. B. Tauris, 2007.

Naccache, Albert. "L'industrie de la villegiature au Liban" [The tourism industry in Lebanon]. *La revue phénicienne* 1, no. 6 (1919): 208–213.

Naff, Alexa. "Lebanese Immigration into the U.S: 1880 to the Present." In *Lebanese in the World: A Century of Emigration*, edited by Albert Hourani and Nadim Shehadi, 141–165. London: I. B. Taurus and Centre for Lebanese Studies, 1992.

Naguib, Nefissa, and Inger Marie Okkenhaug, eds. *Interpreting Welfare and Relief in the Middle East*. Leiden, Netherlands: Brill, 2008.

"News from Syria" (January 7, 1916). *Near East* 10, no. 244 (1916), 260.

"News from Syria" (April 28, 1916). *Near East* 10, no. 260 (1916): 701.

"News from Syria" (May 4, 1917). *Near East* 13, no. 313 (1917): 5.

"News from Syria, a Terrible Record" (February 9, 1917). *Near East* 12, no. 301 (1917): 341.

"News of Syria" (February 2, 1917). *Near East* 12, no. 300 (1917): 317.

"News of the Lebanon" (July 23, 1915). *Near East* 9, no. 220 (1915): 321.

Ó Gráda, Cormac. "Adam Smith and Amartya Sen: Markets and Famines in Pre-industrial Europe." Working paper no. 200218, School of Economics, University College Dublin, 2002.

———. *Eating People Is Wrong, and Other Essays on Famine, Its Past, and Its Future.* Princeton, NJ: Princeton University Press, 2015.

———. *Famine: A Short History.* Princeton, NJ: Princeton University Press, 2009.

Ó Gráda, Cormac, and Andrés Eiríksson, eds. *Ireland's Great Famine: Interdisciplinary Perspectives.* Dublin: University College Dublin Press, 2006.

Özdemir, Hikmet. *The Ottoman Army, 1914–1918: Disease and Death on the Battlefield.* Salt Lake City: University of Utah Press, 2008.

Özveren, Eyüp. "Beirut: Port-Cities of the Eastern Mediterranean (1800–1914)." *Review (Fernand Braudel Center)* 16 (1993): 467–497.

Pamuk, Şevket. *A Monetary History of the Ottoman Empire.* New York: Cambridge University Press, 2000.

———. "The Ottoman Economy in World War I." In *The Economics of World War I*, edited by S. N. Broadberry and Mark Harrison, 112–136. New York: Cambridge University Press, 2005.

Panian, Karnig. *Goodbye, Antoura: A Memoir of the Armenian Genocide.* Stanford, CA: Stanford University Press, 2015.

Philipp, Thomas. *The Syrians in Egypt: 1725–1975.* Wiesbaden, Germany: Steiner, 1985.

Pollard, Lisa. "Egyptian by Association: Charitable States and Service Societies, circa 1850–1945." *International Journal for Middle East Studies* 46 (2014): 239–257.

"The Position in Syria" (September 7, 1917). *Near East* 13, no. 331 (1917): 365.

Proctor, Tammy M. *Civilians in a World at War, 1914–1918.* New York: New York University Press, 2010.

Al-Qattan, Najwa. "Fragments of Wartime Memories from Syria and Lebanon." In *Syria in World War I: Politics, Economy, and Society*, edited by Talha Çiçek, 130–149. London: Routledge, Taylor & Francis, 2016.

———. "Historicising Hunger: The Famine in Wartime Lebanon and Syria." In *The First World War and Its Aftermath: The Shaping of the Middle East*, edited by T. G. Frazer, 111–126. London: Gingko Library, 2015.

———. "*Safarbarlik*: Ottoman Syria and the Great War." In *From the Syrian Land to the States of Syria and Lebanon*, edited by Thomas Philipp and Christoph Schuman, 163–173. Beirut: Argon Verlag Wurzburg, 2004.

———. "When Mothers Ate Their Children: Wartime Memory and the Language of Food in Syria and Lebanon." *International Journal for Middle Eastern Studies* 46 (2014): 719–736.

Quilty, James, M. "Bridging the Dichotomy: Socio-Economic Change and Class Consolidation in Ottoman Beirut and Damascus." Master's thesis, Simon Fraser University, 1992.

Al-Qissis, Antwan, ed. *Lubnan fi al-Harb al-'Alamiyya al-Ula* [Lebanon during the First World War]. Beirut: Manshurat al-Jami'iyyat al-Lubnaniyya, 2011.
Rabinow, Paul. *Anthropos Today: Reflections on Modern Equipment*. Princeton, NJ: Princeton University Press, 2003.
Rabinow, Paul, and Nikolas Rose. "Biopower Today." *BioSocieties* 1 (2006): 195–217.
Rangasami, Amrita. "Failure of Exchange Entitlements' Theory of Famine: A Response." *Economic & Political Weekly* 20 (1985): 1747–1752.
"Relief for Syria" (February 16, 1917). *Near East* 12, no. 302 (1917): 364.
Remoulière, J. de la. "L'oeuvre du ravitaillement civil de Beyrouth" [The work of provisioning Beirut's civilians]. *La revue phénicienne* 1, no.1 (1919): 55–57.
Rida, Ahmad. *Mudhakkirat lil-Tarikh; Hawadith Jabal 'Amil, 1914–1922* [Memories of history: Events of Jabal 'Amil, 1914–1922]. Beirut: Dar al-Nahar, 2009.
Rieff, David. *A Bed for the Night: Humanitarianism in Crisis*. New York: Simon & Schuster, 2002.
Robert, Jean-Louis. "The Image of the Profiteer." In *Capital Cities at War: Paris, London, Berlin 1914–1919*, edited by J. M. Winter and Jean-Louis Robert, 1:104–132. New York: Cambridge University Press, 2007.
Rollet, Catherine. "The 'Other War' I." In *Capital Cities at War: Paris, London, Berlin 1914–1919*, edited by Jay Winter and Jean-Louis Robert, 1:421–455. Cambridge: Cambridge University Press, 1997.
Rosenberg, Emily. "Missions to the World: Philanthropy Abroad." In *Charity, Philanthropy, and Civility in American History*, edited by Lawrence Friedman and Mark McGarvie, 241–258. Cambridge: Cambridge University Press, 2003.
Rosenthal, Steven. "Foreigners and Municipal Reform in Istanbul." *International Journal of Middle Eastern Studies* 11 (1980): 227–245.
———. "Urban Elites and the Foundation of Municipalities in Alexandria and Istanbul." *Middle Eastern Studies* 16 (1980): 125–133.
Ruppin, Arthur. *Syrien als Wirtschaftsgebiet* [Syria as an economic zone]. Berlin: Kolonial-Wirtschaftliches Komitee, 1917.
Sa'id, 'Abdallah, "Tatawwur Harakat al-As'r wa-l-Ujur" [The evolution of price and wage fluctuations]. In *Lubnan fi al-Harb al-'Alamiyya al-Ula* [Lebanon during the First World War], edited by Antwan al-Qissis, 373–406. Beirut: Manshurat al-Jami'iyyat al-Lubnaniyya, 2011.
Salam, Salim 'Ali. *Mudhakkirat Salim 'Ali Salam (1868–1938)* [The memoirs of Salim 'Ali Salam (1868–1938)]. Beirut: Al-Dar al-Jami'iyya, 1982.
Salibi, Kamal S. "Beirut under the Young Turks: As Depicted in the Memoirs of Salim 'Ali Salam." In *Les Arabes par leurs archives* [The Arabs through their archives], edited by J. Berques and D. Chevallier, 193–216. Paris: Centre national de la recherche scientifique, 1976.

———. *A House of Many Mansions: The History of Lebanon Reconsidered*. Berkeley: University of California Press, 1988.

———. *The Modern History of Lebanon*. New York: Frederick A. Praeger, 1965.

Samson, Anne. *World War I in Africa: The Forgotten Conflict among the European Powers*. London: I. B. Tauris, 2013.

Samuel, Raphael. *Theatres of Memory*. London: Verso, 1994.

Sanborn, Joshua A. "Unsettling the Empire: Violent Migrations and Social Disaster in Russia during World War I." *Journal of Modern History* 77 (2005): 290–324.

Scheper-Hughes, Nancy. *Death without Weeping: The Violence of Everyday Life in Brazil*. Berkeley: University of California Press, 1992.

Schilcher, Linda. "Famine in Syria, 1915–1918." In *Problems of the Middle East in Historical Perspective: Essays in Honour of Albert Hourani*, edited by John Spagnolo and Albert Hourani, 229–258. Reading, UK: Ithaca Press, 1996.

Schneer, Jonathan. *The Balfour Declaration: The Origins of the Arab-Israeli Conflict*. London: Bloomsbury, 2010.

Scott, James C. *Weapons of the Weak: Everyday Forms of Peasant Resistance*. New Haven, CT: Yale University Press, 1985.

Sefi, Alexander. "The Plight of Syria" (June 23, 1916). *Near East* 11, no. 268 (1916): 175.

Sehnaoui, Nada. *L'occidentalisation de la vie quotidienne à Beyrouth, 1860–1914* [The Westernization of everyday life in Beirut, 1860–1914]. Beirut: Editions Dar an-Nahar, 2002.

Seikaly, Sherene. *Men of Capital: Scarcity and Economy in Mandate Palestine*. Stanford, CA: Stanford University Press, 2016.

Sen, Amartya. *Poverty and Famines: An Essay on Entitlement and Deprivation*. Oxford: Oxford University Press, 1981.

Sewell, William H. *Logics of History: Social Theory and Social Transformation*. Chicago: University of Chicago Press, 2005.

Shahadah, Salim Jurj. *Kitab al-Harb al-Kabir* [The long history of the war]. New York: Al-Majalla al-'Arabiyya, 1917.

Sharif, Malek. *Imperial Norms and Local Realities: The Ottoman Municipal Laws and the Municipality of Beirut (1860–1908)*. Beirut: Orient-Institut Beirut, 2014.

Shaw, Stanford J. *The Ottoman Empire in World War I*. Ankara: Turkish Historical Society, 2006.

Shibaru, Issam Muhammad. *Jam'iyyat al-Maqasid al-Khayriyya al-Islamiyyah fi Bayrut (1878–2000)* [Islamic Association for Benevolent Intention in Beirut (1878–2000)]. Beirut: Dar Misbah, 2000.

Singer, Amy. "Serving Up Charity: The Ottoman Public Kitchen." *Journal of Interdisciplinary History* 35 (2005): 481–500.

———. "Special Issue Introduction: Politics of Benevolence." *International Journal of Middle East Studies* 46 (2014): 227–238.

Slim, Souad. *The Greek Orthodox "Waqf" in Lebanon during the Ottoman Period*. Beirut: Orient Institute, 2007.

Solnit, Rebecca. *A Paradise Built in Hell: The Extraordinary Communities that Arise in Disasters*. New York: Viking, 2009.

Spagnolo, John P. "Mount Lebanon, France and Daud Pasha: A Study of Some Aspects of Political Habituation." *International Journal of Middle East Studies* 2, no. 2 (1971): 148–167.

"State of Medical Education in Turkey." *American Journal of Medical Science* 17 (1849): 233.

"The State of Syria" (July 15, 1915). *Near East* 9, no. 219 (1915): 303.

Strachan, Hew. *Financing the First World War*. Oxford: Oxford University Press, 2004.

Suny, Ronald Grigor. *"They Can Live in the Desert but Nowhere Else": A History of the Armenian Genocide*. Princeton, NJ: Princeton University Press, 2015.

"Syria and the Lebanon." *Near East* 12, no. 297 (1917): 245.

"Syria and the Lebanon." *Near East* 12, no. 299 (1917): 292.

"La syrie martyre" [Syrian martyrdom]. *Oeuvre des écoles d'Orient* 332 (1917): 192.

Tamari, Salim. "The Short Life of Private Ihsan: Jerusalem 1915." *Jerusalem Quarterly* 30 (2007): 26–58.

———. *Year of the Locust: A Soldier's Diary and the Erasure of Palestine's Ottoman Past*. Berkeley: University of California Press, 2011.

Tanielian, Melanie Schulze. "Disease and Public Health (Ottoman Empire/Middle East)." In *1914–1918-Online: International Encyclopedia of the First World War*, edited by Ute Daniel, Peter Gatrell, Oliver Janz, Heather Jones, Jennifer Keene, Alan Kramer, and Bill Nasson. Berlin: Freie Universität Berlin. Last updated October 8, 2014. DOI: 10.15463/ie1418.10466.

———. "Feeding the City: The Beirut Municipality and the Politics of Food during World War I." *International Journal of Middle East Studies* 46 (2014): 737–758.

———. "Food and Nutrition (Ottoman Empire/Middle East)." In *1914–1918-Online: International Encyclopedia of the First World War*, edited by Ute Daniel, Peter Gatrell, Oliver Janz, Heather Jones, Jennifer Keene, Alan Kramer, and Bill Nasson. Berlin: Freie Universität, Berlin. Last updated October 8, 2014. DOI: 10.15463/ie1418.10322.

———. "Politics of Wartime Relief in Ottoman Beirut." *First World War Studies* 5 (2014): 69–82.

Tauber, Eliezer. *The Arab Movements in World War I*. London: Frank Cass, 1993.

———. *The Emergence of the Arab Movements*. London: Frank Cass, 1993.

Thompson, Elizabeth. *Colonial Citizens: Republican Rights, Paternal Privilege, and Gender in French Syria and Lebanon*. New York: Columbia University Press, 2000.

———. *Justice Interrupted: Historical Perspectives on Promoting Democracy in the Middle East*. Washington, DC: US Institute of Peace, 2009.

Tibawi, Abdul Latif. *A Modern History of Syria, including Lebanon and Palestine*. London: Macmillan, 1969.

Tilly, Charles. "War Making and State Making as Organized Crime." In *Bringing the State Back*, edited by Peter Evans, Dietrich Rueschemeyer, and Theda Skocpol, 169–186. Cambridge: Cambridge University Press, 1985.

Tilly, Louise A. "Food Entitlement, Famine, and Conflict." *Journal of Interdisciplinary History* 14, no. 2 (1983): 333–349.

Townshend, Charles. *Desert Hell: The British Invasion of Mesopotamia*. Cambridge, MA: Belknap Press of Harvard University Press, 2011.

Traboulsi, Fawwaz. *A History of Modern Lebanon*. London: Pluto Press, 2012.

Tucker, Jonathan B. *Scourge: The Once and Future Threat of Smallpox*. New York: Atlantic Monthly Press, 2002.

"Typhoid Fever: Its Symptoms and Treatments." *Al-Muqtataf* [Anthology] 47 (August 1915): 181.

US Bureau of Manufactures. *Daily Consular and Trade Reports*. Washington, DC: Department of Commerce and Labor, Bureau of Manufactures, 1910–1914.

Van Dyck, W. T. *Syllabus of Lectures on Hygiene for the Use of Students of the Syrian Protestant College*. Beirut: n.p. 1916.

Van Leeuwen, Richard. *Notables and Clergy in Mount Lebanon: The Khazin Sheikhs and the Maronite Church, 1736–1840*. New York: E. J. Brill, 1994.

———. "The Political Emancipation of the Maronite Church in Mount Lebanon (1736–1842)." Middle East Research Associates Occasional Paper no. 8, Amsterdam: Middle East Research Associates, 1990.

Vincent, C. Paul. *The Politics of Hunger: The Allied Blockade of Germany, 1915–1919*. Athens: Ohio University Press, 1985.

Volk, Lucia. *Memorials and Martyrs in Modern Lebanon*. Bloomington: Indiana University Press, 2010.

Vuaille, Jerome. "La famine à Beyrouth" [The famine in Beirut]. *Les missions catholiques* 50, no. 2581 (1918): 553–554.

Walker, Dennis Patrick. "Clericist Catholic Authors and the Crystallization of Historical Memory of World War I in Lebanonist-Particularist Discourse, 1918–1922." *Islamic Studies* 48, no. 2 (2009): 219–260.

———. "The Role of Ilyas Butrus al-Huwayyik in the Emergence of Lebanon as a Separate State." *Journal of Pakistan Historical Society* 50, no. 2 (2003): 109–123.

Wallach, Jennifer Jensen. *How America Eats: A Social History of U.S. Food and Culture*. Lanham, MD: Rowman & Littlefield, 2013.

Watenpaugh, Keith David. *Bread from Stones: The Middle East and the Making of Modern Humanitarianism*. Oakland: University of California Press, 2015.

Watts, Michael. *Silent Violence: Food, Famine and Peasantry in Northern Nigeria*. Berkeley: University of California Press, 1983.

Watts, Michael J., and Hans G. Bohle. "Hunger, Famine and the Space of Vulnerability." *GeoJournal* 30, no. 2 (1993): 117–125.

———. "Spaces of Vulnerability: The Causal Structures of Hunger and Famine." *Progress in Human Geography* 17, no. 1 (1993): 43–67.

Weber, Max. *The Sociology of Religion*. Translated by Ephraim Fischoff. Boston: Beacon Press, 1963.

Weindling, Paul. "The First World War and the Campaigns against Lice: Comparing British and German Sanitary Measures." In *Die Medizin und der Erste Weltkrieg* [Medicine and the First World War], edited by Wolfgang Uwe Eckart and Christoph Gradmann, 227–240. Pfaffenweiler, Germany: Centaurus-Verlagsgesellschaft, 1996.

White, Benjamin Thomas. *The Emergence of Minorities in the Middle East: The Politics of Community in French Mandate Syria*. Edinburgh: Edinburgh University Press, 2011.

Whiting, John D. "Jerusalem's Locust Plague." *National Geographic* 28 (1915): 511–550.

Wiegand, Theodor. *Halbmond im letzten Viertel: Archäologische Reiseberichte* [Half moon in the last quarter: Archaeological travel reports]. Mainz am Rhein, Germany: Verlag P. von Zabern, 1985.

Williams, Elizabeth. "Economy, Environment, and Famine: World War I from the Perspective of the Syrian Interior." In *Syria in World War I: Politics, Economy, and Society*, edited by Talha Çiçek, 150–168. London: Routledge, Taylor & Francis Group, 2016.

Winter, J. M. "Paris, London, Berlin 1914–1919: Capital Cities at War." In *Capital Cities at War: Paris, London, Berlin 1914–1919*, edited by J. M. Winter and Jean-Louis Robert, 1:3–24. New York: Cambridge University Press, 2007.

Winter, J. M., and Jean-Louis Robert, eds. *Capital Cities at War: Paris, London, Berlin 1914–1919*. New York: Cambridge University Press, 2007.

Woman's Foreign Missionary Societies of the Presbyterian Church. "Editorial Notes." *Women's Work: A Foreign Missions Magazine* 31, no. 7 (1916): 146.

Woodward, David R. *Hell in the Holy Land: World War I in the Middle East*. Lexington: University Press of Kentucky, 2006.

Yalman, Ahmet Emin. *Turkey in the World War*. New Haven, CT: Yale University Press, 1930.

Yamin, Antun. *Lubnan fi al-Harb: Aw, Dhikrat al-Hawadith wa-l-Mazalim fi Lubnan fi al-Harb al-'Umumiyya, 1914–1918* [Lebanon during the war: Memory of the events and injustices in Lebanon during the World War]. 2 vols. Beirut: al-Matba'a al-Adabiyya, 1919.

Yıldırım, Onur. "Bread and Empire: The Working of Grain Provisioning in Istanbul during the Eighteenth Century." In *Nourrir les cités de Méditerranée, antiquité–temps modern* [Feeding the cities of the Mediterranean, antiquity–modern times], edited by Brigitte Marine and Catherine Virlvouvet, 37–42. Paris: Maisonneuve a. Larose, 2002

Zachs, Fruma. *The Making of a Syrian Identity: Intellectuals and Merchants in Nineteenth-Century Beirut*. Boston: Brill, 2005.

———. "Transformations of a Memory of Tyranny in Syria: From Jamal Pasha to 'Id al-Shuhada', 1914–2000." *Middle Eastern Studies* 48, no. 1 (2012): 73–88.

Ziadeh, Nicola. "A First-Person Account of the First World War in Greater Syria." In *The First World War as Remembered in the Countries of the Eastern Mediterranean*, edited by Olaf Farschid, Manfred Knopp, and Steven Dähne, 265–278. Würzburg, Germany: Ergon, 2016.

Ziser, Eyal. *Lebanon: The Challenge of Independence*. London: I. B. Tauris, 2000.

Zurbrigg, Sheila. "Hunger and Epidemic Malaria in Punjab, 1868–1940." *Economic and Political Weekly* 27 (1992): 2–26.

Zürcher, Erik. *Arming the State: Military Conscription in the Middle East and Central Asia, 1775–1925*. London: I. B. Tauris, 1999.

———. "Between Death and Desertion: The Experience of the Ottoman Soldier in World War I." *Turcica* 28 (1996): 235–258.

———. "The Ottoman Conscription System, 1844–1914." *International Review of Social History* 43 (1998): 437–449.

INDEX

Page numbers in italics refer to figures and maps.

Aaronsohn, Aaron, 271n6
Aashqut, 112
Abdul Hamid II, 271n131
'Abeih, 147, 150, 304n120
Acre, *xvi*, 40, 124
Adana, *xvi*, 69, 125, 193, 214
Adham Bey, 89
Administrative Council (AC): creation of, 38, 40, 42, 269n91; level of food distribution by, 116; power issues facing, 44–45, 138, 270n114; reliance on religious networks, 116; and Salim 'Ali Salam, 188; sectarian composition of, 38, 122; sidelining of, 111, 121–122, 124, 131, 254; significance of, 45–46; suspected of colluding with Britain and France, 121
African famines, 143
agricultural industry/production: changes to, prewar, 30, 32, 33; decline in cultivated area for, 69–70, 72, 105, 106, 276n130, 277n131; employing men for, as part of ARC relief efforts, 223; failure to address decline in, 24–25; Jamal Pasha's demands on, 103–104; lack of incentive to increase, 105; laws mandating, 102, 105–106, 283nn124–128; limited, 3; maritime blockade and, 60; by Maronite community, church regulation of, 118; meeting addressing, 98–99; men conscripted from areas of, 68; prioritizing, 106; reform of, call for, 99; wages in, and purchasing power, 73–74
Aintoura, 197
Ajay, Nicholas, 121
Akın, Yiğit, 277n141
Akkar, 112
Aleppo: and administrative divisions of the Ottoman Levant, *xvi*; ban on grain exports from, 82; blame cast on, for the famine, 243; cholera in, 157, 158, 292n89; deaths from disease in, 158; decline in cultivated area, 69; disease in, 146; grain shipments from, 64, 79, 80, 99; having good connections to, benefit of, 190; and the locust plague, 271n7; men conscripted from, 68; price increases in, 100; and railways, *xvi*, 32, 34, 64; surplus of grain in, 62, 83; syndicate-run provisioning in, 100–101
Alexandria, 134, 267n51, 288n104, 295n15
'Aley, 32, *39*, 122, 125, *152*, 189, 190, 209

Allenby, Edmund, 127, 128, 235, 237, 286n74
American Committee for Armenian and Syrian Relief (ACASR), 205, 225
American Mission Press (AMP), 204, 207, 212–213, 217, 218, 219–221, 250
American Red Cross (ARC), Beirut chapter/committee: bound by norms and practices of the ICRC, 208; chapter establishment, 300n8; estimation of deaths from famine, 244; executive committee composition, 204, 217; focusing relief efforts on Mount Lebanon, 222–225; funding of, 204–205; legitimacy and, 18; local relief efforts of, 206, 210–213, 301n45; medical relief campaign for the military, 206–209; ordered to suspend relief work, 98, 216–217; postwar relief efforts of, 250–251; and prohibition of their relief efforts, 216–217; sanitation efforts partially funded by, 167, 184, 211; and support from US headquarters, 204, 205; on women left as heads of households, 74
American-Syrian Chamber of Commerce, 267n61
American Tobacco Company, 219
American University of Beirut (AUB), 22, 172, 264n94. *See also* Syrian Protestant College
Anatolia, 98, 121, 146, 205, 216, 265n4
Anfeh, *152*, 197
Annales school, 272n22
Antelias, 141, 142, *152*
Antonius, George, 255, 261n11
'Aqil, Khalil, 121
Arab, Emile, 242, 306n21
Arab Girl's Awakening Society (Jam'iyyat Yaqzat al-Fatat al-'Arabiyya), 193, 251
Arabian Peninsula: maritime blockade affecting, 59; Ottoman military battles in, 104, 236, 260n9; reign over, 6
Arabic diaspora press, 4, 19, 97, 135, 264n96, 284n34, 288n109, 288n111
Arabists, 44, 96, 188, 190, 280n51
Arab nationalism, 6, 92, 187, 255, 308n80
Arab reformers, public execution of, 6, 190, 253, 255. *See also* martyrdom

Arab Revolt, 9, 236, 256
al-Ardati, Najib, 148
archival records, issues involving, 18–21, 110, 273n57, 288n109
Argentina, 128, 135, 264n96, 288n111
'Arida, Nasib, 5
Armenian Relief Committee, 205, 300n15
Armenians: convent of, on the committee formed to provide food, 284n25; genocide perpetrated against, 8, 69, 146, 205, 232, 243, 252, 260n8; and the severing of kinship bonds, 246; volunteer unit mostly comprised of, 127
arrests. *See* imprisonment/arrests
Asfar family, 75
Ashqut, *39*, 112
Ashrafieh, 183
al-Asir, Hasan Bey, 157
Audoin-Rouzeau, Stephane, 260n8
Australia, 59, 235
Austria, 27, 30, 155, 229
Austria-Hungary, 2, 58. *See also* Central Powers
'Awdah, Nahla, 179
Ayyub, Shukri, 237
'Aziz Bey, 90
'Azmi Bey: appointment of, 90, 96; charitable societies approved by, criteria for, 175; and control over food provisioning, 95–96, 98–99, 100–101, 107, 185, 217, 230; and extension of state power, 174; failed efforts of, 101, 250; infrastructure improvements of, 167–169; Ottoman Imperial Bank, 130; prohibition of all foreign relief efforts ordered by, 216, 221; and public health efforts, 141, 149; and relationships with prominent families, 184, 185, 190; suspicions held by, 90, 125, 191, 216, 219, 220; women's charitable relief work supported by, 173, 191, 193–194, 198, 299n100

Baabda, *39*, 150, *152*, 237, 290n33
Baalbek, 125
bacteria/microbes, 142, 146, 147. *See also* disease
Bahjat Bey, 99, 291n49

INDEX 329

bakeries and shops, 79, 82, 83, 94, 95, 99, 278n2
Bakhus, Naʿum, 121
Balfour Declaration, 10, 256
Balkan Wars, 29, 56, 63, 66, 70, 147, 166, 169, 266n18
Balta Liman Convention, 28
Barton, James, 233
Bashir II, 27, 37
Bashir III, 268n74
Batrun, *39*, 109, 110, 121, *152*
Bayhum, ʿAdila, 193, 195, 251
Bayhum, Ahmad Mukhtar, 80, 81, 91, 92, 93, 98, 173, 187, 193, 236–237, 252–253, 278n7
Bayhum, Amina, 251
Bayhum, Hasan, 91, 280n61
Bayhum, Ihsan, 251–252
Bayhum, Najila, 193
Bayhum, ʿUmar, 184
Bayhum family, 75, 91, 95, 240
al-Baylani, ʿAli Riza, 120
Becker, Annette, 260n8
Beersheeba, 208, 209
Beirut: access routes to, 24, 32–34; and administrative divisions of the Ottoman Levant, *xvi*, 40; American products marketed in, 33, 267n61; Arabic press archives in, 264n96; and archival records, 18, 19; aspirations for independence in, 252; banning interior shipments of food to, 56, 64–65; charitable giving in, changes to, 47–49, 174–175, 176–177; cholera in, 158; civilian casualties of war, 2; and climate, 53; close connection between Mount Lebanon and, 24, 29; commission expanding Jamal Pasha's control into, 149; competition for political power and status in, 16; and conscription, 66–67, 150–151; cooperation between Mount Lebanon and, difficulty of, 118–119; cultivated area of, decline, 69; deaths from disease in, 2, 158; deaths from famine in, 2; demolitions in, 142, *168*, 169; disease in, 3, 141–142, 143, 148–149, 289n2, 290n44; disinfection stations in, *152*; dismissal of relief efforts in, taking issue with, 8–9; division of, into relief districts, 210; doctor shortage in, remedies for, 151, 291n59; earthquake in, 235, 305n2; economic changes in, during the nineteenth century, 28–30, 31, 32, 49; under Egyptian rule, 27, 266n23; famine in, 3, 4, 54, 147; and fears of foreign coastal invasion, 55; female volunteerism in, 191, 193–195, 196; and food supply lines, 62; French military occupation of, 237–238, 239; German relief work in, 202–203, 203; growth and modernism of, period of, 28–29; hospitals in, 151, 162–163, 214; immediate aftermath of the war in, 238, 306n9; important political actors in, 46; income/wages in, 72, 73–74, 86; independence of, 237; infrastructure improvements in, 167–169; international relief work in, 203, 204–205, 206, 210–213, 217–222, 226–227, 231–232, 250, 300n8; key exports from, 30; land sales in, involving the Maronite Church, 132; lice in, prevention of, 166; local charitable societies in, 48–49, 173–174, 177–180, 181–182, 182–183, 185–186, 186–187, 191, 193–195, 197, 198–199; locust plague in, 52; malaria in, 166–167; and maritime blockades, 56–57, 59, 60, 61, 218; media in, 43, 79, 80, 82, 83–84, 85, 86–87, 88, 90, 96–97, 120–121, 154, 162, 211, 212, 247, 248; migration from, 55, 68; migration to, 29; military defense of, claims of, 120; military transport of grain to, 101; mobilization of civilian resources in, 11; municipal provisioning efforts in, 79, 81–84, 85–87, 92, 93–95, 106–107, 247, 248–249; museum in, statue on display at, 257; and the *mutasarrifiyya* of Mount Lebanon, *39*; physical landscape of, descriptions of, 26; political changes in, 35, 40–42, 49; population figures, 29, 261n12, 266n31; population growth, 29, 41; and positioning of Ottoman troops in Mount Lebanon, 120; postwar relief efforts by France in, 238, 239–240; primary admissions

to hospitals in, 151; prioritizing the military in, 63; profiteering in, 74–76; prohibition of American relief efforts in, 98, 194, 216–217; as a provincial capital, 2, 42, 175, 236; and provincial politics, 44–45, 270n114; public hanging of Arab reformers in, 6, 190, 253, 255; public health administration in, 143, 147–148, 149, 150, 151; racetrack in, 184, *185*; rationing in, 96–98; region responsible for feeding, under Jamal Pasha's plan, 104; reliance on trade in, 57–58; religious composition of, 29, 269n93; remittances processed through, 32, 217–222, 267n56; requisitioning of supplies for the military in, 71; resisting Ottoman rule in, 6; response to health interventions in, 170; retreat of Ottoman officials from, 236, 237; rise of opposition in, 43; sanitation improvements in, 167; sidelining of the municipal council in, 95–96; silk industry and, 30, 60; smallpox in, 159, 160; soup kitchens in, 101, *152*, 228–229, 240, 247, 250; state failure to alleviate the situation in, 105; and state power, 13, 14; suspension of foreign relief work in, 98; syndicate-run provisioning in, 99–101; and tourism, 32; trade growth in, 29–30, 31, 266n37; transportation services in, lack of, 66; typhus in, 156–157; vaccination in, 159, 161; *vali* (governor-general) of, 40–41; vegetable marketplace, *78*, 80; view looking out toward Mount Sannine from, *22*, 23–24; vulnerability of, to famine, 10, 26, 34, 266n28; war taxes in, 70, 71; waste management in, 165; and water contamination, 163–164.

Beirut-Aleppo joint-stock company, 100–101

Beirut Chamber of Commerce, 82, 84, 91, 188

Beirut-Damascus railroad, 24, 32, 34, *39*, 64, 80, *152*, 268n65

Beirut-Damascus road, 235, *236*, 268n64, 280n61, 304n120

Beirut Industry Shelter, 251

Beirut Reform Society (Jam'iyyat Bayrut al-Islahiyya), 43, 89, 91, 92, 184, 187, 188, 190

Beirut Water Company, 294n123

Beit ad-Din, *39*, 44, 285n36, 290n33

Beit Marie, 32, *39*

Bekaa, 112, 193

benevolence, 14. *See also* charitable giving; humanitarian aid/war relief

Bengal, 25, 54, 55, 76

Berlin, 34, 63

Berlin-Baghdad Railway, 34

Bernstoff, Johann Heinrich von, 227

Bhamdun, 32, *39*, 287n82

biopolitical state, 14–15

births, 149, 150, 292n79

bitter vetch, 94–95, 281n74

Bkirki, 37, *39*, 112, 118, 131, *152*

black market, 71, 75, 86, 94, 99, 100, 105

Bliss, Frederick, 217

Bliss, Howard, 19, 62, 96, 151, 204, 206, 216, 232, 270–271n130, 300n9

Bliss family, 212

Bohle, Hans, 15, 25, 49

Bourdieu, Pierre, 49

Boyer, Benoît, 161, 163–164, 294n123

Brecht, Berthold, 74–75

Briand, Aristide, 127, 133

bribery, 64, 83, 100, 105

Briggs, Charles, 291n66

Britain: Administrative Council suspected of colluding with, 121; aiding the Arab Revolt, 236; blockade of Germany, 58; and colonialism, 54, 55, 266n28; countering influence of, in Mount Lebanon, 45; drawing a new political map of the Middle East, 238; and Egyptian expansionism, 28; employing famine as weapon of war, 58, 59; and health clinics in Mount Lebanon, 147; influence of, in comparison to Germany, 202; military push toward Beirut by, 235; missionaries from, 48, 217, 270–271n130; occupation of Beirut, 237, 239; Ottoman military campaigns against, 260n9; propaganda against Germany, 287n102; reluctance to intervene in Mount Lebanon, 126; remittances from, processing, 217;

retention of medical faculty from, 206, 209, 301n41; review of wartime naval policy, 58; and the Sykes-Picot negotiations, 10, 237; trade with Beirut, 29; and travel through Beirut, 32; and the Treaty of Balta Liman, 28. *See also* Entente Powers

brothels. *See* prostitutes/brothels

Brumana, 32, *39*, *152*, 201, 224, 225, 228

buildings, demolition of, 142, *168*, 169

bureaucratization, 144, 202

al-Bustani, Butrus, 270n128

Cahen, George, 145

Cairo, 119–120, 122, 123, 132, 133–134, 135, 137, 190, 267n51, 288nn104–105

Caix, Robert de, 242

cannibalism, 4–5, 113, 226, 261n23

capitalism, 27

carriage roads, 24, 275n103

Catholics: appeal to, in France, for donations to relief efforts, 243; committee of, made up of various convents, formation of, 116–117, 284n25; confiscated institutions of, 213; mandating, to serve in government post, 38; missionary work of, 48, 202, 213, 214, 271n130. *See also specific Catholic institutions/organizations/groups*

Caucasus Campaign, 260n9

censorship, 12, 88–90, 176, 218, 280n46

Central Commission for Provisioning, 103, 282n112, 282n113

centralization, 27, 34–35, 49, 82, 263n68

Central Powers, 2, 11, 209, 213. *See also* Austria-Hungary; Germany

charitable giving: changes in, 47; as an integral part of religious piety, 176; motivation for, most often, 186; political character of, 17–18; power of, 17; primary sources of, 47; traditional forms and institutions of, challenges to, 212; undermining of, 175

charitable societies/associations (*jamʿiyya khayriyya*): and competition from foreign philanthropists, 212; constriction of aid provided by, 181–182; financing of, 47, 48, 177–179, 179–180; fund-raising efforts, 47, 179; governing bodies of, 48, 295n13; hospitals associated with, 178, 296nn21–22; as political gathering centers, 45; power politics and social demographics involving, 182–191, 253; property confiscations, 132, 181; rise of, 45, 47–49, 174–175, 176–177, 270n126; schools associated with, 178, 296n26; secularism of, 45, 295n13; sidelining of male-dominated, 175, 186, 187, 191, 198; systemic studies of, lack of, 270n129. *See also specific groups/organizations*

Cheiko, Louis, 143, 155, 289n9, 292n89

Chickering, Roger, 18, 264n93, 299n117

childhood vaccination, 159, 160, 293n102

children: education of, 48–49, 177, 195, 196, 295n11; employment of, 222; healthy, decline of, 149; and the horrors of famine, 3–4, 5, 113, *245*, *246*; mobilization of, for war effort 106; organizing government-supported relief work for, 173; and rationing, 96, 97, 98; selling, 135; shelters and care for, 194, 195, 196, 201; soup kitchens and, 200, 201, 229; in the vegetable markets, *78*, 80; vocational training for, 224–225. *See also* orphans/orphanages; schools

cholera, 142, 143, 145, 147, 150, 151, 153, 154, 156, 157–158, 160, 163, 292n83, 292n89

Christian nationalism, 188, 244

Christians: Beirut district/neighborhoods mainly comprised of, 183, 195; conscription, 68; French meddling on behalf of, 56; genocide perpetrated against, 12, 113, 137, 205, 242, 243; charitable giving 47, 176; and the locust plague, 51; migration 55, 29; as most affected by famine, 253; organization bringing together Muslims and, 43; Ottoman suspicions of, 56; population in Mount Lebanon, 268n75; protection of, promises for, 36; publication of, 248; reaction of, to the arrival of French troops into Beirut, 237; relationship of the CUP to wealthy families of, 184; sculpture of female mourners representing both Muslims and, *xviii*, 1; secret French provisioning scheme designed to

influence, 127; soup kitchens and, 229; tensions between Muslims and, 56, 254; women-run charitable relief work, 194. *See also specific Christian denominations/organizations/groups*
Çiçek, Talha, 14, 44, 263n68, 277n132
civil wars, 18, 20, 38, 56, 147, 257
claim fraud, avoiding, 210, 211
cleaning battalions, 149, 167, 169, 184
climate, 53, 60, 272n16
coal industry, 29–30
coal supply, 64
Cochrane, Yvonne Sursock, 297n64
colonialism, 1, 10, 26, 54, 55, 213, 238, 239, 244, 245, 266n28
Committee of Union and Progress (CUP): blamed for the Sarikamish defeat, 263n61; charitable societies approved by, criteria for, 175; coup staged by, 43–44, 89, 188; editorial critiques of, 89, 280n51; European paternalism and view of, 203; France's attempts to undermine, through provisioning efforts, 127; intentions of, toward Christians, common view of, 113; issues with the municipal councils, 82; narratives using the famine to highlight the tyranny of, 242–244; and newly elected members of the Administrative Council, 122; perceptions of Syro-Lebanese diaspora, 119–120; position on Arabists, 188–189; and relationships with prominent families, 183–184, 187, 189, 253; as the ruling party, representative of, 6; seeing war as opportunity, 55; strategies used by, justified by war, 55, 57; and suspicions of missionary schools, 214, 215
compliance, 15, 17, 18, 57, 67, 94, 103, 118, 145, 160, 170
Compulsory Cultivation Law, 105–106, 283nn124–128
confiscation: of animals, 65; of food, 65, 70, 71, 102, 129, 137; of money, 150, 216, 237; of properties, 132–133, 144–145, 150, 151, 169, 175, 180–181, 206, 241, 293n116
conscription: employment of women resulting from, 192; exemption from, 38, 56, 65, 67, 68–69, 106, 123, 148, 151, 209, 276nn124–125; of farmers, agricultural production and, 69; hiding from, 65, 67–68, 119, 125–126, 151; of medical professionals, 148, 149, 150, 290n39; of pack animals, 65–66, 68; process of, for men, 11, 66–69, 276n109; reckless, 69; result of, for average families, 74; of students in medical school, 150, 291n55; suffering caused by, blame for, 256; universal, 66, 275n108
Corm, Charles, 240, 242, 243, 244, 247, 248, 306n21
councils. *See* Administrative Council (AC); municipal council; provincial council
coup, 43–44, 89, 188
court-martials, 90, 121
Coury, Alfred, 242, 244
Crawford, James Steward, 217
crime, 4, 76, 263n58
Crimean War, 266n18
croup, 156
currency exchange rate, 60, 61, 72, 218, 219, 227, 228
currency value, 25, 100, 104, 110, 115, 218, 219, 265n8, 283n120, 299n100
Cyprus, *xvi*, 126, 127–128, 286n75

Damascus: access to Beirut from, 24; and administrative divisions of the Ottoman Levant, *xvi*, 40; banning food exports from the interior, 64–65, 82; bishop of, exile of, 125; blame cast on, for the famine, 243; charitable society extending help into, 295n15; cholera in, 157, 158; deaths from disease in, 158; decline in cultivated area, 69; independence of, 236, 237; Lebanese government officials called to, 121; marking the Ottoman retreat, 236; men conscripted from, 68; migration of Muslims to, 55; and mobilization of troops, 67; Ottoman troops moved from, 120; public hangings in, of Arab reformers, 6, 190, 253; and railways, *xvi*, 24, 32, 34, *39*, 64, 80, 268n65; requisition orders transmitted to, 70; resisting Ottoman rule in, 6; smallpox in, 159

INDEX   333

Damur, 5, *152*
Dana, Charles A., 204, 212, 217–218, 219–220, 221–222, 304n117
Darian, Yusuf, 133, 137, 288n117
Da'uq, 'Umar, 98, 173, 195, 236, 251
Dayr al-Qamar, *39*, 121, *152*
deaths: from disease, 2, 76, 90, 136, 142, 143, 145, 147, 155, 160, 209; potential, from toxic food additives, 94, 135; recording, 150, 292n79; from famine, 2, 4, 21, 54, 76, 111, 112, 113, 120, 136, 142, 143, 209, 244, 261n11; from warfare, 2, 235, *236*, 260n8. *See also* executions; genocide
death sentences, 134, 151
debt/borrowing, 55, 115, 131, 132, 133, 272n28
Decentralization Party (Hizb al-Lamarkaziyya), 43, 89, 90, 119–120, 188, 190, 280n55, 285n54
decentralization 27, 43, 81
Deir Zor, 146
demolitions, 142, *168*, 169
demonstrations, 55, 97, 193
Deringil, Selim, 27
deserters, 67, 130, 146, 150, 151, 289n24
diaspora communities. *See* Syro-Lebanese diaspora
digestive disease, 147, 290n31
Diman, *39*, *108*, 109, *152*
disease: absence of, defining health as, 151; connection between famine, war, and, 142–143, 145–147, 153; deaths from, 2, 76, 90, 136, 142, 143, 145, 147, 155, 160, 209; distinguishing between types of, issue of, 156–157, 292n83, 292n87; migration and, 146; prevention of, 145, 151; recording, system of, 292n79; regulation of, 147–148, 151, 153, 160, 290n35; reliable statistics for, as an issue, 143; reporting, responsibility for, 147, 153, 160; struggle against, as a contested domain, 9; susceptibility to, 3, 143, 145, 290n29, 290n31; treatment of, 141, 149, 153; upsurge in, 144; war against, goal of, 145. *See also specific type of disease, contributing/causal factors, and prevention efforts*
disinfection, 151, 163
disinfection stations, *140*, 142, *152*, 153, 165–166

distributive charity, 47, 175, 177, 196, 295n11
Djelal Bey, Mehmet, 64
Dodge, Bayard, 8–9, 12, 52, 65–66, 69, 75, 150, 158, 194, 195, 202, 204, 205, 210, 211, 212, 222–223, 250–251
Dodge, Cleveland, 205, 206, 212
Dodge, Mary Bliss, 250
Doizelet, 240
Doolittle, George C., 207
Dorman, Mary Dale, 204, 216–217, 300n9
Dray, Arthur, 224, 228
Druze: under decentralization, 27; and famine, 112; and Maronite tensions, 35–36, 38, 268n74; outside government control, 104; population in Beirut, 29; postwar criticism of the Maronite patriarch, 254; representation of, on the Administrative Council, 269n91
dysentery, 156, 163

Eastern Catholic Syriac Church, 29
Eddé, Carla, 247, 248
Edip, Halide, 3, 174, 299n108
Edkins, Jenny, 74
education: of poor children, 177, 195, 196, 295n11; primary language in, issue of, 44; reform of, call for, 99; of women, 48–49, 187, 249, 251, 270–271n130, 271n133. *See also* public health education; schools
Education Society (Jam'iyyat al-Tahdhib), 270n128
educators, 10, 51, 54, 203, 204, 209, 250
Egypt: and administrative divisions of the Ottoman Levant, *xvi*; aspirations for independence in, 252; diaspora community in, 19, 127, 133–134, 137, 221, 284n34; disease in, 157; and divine punishment in sacred texts, 271n11; expansion into Greater Syria and occupation, 27, 28, 266n18, 269n100; famine in, 265n8; French officials in, assistance from, 240; independence movement in, 188; maritime blockade impacting trade with, 59; media in, 19, 134, 135, 221, 264n96, 284n34, 287n102, 288n111; and Ottoman tensions, 27, 28, 34; religious leaders in, involved in Syrian relief

committee, 134, 136–137, 287n104; rule of, oppressive and exploitative, 27, 266n23; tourists from, 32
Egyptian Expeditionary Force, 286n74
elections, 38, 269n91
Eley, Geoff, 16, 176
elites, 13, 21, 40, 42, 45, 47, 48, 49, 85, 87, 138, 174–175, 175, 176, 177, 182, 191, 196, 232, 249, 252, 266n22, 267n51, 291n49. *See also* notables
emigration, 31, 68, 198, 221, 256, 267nn51–53. *See also* migration; Syro-Lebanese diaspora
employment department, creation of, 210, 301n46
employment efforts: for children, 222; for men, 167, 184–185, 211–212, 222–223, 223–224, 301n46; for women, 174, 193, 194, 195, 196, 201, 210, 222, 224, 301n46
Entente Powers: closure of banks/postal services associated with, 218; diaspora communities wanting to join forces with, 119–120, 122–123, 127–128, 135, 285nn52–54; and inhabitants of Mount Lebanon willing to help, 125, 126, 254; maritime blockade by, 3, 58–59, 68, 84; warships of, presence of, 56, 58. *See also* Britain; France; Russia
entitlement, 16, 25, 49, 63, 71, 177, 239, 265n8
Enver Pasha, 57, 65, 66, 192
Europe: ARC in, 205; codification of war crimes, 263n58; employment of women in, 196; hospitals in, primary admissions in, 151; influence of, maintaining, desire for, 213; investors/investment from, 27, 33–34; markets in, 29, 30, 31; meddling in Mount Lebanon, 36, 56; media report on refugees, 68; new political map drawn based on interests of, 238; paternalism of, CUP's view of, 203. *See also specific European countries*
excommunication, 40, 45, 118
executions, 6, 14, 90, 124, 125, 138, 189, 190, 193, 194, 253, 255, 308n80, 308n82
exemption taxes, 67, 68–69, 276n125
exile, 6, 14, 28, 90, 98, 121, 125, 131, 138, 165, 189, 206, 213, 216, 251
expansionism, 27, 28, 232, 245

exports/imports. *See* trade
expropriation. *See* confiscation

Faisal, 236, 237, 251
Faisal-Clemenceau accords, 253, 308n70
family bond, break in. *See* kinship bonds, severing of
famine: in Africa, 143; in Bengal, 25, 54, 76; connection between disease, war, and, 142–143, 145–147, 153; deaths from, 2, 4, 21, 54, 76, 111, 112, 113, 120, 136, 142, 143, 209, 244, 261n11; disputing the inevitability of, 62–63; horrors of, 3–5, 113, 226, 238, 244, 245–247, 261n23; largely futile responses to, reasons for studying and writing about, 21; in Lebanese memory and history, 6–7, 241–257, 308n80, 308n82; man-made, 2, 5, 24–25, 103, 265n4, 265n8; micro-study of, focus in, 8–9; mourning the victims of, monument symbolizing, xviii, 1, 5, 256; paradox of, 8; recalling the, as politically problematic, 252–255; significance of, 5–6, 76–77; social capital possessed by victims of, 17; as a strategy of warfare, 54–63, 76; as a term, searching archival records and issues with, 19; theories of, shift in, 24–25, 74, 265n4; and vulnerability, 10, 25–26, 26–32, 34, 49, 54, 143, 147, 266n28, 290n29. *See also specific contributing/causal factors and responses to famine*
farmers/farming. *See* agricultural industry/ production
Faroqhi, Suraiya, 84
Fawaz, Leila, 29, 31
feminism, 191–192
fines, 89, 93, 95, 106, 159, 160, 164, 165
flies, 156, 163
food: additives to, 94–95, 135; and digestive disease, 147, 290n31; confiscations of, 65, 70, 71, 102, 129, 137; and fraud, 94–95, 115; history of, literature on, and change in how eating is framed, 272n22; importance of, 53; poisoning from, 113, 135; surplus of, 62, 70, 80, 83, 103, 274n74. *See also* famine, provisioning
foreign debt, 55, 272n28

foreigners: in Beirut, 29, 32; exit tax on, 71; expulsion of, 90, 98, 131, 206, 213; as important agents of provisioning, 46. *See also specific people and countries*
foreign exchange rates. *See* currency exchange rate
foreign institutions, seizure of, 132, 144–145, 206, 293n116
foreign medical experts, 154–155
foreign missionaries, 48, 132, 175, 270–271n130. *See also specific missionary groups*
foreign relief work: new social reality forged by, 212; ordered suspension of, 98, 216–217; potential benefit to nations engaged in, 202. *See also specific international organizations/groups*
Foucauldian *dispositif*, 87, 280n42
France: Administrative Council suspected of colluding with, 121; as an ally to the church, 45, 254; American relief work in, German support for, 231; appeal to Catholics in, for donations to relief efforts, 243; archival records in, 18; and aspirations for independence in Mount Lebanon, 188; and Catholic missionaries, 48, 213, 214; and colonialism, 1, 244, 245; confiscation of German property, 241; conspiring with, consequences for, 90, 189; countering influence of, in Mount Lebanon, 45; diaspora communities wanting to join forces with, 122–123, 127–128, 285nn53–54; drawing a new political map of the Middle East, 238; embassy in the United States, 122; employing famine as weapon of war, 59; expulsion of colleges/professors from, 206; and the Faisal-Clemenceau accords, 253, 308n70; influence of, in comparison to Germany, 202; intervention in Mount Lebanon's civil war, 38, 56; Lebanon's independence from, 260n1 (Intro.); limited help from, 128, 251; Maronite Church's connection with, Ottoman concern over, 119, 125, 126, 127; merchants of, 270n114; mobilization for war in, 67; on the moral obligation of communal sacrifice, 279n38;

occupation of Beirut, 237–238, 239, 247–248, 252; Ottoman military campaigns against, 260n9; postwar relief efforts by, 238, 239–240, 244, 246, 247, 248; promoting their position of a postwar Greater Syria, 137; provisioning scheme of, using neutrality of the United States, 127, 137; railway building by, 34, 268n65; reluctance of, to intervene in Mount Lebanon, 122, 123, 125–128, 137–138; road building by, 33, 268n64; seeking money from, for the Maronite community, 133; sidelining, Germany's efforts at, 213–215; silk industry and, 60; and the Sykes-Picot negotiations, 10, 237; trade with Beirut, 30; urban improvement proposed by hygienists from, 167. *See also* Entente Powers
francophilism, 131, 240, 242
fraud, 85, 94–95, 115, 210
free market, 85, 101–102, 282n103
French Asia, Committee of, 245
French Mandate, 181, 239, 244, 249, 252, 254, 256
French Medical Faculty, 148, 161, 162, 206, 293n116
French Red Cross, 126
fumigation, 165, 166, 294n136

Gallipoli Campaign, 12, 67, 260n9, 263n61
gender roles, normative, break in, 246
General Assembly (GA) meetings, 98–99, 149, 158, 159, 160–161, 291n49
General Directorate of Provisioning, 282n104, 282n112
genocide, 8, 12, 69, 113, 137, 146, 205, 232, 242, 243, 252, 260n8
Georges-Picot, François, 10, 55, 66–67, 90, 119, 122, 125, 126–127, 237, 286n69
Germany: agent of, 62, 274n75; archival records in, 18; and the ARC medical relief campaign, 209; blame cast on, for the famine, 243; Catholic, 202, 213–215; citizens of, in Beirut, funding from, 229; and colonialism, 203; debt payments to, 272n28; development of provisioning in, 283n129; dissemination of medical and health information

from, 155; hospitals of, 145, 209, 228, 229; involvement of, in relief efforts, factors in, 202, 231, 232; last-minute relief efforts by, 226–231; local relief efforts in, study of, 299n117; maritime blockade of, 58; medical supplies provided by, 166; missionaries from, 202, 209, 214, 215–216, 226, 228–229, 241, 271n130; Ottoman reliance on trade with, 58; prioritizing the military in, 63, 65, 229; propaganda against, 287n102; propaganda for, 228, 229, 231, 232; and property confiscation by the French in Beirut, 241; Protestant, 202, 214; reported food and grain supply to, 62, 274n74; retreat of, from Beirut, 240–241; role of, in the Ottoman Empire, debate over, 202–203; and persecution of religious leaders and outspoken clerics, 286n63; trade with Beirut, 30; undermining, attempts at, 230; vaccination in, and the military, 160; view of American relief efforts, 225, 227, 231. *See also* Central Powers
Ghandur, 'Abdl Hamid, 193
Ghanim, Shukri, 122–123
Ghosta, 117
Gibran, Khalil, 243
Gill, Rebecca, 9
globalization, 27, 28, 29, 30, 34
Grand Serail, 237
Greater Lebanon, 244, 248
Greater Syria: advertising by Americans in, 267n61; altered living conditions in, due to WWI, effect of, 145; civilian casualties of war, 2; commission tasked with surveying, on postwar political desires, 244; cultivated area of, 69; devastating famine in, increased state nervousness arising from, 90; and Egyptian occupation, 27, 28, 269n100; famine in, 2, 53, 261n11, 272n16; food additive grown in, 94; geographic area of, 260n10; grain production in, 61–62; impending anti-Ottoman rebellion in, fear of, 90; infrastructure improvements for, 169, 184; movement of troops over entire span of, effect of, in terms of disease, 146; postwar, France promoting their position in, 137; provincial borders of, reconfiguration of, 40; as a provisioning zone, 103, 283n115; reign over, 6; replacement of most governors in, 96; reported surplus in, 62, 80, 104, 274n74; rise of opposition in, 44; transformation of women's charities in, 196; transportation of food in, 3. *See also* Beirut; Levant; Mount Lebanon; Palestine; Syria
Great Powers, 36, 203
Great War. *See* World War I
Greece, willingness to supply weapons to Mount Lebanon, 126, 286n69
Greek Catholic Charity Association (Jam'iyyat al-Khayriyya lil-ta'ifa al-Rum al-Kathulik), 48, 175, 177, 178–179, 180, 181, 182, 295n15, 296n27, 296n32, 297n39
Greek Catholic Church: leaders and outspoken clerics of, persecution of, 124–125; missionary order in Mount Lebanon, 112; properties of, 180, 296n38; and support for Syrian relief committee in Egypt, 136–137, 287n104
Greek Catholics: migration of, 112; population in Beirut, 29; representation of, on the Administrative Council, 269n91
Greek Orthodox: population in Beirut, 29; prominent families, 178, 296n20; representation of, on the Administrative Council, 269n91; schools for girls, 49, 271n133; and support for Syrian relief committee in Egypt, 287n104
Greek Orthodox Benevolent Society (Jam'iyyat al-Khayriyya al-Urthuduxiyya), 48, 175, 177, 178, 179, 180, 182, 186, 295n11, 295n17, 296nn25–26, 296n37, 297n55
Greek Orthodox Society for Aiding the Sick of the Hospital St. George (al-Jam'iyyat musa'da al-Marda fi Mustashfa al-Qadis Jirjis). *See* Society of St. George
Grobba, Fritz, 62, 63–64, 68, 69–70, 98, 104, 130, 274n75, 276n130, 277n131

Haifa, 34, 62, 214
al-Hakim, Yusuf, 75, 125, 196–197

INDEX

Halim Bey, 123
Hama, *xvi*, 32, 34, 68, 83, 104, 283n118
Hamdi, Fuad, 150, 151, 157, 160, 163
Hanike, Luise, 209
Hanssen, Jens, 291n49
Haqqi Bey, Isma'il, 143, 236–237, 289n10
Harissa, *39*, 112, 116, 117, 130, 138, *152*
al-Hashimi, Husayn Ibn 'Ali, 9, 236
Haskell, Mary, 243
Hauran, *xvi*, 68, 69–70, 91, 104, 112, 146
Hazim, Abu Bakr, 89, 188
health, defined, 151. *See also* disease; provisioning
health commission, 147, 149, 154, 158–159, 161, 164, 165, 167, 169, 170
health inspections, 145, 149, 158, 160, 161, 163, 169, 170, 290n45
Hejaz railroad, *xvi*, 34
Hejaz region, Ottoman military battles in, 104–105, 260n9
Hertling, Georg von, 227
hierarchical order, 186
Hitti, Philip, 256
hoarding, 72, 75, 76, 82, 86, 93, 102, 129
Hoffmann, Hermann, 226–227
Hollis, Stanley, 59, 60, 71, 204, 217, 220, 225, 273n57
home front, meaning of, 3
Homs, *xvi*, 32, 34, 68, 83
hospices. *See* shelters/hospices
hospitals: attached to mosques, 47; charitable, 178, 296nn21–22; contraction of services provided by, 162, 294n119; in Europe, primary admissions in, 151; foreign, seizure of, 144–145, 206, 293n116; French aid for, 240; German, 145, 209, 228, 229; military, 147, 150, 209, 214, 290n33, 290n38; Ottoman, 162, 215, 293n116; overcrowding in, 162; primary admissions to, 151; records from, 143, 155; shortage of, 162; size/capacity of, 162–163, 294n120; SPC associated, 143, 151, 162, 206, 292n72, 294n119; undermining of, 162
Hourani, Albert, 35, 46
Hub, 109, 114, 115
humanitarian aid/war relief: as an act of protection, 14; goal of private and public mobilization for, 15–16; legitimacy and, 18; limited historical attention to, 8–9; as need-based, 177; reasons for studying and writing about, 21. *See also specific state, local, and international actors involved in providing aid/relief*
humanitarianism: of the biopolitical state, 14; modern, birth of, 202
hunger, extreme. *See* famine
Hunt, Nancy Rose, 13, 14
Husni Bey, 143, 149, 150, 156, 157, 158, 161, 164, 165–166, 292n79, 292n83
al-Huwayyik, Ilias Butrus, 45, 109, 110, 113, 114, 115, 118, 125, 128–129, 129–130, 131, 132–133, 135, 138, 242, 253–254, 260n3, 288n109
Huwayyik, Yusuf (priest), 125
Huwayyik, Yusuf (sculptor), *xviii*, 1, 5, 256, 257, 260n3, 261n30
hygiene, 144, 153, 155, 157–158, 161, 166

Ibn Khaldun, 24–25, 265n5, 265n8
Ibn Taghribirdi, 25, 265n8
immigrants, returning, 31, 61. *See also* emigration
imperialism, 27, 29, 203, 204, 231, 232, 239, 247
Imperial Ottoman Office for Provisioning, 102, 282n104
import/exports. *See* trade
imprisonment/arrests, 6, 89, 90, 93, 95, 98, 102, 106, 125, 138, 151, 160, 165, 189, 190, 216, 217, 222
income taxes, 71
income/wages, 54, 72, 73–74, 86
independence movements, 27, 43, 122, 188, 242, 266n18. *See also* Decentralization Party
individual giving/endowments, 47
infant mortality, 149
infectious disease. *See* disease
inflation, 115, 226, 283n120
infrastructure improvements, 33–34, 161, 167–168, 180, 183, 184
inoculations. *See* vaccination
institutionalization, 47
interest rates, 132
International Committee of the Red Cross (ICRC), 208

Islam, leader of, and support for Syrian relief committee, 287n104. *See also* mosques; Muslims

Issawi, Charles, 266n31

Istanbul: first municipality established in, 269n100; grain shipments to, 62; and the locust plague, 271n7; and rail connection, 268n65; as seat of the Ottoman central government, 2; soup kitchens in, 227; vaccination campaign in, 293n102; vaccines prepared in, 160

Italy, 30, 32, 60

'Izzadin, Mustafa, 99, 100–101, 283n118

Izzedine, Muhammed Effendi, 222

Jabal al-Druze, 104

Jackson, Simon, 247

Jalakh, Salim, 151

Jamal Pasha: actions of, as a trigger for local resistance and activism in the diaspora, 288n110; at the American University of Beirut, *172*; and the ARC medical relief campaign, 206–207, 208, 209; ban on interdistrict/interprovincial trade, 56, 65, 101, 255; blame cast on, for the famine, 243, 255, 256; direct provisioning efforts by, 103–104, 105, 111, 283n118; and extension of state power, 174; health commission created by, 149; Huwayyik's access to, 118, 129–130, 131, 254, 286–287n82; and infrastructure improvement, 169, 184; and the Kaiserwerth, 215; legacy of, 8; and the locust plague, 271n6; policies of, framing, 13–14, 263n68; port closure by, 56–57; position on Arabists, 188–189; postwar memoir of, response to accusations in, 243; and price regulation, 101; promising to furnish provisions, 62, 101, 130; provisioning zone assigned to, 103, 283n115; public execution of reformers ordered by, 6, 190, 253, 255; reign and rule of, 6, 96, 189; and relationships with prominent families, 183, 184, 186, 187, 189–191; on requisitioning in *Memories of a Turkish Statesman*, 71; and retention of British medical faculty, 206, 209, 301n41; in society, 15; strengthening Ottoman control over Mount Lebanon, 111, 120–122, 123, 124, 125, 254; and supplying local churches, 116, 117–118; suspicions held by, 90, 123, 125, 189, 191, 194, 285n54; women's charitable relief work supported by, 173, 174, 191, 193, 194, 195, 198, 299n108; and women workers' brigades, 193

Jbeil, *39*, 110, 121, *152*

Jerusalem, *xvi*, 51, 121, 271n5

Jesuit order, 143, 155, 240, 254, 289n9

Jews, 10, 29, 229, 251, 287n104

Jezzin, 36, *39*, 121, *152*

job scarcity, 74

Johanniter hospital, 145, 209, 228, 229

Johnson, Michael, 295n13

Junieh, *39*, 56, 112, 117, 123, *152*, 228

Kaddourah, Ibtihaj, 249, 251

Kaiserwerth Diocese/deaconesses, 207, 209, 215–216, 241, 271n130

Kamil Pasha, 188

Kan'an, Ibrahim Na'um, 4, 97–98, 245, 261n23, 281n90

Kandiyoti, Deniz, 192

Kemal, Mustafa, 12, 263n61

Kemal Bey, 282n104

Khalidi, Rashid, 35

Khan 'Abdl-Salam, 181

Khan al-Babir, 181

Khater, Akram Fouad, 267n52

Khazin family, 37, 266n22

Khuwairi, Butrus, 242

King-Crane Commission, 244, 249, 251

kinship bonds, severing of, 4, 112, 134–135, 245, 246, 307n43

Kisrawan, 4, 37, *39*, 112, 124, *152*, 228, 266n22

Knabenshue, Paul, 137, 288n117

knowledge, history as a hybrid form of, 20

Knüsermann, Lina, 209

Kouyoumdjian Pasha, Ohannes, 65, 118–119, 120, 121, 122, 123, 193, 282n99, 285n36

Kura, *39*, *152*, 196–197

al-Lam, Ra'if Abi, 98

land, seizure of. *See* property confiscation

land sales, 115, 131, 132

Lansing, Robert, 225, 288n117
Larsson, Lewis, 51–52, 271n5
Latakia, *xvi*, 40, 62
Law for Public Education, 271n131
Law of Military Obligation, 66, 70
Law on the Liabilities of Physicians, 148, 290n39
Law on the Method of War Taxes, 70
Lawrence, T. E., 9
League for the Liberation of Lebanon and Syria, 127
League of Nations, Article 22 of, 251
Lebanese Alliance, 119–120
Lebanese Civil War (1975-1990), 18, 20, 257
Lebanese famine, 21
Lebanese Mandate. *See* French Mandate
Lebanese nationalism, 244, 251–252, 255, 308n80
Lebanese Society of Paris (Comite? libanais de Paris), 123, 285n53
Lebanon: archival records in, 18–19, 20–21; aspirations for independence in, 242, 249–250, 251; day for commemoration of WWI in, focus of, 6–7; end of Ottoman rule in, 1; founder of modern, 254; under French colonial rule, 1, 253, 308n70; history textbooks in, 7, 308n82; independence from France, 260n1 (Intro.); media coverage in, 5; modern day, geographic area including, 260n10; monuments depicting the experience of, in WWI, *xviii*, 1, 5, *234*, 256–257; postwar estimate of famine deaths in, 244; press coverage of the famine in, archives of, 19. *See also* Beirut; Greater Syria; Mount Lebanon
Lebanon League of Progress, 122
Legion d'Orient, 127–128, 286n75
legitimacy, 16, 17–18, 46, 80, 81, 87–90, 101, 107, 144, 174, 176, 186, 189–190, 237, 238, 239, 247, 252, 254
Levant: independence movements in, 43; Ottoman, administrative divisions of, *xvi*, 24; and petroleum, 33; reluctance of France to engage the Ottomans in, 126; wartime famine in Bengal and Ottoman, similarities of, 54. *See also* Greater Syria

lice, 142, 146, 154, 156, 158, 165–166, 294n134, 294n136
literary associations, 48, 270n128
livestock, reduction of, 66
locust plague, *50*, 51–53, 62, 256, 271n11, 271nn6–7
Longrigg, Stephen, 256
looting, 71, 79, 146, 277n141, 278n2
Ludendorrff, Erich, 262n53
luxury items, 60, 61, 85, 87, 211, 274n70

Ma'an family, 27
madness of hunger (*delirio de fome*), 135, 288n107
Mahmersh, 109–110
Makdisi, Ussama, 203, 232
malaria, 145, 147, 150, 151, 154, 156, 164, 166–167, 290n41, 292n83
malnutrition, 98, 142, 146, 147, 290n29. *See also* famine
Malthus, Thomas R., 74, 265n4
Mann, Nellie Miller, 23, 26
manufacturing industry, 30, 31
al-Maqasid (Sunni charitable association), 48–49, 175, 177, 186–187, 188, 189, 295n13, 298n73
al-Maqdisi, Jirjis, 242–243
al-Maqrizi, Taqi ad-Din, 25, 265n8
maritime blockades, 3, 56–57, 58–61, 62–63, 64, 84, 112, 137, 166, 218, 256, 273n51
Maronite Church: and the Administrative Council, 40, 269n93; aid/provisioning efforts of, 109–110, 111, 113–116, 117–118, 129, 130–131, 132, 133, 138–139, 287n89; ally to, 45, 254; amount of aid spent by, 114, 115–116; appeasement by, 124, 125, 128, 254; application to protect both property and patriarch of, 132–133; common criticisms of, 113, 114; and connections to France, Ottoman concern over, 119, 125, 126, 127, 138; convents of, on the committee formed to provide food, 284n25; courting the state, reasons for, 128–131, 138; historical autonomy of, 287n96; increasing power of, 36, 37–38, 111, 139; independence of, safeguarding, 40; Jamal Pasha's suspicion of, 125; leaders and outspoken

clerics of, persecution of, 125, 286n63; legitimacy and, 18; opposition to, rise of, 44–45; overlords of, prior to reforms, 37, 268n85; patriarchate of, 37, 112; patriarch position in, emerging power of, and history, 37; prioritizing shipments to, 117–118; quest for money, 115, 131–132; reassertion of, postwar, 253–255; regulation of aid provided by, 114–115; regulation of community food production and sales, 118; seeing famine as opportunity, 129; self-blame of, presentations of, 129; spiritual relief offered by, 112–113, 129; and support for Syrian relief committee in Egypt, 287n104; view on Muslim appointed as *mutasarrif*, 123

Maronites: assessment of, reporting on, 109–110; under decentralization, 27; diaspora community in Egypt, 127; and Druze tensions, 35–36, 38, 268n74; population in Beirut, 29, 269n93; representation of, on the Administrative Council, 269n91; secular, postwar criticism by, of the patriarch, 254; sympathies toward France, 56

Mar Sema'an survey, 112

martial law, 6, 14, 56, 169, 176

martyrdom, 1, 6–7, 99, 253, 255, 257, 308n82

Martyr's Square (Sahat al-Shuhada'): monuments in, *xviii*, 1, 5, *234*, 256–257; name of, 1, 260n2 (Intro.)

Matn, 5, 36, *39*, 52, *152*, 292n78

Mayer, Hanna, 209

Mazzacurati, Renato Marino, *234*, 257

McGilvary, Margaret, 57, 119

McMahon, Henry, 9

measles, 156

media/press coverage: of actual profiteers, 90–91, 94, 95; of Administrative Council members' dismissals/resignations, 121; of American relief efforts, 211, 212; British propaganda impacting, in Egypt, 287n102; censorship of, 12, 88–90, 176, 280n46; of disease deaths, 136, 158; of families facing existential crisis, 134–135; of famine deaths, 136, 288n111; of the "flour/wheat issue" in Beirut, 79–80, 82, 83–84; of France's humanitarian/relief work, 242, 247, 248; and fundraising efforts by Syrian diaspora relief committees, 133–134, 135–137, 288n111; health education through, 153, 154, 157, 291n67; of hospital conditions, 162; increasingly vocal, 43, 45; of Kouyoumdjian's resignation, 123; of the locust plague, 51; of the Maronite patriarch, 125, 254; of mobilization, 66; on the moral obligation of communal sacrifice, 279n38; of the municipality, 86, 87, 88, 89, 92–93, 95, 107; of Ottoman troops in Mount Lebanon, 120–121; of prices, 85, 86, 87, 95, 279n29; of promised shipments to Mount Lebanon, 130; of property taxes, 181; public health announcements through, 157, 159; of public health efforts, 142; to publicize remittances, 221; of rationing, 96–97, 98; of refugees, 68; of Regulations for Communicable Diseases, 147, 153; of sculpture depicting Lebanese experience of WWI, 5; and secularism, 45; of smallpox, 160; of the Syrian Ladies' Association, 193; of vaccination campaign, 159; visual and textual, of suffering, 245–246; of voluntary quarantine, 162; of women as heads of households, 74. *See also* Arabic diaspora press

medical experts, 148, 153, 154–155, 156, 159, 163, 165

medical professionals: advertisements by, 151, 291n68; and the aftermath of civil war, 147; conscription of, 148, 149, 150, 290n39; decision making by, 141; foreign, submitting a list of, 145; ignorance of, 156–157; international relief work organized by ARC and, 206–209; mandated volunteering by, 151; media targeting, for discussions of disease, 154; in Mount Lebanon, 150; registration of, 148; shortage of, 151, 162, 166–167, 291n59; teaching, 290n38; women as, 191

medical schools: conscription of students in, 150, 291n55; instruction on hygiene in, 155

Mediterranean region: Beirut's importance to, 28, 30, 32; boomtown in, 29; and natural disasters, 53; trade blockage in, 3, 56, 58–59
Mediterranean Sea, *xvi*, 24, *39*, 52, *152*. *See also* maritime blockades
Mehmet 'Ali, 27, 28
Melkite Greek Catholics Church, 112
Méouchy, Nadine, 248
merchant class, 31, 35, 42, 81, 269n106. *See also* notables
Mesopotamia, 103
Mesopotamian Campaign, 260n9
mice/rats, 142
microbes/bacteria, 142, 146, 147. *See also* disease
middle class: as important agents of provisioning, 46; new, emergence of, 44
Middle East, 5, 7, 9, 16, 47, 53, 197, 233, 238, 256, 263n60
Midgal, Joel, 13, 15, 17
migration, 29, 55, 76, 112, 146. *See also* emigration; refugees; Syro-Lebanese diaspora
militarization, 143, 176
Ministry of Education, 44, 99
Ministry of Forestry, Mining, and Agriculture, 69
Ministry of Health, 159, 160
Ministry of War, 192
missionaries, 8, 48, 51, 112, 132, 175, 202, 209, 210–213, 214, 215–216, 217, 220, 226, 228–229, 232, 241, 270–271n130, 287n104
missionary schools, 48, 55, 214, 215, 271n130
Mkhaysh family, 75
Modern History of Lebanon (Salibi), 256, 308n80
modernism, 28
monetary aid, 47, 110, 115, 115–116, 182, 211, 248, 295n11. *See also* remittances
money confiscations, 150, 216, 237
morality, 87, 92, 97, 163, 164, 279n38
Morgenthau, Henry, 6, 205
mortalities. *See* deaths
mortgage loans, 115, 131, 133
mosques, 47, 297nn44–45
mosquitoes, 146, 164
Mouawad, Youssef, 253

Mount Lebanon: and administrative divisions of the Ottoman Levant, *xvi*; and archival records, 18; aspirations for independence in, 43, 122, 125, 188; autonomy of, 6; banning interior shipments of food to, 64–65; Beiruti migration to, 55, 68; charitable giving in, changes in, 47–49; cholera in, 147, 157, 158; and the Christian nationalism movement, 244; church provisioning efforts in, 109–110, 111, 113–116, 116–118, 129, 130–131, 132, 139; civilian casualties of war, 2; civil war in, 38, 56, 147; and climate, 53; close connection between Beirut and, 24, 29; coal industry in, 29–30; competition for political power and status in, 16; and conscription, 67; cooperation between Beirut and, difficulty of, 118–119; deaths from disease in, 2, 136, 158; deaths from famine in, 2, 4, 136; under decentralization, 27; disease in, 3, 143, 146; disinfection stations in, *152*, 165–166; dismissal of relief efforts in, taking issue with, 8–9; division of, into relief districts, 240; economic changes in, during the nineteenth century, 30–32, 49; effects of WWI felt early on in, 2; under Egyptian rule, 27, 266n23; elections in, 38, 269n91; and emigration, 31, 267nn51–53; European meddling in, 36, 56; exemption from conscription, 38, 65, 68, 148; famine in, 3, 4, 5, 54, 129, 147, 243; and fears of foreign coastal invasion, 55; and food supply lines, 62; and fundraising efforts by Syrian diaspora relief committees, 134, 136, 288n111; German relief work in, 202; Greek willingness to supply weapons to, 126, 286n69; hospitals in, 290n33; and the immediate aftermath of the war, 238, 306n9; important political actors in, 46; interior grain-producing areas and food supply in, 118; international relief work in, 222–225, 231–232, 250; and *kaymakams* (subgovernors), 38, 121; local charitable efforts in, 196–197; locust plague in, 52; malaria in, 164, 166; and maritime blockades, 56–57, 60, 61, 112; media coverage in, 45, 157; migration from, 29; migration to, 55; military transport of grain to, 101; militia in, 285n36; mobilization of civilian resources in, 11; as most affected by famine, 253; *mutasarrif* (governor) of, 38, 44, 123; and one of the key scholarly projects of the time, 143, 289n10; political changes in, 35–40, 49; population figures, 156; prices in, 72, 73, 100; primary sources of income in, 31–32; prioritizing the military in, 63, 230; profiteering through, 74–76, 82, 90; public health administration in, 147, 150; refugees in, 68; region responsible for feeding, under Jamal Pasha's plan, 104; reliance on trade in, 57–58; religious composition of, 35–36, 268n75; reluctance of France to intervene in, 122, 123, 125–128; and remittances from emigrants, 31, 32, 61, 267n56; reshaping of the political landscape of, 111; response to health interventions in, 170; retreat of Ottoman officials from, 237; returning immigrants, 31; rise of opposition in, 44–45; roads in, 33; as a semiautonomous province (*mutasarrifiyya*), xvi, 2, 27, 38, *39*, 40, 56, 119, 123, 256; silk industry in, 30–31; smallpox in, 159; soup kitchens in, *152*, 222, 224, 225; state failure to alleviate the situation in, 105; and state power, 13, 14; strengthening Ottoman control over, 119–124; syndicate-run provisioning in, 100–101, 117; and the Tanzimat, 36–37; and tourism, 32; troop movement in, 120, 121; typhoid in, 147; typhus in, 146, 155–156, 165; vaccination in, 159, 161; view looking out toward, from Beirut, *22*, 23–24; vulnerability of, to famine, 10, 26, 34, 266n28; water contamination in, 164.

Muhyi ad-Din, Husni, *See* Husni Bey Mukarzal, Naʿum, 288n112
Mukherjee, Janam, 7
Mumtaz Bey, 237
municipal council: appointment of wartime health administrators, 148; blame cast on, for the famine, 249; eligibility for and composition of, 41–42, 85, 253, 269n106; establishment of, 41; failed efforts of, 101, 107; gender and, 48; legitimacy of, 81, 87–90; media coverage of, 86, 87, 88, 89, 92–93, 95; postwar relief efforts of, 247, 248–249; provisioning efforts of, 79, 81–84, 85–87, 92, 93–95, 106–107; sidelined as the city's chief provisioner, 96, 97, 98, 107; significance of, 45–46; social position of members, 91–92
municipal government, establishment of, 41, 269n100. *See also specific municipalities*
municipal health department, 141–142, 144, 148, 149, 151, 154, 159, 160, 161, 166
municipal hospitals, 144–145
Municipal Law/Municipality Law, 41–42
Munif Bey, ʿAli, 100, 123–124, 150, 222, 282n99
Murphy, Starr, 204, 300n15
Muslims: Beirut district/neighborhoods mainly comprised of, 193, 195; and conscription, 68; daughters of notable, petition signed by, 252; election of, to the Administrative Council, 122; emigration of, 55; genocide perpetrated against, 243; importance of charitable giving to, 47; integral part of religious piety for, 176; and media censorship, 90; organization bringing together Christians and, 43; population in Beirut, 29; population in Mount Lebanon, 268n75; relationship of the CUP to wealthy families of, 184; sculpture of female mourners representing both Christians and, *xviii*, 1; secret French provisioning scheme designed to influence, 127; soup kitchens and, 229; tensions between Christians and, 56, 254. *See also specific Islamic sects and Muslim organizations/groups*
mutasarrif (governor), 38, 44, 123
mutasarrifiyya, xvi, 2, 27, 38, *39*, 40, 56, 119, 123, 256. *See also* Mount Lebanon
Mutius, Gerhard von, 56, 68, 71, 72, 75, 83, 90, 123, 226, 227–228
Mutterhaus, 209
Muzaffar Pasha, 45

INDEX

Nabeer, Fatmeh, 251–252
Nablus, *xvi*, 40
Naccache, Albert, 243
al-Najjar, Salim, 122
nationalism, 6, 12, 27, 36, 44, 92, 187, 188, 244, 255, 256, 280n51, 308n80
natural disasters, 3, 53, 103, 272n16. *See also* locust plague
Near East Relief, 197
Nelson, William, 71
nervous state, 13, 14–15, 90, 239
newspapers/journals. *See* Arabic diaspora press; media/press coverage
New York, diaspora community in, 122, 123, 127, 136, 137
Nickoley, Edward, 3, 75–76, 97, 155, 156, 158
nonsectarianism, 27, 134, 177, 193
notables, 27, 31, 35, 37, 41, 42, 43, 44, 46, 68, 75, 91, 178, 179, 236, 240, 249, 252, 274n70. *See also* elites
Nucho, Naimeh, 207
nurses, 207–208, 209, 214, 229

oil/petroleum, 33, 87
orphans/orphanages, 49, 74, 112, 155, 195, 197, 215, 224–225, 244, 246, 252, 299n108, 303n77
Ottoman embassy, 44, 183
Ottoman Empire: abrogation of capitulatory agreements with foreign powers, 55, 57; actions of, significance of, both locally and internationally, 10, 11; administrative divisions of, in the Levant, *xvi*, 24; and the basis for humanitarian aid/relief, 177, 295n16; blame cast on, for the famine, 243, 255, 256; civilian casualties of war, 2, 21, 260n8; decision to ally with the Central Powers, 2, 11; decline and tyranny of, normative accounts of, complicating, 9; empire-wide civilian provisioning, 81, 85, 102–103, 103–106, 253; end of, 1, 21, 235–236, 263n61, 305n2; entrance into the war, 2; failed efforts of, 107, 250; finances of, during wartime, 57; food crisis in, 2–3; and foreign debt, 55, 272n28; as a governmentalized state, in society, 13, 15; history of famine in, 265n4; lack of patriotism in, 67–68; mobilizing civilians for the war effort in, 54, 70–72; and natural disasters, 53; no-dissent policy of, 124–125; opposition to, rise of, 43; and petroleum, 33; political restructuring in, 34–35; price regulations in, history of, 84; profound changes during the nineteenth century, 26–28; railways in, and number of trains in operation, 34; reduction of livestock in, 66; reforms in, period of, 36; reliance of, on free markets, 101–102; role of Germany in, during and after the way, debate over, 202–203; sovereignty of, challenges to, 27, 46; stance of, toward neutral countries, 56, 57; and tensions with Egypt, 27, 28, 34; tyrannical rule of, 6, 13; vaccination in, 293n101. *See also specific Ottoman provinces/districts and government bodies/officials*
Ottoman Imperial Bank, 83, 218–219, 282n112, 282n113
Ottoman military: and the ARC medical relief campaign, 206–209; casualties of war, 2, 235, *236*, 260n8; cleaning battalions of, 149, 167; and court, 56, 90, 102, 122, 125, 150, 151, 189, 296n20; and deaths from famine, 120; and deaths from disease, 90, 145, 160; desertion in, 67, 130, 146, 150, 151, 289n24; empire-wide requisitioning for, 11, 54, 70–71, 72, 102, 113, 256; experiencing disease on the battlefront, 145; financing of, 181; grain shipments transported by, 101; health officials for, 151; hospitals of, 147, 150, 209, 214, 290n33, 290n38; and its court, 189, 296n20; limited geographical area involved in engagement of, 2; major campaigns of engagement, 104, 236, 260n9; malnutrition in, 146; mobilization of, 2, 11, 54, 63–66, 66–67, 69, 113, 260n7, 277n132; movement of troops into Mount Lebanon, 120, 121; preventing entry of food into Lebanon, 137; prewar squadron in Mount Lebanon, 285n36; prioritizing provisioning of, 63, 64–65, 72, 76, 103, 104–105, 229, 230, 256; recruitment difficulties, 65, 67–68;

sacrifice of soldiers in, 99; troop movement by, 56, 146, 292n89; Turkish official history of WWI and, 12, 263n62; unsanitary condition of, 146, 164; and vaccination, 159; and women workers' brigades, 192, 193. *See also* conscription
Ottoman nationalism, 36
Ottoman Public Health Council, 293n102
out-migration. *See* emigration

pack animals, 65–66, 68, 104–105
Palestine: and the Balfour Declaration, 10; decline in cultivated area, 69; German contribution to Ottoman campaign in, 231; immigration of Jews to, women's position on, 251; locust plague in, 50, 51–52; and military provisioning, 105; modern day, geographic area including, 260n10; as a purchasing zone, 104, 283n118, 297n64; refugees in Lebanon from, 68; Syro-Lebanese men joining the Legion d'Orient in, 128
Palestine Campaign, 260n9, 286n74
Palestine-Syrian Relief Committee, 205
Pamuk, Şevket, 101, 272n28
paradox, 8, 16, 28, 36, 176
Paris: balancing the military and citizens in, 63; decision making in, following the armistice, 238; diaspora community in, 123, 127; hospital system in, 294n120; Ottoman embassy in, 44, 183
Paris Peace Conference, 242, 254
participation, 15, 16, 17, 18, 26, 37, 43, 48, 128, 176, 179, 183, 189, 193, 233, 250, 252
Patch, James Alfred, 204, 217
paternalism: crisis of, 175, 246, 256; European, 203, 256
patriotic feminism, 191–192
Paulists. *See* St. Paul order
Persia, Ottoman military campaign in, 260n9
petroleum/oil, 33, 87
philanthropic organizations. *See* charitable societies
photography, 245, 246
Piépape, Philpin de, 237–238, 240, 247
plague, 141–142, 145, 151, 289n2, 292n83
police departments: corrupt, 94; creation of, 269n100; enforcing public health initiatives, 148; providing security for food distribution, 94, 101; rationing conducted by, 96–97; and vaccinations, 159. *See also* imprisonment/arrests
politics of provisioning, 8–9, 16–18, 21, 24, 26, 35, 45–46, 49, 77, 80, 81–82, 110, 118–119, 139, 143, 174, 202, 238, 239, 247, 249, 252, 253, 254. *See also specific actors involved in provisioning*
Pollard, Lisa, 270n126
postwar political landscape: narrative account of, 247–249, 253; shaping of, contributing to, 5, 9, 17–18, 21, 107, 111, 233, 241, 257
Poverty and Famine (Sen), 25
power: juridical, 13, 16; over life, 14, 15; relational, 17.
power currency, provisions as, 17
practical philanthropy, 177
Presbyterian Church, 221
Presbyterian Mission, 204, 218, 221. *See also* American Mission Press
press coverage. *See* Arabic diaspora press; media/press coverage
price controls/regulations, attempts at, 83–87, 92, 93–95, 99–100, 101, 102, 103–104, 105, 167, 240, 248
price increases, 3, 19, 24, 25, 54, 60–61, 64, 66, 72, 73, 75, 76, 80, 82, 84, 86, 100, 101, 110, 115, 116, 167, 198, 218–219, 226, 265n8, 275n89, 275n103, 279n29
professionalization, 47, 202
profiteering, 18, 72, 74–76, 82, 86, 87, 90–91, 94, 95, 102, 167, 184, 190, 196, 237, 239, 253, 256, 282n104. *See also* bribery; price increases
propaganda, 122, 202, 228, 229, 231, 232, 287n102
property confiscation, 65, 132–133, 144–145, 150, 151, 169, 175, 180–181, 206, 241, 293n116
property sales, 180
property tax, 42, 162, 181, 182, 297n52
prostitutes/brothels, 148, 149, 163, 290n42, 290n45
protection, 14
Protestants: in Jerusalem and Egypt, lead-

ers of, and support for Syrian relief committee, 287n104; missionary work of, 48, 202, 210–213, 232, 271n130. *See also specific Protestant institutions/organizations/groups*
provincial council, 41, 42, 45, 82
provincial departments, 40, 269n98
provincial health director, 141–142, 148, 149, 154, 162
Provincial Law (1864), 40
Provisional Grain Act, 102, 282n107
provisioning: as a contested domain, 6, 9; food and health, contrast between, 169–170; importance of, 14, 46; initial absence of, response to, 9; politics of, 8–9, 16–18, 21, 24, 26, 35, 45–46, 49, 77, 80, 81–82, 110, 118–119, 139, 143, 174, 202, 238, 239, 247, 249, 252, 253, 254; power of, 17; reasons for studying and writing about, 21; relief in the form of, attention to, reason for, 8–9; sociopolitical significance of famine and, 5–6; state in society approach and, 13, 15; and state power, 14. *See also specific aspects of food and health provisioning*
provisioning zones, division of the empire into, 103
public health administration, 144, 147–148, 149–150, 161, 169, 291n49. *See also* health commission; health inspections
public health announcements, 144, 151, 153, 154, 157, 159, 160, 165
public health departments, 150, 269n100, 294n120. *See also* municipal health department
public health education: focus of, 153, 161; prioritizing, 153–155, 291n65; resistance to, 169; through the media, 153, 154, 291n67
punishment, 65, 67, 83, 93, 144, 153, 160, 170, 188, 271n11, 277n141. *See also specific type of punishment*
purchasing power, study of, 73–74, 277n152
purchasing zones, creation of, 104, 283n118

Qabbani, 'Abd al-Qadir, 144–145
al-Qattan, Najwa, 5, 242, 261n23
quarantines, 141, 142, 151, 161–162, 163, 169

Qur'an, 95, 271n11

Rabinow, Paul, 280n42
railroads, *xvi*, 24, 32, 33–34, *39*, 64–65, 67, 80, 83, 101, 146, *152*, 268n65, 275n89
railway company, 91, 280n61
Ras Beirut, 159
rationing, 96–98, 182
rats/mice, 142
Red Crescent, 208, 222, 250, 283n126
Red Cross: focus on efforts of, in studies of WWI, 197; formation of, 47; French, 126; insignia of, wearing, *207*, 208. *See also* American Red Cross (ARC), Beirut chapter/committee
Red Sea, 59
red tape, 65
Reed, Robert, 301n46
refugees, 21, 41, 68, 69, 146, 158, 193, 246, 247–248, 292n89
refugee shelters, 174, 194, 195, 240
Règlement Organique, 38
Regulation for Communicable Diseases, 147–148, 151, 153, 160, 290n35
relapsing fever, 156, 292n87
religious associations, 48, 175, 181. *See also specific religious associations/societies*
religious endowment (*waqf*), 47, 179–180, 181
religious institutions: and competition from foreign philanthropists, 212; level of food distribution by, 116; prominent associations linked to, 48; shift from, to charitable societies, 47, 176–177. *See also specific churches*
religious networks, government reliance on, 116–117, 138
religious properties, confiscation of, 132–133
religious schools, 48–49, 187
remittances, 31, 32, 61, 217–222, 225, 267n56
Rémy, Father, 240
rental properties, 179–180, 181
requisitioning, empire-wide, 11, 54, 70–71, 72, 102, 113, 256. *See also* confiscation
restricted movement, 12, 61, 64, 142. *See also* exile; maritime blockades; quarantines
Rida Bey, Muhammed, 122, 124, 125, 285n50
riots, 82, 83, 97
road taxes, 71

Rockefeller, John D., 204, 300n15
Rockefeller Institute of Charity, 300n16
Rumia, 112
Russia, 10, 27, 28, 146, 202, 206, 260n9, 295n17. *See also* Entente Powers
Russo-Turkish War, 70, 266n18

al-Saʻad, Habib Pasha, 121, 122, 237
Saadeh, Atman, 207
Saba, Macarios, 137, 288n117
sacrifice, 6, 11, 12, 70, 87, 92, 99, 106, 113–114, 231, 254, 279n38
safar barlik: meaning of, 67, 276n114; Ottoman proclamation using, 66
Saʻid, ʻAbdallah, 73
Salam, ʻAnbara, 173–174, 176, 194–195, 251–252
Salam, Salim ʻAli, 75, 92, 96, 173, 186–187, 187–188, 189–191, 194, 236–237, 252–253
Salam family, 95, 186, 240
Salibi, Kamal, 187, 256, 308n80
Samʻan family, 178
Sami Bey, Bekir, 55, 57, 79, 82, 86, 87, 90, 96, 118, 119, 206
Samuel, Raphael, 20
Sanders, Liman von, 155, 229
sanitary citizens, 153–154, 169, 291n66
sanitation: breakdown in, 143, 146; efforts in, 143; military involvement in, 149, 167; rules and regulations for, 145, 153; strategy of, 161; strengthening, demand for, 144; transformation of, 147
sanitation commission, 161, 164
sanitation workers, 149, 167, 211
Sarikamish defeat, 12, 263n61
Sarkis, Salim Effendi, 288n111
Sayigh, Salma, 299n108
Scheper-Hughes, Nancy, 288n107
Schilcher, Linda, 58, 238, 261n11
Schmidlin, Joseph, 213, 214, 303n72
Schönrock, Magda, 215
schools: academic, charitable efforts moving beyond, 196; attached to mosques, 47; charitable, 178, 296n26; foreigners abandoning, 55; medical, 150, 155, 291n55; missionary, 48, 55, 214, 215, 271n130; religious, 48–49, 187; state-run, 48, 196; vaccinations and, 159

scientific associations, 48, 270n128
Scott, James, 105
Second Constitutional Period, 43
Second Hague Conference, 58
sectarianism, 36, 38, 41, 177
secularism, 36, 37, 40, 44, 45, 111, 138, 175, 202, 214, 254, 295n13
Seikaly, Sherene, 43
self-interest, as a primary motivation, 186
Sen, Amartya, 25, 63, 74, 103, 106, 265n8
service sector, 32
sewage/toilets, 164, 167
sexually transmitted disease, 148–149, 290n44
Shaʻab, Nabih, 166
Shahin, Tanyus, 37
Shaʻiya, Yusuf Milhim (José M. Chaia), 135, 288n109
Sharif, Malek, 42, 269n101
shelters/hospices, 47, 162, 174, 192, 194, 195, 196, 197, 201, 240, 249
Shibli, Butrus, 125, 286n63
Shihab, Fuad, 257
Shihab family, 27
Shiites, 29, 269n91
Shuf, 4, 36, *39*, 52, 73–74, *152*, 266n22, 292n78, 304n120
sickness. *See* disease
sick people, isolation of. *See* quarantines
Sidon, *xvi*, 24, 30, 33, *39*, 40, *152*, 159, 207, 220
silk industry, 30–31, 33, 59–60, 73, 224
sin, 129
Sinai Campaign, 260n9, 286n74
Sinai desert, 208, 209
Singer, Amy, 17
Sleem, Salim, 256–257
smallpox, 150, 153, 156, 159–161, 160
Smith, Adam, 101
smuggling, 56, 75, 102, 103
soap shortage, 158
social capital, possessing, 17
social control, measures of, 17
Society for Aiding the Poor (Jamʻiyyat ʻAwn al-Faqir), 176
Society for Employment of Ottoman Women, 192
Society of St. George, 48, 162, 175, 177, 178,

INDEX

179–180, 181, 182, 185–186, 187, 295n17, 296nn19–23, 296n30, 296n35, 298n65
Solnit, Rebecca, 25
soup kitchens, 3, 101, *152*, 153, 155, 200, 201, 211, 222, 224, 225, 227, 228–229, 240, 247, 250
South America, 32, 127–128, 135, 221, 267n56
Standard Oil Company, 33, 219
St. Anthony monastery, 109, 114, 115, 132
starvation. *See* famine
state formation, 13–14, 263n68
state functions, duality of, 14
state in society, 12–16, 46
state power, 13–14
state-run schools, 48
St. Joseph University, 306n21
St. Paul order (Paulists), 112, 113, 115, 116, 117, 130, 131, 132, 138, 284n25
Strachan, Hew, 57
Strangford, Lady, 23, 26
street-sweeping battalions, 184
strikes, 89, 188
student volunteers, 207, 209, 210, 211
Sublime Porte, 38, 44, 57
subsidies, 133, 240, 248
Suez Campaign, 64, 65, 104, 149, 206, 299n101
Suez Canal, 30
suicide, 76, 247
Sunni Muslim Association for Benevolent Intention (al-Jam'iyyat al-Maqasid al-Khayriyya al-Islamiyya). *See* al-Maqasid
Sunnis, 29, 187, 248, 269n91
Suq al-Attarin, 181, 297n45
Suq al-Barzarakan, 181, 297n44
Suq al-Gharb, 121, 222
Suq al-Haddadin, 181
Sursock, Alfred Bey, 183, 184, 185, 236–237, 297–298n64
Sursock, Catherine, 186
Sursock, Emili, 49
Sursock, Jurji Yusuf, 296n19
Sursock, Michel Bey, 75, 91, 92, 104, 183–184
Sursock, Yusuf Bey, 178, 179, 183, 185–186, 298n65
Sursock family, 75, 95, 178, 183, 184, 185, 186, 240, 297n57

Sursock Museum, 257
surveillance, 12, 56, 86, 94, 124, 125, 144, 158, 161, 176
Susa, Yusuf 'Abdallah, 86–87, 91, 92–93
Sykes, Mark, 10, 237
Sykes-Picot negotiations, 10, 237, 256
syndicates, 99–101, 117
syphilis, 148
Syria: and administrative divisions of the Ottoman Levant, *xvi*, 40; case study failing to mention famine in, 273n51; economic union with, advocating for, 248; Egyptian occupation of, 266n18; German contribution to Ottoman campaign in, 231; interior provinces of, oversupply of food produced in, 61–62, 63; and the locust plague, 52; and military provisioning, 105; missionary movement in provinces of, 27; modern day, geographic area including, 260n10; Ottoman view of Maronites in, 119; political independence of, demand for, 251; press coverage of the famine in, archives of, 19; and railways, 34; refugees in Lebanon from, 68; response to mobilization and conscription in, 67–68; secret treaties concerning, women's position on, 251.
Syriac Church, Eastern Catholic, 29, 124, 284n25
Syrian Central Committee (Comite? central syrien, CCS), 127–128
Syrian Ladies' Association (Jam'iyyat al-Sayyidat al-Suriyya), 176, 191, 193–195, 251, 299n100
Syrian National Congress, 253
Syrian Protestant College (SPC): AMP distancing itself from, 218, 221–222; archival records of, 19; arrests involving employees of, 216–217; employees/students of, observations of, 3, 8–9, 19, 75–76, 98, 153; employment of Red Cross workers, 211; hospital associated with, 143, 151, 162, 206, 292n72, 294n119; Jamal Pasha's visit to, *172*; local relief efforts involving, 206, 210–213, 250; meddling with ARC committee's decision making, 217; medical relief

campaign involving, for the military, 206–209; medical school, 155, 206, 207; nurses training school, 207; promise of furnishing provisions to, 62; renaming of, 264n94; representation of, on the ARC committee, 204, 217, 300n9; retention of medical faculty, 206, 209, 301n41; suggestion by, to employ the poor, 167
Syrian Relief Committee/Fund, 134, 137, 287–288nn104–105
Syrian Scientific Society (Jam'iyyat al-'Ilmiyya al-Suriyya), 270n128
Syrian Society of Arts and Science (Jam'iyyat al-Suriyya lil-Iktisab al-'Ulum wa al-Funun), 270n128
Syro-Lebanese diaspora: activism in, factors instrumental in shaping, 135–136, 288n110; in Egypt, described, 284n34; fund-raising efforts by, 133–134, 135–137, 221, 287–288nn104–105; late start in aid effort by, reason for, 287n102; remittances of, 31, 32, 61, 220–221; willingness to help Entente forces, 119–120, 122–123, 127–128, 285nn52–54, 286n75. *See also* Arabic diaspora press

Tabbara, Ahmad Hassan, 88, 89–90, 91, 92, 107
Tabet, Ayub, 92
al-Tahtawi, Rifa'a, 47
Talat Pasha, 225
Tamimi, Rafiq, 99, 291n49
al-Tannuri, Ignatious, 113, 132, 138
Tannurin, *39*, 109
Tanzimat period, 36–37, 41, 269n101
tariffs, 55, 57
tax collection, 27, 38, 266n22, 269n89
taxes: exemption, 67, 68–69, 276n125; higher, for religious societies, 132, 175; in-kind payment of, 69, 72, 102, 103, 104, 276n125, 282n106; oppressive, 25, 105, 265n8; property, 42, 162, 181; raising, to fund infrastructure improvements, 167; war, 11, 70, 71–72
tax-farming families (*muqata'jis*), 27, 268n85
tax payers, 27, 42
textile industry, 30

Thompson, Elizabeth, 175, 196
Tilly, Charles, 13, 14, 239
tolls, 71
total history, 18, 264n93
total mobilization, 11, 54, 63, 106, 262n53, 263n11
total war, 11–12, 16, 18, 49, 53, 143, 239, 262n53
tourist industry, 32, 61
Trabaud, Albert, 133
Traboulsi, Fawwaz, 44
Trad, Jurji Habib, 178
trade: ban on interdistrict/interprovincial, 56, 65, 101, 255; disruptions to, during wartime, 3, 54, 72; postwar liberalization of, 248; prewar growth in, 29–30, 31, 266n37; reform of, call for, 99; reliance on, for food, 34, 58; and syndicates, 99–101, 117. *See also* maritime blockades
trade treaties/agreements, capitulatory, 28, 55, 57, 213, 256, 266n25
Trad family, 75, 178, 296n20
trading companies, 283n126
Trading with the Enemy Act, 225
trains. *See* railroads
treason, 125, 134, 184, 194, 296n20
Treaty of Balta Liman, 28, 266n25
Treaty of Versailles, 58
Tripoli, 5, 24, 30, 34, *39*, 40, 59, 62, 125, *152*, 156, 220, 226–227
Tripoli-Homs railroad, *39*, *152*
Turjman, Ihsan, 52–53
Turkey, historiography of WWI, 12, 263n62
Turkish nationalism, 12, 44, 280n51
Turkish War of Independence, 12
typhoid, 147, 151, 154, 156, 157, 158, 159, 160, 163–164, 291n67, 292n83
typhus, 143, 145, 146, 151, 154, 155–157, 165, 291n67, 292n72, 294n134

underground mail, 218
United States: advertising products in Beirut, 33, 267n61; Arabic press in, 264n96; archival records in, 18; diaspora community in, 122, 123, 127, 136, 137, 221; direct aid from, failed attempts by Syrian diaspora to secure, 136–137; emigrant journalists in, 136,

288n112; employment of women in, 196; entrance into the war, and the fate of relief work, 225; focus on, and American war relief and humanitarian work, 201–202; France using neutrality of, in provisioning scheme, 127, 137; French embassy in, 122; and health clinics in Mount Lebanon, 147; help blocked from, 194; hospitals of, 145; involvement of, in relief efforts, factors in, 202, 231–232; maritime blockade of, 56–57, 137; media in, 221; missionaries from, 48, 202, 232, 270–271n130, 287n104; official denial of government relief work, 205; opening for, to participate in reconstruction, 233; perception of, during and after the war, 203–204, 212–213, 227, 231–232, 250, 252; prohibition of any aid associated with, 98, 194, 216–217; property of religious groups from, concern over, 132; remittances from, 32, 221; strengthened role of, 18; trade with Beirut, facilitation of, 33, 267n61; unofficial remittances through, 218, 219, 220–221, 225; womanhood in, presentation of, as an ideal, 250
universal conscription, 275n108
al-Unsi, 'Abd al-Rahman, 148, 157
al-'Uraysi, 'Abd al-Ghani, 89, 194, 280n51
US State Department, 205, 217, 218, 225

vaccination, 150, 158–161, 165, 293nn101–102, 293n113, 294n134
vali (governor-general), 40–41
Van Dyck, William Thomson, 153, 155
Van Leeuwen, Marco, 186
vehicle taxes, 71
venereal disease, 148–149, 290n44
victimhood, narrative discourses of, 241–249
violence, 3, 6, 8, 9, 12, 13–14, 29, 38, 41, 71, 76, 101, 146
volunteer associations, emergence of, 47–48, 176, 191, 270n126. *See also* charitable societies
vulnerability, 10, 25–26, 26–32, 28, 34, 49, 54, 143, 147, 266n28, 290n29

Wangenheim, Hans von, 214, 215

war: connection between famine, disease, and, 142-143, 145–147, 153; as a factor in famine, 53–54, 67, 74, 76; famine as a strategy of, 54–63, 76; lines between civilians and soldiers in, issue of, 11–12, 263n58; opportunity seen in, 14, 55; productive power of, 8, 13. *See also specific wars and aspects pertaining to war*
war crimes, 12, 263n58
Ward, Edwin, 206, 207, 208
war paradox, 16, 176
war profiteers. *See* profiteering
war relief. *See* humanitarian aid/war relief
war taxes, 11, 70, 71–72
war theory, 8
War Trade Board, 225
waste management, 164–165, 167
Watenpaugh, Keith, 202
waterborne disease, 157, 161, 163
water contamination, 157, 158, 163–164
Watts, Michael, 15, 25, 49, 266n28
Wemuke, Sophie, 209
Whiting, John D., 51, 271n3
Williams, Elizabeth, 87
Wilson, Woodrow, 136, 203–204, 205, 244, 250, 252
Winter, Jay, 63, 80
womanhood, ideal, 250
women: agricultural wages of, and purchasing power, 73–74; allowances to, as wives/widows of soldiers, 192, 210; blaming, as transmitters of disease, 163; charitable work done by, 48, 49, 176, 191, 193–195, 196, 197, 224, 249, 299n94, 299n100; education of, 48–49, 187, 249, 251, 270–271n130, 271n133; emancipation of, 176, 191–192, 195–196, 298n84; employment/workshops for, aid involving, 174, 193, 194, 195, 196, 201, 210, 222, 224, 301n46; execution of, 193; exemption from conscription, 276n124; as heads of households, 74, 246; and the horrors of famine, 3–4, 5, *245*, *246*; as important agents of provisioning, 46; increasing role of, in charitable work, 48, 49; independence of, 250; international relief work by, 207–208, 209, 210, 211, 250; mandating

agricultural labor for men and, 105; as migrants, 267n52; as missionaries, 22, 271n130; mobilization of, intention of, 106; as mourners, sculpture depicting, *xviii*, 1, 5, 256–257; organizing government-supported relief work for, 173; orphanages run by, 197, 299n108; as a political asset, 17; portrayal of, during rationing, 97, 98; postwar political activities of, 249–250, 251–252; and prostitution, 148, 149, 290n42, 290n45; and the right to vote, 252; and the severing of kinship bonds, 4, 112, 135, 245, 246; and the silk industry, 31, 224; in the workforce, entrance of, 48, 176, 191, 192, 196. *See also specific women involved in aid/relief work*

work, value of, 251. *See also* employment efforts

World War I, 110; aftermath of, factors affecting sociopolitical standing in, 5–6; altered living conditions due to, effect of, 145; casualties in, 2, 235, *236*, 260n8; combined with famine, vulnerability arising from, 143; day for commemoration of, focus in, 6–7; decentering the history of, 10; and the emancipation of women, 176, 191–192, 195–196, 298n84; escalation of, 90; exclusionary historiography of, 7, 8, 12, 53, 197, 255–256, 255–257, 263n60, 273n51; exigencies of, as a productive force, 8–9; inclusionary historiography of, working toward, 7, 12, 257, 263n60; increasing efforts to address public health and sanitation in, 169; and the meaning of "home front," 3; in the Middle East, diplomatic stunts during, 9–10; monuments expressing Lebanese experience of, *xviii*, 1, 5, *234*, 256–257; periphery of, centrality of the, 10–12; predictions about duration of, 277n132; state of Lebanese cities and villages following, 21; total mobilization in, 11, 262n53, 263n11; as a total war, defining, 11–12, 18, 49, 53, 143, 262n53; understanding the global scope of, need for, 10; viewing, through the lens of famine, 10–11, 21. *See also specific wartime actions and countries involved in the war*

Yalman, Ahmed Emin, 192
Yamin, Antun, 4–5, 184, 242, 242–243
Yazbek, Yussef Ibrahim, 308n82
Yıldırım Army Group, 228, 230
Young Arab Society (Jam'iyyat al-'Arabiyya al-Fatat), 43
Young Turk Revolution, 26, 43, 127, 299n94

Zahle, *39*, *152*, 220, 292n78
Zaynieh, Khalil, 92
Zionist movement, 10, 238
Zoar orphanage, 215
Zorn, Anna, 209